THE TRADE AND ADMINISTRATION
OF CHINA

THE TRADE AND ADMINISTRATION OF CHINA

By

HOSEA BALLOU MORSE, LL.D.

SOMETIME COMMISSIONER OF CUSTOMS
AND STATISTICAL SECRETARY, INSPECTORATE GENERAL OF CUSTOMS
AUTHOR OF "THE GILDS OF CHINA"
"THE INTERNATIONAL RELATIONS OF THE CHINESE EMPIRE" ETC.

WITH ILLUSTRATIONS, MAP AND DIAGRAMS

THIRD REVISED EDITION

NEW YORK / RUSSELL & RUSSELL

FIRST PUBLISHED IN 1908
REISSUED, 1967, BY RUSSELL & RUSSELL
A DIVISION OF ATHENEUM HOUSE, INC.
BY ARRANGEMENT WITH ANNE E. WELSFORD
L. C. CATALOG CARD NO: 66–24734

PRINTED IN THE UNITED STATES OF AMERICA

DEDICATION

[1907]

THIRTY-THREE YEARS AGO FOUR YOUNG
MEN CAME TO CHINA DIRECT FROM THE
HALLS OF FAIR HARVARD. TO THE OTHER
THREE THE FOURTH DEDICATES THIS
WORK

PREFACE

THIS book is intended to portray the present state of the Chinese Empire, with such record of the past as will show by what process of evolution the existing state has been reached. No attempt is made to forecast the future, or even to refer to the revolution which, under the name of Reform, has been begun. The development of many centuries is to be recast, and within a year or a generation, according as the pace is forced or not, it will assume an unaccustomed garb; and the China of that future day, near or distant, will not be the China of to-day. Whether this revolution will follow the precedent of the English Revolution or of the French, whether it will proceed by logical development from step to step, or will rush on a headlong course, will depend upon the wisdom and self-restraint of the leaders in the government, and in the last resort upon the nature of that public opinion which will be created in the Chinese people. But, just as the history of the England of the Georges cannot be well understood without some knowledge of the Stuart period, and as an acquaintance with the France of the Kingdom and the Empire is necessary to a comprehension of the France of the Third Republic, so also, to understand the China which the student of the future will know, he must be able to study its past. The China of to-day is, with minor differences, the China of the past ; and in this book it is hoped that the future student will find, within the limits of the dozen subjects treated, a succinct account of the foundation on which the China of the future will be erected.

I have written also for the reader of to-day. I can add little to the knowledge of the sinologue ; but the great majority of the men of Western countries living in China know little of the people among whom their lives are spent, or of the Empire within whose borders they pursue their avocations. Much interest, too, has been aroused of late in the home lands in the study of Chinese affairs, and we have seen members of Parliament and of Congress manifesting an intelligent interest and some adequacy of knowledge in matters connected with the Orient. All those classes will, I hope, find in these pages some information on subjects on which they may seek knowledge.

Excuses must be made to American readers for giving the equivalence of Chinese currency values in English currency only. The statements of value go back over half a century, and readers must remember the state of the American currency from 1861 to 1879.

To the number of works on China I venture to add this one, and to commit it to the kindly attention of the reading public, in the hope that in its pages they will find information not readily accessible in other works.

H. B. M.

SHANGHAI,
December 1907.

PREFACE TO SECOND EDITION

THE revolution has come, but it is yet too soon to declare if it will be destructive or constructive. China, however, remains unchanged, and a knowledge of the China of the past is as necessary as ever to an understanding of the China of the future. In this belief this second edition is prepared for a public which has given a kindly reception to its predecessor.

H. B. M.

GUNTEN, LAKE OF THUN
October 1912.

PREFACE TO THIRD EDITION

THE continued demand for this work confirms me in my belief that a knowledge of the China of the past, on which is to be modelled the China of the future, is considered desirable by those who are interested in the country.

While the volume was being revised, and as it goes to press, China is everywhere in a disturbed state, divided against itself, with a weak government dominated by a lawless soldiery; at the same time the world is distracted to such an extent that none but well-organised and well-administered nations can hope to win through. And yet the Chinese have shown in their three thousand years of history that there is a vitality in the people which enables them to emerge from troubles as great, even, as those which now threaten themselves and the whole world. A true friend of China, Sir Robert Hart, once wrote :—

" The country will stagger onwards through all sorts of mistakes, but it will be an advance always, and, provided wisdom increases with strength, I don't think the latter will be misused more than, or even as much as, is the case elsewhere."

That the wisdom which gives strength may increase, and that the strength which wisdom gives may be used for good, is the fervent wish of every true friend of China.

The oldest surviving nation in the world is, in some respects, the youngest. While in past centuries the West has learned much from the East, now, in this twentieth century of unrest and progress, of democracy and strong government, the East must learn of the West. In this task of instructing the East in the principles of modern thought and the methods of modern science, the United States of America have taken a leading part, worthy of all praise. If England and France could do as much, not even the time-honoured conservatism of China could resist the united impulse given by the three great democracies of the West; and the whole world would be the gainer.

H. B. M.

CAMBERLEY,
April 1920.

CONTENTS

xi

ILLUSTRATIONS

xiii

NOTE

Currency.—In the following pages the value of commodities is expressed in taels of silver as accepted at the Custom House. The gold exchange value of these Haikwan or Customs taels (symbol Tls.) has been as follows :

In 1864	..	80 pence English currency (6s.	8d.)
,, 1874	..	76 ,, ,, ,, (6s.	4d.)
,, 1884	..	67 ,, ,, ,, (5s.	7d.)
,, 1894	..	38 ,, ,, ,, (3s.	2d.)
,, 1904	..	34 ,, ,, ,, (2s.	10d.)
,, 1911	..	32 ,, ,, ,, (2s.	8d.)
,, 1918	..	63 ,, ,, ,, (5s.	3d.)

In the first months of 1920 it rose to 106 pence (8s. 10d.) in English currency, which was then depreciated about 30 per cent.

Weight.—Weights are expressed in piculs, catties, and taels.

One picul = 133⅓ lb. av. = 60·453 kilogrammes.
$\begin{cases} 1\frac{1}{5} \text{ cwt. English.} \\ 1\frac{1}{3} \text{ cwt. American.} \end{cases}$

16·8 piculs =	1 long ton.
15·0 ,, =	1 short ton.
16·54 ,, =	1 metric ton.
One catty =	1⅓ lb. av. = 604·53 grammes.
One tael =	1⅓ oz. av. = 583·3 grains.
,, =	37·783 grammes.

xv

The Trade and Administration of China

CHAPTER I

SKETCH OF CHINESE HISTORY

THE autochthonous peoples of China are still to be found in the various tribes of Miaotze, Lolo, To, Li, and others occupying the mountainous districts of the provinces of Kweichow, Szechwan, Yunnan, Kwangtung, and Kwangsi, and of the island of Hainan, driven there for refuge by the conquering Chinese, and preserving their own customs and habits. They have generally preserved their own tribal government and given but a nominal submission to the established government of the country, and, in modern times, have never been prominent in brigandage or in rebellion.

The Chinese came into the country at a date which, in the absence of any positive proof, may be assumed to have been about B.C. 2500. They first settled with their flocks in what is now the province of Shensi, west of the Yellow River, and from there spread to the east and south of that river. From this region they followed the valleys, first westward by the valley of the Wei toward Szechwan ; then, crossing the Yangtze, they occupied the basin of Kiangsi, draining into the Poyang Lake ; and later, by the Tungting Lake and the valley of the Siang, they occupied

Hunan and penetrated into the Two Kwang. Their absorption of the kingdom of Wu, stretching along the sea coast from the Yangtze south, was accomplished during the Han dynasty.

The age of the Five Rulers begins with the reign of Fu-hsi (B.C. 2852), who taught the people to fish with nets, to rear domestic animals, and to play on musical instruments ; he also regulated the marriage laws and invented hiero-glyphic writing. His successor was Shen-nung (B.C. 2737), who taught the people agriculture and herbal medicine. He was followed by Hwang-ti (B.C. 2697), who devised the Chinese calendar and introduced the rearing of the silk-worm. The fourth was the great Yao (B.C. 2356), who associated with himself in the government Shun and Yü. These three, whose doings were recorded by Confucius and Mencius, governed wisely and increased the happiness of their people ; but their chief claim to fame is derived from their control over great floods which devastated the country, and from a system of canals by which the land was drained and reclaimed. Yao handed down the government to Shun (B.C. 2255–2205) and he in turn to Yü, by whom the Hsia dynasty was founded.

The Hsia dynasty lasted from B.C. 2205 to B.C. 1766, when it was overthrown by a rebellion raised by Tang, the Prince of Shang, who founded the Shang or Yin dynasty. This was overthrown in B.C. 1122 by Wu Wang, the Duke of Chow, who founded the Chow dynasty, which endured until B.C. 255. Then followed a period of confusion until, in B.C. 221, the Duke of Tsin established himself on the throne.

During the Chow dynasty the administration of public affairs received a high degree of organisation. A currency was introduced, the token simulacra of swords and spades, which had formed the medium of exchange, being replaced by token coins of copper, round and flat, with a hole in the middle, the earliest of this form being assignable to about B.C. 660. The government was not yet in name an Empire ;

but the overlord governed through a feudal nobility of graduated rank (duke, marquis, count, etc.), the members of which were in command each of an assigned district, as was the case in the Holy Roman Empire in Europe ; and, as in that Empire in its latter centuries, these feudal nobles by degrees asserted their semi-independence, giving only a nominal allegiance to their sovereign.

The Chow dynasty was distinguished by the teaching of the three great philosophers Laotze, Confucius, and Mencius, who were, respectively, contemporaries of Socrates, Plato, and Aristotle.

Laotze (the " Old One ") was born about B.C. 604, in the eastern part of what is now Honan. His name records the tradition that at birth he was already an old man, with bald head and a beard. His system of philosophy is mystical, teaching men to live in harmony with " Tao " (Right or Reason), the great absolute impersonal principle which is the source of all things and immanent in all things. Taoism, one of the religious cults of China, claims him as its founder.

Confucius (Kungfutze) was born B.C. 551 in the dukedom of Lu, in the south-western part of Shantung. He collected and edited the writings and historical records of the past, giving lectures on them to his pupils. A minister of the Duke of Lu, he left the Court when he failed to persuade his master to govern according to the practice of the wise men of old (a Clarendon to a Charles II), and visited Court after Court of the feudal rulers, seeking in vain for a prince wise enough to accept his counsels. His philosophy was collected by his disciples of a later age and has served as the ethical guide of the Chinese race for over two thousand years. He died in B.C. 479 ; his lineal descendant was created an hereditary duke in the Tang dynasty ; and he himself was canonised by Imperial decree in 1906.

Mencius (Mengtze), also a native of the state of Lu, was born B.C. 372. In some ways he was a more original thinker than Confucius, whom he called his master ; but

in the eyes of the Chinese race his chief claim to fame comes
from his having collected and annotated the sayings of the
Master, and taught the Master's system of philosophy.

The Tsin dynasty was established B.C. 221 by the Duke
of Tsin, who was the first to adopt the title of Hwangti
or Emperor ; it ended soon after the death of its first
Emperor, B.C. 209, but in that short space of twelve years
much was accomplished. The Empire was extended until
it included from the Great Wall on the north to the Yangtze
on the south, and from the Yellow Sea on the east to
Szechwan on the west. The feudal system was abolished
and the government centralised. The currency and the
standards of weight and measure were reformed. During
this reign the Great Wall of China, the marvel of future
ages, was greatly extended. It stretches, through a length
of 1,500 miles, from 98° to 120° E. longitude, and was designed to protect the Empire from the incursions of the wild
Tartar tribes on the north, who had then begun to be a
menace to the Chinese and who dominated the Empire
during many of the centuries following. The Emperor
entirely reorganised the nation, and, desiring that it should
look forward and not back, he decreed that all books and
records relating to the past should be burnt. In this he
succeeded only in making his name execrated by scholars
in all future ages ; but his reforms stood the test of time,
and, in its organisation, China retained his impress for
two thousand years.

The Han dynasty was established B.C. 206 by Liu-pang,
Prince of Han. It carried Chinese arms and civilisation
south of the Yangtze (Kiangsi, Hunan, Kweichow, Kwangsi,
and Kwangtung), following the lines through the Poyang
and Tungting Lakes ; and it also included Kansu in its
dominion, and subjugated the northern part of Korea.
Through Kansu the Chinese thus came, by the trans-Asian
trade routes, into communication with the West. This
period is looked back to as the Golden Age of Chinese history ;
and " Sons of Han " is the name given to themselves to

this day by the Chinese, except the Cantonese, who call themselves " Sons of Tang." During this period, too, the incursions of the Tartar tribes became more troublesome, the most insistent being the Hiung-nu, to whom for many years the Han Emperors paid an annual subsidy of silks, rice, and wine.

The Han dynasty came to an end A.D. 25, and a period of two centuries of confusion followed. In this were distinguished the three great traitors of Chinese history, Wang-mang, Tung-cho, and Tsao-tsao. This was followed by the romantic and chivalrous period of the " Three Kingdoms" (A.D. 221-265)—the kingdom of Wei, comprising the central and northern parts of the Han Empire; Wu, bordering the Yangtze and comprising Hunan, Hupeh, Kiangsi, Anhwei, Kiangsu, and Chekiang ; and Shu, including Szechwan and adjacent territory. These kingdoms waged incessant war with each other ; but finally the kingdom of Wei was victorious and, absorbing the others, its ruler established the Western Tsin dynasty (A.D. 265-317). During the whole of this time the country was subject to the incursions of the Tartars, who seemed to consider the Great Wall as only an incitement to invasion, and to regard with scorn the weak pretensions of the " man behind the wall." Finally the Chinese rulers were driven from their capital at Kaifeng and pushed south of the Yangtze, the Tartars holding the country to the north ; and in that southern territory, with the capital at Nanking, there was a succession of weak and short-lived dynasties—Eastern Tsin (317-420), Sung (420-479), Tsi (479-502), Liang (502-557), Chen (557-589) and Sui (589-618)—each throne set up by a strong commander and lost by his degenerate successor.

The Tang dynasty (618-907) is another glorious period of Chinese history. Its founder remodelled his army and was able to drive back the Tartar invaders, establishing his capital at Changan in Shensi ; he reorganised the government and re-established order ; he brought the Cantonese under more perfect control; and he encouraged the study of the Confucian classics, declaring that " Confucian thought is to the Chinese what the water is to the fish." The culminating point in this period was the domination of the Empress Wu-how, who first ruled jointly with her husband, the Emperor Kao-tsung (650–684) and then as Empress Dowager-Regent for her son Chung-tsung, until in 705 she was forced by advancing age to abdicate her power. Her ability has been recognised by the Chinese, but her memory has been execrated because of the impropriety of her conduct in presuming to govern the Empire. In fact, however, she was the last of the strong rulers of the dynasty, and for the remaining two centuries the throne was for the most part filled by men weak in character and of small capacity. Literature flourished and the arts advanced; but the country was disturbed by internal rebellions and Tartar incursions. Korea was fully conquered in 667 and reduced to a vassal state, remaining in that position until 1895; this secured the north-eastern frontier, but along the northern border for more than two centuries there was no peace.

Nestorian priests, coming from Persia, brought the first teaching of Christianity into China during this period. They were favourably received; and by Imperial sanction a stone tablet recording the tenets of their Church was erected at Sianfu in Shensi.

After the Tang dynasty followed the period of the Five Dynasties (907–960)—Later Liang, Later Tang, Later Tsin, Later Han, and Later Chow—a period of military despotism.

The Sung dynasty followed in 960. Peace was again restored and order established, and for a time one ruler governed the whole Empire. The incursions of the Tartar tribes were, however, soon resumed; and in 1125 the Kin or Nü-chen Tartars—" the Golden Horde "—gained the predominance and made serious inroads upon the Imperial domain. At an early date they seized the capital, Kaifeng, and required the Emperor to pay an annual tribute ; and in no long time they drove the Imperial forces south of the Yangtze, establishing their own dominion over the territory to the north of the great river. The Chinese rulers of what is called in history the Southern Sung dynasty set up their capital at first at Nanking, and afterwards at Hangchow. Incessant war was waged between the North and the South, between the Chinese dynasty of the Southern Sung and the Golden dynasty of the Tartars, across the moat of the Yangtze, but neither side succeeded in gaining ground ; and the Yangtze remained the frontier until the establishment of the Yuan dynasty of the Mongols in 1280.

The Mongols, originating in the district south-east of Lake Baikal, made their first assaults on the northern frontier in 1135. Under Genghis Khan (1162) they entered on their marvellous career of conquest. He first consolidated the loosely knit Mongol confederacy, and then made many successful raids into Northern China. In 1213 three expeditions, one under Genghis himself, overran the country, subjugating as far as the Shantung peninsula. Next the Mongols set out to conquer Asia. They subjugated the country to the south-west of China, pierced the mountain passes of the Himalayas, won a great victory on the Indus, and carried their victorious arms to the borders of the kingdom of Poland. Whenever Genghis conquered a city, he razed it to the ground and put its inhabitants to the sword. Genghis was succeeded in 1229 by his son, Ogotai Khan, who continued his father's career of conquest. He repeated the raid into Europe, pursuing his victorious course through Russia, Poland, and Hungary.

The Chinese Emperor Li-tsung (1225–1265) saw in the rise of the Mongols an opportunity to throw off the domination of the Golden Tartars ; and, setting dog to eat dog, he made an alliance with the Mongol leader. Their combined armies overcame the forces of the Golden dynasty and conquered the country north of the Yangtze still in its possession ; but when the Chinese Emperor proposed to reoccupy Kaifeng and re-establish there the capital of his Empire, he found that the Mongols saw no reason for surrendering conquests which their arms had made, and was summoned to return to his former domain in the south. War was thereupon declared between the allies, and the Mongols entered upon the subjugation of Southern China. Their forces were victorious, and the Chinese Emperor was driven to his last refuge in the island of Yaishan, south of Canton ; there he was blockaded, and finally, to avoid falling into the hands of his enemies, he and all his family committed suicide by throwing themselves into the sea.

This established the Yuan dynasty (1260–1368), which again, and for the first time under Tartar rule, reunited the whole of China under one sovereign. The consolidation of the Empire was mainly effected by Kublai Khan (1260-1295). He failed in an attack on Japan, his sea power being inferior to that of the island Japanese ; but, after subjugating the Chinese provinces, and adding Yunnan to his domain, he conquered Annam and Burma and maintained his northern frontier. Annam became a vassal state, its king soliciting investiture from Peking (where the Mongol capital was established) and sending periodic tribute until it became a dependency of France—Cochin China in 1864, Tonkin in 1885. Burma became a tributary state and sent tribute until the end of the nineteenth century. China was, however, but a part of the Mongol dominion ; in its whole extent it spread from the Black Sea on the west to the Yellow Sea on the east, and from the northern border of Mongolia to the southern limits of Annam.

The collection of tribute and its transmission to Peking were among the most important functions of the Mongol administration ; and one of the first steps taken by Kublai was the improvement of the communications between the north and the south. As a preliminary measure a canal was made from Kiaochow to the Gulf of Pechihli, cutting off the Shantung peninsula and its stormy circumnavigation. Then the Grand Canal was taken in hand. This magnificent channel of commerce was begun as early as B.C. 489, and then extended to the territory south of the Yangtze ; under the Southern Sung its southern part, from Hangchow to Chinkiang, was much improved ; and now, by Kublai, the northern part was restored and its course extended on to Tientsin, from which city the Peiho provides a good water route to Peking.

During the reign of Kublai, in 1271, the Venetian traveller Marco Polo first arrived in China, and on his return to Europe gave to the world the first of the many accounts of the wonders of that Empire. In many respects the civilisation of China was then ahead of that of Europe, and his report opened up a new realm of thought.

In conquering the country the Mongols had no thought of modifying the civilisation of the Chinese, in all respects far higher than their own ; and they recognised that their own talents lay solely in the direction of arms, and that they could not supply the qualities demanded for a civil administration. The actual administration, under the Mongols, as later under the Manchus, was in the hands of Chinese, habituated to the ways of government and finance ; and the nominal masters of the Empire, based on their northern home and guarded by garrisons stationed at a few strategic points, settled down to a life of luxury, supported by the tribute which was levied on the conquered people. This tribute was mainly in the produce of the country—silks for currency, and rice and other grain for subsistence—the contributions in circulating medium of exchange consisting almost entirely of cowrie shells. Of silver and of copper coins but little came into the treasury otherwise than by plunder ; and the needs of the Imperial Government, other than those provided by the tribute in kind, were supplied by issues of irredeemable paper money, of which during most of the short hundred years of the Mongol dynastic rule the annual emissions amounted to the enormous sum of forty million taels.* The distress resulting from this

* Cf. Chap. V.

financial condition, combined with the iron rule of the barbarous conquerors, soon brought the dynasty to its fall;
and the rebellious Chinese found a leader of ability in Chu
Yuan-chang (born 1328), who had spent his early life in a
Buddhist monastery, and now, inspired by patriotism,
emerged from his retirement to fight the oppressors of his
country.   Under his leadership the Mongols were driven
from the soil of China, and, in 1368, he declared himself
Emperor and established the Ming dynasty (1368–1644),
restoring Chinese rule over the Chinese people.

The first Ming Emperor assumed the title of Hungwu
and established his capital at Nanking; but, with the continued pressure of the Mongols and other Tartar tribes on
the northern frontier, it was transferred to Peking in 1421
by the third Emperor, Yunglo, by whom the famous porcelain pagoda was erected at Nanking as a solatium to its
people and a memorial to his father, whose tomb was there.
This pagoda was destroyed by the Taiping rebels in 1853
as being an instrument of idolatry.   Notwithstanding the
constant conflicts on the northern frontier, internal order
was soon restored; and the earlier reigns of the dynasty
were marked by great prosperity and splendour.   The
currency was restored, trade prospered, the arts flourished,
and scholarship was fostered; and at the same time the
power of the Empire was maintained over the vassal states
coterminous with China.   It was demonstrated to the
people of China that Chinese could govern their country and
govern it well; and the Ming period, the period of the finest
Chinese porcelain, shares in the Chinese mind in the glory of
the Han and Tang periods of an earlier date.

It was during the Ming period that European traders
first entered into trade relations with the Chinese Empire *
—the Portuguese in 1516, the Spanish from the Philippines
in 1575, the Dutch in 1604, and the English in the dying
days of the dynasty in 1637; the Portuguese traded solely
at Canton, the Spanish permitted the Chinese to trade with

* Cf. Chap. IX.

them at Manila, and the Dutch and English traded at first at Amoy and in Formosa.

The first Christian missionary, after the Nestorians, to arrive in China was St. Francis Xavier, the first disciple of Ignatius Loyola, the founder of the Jesuit Society. The jealous regard of the Chinese for their own institutions denied him access to the mainland ; and, after a glorious crusade to Japan, he died on the island of Shangchuen (now called St. John's Island), south of Canton, in 1553, without having set his foot on the mainland. He was followed by Michael Roger and Matteo Ricci, who were more successful in their attempts to settle and preach on the mainland, Father Ricci even succeeding, in the closing years of the century, in obtaining a lodgment in Nanking. During the last reigns of the Ming dynasty the Jesuit missionaries obtained a footing at the Imperial Court, and this was maintained during the first two reigns of the Tsing dynasty ; the most prominent among them were Adam Schaal and Verbeest, to whom was entrusted the care of compiling the calendar. Of the beautiful bronze astronomical instruments which were removed from their home on the walls of Peking, and carried to Europe in 1900, the older pieces dated back to the Mongol period, but the greater number, and of finer finish, were of the Ming period, one having been sent as a present from Louis XIV of France to the Ming Emperor.

The Ming dynasty finally fell, as the result of successful rebellion by ambitious Chinese generals ; but the profit was reaped by the Manchus, a Tartar tribe occupying what is now the province of Kirin. In 1618 the Ming Emperor, Wanli, interfered in a faction fight among the Manchus, espousing the cause of Nikan. The Manchu chief, Nurhachu, having overcome his rival, at once invaded Chinese territory and occupied the Liaotung peninsula. Defeating the Chinese troops, he then took the city of Liaoyang, the inhabitants of which were forced to shave the front part of their heads and to plait their back hair into a queue after the Manchu custom ; and this rule was enforced whenever the Manchus later gained possession of a Chinese city. Nurhachu then advanced to force the passage of the Great Wall, where it touches the sea at Shanhaikwan, but was unable to take the city of Ningyuan, which barred his way and was well defended by the Chinese troops, who were aided by cannon supplied by the Portuguese in Macao. The greater part of Manchuria was, however, brought into subjection by the Manchus.

Meantime the country was rent by civil war, two Chinese generals having in 1630 raised the standard of rebellion. Chang Hsien-chung, starting from Shensi, conquered the country to the west and south, and established himself as sovereign in Szechwan, where for some years he was left undisturbed. Li Tze-ching, starting from Shansi, marched on Peking, defeating the Ming troops sent to bar his way, and gained possession of the capital. He then assumed the title and dignity of Emperor, whereupon the last of the Ming emperors, Chwanglieh-ti, committed suicide by hanging himself.

Under ordinary circumstances this would have left the victorious general in possession of the throne and enabled him to found a new dynasty. But a loyal general of the Ming Emperor, Wu San-kwei, resolved to avenge the death of the Emperor, and for that purpose called in the Manchus to aid him in dispossessing the successful rebel ; and the allied forces of the Manchus and the Chinese army loyal to the dynasty together gained a decisive victory. The fruits of victory were reaped by the Manchus, whose chief, a minor at the time, was placed on the throne, thereby establishing the Tsing dynasty (1644–1912). After the subjugation of the Empire was completed, Wu San-kwei was rewarded with the satrapy of Yunnan and Kweichow, to be held in feudal tenure ; but, exciting the jealousy of Kanghi and fear lest he should set up an independent kingdom, he was summoned to Peking. He refused, declaring that he would come only at the head of eighty thousand soldiers ; this was treated as contumacy and rebellion, an expedition was sent to reduce him to obedience, and he died in 1678.

The reign of the first Emperor, Shunchih (1644–1661) was spent principally in conquering the provinces. This task was still uncompleted at his death, many Ming princes and partisans being still in arms in the south and west, and the final conquest and pacification were completed by his successor, the great Kanghi (1662–1723). The conquest may be considered to have been accomplished in 1683, in which year Formosa, then recently colonised by settlers from southern Fukien, was first brought into subjection to the Chinese throne. That island had first, within the previous hundred years, been colonised from Amoy ; it was then taken and held from 1624 by the Dutch ; they were dispossessed in 1662 by Koxinga, of the name-clan of the imperial family of the Ming, who made good his hold on Amoy and Formosa ; and he in turn by the Manchu forces, under the Emperor's own leadership, in 1683.

The Manchus imitated the Mongols in leaving the civil administration of the Empire to a great extent in the hands of the Chinese.* They organised the whole of modern Manchuria on the military basis, and converted Peking into an armed camp, with the Emperor's tent in the middle, surrounded by the troops of the Imperial clan, that in turn surrounded by the main body of the Manchu army,† with the Chinese inhabitants (the sutlers of the army) segregated in a separate city, dominated by the walls of the Manchu city, as shown in the diagram. (See next page.)

They further established military colonies in twenty-five cities of Chihli, as an inner line of defence, and selected a dozen important strategic points ‡ in the other provinces at which military colonies were settled to serve as outposts in holding the Empire in subjection. Certain lucrative posts were reserved for Manchus, and an indefinite number of posts in the ordinary administration, latterly not exceeding a fifth of the total, were held by Manchus ; otherwise the civil

* Cf. Chap. II.   † *Ibid.*   ‡ *Ibid.*

administration was in the hands of the Chinese, the nominally subject race. The Court and the Manchu army (consisting of all adult male Manchus) were maintained from the grain tribute, the land tax, the salt gabelle, and a few minor tributes, the grain tribute being sent in kind to Peking to be issued as rations to the army. The taxation covered by these heads was light, and the conquered race was not discontented with its subjection, so long as the government was strong, official corruption was kept in check, and justice and protection secured to the subject.

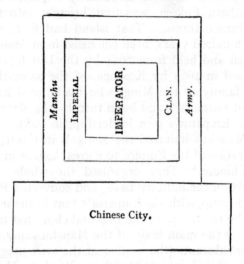

The reign of Kanghi was one of great splendour. The arts flourished, and Kanghi porcelain was equal to that of the best Ming period. Order was maintained, and throughout the Empire the farmer and trader enjoyed full security in their occupations. The vassal states recognised his overlordship without question. Scholarship was encouraged ; the Emperor himself was no mean scholar, and under his patronage were published the great Kanghi dictionary, and an encyclopedia of universal knowledge in 6,026 fascicules. He himself composed the sixteen maxims, known as the

Sacred Edict, which, afterwards expanded and annotated by his successor Yungcheng, have since that time been expounded in the city temple of every city in the Empire.

He was succeeded by Yungcheng (1723–1735), whose reign was also one of great prosperity and good administration.

The Roman Catholic missionaries, barely tolerated at first by the Ming emperors, had later obtained a footing at court. Shunchih, the first Manchu Emperor, was much interested in their accounts of their religion and civilisation ; and under Kanghi they attained to positions of great importance in the Imperial administration. Though jealous of any attempt to introduce unaccustomed practices, he was much inclined to lend a willing ear to what they had to say, until he was suddenly aroused by a question of mere terminology. The proper rendering into Chinese of the term " God " formed a subject of dispute between the Jesuits and the Dominicans ; the Emperor interested himself in the disputation, and gave his decision in favour of the interpretation desired by the Jesuits. The Dominicans, however, appealed to the Pope ; and, as the Jesuits were then in disfavour at the Papal court, the Emperor's judgment was reversed. The Emperor was dissatisfied that his knowledge of his own tongue should be questioned by a Western barbarian ; and he and his Ministers were startled on discovering that an appeal from his judgment on a question of Chinese polity could be carried to the tribunal of an Italian priest. He therefore withdrew the light of his countenance from the missionaries, and an exceptionally favourable chance of converting the Empire to Christianity was lost. His successor Yungcheng went further and, in 1727, issued an edict prohibiting the propagation of the Christian faith and confiscating the property of the missions. This prohibition was withdrawn in 1844.

Calvinist pastors entered Formosa in the train of the Dutch, and shared their fate in being driven out in 1662. A number of them were then beheaded or crucified by the officers of Koxinga.

Yungcheng was followed by Kienlung (1736–1796). There were some internal disorders during his reign, but on the whole the administration was effective, and the country prospered. He conquered and annexed eastern Turkestan, and reduced Burma, which had rejected his suzerainty, to subjection. The Gurkhas having invaded Tibet, he dispatched an army into that country and drove them back into Nipal, restoring Tibet to obedience to the Chinese rule.

During the reign of Kienlung the foreign trade of Canton developed and assumed great proportions,* the nations of the West sending their ships and traders to obtain the tea and silk of the Celestial Empire. It was during this period, in 1784, that the Americans entered the commercial field, in which they were soon to occupy a place second only to that of the English ; and by the end of the reign all the trading nations of the West were represented in the factories at Canton.

Kienlung abdicated in 1796, after a reign of sixty years, in order that he might not exceed the limits of the reign of his grandfather, Kanghi. With the accession of Kiaking set in the degeneration and degradation of the Empire. The court became corrupt, the administration ceased to be efficient, corruption among the mandarinate went unchecked, justice and protection were no longer assured to the people, the secret societies awoke from their dormant state, and dissatisfaction manifested itself in many parts of the empire. At Canton trade flourished and the foreign merchants increased in numbers ; but their trade, grown to larger proportions, was brought under more complete control, while their personal freedom was restricted by many vexatious regulations, some petty and annoying, others making of the trade a close monopoly in the hands of the officials at Canton.

In 1796 Imperial edicts strengthened the old prohibition (originally proclaimed in 1729) against the smoking of opium—up to the end of the eighteenth century smoked

* Cf. Chap. IX.

entirely in conjunction with tobacco ; and in 1800 an edict was issued prohibiting the growing of the poppy in China, and the importation of foreign opium. These restrictions changed, in immaterial ways, the machinery of trade, but they were not enforced, and they in no way diminished the use of the drug.

Taokwang (1820–1850) attempted to check the corruption of the Court, and to amend the evils of the administration ; but the task was impossible. He succeeded to a rotten administration ; the finances were disordered by a succession of minor rebellions in one after another of the provinces ; he obtained but weak support for reform among his officials, who were the most in need of being reformed ; his army had degenerated ; and he was helpless in presence of the Augean mass of corruption which it was his task to sweep away.

The restrictions on the trade of Canton were made more strict and the monopoly more close. The trade of the nations of Europe was under the control each of an East India Company of its own nation, and this system provided some small degree of check on the working of the Chinese monopoly. But, by the year 1830, fully nine-tenths of the trade was in the hands of the English and Americans. Of these, the English were compelled to trade through, or by the licence of, their East India Company—they could trade with India and other Asiatic countries under licence, but the trade with their home country, including the entire trade in the main staples of tea and silk, was absolutely prohibited to them. The Americans, on the other hand, were free to trade where they would ; even the trade between China and Europe, denied to the English, was open to them. An agitation for freedom of trade started in England, and in 1833 the monopoly granted to the English East India Company was abolished.

This brought China face to face with the English Government, without the intermediary of an incorporated company ; and in 1834 Lord Napier was sent to Canton to settle

2

the many subjects of friction and dispute between the two countries. He was not allowed to get so far as to open negotiations ; he was met at the outset by a refusal to treat him as an envoy of a friendly Power, enjoying a position of equality with China ; he was refused an interview with the Viceroy, who required him to formulate his demands through the committee of Chinese merchants through whom the trade monopoly was worked ; his letters were not received, and he was required to present his written communications in the form of a humble petition ; and coercion was applied to the English merchants and their trade to force him to leave Canton. For public reasons he complied with this last order, and returned to Macao, where he died, from fever and vexation of spirit, just three months after his first arrival in Chinese waters.

During this same year died Robert Morrison, who had arrived in Canton in 1807, the first Protestant missionary to be sent from England. He was not allowed to preach the Gospel ; but, under the protection of a nominal post under the English East India Company, he studied the Chinese language, and gave to the world a translation of the Bible and a dictionary which has been the basis of most of the lexicons compiled since by others. The next to follow him was Elijah Colman Bridgeman, sent from America, arriving in Canton in 1829. He founded the *Chinese Repository*, a monthly magazine published at Canton from 1831 to 1851 ; and originated in 1857 the Shanghai Asiatic Society, being its first president. Other Protestant missionaries followed, and in 1845 they numbered sixty, of whom (with one German) two-thirds were American and one-third British. In 1907, the centennial anniversary of Robert Morrison's arrival, the Protestant missionaries, including all independent workers, men and women, but excluding wives and children, exceeded four thousand in number, of whom about a half were American, four-tenths British, and one-tenth of other nationalities.

The Emperor Taokwang took the opium question much

to heart. The restriction on its import had in no way diminished the quantity ; the ships under all the foreign flags (excepting only the ships of the English East India Company) continued to bring it, but, instead of coming into port, they remained outside port limits and delivered it there to Chinese buyers ; and the officials continued to levy their tax on it, but it was for their own profit and not for the public fisc. In 1836, in order to combat the evils of a clandestine trade, the question was seriously debated at Peking whether it was not better to legalise the trade, but it was decided in the negative. In this decision the Emperor had against him practically all the tax-collecting mandarins, but in Lin Tse-sü he found a man after his own heart, prepared to over-ride all obstacles and so extirpate the curse. He was appointed High Commissioner for this purpose in 1839 ; and, on his arrival at Canton, put an embargo on the foreign trade, and placed the English Superintendent and the foreign merchants of all nationalities in close confinement in their houses, deprived of food, fuel, water, and servants, and demanded that the opium then in the " outside waters " be brought in and surrendered to him. With the foreign residents held as hostages for the execution of this command, the English Superintendent, to secure their release, ordered all opium then in Chinese waters to be surrendered to him on behalf of the British Government, and he in turn surrendered it, to the amount of 20,291 chests, to the Chinese authorities, who destroyed it to the last ounce. Commissioner Lin then demanded that each foreign resident should sign a bond undertaking, for himself, his Government, and all foreign merchants, that there should be no more trade in opium. They were willing, in their state of duress, to sign for themselves individually ; and, when the High Commissioner found he could obtain no more, he released the imprisoned foreigners and allowed them to take refuge on board their ships at Hongkong. In the war which followed the Chinese were uniformly beaten ; Canton, Amoy, Ningpo, Chapu, Shanghai, and Chinkian were taken by the British plenipotentiary, Sir Henry Pottinger, with Admiral Sir William Parker in command of the fleet; and on August 29th, 1842, was signed the treaty of Nanking, by which the Chinese conceded all that was demanded.

To the Chinese opium appeared to have been the sole cause of the war, and they honestly could not understand that any other cause existed. To their expressed surprise * the opium question was not included in the English demands formulated at Nanking, and they were informed that they could regulate the trade according to their own laws, on condition that, in doing so, they did not injuriously affect the persons or the other property of foreign merchants. The treaty settled the equal status of nations, and guaranteed security to the persons of their representatives and merchants; abolished the monopoly of trade, and permitted foreign representatives to communicate direct with the Chinese officials; designated five ports (Canton, Amoy, Foochow, Ningpo, and Shanghai) at which foreign merchants might erect residences and warehouses and conduct their trade; provided for a uniform and published tariff of customs duties, in lieu of the previous exactions, unknown in amount and uncertain in their incidence; and exacted an indemnity of twenty-one million dollars for the expenses of the expedition and as compensation for the opium surrendered to obtain the release of the persons illegally detained. The provisions of this treaty, imposed at the cannon's mouth, indicate clearly enough what were the motives which led the British Government to take up arms.

The concessions obtained under this treaty for the British were expressly extended to all other nations. In 1844 the United States of America negotiated a similar treaty, by which the principle of extraterritoriality † was more clearly defined; and in the same year France also made a similar treaty. Under the new treaties the foreign

* "Is this all?" as the principal Chinese negotiator, Kiying, said to Sir H. Pottinger.

† Cf. Chap. VII.

trade developed ; but their spirit was not fully accepted by the Chinese and, in the succeeding years, there were much hostility and friction. The Canton Viceroy, Yeh Ming-chin, in particular showed himself hostile on all occasions, never once consenting to grant an audience to the foreign Envoys, British, American, or French, who requested one ; and finally in 1856 he provided a fresh *casus belli* by illegally seizing some reputed pirates on a ship, the lorcha *Arrow*, flying the British flag, for which he refused reparation, or even explanation.

In the meantime Hienfeng (1851–1861) had come to the throne, succeeding to an Empire rent by rebellion and rotten with corruption. The greatest of the rebellions was that of the Taiping. This originated in north-eastern Kwangsi, and soon found a leader in Hung Siu-tsuen. He had been instructed by an American Baptist missionary in the tenets of the Christian faith ; and, though his beliefs were soon dominated by the practices of an Oriental despot, at the outset he formed a band of devoted adherents, rigid in their observances, unconquerable in battle, and comparable only to Cromwell's Ironsides. Breaking out from Kwangsi in the spring of 1852, he advanced north through Hunan, conquering as he went, but was unable to take Changsha. Yochow and Hanyang fell to his troops in December 1852, and Wuchang in January 1853. Thence he pursued his conquering advance down the Yangtze, gathering adherents as he went, and devastating and plundering the country ; and, on March 19, captured Nanking, which he made the capital of the new Taiping empire. For the time his troops advanced no further to the east ; but an army was sent north to attack Peking. It defeated every army sent to oppose it, and established a fortified camp within twelve miles of Tientsin ; but it was a spent force, and in 1854 its remnants were driven back to the south. Other associated risings were also successful, and in 1854 the Imperial Government was undisputed master of scarcely a province in the Empire.

This was the time selected by the Canton Viceroy to irritate the three Western Powers, who were then united in making joint representations to the Chinese Government, and in demanding a revision of the treaties and better protection to foreign lives and property. The American representative could take no positive action, since his instructions forbade him to proceed to the use of force, the declaration of war lying with Congress and not with the President ; but France was provided with a *casus belli* by the murder of the missionary Chapdelaine, the rightfulness of which was upheld by Viceroy Yeh, who refused any reparation, and, when it came to the clash of arms, France stood by the side of England. Canton was taken by the allies at the end of 1857, just twelve months after the Viceroy had burned the foreign factories there. The forces then proceeded to the Peiho, at the mouth of which stood the Taku forts, which were taken almost without a blow ; and they advanced at once on Tientsin, with the American and Russian Envoys in close attendance. There was no long hesitation, and the negotiations were not protracted. With the Empire torn asunder by rebellion, the prestige of the Imperial Government was shattered by the armed force of the English and French, and the conditions imposed were accepted. In June 1858 the Treaties of Tientsin were signed, the first by Hon. Wm. B. Reed on behalf of the United States, the second by Count Putiatin for Russia, then by the Earl of Elgin for England, and the last by Baron Gros for France.

One article of the British treaty provided for the continued residence of the British Envoy (and therefore of all foreign Envoys) at Peking ; but, on the earnest solicitation of the Chinese negotiators, Lord Elgin consented to defer the execution of this condition, substituting for it a stipulation that the ratifications of the treaty should be exchanged at Peking. When, in June 1859, the Envoys of the four Powers came to exchange the ratifications, they were refused a passage past the Taku forts. The French forces were engaged in operations against Annam, and the only fleet present was the British. An attempt by these to force the passage was repulsed with heavy loss. It was on this occasion that the American Commodore Tatnall declared that " blood is thicker than water," when he sent boats to tow the wounded English marines out of the line of fire, and went himself, amid the dropping shot, to inquire for the welfare of the English admiral, who had been wounded.

The English and French proceeded to carry their undertaking to its end, and sent a joint expedition, again with Lord Elgin and Baron Gros as plenipotentiaries. The allied force took the Taku forts, after some resistance, on August 21st, 1860, occupied Tientsin, and took Peking. At Tungchow a party of English and French were captured by the Chinese, while engaged in peace negotiations ; some were murdered and all were tortured, and as punishment for the act of treachery, the Emperor's summer palace at Yuenmingyuen was destroyed by fire. By the Convention of Peking, which was then signed, the indemnities were increased and it was provided that the foreign Envoys should reside in Peking.

The treaties of 1858 and 1860 made a definite settlement of the relations between China and Western nations ; up to 1842 it was China which dictated absolutely the conditions of trade, but since 1858 they have been dictated by the West. The opium question was then settled by the legalisation of the traffic. The smuggling had reached scandalous proportions, demoralising the officials whose duty it was to enforce the law and the merchants to whom it was a forbidden trade. The American Envoy was appalled by the demoralisation, and suggested legalisation as the lesser of two evils. Lord Elgin, who was in a position to dictate terms, was reluctant to take the initiative ; but the Chinese negotiators were ready to relieve the financial difficulties of the Empire by securing for the Treasury the revenue which prohibition only diverted into private pockets ; and the trade was legalised by including opium in the tariff which was appended to the treaty.

Meantime the Taiping rebellion maintained its ground. For some years the Heavenly King remained quiet, with his capital, Nanking, as the eastern outpost of his Empire ; but the devastation and depopulation of the country dominated by his anarchical rule drove him to seek new bases of supply, and, in 1860, the Taiping forces broke into the rich and hitherto undevastated country between Nanking and the sea. They captured Soochow and Hangchow, and the intervening country, but evacuated Hangchow, leaving the corpses of 70,000 of its inhabitants massacred within its walls. They then marched against Shanghai ; but the foreign Envoys had decided to protect, against Imperialists and rebels alike, the neutrality of that centre of foreign trade ; and, on August 18th, while the allied troops were advancing to take the Taku forts from the Imperial forces, the allied troops were engaged in defending Shanghai from the Taiping assault. Shanghai was, however, an oasis in a desert of Taiping devastation, and the only successes obtained against their armies were gained by a force organised and led by the American, Frederick T. Ward. To this force was given by Imperial decree the title of " The Ever-Victorious Army." Ward was killed in action in 1862, and after the American Burgevine and the English Holland had tried to wield the baton of leadership, the British authorities lent the services of Captain Charles G. Gordon—" Chinese Gordon." He continued the ever-victorious career initiated by Ward, and recaptured city after city, until finally Changchow was retaken. Gordon then resigned his command, refusing all reward, except the Imperial insignia of the Yellow Jacket and military rank. The back of the rebellion was broken, and in the spring of 1864, after an investment, not always very close, of eleven years, Nanking was taken by the Imperial forces, the Heavenly King committing suicide.

Then followed twenty years of recovery, with no important events, but with a great development of trade. The event most worthy of special note was the mission to foreign

Powers, at the head of which was Mr. Anson W. Burlingame, with two Chinese associates. He had been Envoy of the United States during the period of reconstruction, and on his resignation in 1867 he undertook to establish the relations between China and the West on a new basis. China was not yet, however, sufficiently advanced to enter on equal terms into the comity of nations, and this was manifest to the sober sense of the Western Governments.

In 1870 occurred the massacre of Tientsin. For some time before anti-foreign and anti-Christian literature had been freely circulated, and the feelings thereby excited were stirred to frenzy by reports that the sisters of the (French) Roman Catholic orphanage were in the habit of kidnapping children, and using their hearts and eyes to compound the marvellously effective Western medicines. A riot ensued in which the orphanage and cathedral were burned and all of French nationality who could be found were murdered with horrible mutilations. France was then engaged in war with Germany, and the settlement demanded gave reparation for the murders, but not for the anti-national animus manifested.

In 1873 the Emperor Tungchih (1863–1874) attained his legal majority, and on June 29th the first Imperial audience was granted to the foreign Envoys. This was a notable concession, but after all only a half-concession, as the audience took place in the Pavilion of Purple Light, a hall ordinarily used for receiving the Envoys of tributary nations.

In 1876 Mr. A. R. Margary, of the British consular service, was murdered in Yunnan. By the Chefoo Agreement, signed on September 13th, reparation for the murder was given, a better method of regulating the opium traffic was agreed to, and the jurisdiction in mixed cases was placed on a better footing.

In 1883 France undertook the conquest of Tonkin, and in so doing came into conflict with the suzerain Power. In 1884 the Chinese fleet in the port of Foochow was destroyed by the French fleet, which had entered the anchorage before the outbreak of hostilities. Formosa was then attacked, but was successfully defended by the Chinese. An inconclusive war was closed by a treaty, signed June 9th, 1885, by which the French claim to Tonkin was recognised, while France abandoned all other demands on China.

Korea had been a vassal state under the suzerainty of the Chinese Emperor since the year 667 ; but the subjection was little more than nominal, being made manifest chiefly by the formal approval and investiture of each new Korean King, and the annual sending of tribute. The suzerain Power generally maintained the land frontier, but gave no protection against the incursions of the Japanese, the most notable of which was that under Hideyoshi in 1592 ; and in that year a Japanese settlement was founded at Fusan. In 1876 an unprovoked attack on Japanese gunboats led Japan to send an expedition against Korea, and as a result three Korean ports were opened to Japanese trade under conditions of extraterritoriality. As a measure of protection against this, China required Korea to open these ports on the same terms to the trade of all nations. Much disorder followed, and on one occasion, in 1882, the Japanese Legation was attacked and burned to the ground. Japan sent troops to Chemulpo to demand reparation, whereupon China despatched a force to Seoul to maintain order. A clash seemed imminent, but the matter was settled by a *modus vivendi* established by Li Hung-chang and Count Ito. On the ground that disturbances existed along the frontier of her Siberian possessions, Russia moved her troops in the direction of Korea ; as a counter-movement the British fleet occupied Port Hamilton, an island south of the southern point of Korea, but it was abandoned in 1887.

In 1894 China sent troops to Korea to suppress disorder which had broken out, and Japan answered by sending a force to maintain the independence of Korea. Both nations were fully equipped ; but Japan had fully imbibed the spirit of Western military methods, while China had acquired only the material. The Japanese forces on land were uniformly victorious, and drove the Chinese out of Korea, across the Yalu and through eastern Manchuria, with scarcely a check. In the naval battle off the mouth of the Yalu the Japanese gained a great victory, owing to the inferior quality of the Chinese ammunition. The Japanese forces then assaulted and captured the stronghold of Port Arthur; and at Weihaiwei they captured the forts and many of the ships remaining to China, after a gallant defence by Admiral Ting Ju-chang. The war was closed by the Treaty of Shimonoseki, signed April 17th, 1895, by which it was recognised that Japan occupied a status on an equality with any Western power; the independence of Korea was admitted; the Liaotung peninsula, Formosa, and the Pescadores were ceded; an indemnity of two hundred million taels was exacted; and further Chinese ports, all inland, were to be opened to foreign trade. Ultimately, on the joint demand of Russia, France, and Germany, the cession of the Liaotung peninsula was waived, in exchange for an additional indemnity of thirty million taels.

China seemed to have reached her lowest depths, and the European Powers began to provide against the impending break-up of the Empire. In 1897, as compensation for the murder of two German missionaries in Shantung, Germany demanded and obtained a " lease " of Kiaochow. Then in 1898, in rapid succession, "in order to restore the balance of power in the Ear East," Russia obtained a lease of Port Arthur, England of Weihaiwei, and France of Kwangchowwan. In 1899 Italy demanded the lease, on the same footing, of Sanmen Bay in Chekiang. This was too much: Italian interests in China were of the smallest, and Italy had never displayed her strength in Chinese waters; and China, weak and disorganised as she was, peremptorily refused the demand. No evil consequences followed on this refusal, and the patriotic party was much elated.

China had slumbered for half a century, but the awakening seemed at last to have come. The Young China party believed that only by radical reforms could the Empire be saved; and one of the most ardent of their number, Kang Yu-wei, gained the ear of the Emperor. He was carried away, and issued edict after edict, intended to transform in a few months the institutions based on thousands of years of settled government, and to correct the abuses engendered by a century of corrupt administration. The tried Ministers of State took alarm, the Empress Dowager emerged from her retirement and soon restored the Emperor to his natural obedience, and the wave of impulsive reform was checked. But the feeling of discontent among the people was too strong to be suppressed, and in 1900 it manifested itself in the vague and aimless national and anti-foreign rising known as the Boxer * Outbreak.

The Boxer movement came as a bolt from the blue, with no warning, and soon the foreign communities at Peking and Tientsin, including the foreign Envoys at Peking, were beleaguered by many thousands of armed fanatics, determined on their extermination and the uprooting of all foreign influence. The whole world stood aghast. No such crime against the comity of nations had been committed within historical times, and thousands of troops were sent by the principal Western Powers to the succour of their besieged countrymen and their imperilled Envoys. The defence of the beleaguered communities was gallantly maintained, under conditions which recall the siege of Lucknow in 1857 ; but they were in daily peril for nearly three months. One attempt to relieve them was made by an international contingent of 2,000 sailors of all nations under the British Admiral Seymour ; but, while they were on the march, the Taku forts were attacked and taken on June 16th, by the foreign fleets,

---

* The movement was conducted by a secret society named the " Yi-ho " society, which, by its sound, might be interpreted either the " Society of Justice and Union " or the " Society for Pugilistic Exercises." Cf. German Turnverein of 1813.

and the relieving force then found itself confronted by the Imperial troops, who had at once made common cause with the raw Boxer levies, and it found its way back to Tientsin in great peril and difficulty. Finally the troops of the principal Powers—American, British, French, Japanese, and Russian—gathered in their thousands, and after taking the city of Tientsin and driving the Chinese from its defences, they advanced on Peking, which they entered on August 14th. The armed bands besieging the Legations dispersed, and the Court and Government, guilty at least of constructive complicity, fled, making their way to the old historical capital of Sianfu. Peking was then most effectively looted ; and punitive expeditions in the vicinity soon reduced the inhabitants to a condition of bewildered submission, all troops having safely escaped to a distance. The punitive expeditions were renewed on the arrival of Graf von Waldersee, who had been designated as senior commander, but who arrived after the peasantry had been cowed to submission.

While the Court and the Ministers at Peking had generally elected to ride on the wave of Boxer enthusiasm rather than be submerged beneath it, the great Viceroys—Li Hung-chang at Canton, Liu Kun-yi at Nanking, and Chang Chih-tung at Wuchang—saw the criminal folly of the outbreak and did what they could to preserve the Empire from its consequences. Two Chinese ministers went so far as to modify telegraphic instructions sent in the Emperor's name to " exterminate all foreigners," and to convert it into " protect all foreigners " ; the two Yangtze Viceroys entered into a *modus vivendi* by which foreigners were guaranteed against disturbances in their jurisdiction, provided that foreign operations were confined to the north ; and the aged Li Hung-chang, for thirty years the principal authority in the administration of the Empire, hastened from Canton to Peking to assume the rôle of negotiator in the final settlement.

During the outbreak the lives of all foreigners in the

north were in imminent peril. Baron von Kettler, the
German Envoy, was murdered on June 20th, while on his
way to the Ministry of Foreign Affairs ; many of the foreigners
at Peking and Tientsin were killed and wounded during the
sieges, and many more emerged with health shattered by
enteric and other consequences of privation and exposure.
Of the missionaries in Shansi, Shantung, and Chihli some
hundreds were killed with barbarous cruelty, the Governor
of Shansi, Yüsien, being present at some of the massacres ;
and the " secondary devils," the Chinese converts, were a
special object of hostility.

The settlement provided for reparation for the murder
of the German Envoy ; the execution of the principal
leaders and the officials actively responsible for the murder
of foreigners ; the demolition of the Taku forts ; the
establishment of permanent foreign garrisons in the
Legations and on the route from Peking to the sea ; the
clearing of a Legation quarter in Peking ; and an international indemnity of £67,500,000 (amounting with interest
to a total of £147,335,722) payable in thirty-nine years from
1902 to 1940.

The Boxer movement was crushed, but the nationalist
spirit which created it lived in the hearts of the people.
Even the Court was influenced by the force of a public
opinion which had not before existed in China, and with
no long delay took up some of the reforms which it had
resisted in 1898; the Conservative party, which had then
supported it in reaction, was now forced to give its support
to reform.   In 1903 a Ministry of Education was created,
the examinations were remodelled, and primary education
throughout the Empire was placed on a new basis.   Though
the principal initial result was the creation of many thousands of schools without financial support, and the enrol-
ment of millions of pupils without qualified teachers, still
the reform was in the right direction and was of good
augury for future progress.   Modern subjects were substituted for the Chinese classics which had been the sole

foundation of Chinese education. This dethronement of the classics was met, as a protest against the exclusion of China's old civilisation from the education of her youth, by the canonisation of Confucius, as no longer a mere teacher of ethical philosophy, but a saint in heaven ; but even this could not sweep back the wave of progress.

In 1906 the ministries at Peking were reconstructed on a modern basis ; but there was no evidence of any reform in the actual administration of the country, and, with steadily increasing taxes, discontent grew and the nation simmered with rebellion. The nationalist spirit, which in 1900 had as its motto " Safeguard the dynasty, exterminate the foreigner," rapidly became anti-dynastic ; but the risings which occurred were soon suppressed by the forces of the Government with modern weapons at their disposal. The youthful Emperor Kwanghsü died in November 1908 in his thirty-seventh year, and was followed the next day by his adoptive grandmother the Empress Dowager Tsehi, who had guided the ship of state through many storms during forty-four years of a troublous period. On October 10th, 1911, occurred an anti-dynastic outbreak at Hankow, the leaders in which soon gained possession of the tripartite city Wuchang—Hankow—Hanyang. The movement spread rapidly, and independent risings, for the most part bloodless, carried from the Imperial control all of China south of the Yellow River. It was one vast general strike, and it succeeded as strikes succeed in China ; and after a vain attempt by Yuan Shih-kai to preserve the dynasty as a constitutional monarchy, the new Emperor, Hsüan-tung, of the mature age of eight, abdicated the throne. The Republic of China was then proclaimed, with Sun Yat-sen (Cantonese for Sun Yi-sien) as provisional President. With self-denying patriotism he soon resigned, and the leading Chinese statesman of the day, Yuan Shih-kai, was then elected provisional President of the Republic of China.

CHAPTER II

THE GOVERNMENT—IMPERIAL CHINA *

THE government of China is an autocratic rule superposed on a democracy ; but " the East is East and the West is West," and, having applied Occidental terminology to an Oriental system, it becomes necessary to define the terms. When the Mongols under Kublai Khan in the thirteenth century invaded and conquered the country, they became the dominant power and *de facto* rulers of the Empire ; but the daily life of their subjects went on as before, they made no change in domestic and local institutions, and their refusal to be absorbed in the sturdy organisation of the Chinese people, combined with the pressure of heavy tribute and the evils of an irredeemable paper currency, led to their expulsion within a century from the first accession of Kublai to the throne. The native dynasty of the Ming, which then succeeded in the fourteenth century, introduced a better system of government, based on learning and statesmanship, but made no change in its external form ; and the relations between ruler and subject remained unaltered.

The Manchu dynasty of the Tsing, coming to power in the seventeenth century, was based primarily on force of arms ; but even their conquests were effected by armies composed as much of Chinese troops, stiffened by Manchu battalions and led by Manchu officers, as of the all-conquering Manchu bowmen. In their civil government the Tsing emperors

* This chapter is no longer entirely applicable to the present (1920). It is, however, left unchanged in the present tense, though it has now to be read mainly in the light of history.

32

and their Manchu advisers had the wisdom to recognise that their own people, unlettered and without the training of generations in the science of governing, were unequal to the task of providing an administration which could stand by its own strength ; and from the very beginning, before the smoking ruins which marked their military progress were cold, they not only continued the system and forms of their predecessors, but associated with themselves, in the administration, the literate class of their Chinese subjects ; and the mode of living and customs of the people remained unchanged. Garrisons were established at certain strategic points to maintain the conquest ; certain posts in the central government were reserved for Manchu nobles and leaders ; certain " milking " posts were created to tap the wealth of the provinces ; and the Court, the Manchu nobles, and the Manchu garrisons at Peking and elsewhere were maintained by tribute drawn from the provinces. Apart from this the government of the country has been more in the hands of the Chinese than of their conquerors, and the civil service has been a *carrière ouverte aux talents.* Some allowance must be made for the predilection of the ruling powers for men of their own race, and it is only natural that, in the exercise of patronage, Manchus should be somewhat preferred. This preference is now shown less frequently than in the past, as the Manchus have become more and more assimilated in thought and in training to the Chinese, and of late years the proportion of Manchus holding Imperial appointments in the provinces has not exceeded one fifth, while the numerous and important extra-official posts created by modern conditions are seldom held by Manchus. To apply American terminology to things Chinese, the Municipal and State (provincial) government is almost entirely in the hands of the Chinese, while the Federal (Imperial) administration is influenced and controlled as much by Chinese as by Manchu minds, with the further proviso that full weight is given in the Emperor's Council Hall to the shrewd brains of his Chinese counsellors.

3

The American simile may he carried even further, but the Western reader must be cautioned not to apply it except as specifically indicated. American government stands firm-based on the town meeting. This was generally true in De Tocqueville's time (except for the county system of the Southern States), was passably true at the time of Bryce's inquiry, and is true to-day of the country village communities. It is also true, *mutatis mutandis*, of village communities in China to-day, following the precedent of many centuries. The village elder, Tipao, is appointed " with and by the advice and consent " of the villagers, and represents them in all official and governmental matters, being also the ordinary channel of communication of official wishes or orders to his fellow villagers. The American citizen has few direct dealings with any but his township officials so long as he pays his taxes and is law-abiding, and, officially, hardly knows of the existence of the Federal Government, unless he has to deal with the Custom House, or wishes to distil whisky or brew beer. This may be said also of the Chinese villager, and, moreover, few civil suits are brought before the official tribunals in China, while the government exercises no control over distillation. The American federal system finds its counterpart, too, in some respects, in the semi-independence of the central and provincial administrations ; but the means of providing for the maintenance of the Imperial Government resemble much more closely the German system, based on a combination of Imperial taxes and matriculations assessed on the federated states.

The civil government of China may be considered under four divisions :

(i)   The Emperor and his Court, and the Manchu nobles.

(ii)   The Central Metropolitan Government.

(iii)   The Provincial Administration.

(iv)   The Township and Village.

To explain clearly the system of Chinese administration, it would be wise to begin with the foundation and trace it up to the top; but in many ways it is more convenient to trace the stream from its mouth through its many ramifications to its sources.

I. THE COURT

The *Emperor* rules by divine right. His is no empty " Dei gratiâ," based on a parliamentary title, or an election by a Diet or by allied kings and princes. He is himself the Son of Heaven, and, when he dies, he " mounts the Dragon chariot to be a guest on high." He is the Divus Augustus of his Empire, reverenced, in letter and in spirit, by his subjects. He worships only at the Altar of Heaven and the Altar of Earth, apart from his reverential worship of the shades of his ancestors; but he commands his Ministers to propitiate the Guardian Dragon of the River in times of flood, and the Spirits of the Air in times of drought, and leaves to his subjects their worship of Buddhist deities and their adhesion to Taoist tenets, or even to Christian and Mussulman practices, so long as they remain a matter of religion only. Apart from the result of military usurpation, he is selected by his predecessor, or by the Imperial family acting under such inspiration as moves a Papal Conclave. He is usually a son of his predecessor, but is seldom the eldest, the Asiatic practice of selecting the fittest among certain qualified princes of the blood being followed. Not one of the Emperors of the present dynasty (except Tungchih, an only son) was the eldest son of his predecessor: Kanghi was the third son of Shunchih; Yungcheng (1723–1735) was the fourth son of Kanghi, and was driven to imprison some of his brothers, and to banish others, because they rebelled against him on his accession; Kienlung was the fourth son of Yungcheng. Among the sons of the Emperor, one of those by the Empress Consort might, other things being equal, be preferred; next in order of choice come the sons of the Secondary Consorts, and next the sons of concubines; but the son of a concubine might be preferred to others, and all are equally recognised as the

sons of their father. Failing a son, the choice would be
among the other princes of the Imperial family, but restricted by the necessity, if possible, of going a generation
lower in order that the selected prince might be adopted as
the son of the decedent Emperor, and so be qualified to
perform the due ceremonies before the ancestral tablets.
This principle was violated on the death of Tungchih in
January 1875, his successor, Kwanghsü—adopted as his son
and successor—being natally his father's brother's son ; and
the *coup d'état manqué* of January 1900 was based upon the
alleged necessity of providing an Emperor of the next generation below, to carry on fitly the ancestral worship, and so to
avert disaster from the Empire. Princes of the blood of
the same generation have their first personal name the same
(as Albert Edward, Albert Henry, Albert Charles) ; the
Emperor Tungchih was " christened " Tsai-shun, and his
successor, the Emperor Kwanghsü, Tsai-tien ; in the next
generation we have the heir presumptive, selected in 1900,
Pu-chun, the prince who went to St. Louis in 1903, Pu-lun,
and the present Emperor, Pu-yi, whose reign title is Hsüan-
tung. To his people the sovereign is " The Emperor,"
" His Sacred Majesty," " Lord of a myriad years," " The
Son of Heaven " ; his personal name is never mentioned
from the moment of his accession, and even its distinctive
initial word must be avoided for ever thereafter, a synonym
or a modified form being used : just as, for example, with
a King Harry, now or at some past time during the present
dynasty on the throne, it would not be permissible to
" harry " the enemy, but some synonym, if possible one
having a similar sound, would be used instead. Each
Emperor selects a " year indicator " or " reign title," by
which to indicate the years of his reign, 1906 being the
thirty-second year of the period Kwanghsü (Continuation
of Glory) ; and foreigners, from indolence, commonly use
this reign title as if it were the personal name of the sovereign, speaking ordinarily of His Majesty Kwanghsü. Under
previous dynasties the Emperors frequently changed their

reign title, but this has happened only once under Manchu rule—in 1861, when the first reign title of the infant Emperor was changed, concurrently with a *coup d'état*, from Kisiang (Favouring Fortune), to Tungchih (Peace and Order). On his death the Emperor is canonised, and receives a temple name, by which he is known in history ; the temple name of the Emperor we know as Tungchih is Mu-tsung Yi Hwang-ti, " Our Reverent Ancestor the Bold Emperor." The Emperor's writ runs throughout the extent of his dominions, and his edicts and rescripts are the law of the Empire ; this is true also of the writs and Orders in Council of the King of Great Britain and Ireland, and the restrictions on the acts of the two sovereigns differ only in degree and kind. The Emperor is bound, in the first place, by the unwritten constitution of the Empire, the customs which have come down from time immemorial, through generations of both rulers and ruled, and further by established precedent as defined in the edicts of his predecessors, even those of previous dynasties. Then he is bound by the opinions and decisions of his Ministers, whose position and weight differ from those of Ministers of constitutional monarchies only in the mode of their selection and retention in office. Finally, shut up within the walls of his palace, he is more sensible of the daily pressure brought to bear upon him by his personal entourage than his brother sovereigns in the West ; but it must be said of the Manchu rulers that eunuchs have had less influence at Court than under previous dynasties. A strong Emperor may assert his own will, and, given a suitable opportunity and a justifying emergency, may override the constitution as Abraham Lincoln did under similar circumstances ; but when an ordinary ruler tries it, the result is what happened in 1898, when the Emperor Kwanghsü undertook to modify in a few months the development of many centuries, and impetuously instituted reforms for which the Empire was not then ready. The Emperor is also the source of honours and of office ; but this is no more literally true in

China than in any other country where patronage is exercised from above.

The *Empress* Consort is chosen by the Emperor (with perhaps some forcing of the cards) from a bevy of candidates selected by his Ministers from the families of Manchu nobles ; and from the same selection, then or later, he chooses Secondary Empresses, not commonly exceeding four in number.   The concubines are not limited in number by any law or custom, and are selected from the daughters of Manchu nobles and freemen.   The Dragon is the armorial emblem of the Emperor, and the Phœnix of the Empress Consort, and her title of respect is " Mother of the State." When the Emperor Hienfeng (properly Wentsung Hien Hwangti) died in 1861, he left only one son, five years old, to succeed him, born, not of the Empress Consort, but of the Secondary Empress, the late Empress Dowager. Motherhood is divine in China, and it was quite in accordance with law and custom that the Regency over the infant Emperor should be exercised jointly by the Dowager Empress Consort (the " Eastern Palace," the east or left being the side of honour), and the Empress Mother (the " Western Palace "). Only one of the two, however, had capacity for government, and the Semiramis of the Far East, the Empress Mother, exercised alone the real power, even before the death in 1881 of her colleague in the regency, supported then and after by the counsel of Prince Kung, brother of Hienfeng.   The regency was determined in 1873, when the young Emperor, Tungchih, then seventeen years old, was declared of age, and was again resumed in 1875 (January), on the death of Tungchih and the accession of the infant Kwanghsü ; it was again determined in 1889, and again resumed in 1898 ; and the rule of this woman of seventy-one * over the youth of thirty-five, her nephew-adopted-grandson, was strengthened by the capacity of the ruler, the necessity of the state, and the devoted reverence due to parents and grandparents.

* In 1906.

The *Imperial Clansmen* are those who can trace their descent back directly to the founder of the dynasty, Hien-tsu, 1583–1615, and are distinguished by the privilege of wearing a yellow girdle : collateral relatives of the Imperial house are privileged to wear a red girdle. The titles of nobility conferred on members of the Imperial house are of twelve degrees. Sons of an Emperor are created Tsin-wang or Kün-wang, Prince of the first or second order ; their sons descend to Bei-leh, Prince of the third order ; and their sons to Bei-tze, Prince of the fourth order (Prince Pu-lun is of this rank) ; then come four grades of Duke and four of Commanders, until, in the thirteenth generation, the descendants of Emperors are merged in the ranks of commoners distinguished only by their privilege of the yellow girdle.

The *Hereditary Nobility* do not descend in rank with each succeeding generation. Chief among them are the eight " Iron-capped " (or helmeted) Princes, direct descend-ants by rule of primogeniture of the eight princes who co-operated in the Conquest of China ; to them is added the descendant of the thirteenth son of Kanghi. Certain Chinese families also enjoy hereditary titles of nobility, chief among them the Holy Duke of Yen (the descendant of Kung Fu-tze or Confucius), Marquis Tseng (from Tseng Kwo-fan), Marquis Li (from Li Hung-chang) : none of these titles carry with them any special privileges.

II. METROPOLITAN ADMINISTRATION

Of the central government of China, Mayers * says : " The central government of China, so far as a system of this nature is recognised in the existing institutions, is arranged with the object rather of registering and checking the action of the various provincial administrations, than with that of assuming a direct initiative in the conduct of affairs. . . . Regulations, indeed, of the most minute and

* " The Chinese Government," by W. F. Mayers, 1878

comprehensive character, are on record for the guidance of every conceivable act of administration ; and the principal function of the central government consists in watching over the execution of this system of rules. The bestowal of the higher appointments of the civil and military services, and the distribution of the superior literary degrees as rewards for proficiency in the studies upon which the entire polity of the Empire is based, comprise the remainder of the attributes reserved to the government established at Peking. The central government may be said to criticise rather than to control the action of the twenty-one provincial administrations, wielding, however, at all times the power of immediate removal from his post of any official whose conduct may be found irregular, or considered dangerous to the stability of the State."

These words strike the keynote for the part played by the Emperor's Ministers at the capital ; but, written in 1877, they take too little account of the centralising policy forced upon the government by the importance of its foreign relations, and facilitated by the improvement in the means of communication. In its pristine form the government was, a generation only back, as Mayers describes it. When Lord Napier first introduced the element of national sovereignty into China's foreign relations, he found no member of the central administration or Envoy of the Emperor to deal with ; he was not even allowed to come in touch with the Viceroy or the Governor at Canton, but was ordered to communicate through the authorities at Canton, the Co-Hong and the Hoppo. The British treaty of 1842 was signed by the Tartar General of Canton and the Lieutenant-General of Chapu, who, being responsible for resistance to aggression on the coasts of Kwangtung and Chekiang, transferred their headquarters to Nanking to settle matters with the aggressor ; and to them was joined in the signature, though not mentioned as plenipotentiary in the preamble, the Viceroy at Nanking, within whose jurisdiction the negotiations for peace were conducted ; no

Envoy was sent direct from the central government. The American treaty of 1844 was negotiated and signed by the Viceroy at Canton (who alone was named in the preamble) and the Tartar General ; and the French treaty, later in the same year, was signed by the Viceroy alone, the Manchu Commandant having meantime died. Then ensued a period of foreign friction ending in the second war ; and the four treaties negotiated in 1858—the British, French, American, and Russian—were signed by two members of the central administration, both Presidents of Boards, and one of them a Grand Secretary of State.

The hammering of twenty years had welded the Empire together, and the Imperial Government was compelled, in its foreign relations, to act as ruler and not as mere super-visor, and to adopt a more centralised policy. This policy was made the more necessary from the disorganisation into which the provincial administration was thrown by the Taiping rebellion ; and the tendency was increased by the practice of the foreign Envoys in demanding that all important questions, in the settlement of which by the Consuls and the local authorities any difficulty presented itself, should be referred to the capital, and there settled between themselves and the Imperial Ministers ; and the decisions based on such settlements went down to the provinces as orders from Peking. By degrees, as the result of this innovation, the Tsungli Yamen, which had been organised in 1861 as a Ministry of Foreign Affairs, tended more and more to become a body of Cabinet Ministers and to displace the Grand Council. The first members, in 1861, were Prince Kung, uncle of the Emperor ; Kwei Liang, Grand Secretary, who had negotiated the treaties of 1858 ; and Wen Siang, then Vice-President of the Board of War. This number was increased, until, in 1876, there were eleven members, including Prince Kung, as President, including also all the members of the Grand Council, and including none who were not of the Grand Council or were not President or Vice-President of a Board.

Thus was developed a Cabinet, in the sense common to the British, American, and French systems; and the compulsory substitution, in 1901, of a Board of Foreign Affairs and abolition of the Tsungli Yamen, leaving the government without a corporate head, caused the resumption by the Grand Council of its active functions as the deliberating and deciding Cabinet of the Emperor, and the executive head of the government. The Grand Council, however, inherited the centralised power of the old Tsungli Yamen, and the orders emanating from Peking were more direct than of old. In the old days, too, communication was slow, and two or three months might elapse before the authorities at Canton could receive a reply to their request for instructions, with the result that much must be left to the man on the spot. The introduction of steamers brought Canton, Nanking, and Hankow, the seats of the most important Viceroyalties, within a week of the capital; and the extension of the telegraphs, which directly resulted from the Russian difficulty of 1880, brought the most remote of the high provincial authorities into immediate touch with the central administration, and furthered the centralisation which had already become established; and now the Empire is ruled from Peking to an extent unknown while China still played the hermit.

The powers of the central administration are distributed among several Ministries and numerous minor departments; but here, only those having a direct influence in shaping the policy of the Empire will be described. Moreover, as this book is a record of the past and present, and does not forecast the future, it is right, in these days of rapid transformation of a hitherto immovable Empire, to state that this chapter was written in October 1906. In the Imperial administration there are two superior Councils.

The NUI-KO, Inner Cabinet, commonly called Grand Secretariat, was the Supreme Council of the Empire under the Ming Dynasty, but since the middle of the eighteenth century has degenerated into a Court of Archives. Active

membership is limited to six, and confers the highest distinction attainable by Chinese officials. The Grand Secretaries have the title of Chung-tang, "Central Hall" (of
the Palace), the best known in recent years being Li Hung-
chang; under the Ming Dynasty they were designated
Ko-lao, "Elders of the Cabinet" (the Colao of the old
Jesuit narratives). Six honorary titles were once attached
to the Grand Secretariat—Grand and Junior Preceptor,
Tutor, and Guardian; but of these the last only is now
conferred as Junior Guardian of the Heir Apparent, and
that not limited to one incumbent or to Grand Secretaries.
One of the latest to receive the distinction is Sir Robert
Hart, who is thereby entitled to be addressed as Kung-pao,
"Guardian of the Palace."

The KÜN-KI-CHU, "Committee of National Defence"
or "Board of Strategy," commonly called the Grand
Council, is the actual Privy Council of the sovereign, in
whose presence its members, not usually exceeding five in
number, daily discuss and decide questions of Imperial
policy. Its members usually hold other high offices, generally that of President of a Board.

The TSUNGLI YAMEN, described before, was organised
in 1861 and abolished in 1901. The posts of Imperial
Superintendents of Trade for the Northern Seas (the Viceroy
at Tientsin), and for the Southern Seas (the Viceroy at
Nanking), created also in 1861, have continued to be held *
and their functions exercised by those officials.

The actual administration of Imperial affairs is in
the hands of the "Six Boards," later nine in number—
viz. :

    1. LI PU, Board of Civil Office, the dispenser of
    patronage, controlling appointments to all posts in
    the regular hierarchy from District Magistrate (Hsien)
    up.

    2. HU PU, Board of Revenue, controls the receipt

* The Northern superintendency was attached to the Tientsin
Viceroyalty only in 1870.

and expenditure of that portion of the revenue and tribute which comes to Peking, or is under the control of the central administration.

3. LEE PU, Board of Ceremonies, an important Ministry at an Asiatic Court.

4. PING PU, Board of War, controls the provincial forces only. The Manchu military forces are controlled by their own organisation attached to the Palace. This Board also controls the courier service.

5. HING PU, Board of Punishments, a department of Justice for the criminal law only, and dealing especially with the punishment of officials guilty of malpractices.

6. KUNG PU, Board of Works, controlling the construction and repair of official residences throughout the Empire, but having no concern with canals or conservancy, roads or bridges.

The new Ministries additional to the old " Six Boards " were the following :

7. WAI-WU PU, Board of Foreign Affairs, instituted in 1901 in succession to the Tsungli Yamen.

8. SHANG PU, Board of Commerce, instituted in 1903.

9. HIOH PU, Board of Education, instituted in 1903.

These Boards are organised on the same plan. Each has two Presidents—Shang-shu, addressed as Pu-tang, "Hall of the Board "—of whom one is by law Manchu and one Chinese. (An edict issued in 1906 directed that this limitation should no longer be observed.) Viceroys have, *ex officio*, the honorary title of President of a Board, usually of the Board of War. Each Board has also four Vice-Presidents—Shih-lang, addressed as Pu-yuan, " Court-yard of the Board "—two being Manchu and two Chinese (subject to the edict). Governors of provinces have, *ex officio*, the honorary title of Vice-President of a Board, usually of the Board of War. They all have an equipment of Secretaries,

Overseers, Assistants, etc., *quant. suff.*, and are divided into sub-departments according to their needs.

Other departments of the government exist at Peking, with functions not limited to any one Board or one branch of the affairs of State ; but only the more important need be mentioned.

TU-CHA YUAN, " Court of Investigation," commonly called the Court of Censors. Viceroys have the honorary title of President, and Governors of Vice-President, of the Censorate. The " Censors " remind one somewhat of the Censors and somewhat of the Tribunes of Ancient Rome ; their duty is to criticise, and this duty they exercise without fear, though not always without favour.

TUNG-CHENG SZE, " Office of Transmission," deals with memorials to the Throne.

TA-LI SZE, " Court of Revision," exercises a general supervision over the administration of the criminal law.

HAN-LIN YUAN, " College of Literature," exercised control over the education of the Empire until superseded by the Board of Education, and continues to exist as a memorial of a glorious past. It is also charged with the custody and preparation of the historical archives of the dynasty, but many of its records were burnt in 1900.

III. THE PROVINCIAL ADMINISTRATION

It has been explained that the provinces, in actual practice in the past and in theory to-day, occupy a semi-autonomous position *vis-à-vis* the Imperial Government ; in some aspects they may be said to be satrapies, in others to resemble the constituent states of a federation. Either comparison is too sweeping, however, without careful study of the differences. The comparison with states would be more exact if for " state " were substituted " territory,"

such as those of the American Union, which have their
executive and judicial officers appointed by the central power
and removable at its pleasure, but have local autonomy for
the levy of taxes and the administration of the law ; but in
this comparison the difference must always be remembered
between the Occident, which insists on local self-government, and the Orient, which is always governed by the
strong hand. The provinces are satrapies to the extent
that (speaking of the past), so long as the tribute and
matriculations are duly paid, and the general policy of the
central administration followed, they are free to administer
their own affairs in detail as may seem best to their own
provincial authorities. But no satrap has existed under
the present dynasty since its first half-century, when Wu
San-kwei was given the satrapy of Yunnan and Kweichow
as a reward for his services in the conquest, and in the end
had to be brought to subjection as a rebel against the
sovereign power. With much latitude in the exercise of
their power, many restrictions are imposed on the individual
officials.

All officials in the provinces, down to District Magistrate,
are appointed from Peking ; for the lower posts the high
provincial authorities may, and do, recommend ; but it is
Peking which appoints, and it is only the central government which can promote, transfer, or cashier. This keeps
the provincial officials, from the highest to the lowest, in a
proper state of discipline. Appointment to one post is made
for a term of three years ; for Viceroys and Governors this
limitation is often, even usually, disregarded, as when we
see Li Hung-chang holding the Viceroyalty at Tientsin for
nearly thirty years continuously ; but this exception is
explained by the desire to utilise to the utmost the great
experience of these high officials, and by the strong party
backing which put them in their high positions, and which
is strengthened by the patronage which is then at their
disposal. For officials lower in rank the rule is almost
universally followed ; they may be reappointed once, but

at the end of their second triennial term at latest they must
strike root afresh in new surroundings, and, incidentally,
must again contribute to the maintenance of their superiors,
as is explained in Chapter IV. To some especially lucrative
posts appointments are made for one year only.

Another restriction is peculiar to China, and is never
relaxed ; no official is ever appointed to a post in the
province of his birth. The military are an exception, but
they exercise little influence, and Manchuria was up to 1907
governed by Manchus ; otherwise the rule is invariable.
The Chinese never voluntarily abandon the homestead, or
surrender their interest in the ancestral shrine ; and every
official is an alien to the people he rules, often unable to
understand the dialect they speak. He brings his family
connections with him as secretaries and purveyors, and,
if he is a Viceroy or Governor, he brings a bodyguard of
his co-provincials, loyal to his person ; but otherwise he is
surrounded by aliens. No Hupeh man may hold an official
post in Hupeh, nor Kiangsu man in Kiangsu. When Li
Hung-chang left the Viceroyalty at Tientsin, the post to
which he would naturally have gone was the other great
Viceroyalty, that at Nanking ; but his native province,
Anhwei, is in the Nanking Viceroyalty, and hé went to
Canton instead. Tsen Chun-süan, a man of great force
of character, native of Kwangsi, made a name as provincial
Treasurer of Kwangtung, and was promoted to be acting
Viceroy of Szechwan ; in 1903 he was the obviously indicated man to restore order in the Canton Viceroyalty, and
was sent back there ; but though, as a Kwangsi man, he
could rule at Canton as provincial Treasurer of Kwangtung,
he could not be substantive incumbent at Canton of the
Viceroyalty of which Kwangsi forms part, and went therefore as acting Viceroy ; in 1906 he was appointed substantive Viceroy to Yunnan.

Another practice is a matter of policy rather than of
rule, and is only possible in a country where all appointments
are made by a central authority. Parties exist in China

as in other countries, and as in other countries are as often the following of a man as of a principle. In the exercise of patronage at Peking the principle of *divide et impera* in the provinces is followed in this as in other ways. The principle is that which animated Washington in the selection of his first cabinet, and may be understood if we suppose that in the United States the federal government appointed to any state a Republican as Governor, a Democrat as Lieutenant-Governor, a Republican as State Secretary, a Democrat as State Treasurer, and so on. For three decades from 1860 there were two great parties in China, the Hunan men and their adherents, following Tseng Kwo-fan, and later Tso Tsung-tang, and the Anhwei men and their adherents, following Li Hung-chang and Li Han-chang; the former were generally conservative, and the latter generally, but moderately, progressive, and the men of other provinces, disregarding provincial lines, ranged themselves with one or other of these parties. Latterly the Canton party, ultra-progressive, after a check in 1898, has again come to the front. In making provincial appointments care is always taken to balance these parties; and in the general administration, exercising their functions at the provincial capital, an official will seldom be of the same party as his immediate superior or his immediate subordinate, while the appointments to prefectures and magistracies will be fairly divided between the parties. This, of course, implies that the Emperor is able to maintain the same balance of influence in his Ministries, apart from the equilibrium maintained between Manchu and Chinese. In the provinces further equilibrium is maintained by the occasional appointment of Manchus, who are above party, and who number usually about a fifth of the official hierarchy.

With all these balances and checks much more may be left to the local authority, and, so long as the province furnishes its quota towards the maintenance of the Imperial Government and preserves a semblance of order, or settles its disturbances with the means at its disposal, it is left to go its own way and to have a quasi-autonomy. But, while these rights are granted and direct governance is reduced to a minimum, there is also an absence of direct oversight and of holding the provinces responsible for the due performance of their duties. If a breach of the Yellow River occurs in Honan, the Honan authorities must attend to it ; but it is no part of their duty to so direct the work of restoration that the adjoining province of Shantung shall not suffer ; that is the concern of the Shantung authorities. If a rebellion in Kwangsi is held in check, and the rebels, cornered, escape across the Hunan border, " e'en let him go, and thank God you are rid of a knave " ; they are then the affair of the Hunan authorities. Salt-smugglers on the border between Kiangsu and Chekiang have a merry time dodging back and forth across the border, and are brought to book only on the rare occasions when the two provinces loyally join forces. This will be remedied with the further centralisation of power ; but we are dealing with China as it has been and is.

The administrative organisation of each of the provinces is much the same, and the duties of each of the officials will now be described.

TSUNG-TU, commonly called Chihtai, Governor-General, ordinarily styled Viceroy, though there is nothing in the office or its title of the viceregal idea. As *ex officio* President of a Board, he styles himself and is addressed as Putang. He is the highest in rank of the civilian officials of the provincial administration, but in theory ranks after, though he is not subordinated to, the Tartar General, when one is stationed within his viceroyalty ; and he has control over the military forces, other than the Manchu garrison, within his jurisdiction. In some cases he is actually Governor, though with the power and rank of Governor-General, of one province only ; in others he has jurisdiction over two or three provinces, each of which has (by the old theory) its own Governor ; and still other provinces, each with its Governor, are subordinated to no Governor-General. The

distribution is shown by the following table, in which " ex-
Governor " indicates that a Governor was installed up to
1905, in which year an Imperial edict abolished the Governor-
ship of those provinces in which a Viceroy had his seat.

METROPOLITAN PROVINCE :—
Chihli   .. no Governor   Chihli   (Tientsin)
                                    Viceroy.

THREE ADJOINING PROVINCES :—
Shantung   .. Governor   ⎫
Shansi   .. Governor   ⎬ under   no   Vice-
Honan   .. Governor   ⎭ roy.

OUTLYING PROVINCES :—
Kiangsu   .. Governor*   ⎫ Liang-Kiang
Anhwei   .. Governor   ⎬ (Nanking)
Kiangsi   .. Governor   ⎭ Viceroy.
Shensi   .. Governor   ⎫ Shen-Kan   Vice-
Kansu   .. no Governor ⎭ roy.
Fukien   .. ex-Governor ⎫ Min-Che   Vice-
Chekiang   .. Governor   ⎭ roy.
Hupeh   .. ex-Governor ⎫ Hu - Kwang
Hunan   .. Governor   ⎭ Viceroy.
Szechwan   .. no Governor   Szechwan   Vice-
                             roy.
Kwangtung .. ex-Governor ⎫ Liang - Kwang
Kwangsi   .. Governor   ⎭ Viceroy.
Yunnan   .. ex-Governor ⎫ Yun-Kwei   Vice-
Kweichow   .. Governor   ⎭ roy.

For the Eighteen Provinces there are thus eight Viceroys,
and originally fifteen Governors, now reduced to eleven.
The Viceroy, though of higher rank and looming larger in
the eyes of the world, is in the provincial administration

* Not abolished, because the provincial capital, seat of the
Governor, is Soochow, while the Viceregal residence is Nanking.

a superior colleague to the Governor, and in all matters, orders to subordinates or memorials to the Throne, the two act conjointly.

SÜN-FU, commonly called Futai, the " Inspector " or Governor ; addressed as Pu-yuan by virtue of his Vice-Presidency of the Board of War. He is the supreme head of the province, except in so far as his action is restricted by the presence of a Viceroy. The post has been abolished (in 1905) in those provinces in which a Viceroy resides.

PU-CHENG SHIH-SZE, commonly called Fantai, Provincial Treasurer, with some of the functions of a Lieutenant-Governor. He is the nominal head of the civil service in each province, in whose name all patronage is dispensed, even when directly bestowed by the Governor, and is treasurer of the provincial exchequer, in this capacity providing the Imperial Government with a check on his nominal superior, the Governor.

AN-CHA SHIH-SZE, commonly called Niehtai, Provincial Judge. He is charged with the supervision over the criminal law, and acts as a final (provincial) court of appeal in criminal cases, and has jurisdiction over offences by provincial officials. He also supervises in a general way the Imperial courier service.

YEN-YÜN SHIH-SZE, Salt Comptroller, in some provinces, and Yen-yün Tao, Salt Intendant, in other provinces, control the manufacture, movement, and sale of salt under the provincial gabelle, and the revenue derived from it.

LIANG TAO, Grain Intendant, in twelve of the eighteen provinces, controls the collection of the grain tribute, in kind or commuted.

The last four officials, the Sze-Tao (or as many of them as may be found in the province) next below the Governor, constitute *ex officio* the Shan-how Kü, " Committee of Re-organisation," a deliberating and executive Board of provincial government ; and the six enumerated above form the general provincial administration, residing at the capital, except that the Chihli Viceroy now (since 1870) resides at Tientsin, and the Liang-Kiang Viceroy has his seat at Nanking.

Below the Fantai in rank and above the Niehtai is the TI-HIOH SZE, Commissioner of Education, a new post created on the institution of the Hioh Pu in 1903. This is not an administrative post, and its incumbent is not a member of the Shan-how Kü.

The unit for administrative purposes within the province is the Hsien, or district, as will be explained below ; two or three or more (up to five or six) districts collectively form a Fu or prefecture ; and two or more prefectures are placed under the jurisdiction of a Taotai. There are also two other classes, the Chow and Ting, each of two kinds ; the Chow and Ting proper are a superior kind of Hsien, being component parts of a Fu ; the Chihli-chow and Chihli-ting are an inferior kind of Fu, both having as direct a relation to the provincial government as a Fu, but the latter distinguished from the Fu by having no Hsien subordinated to it.

FEN-SÜN TAO, the " Sub-Inspector," commonly translated Intendant of Circuit, and usually called Taotai ; has administrative control over a circuit comprising two or three Fu, or sometimes one or two Fu and a Chihli-chow or a Chihli-ting, and is in certain matters the intermediary of communication between them and the provincial government ; but the circuit is not an official division of the province, and is nowhere marked on any map. He is the civil authority in control of the military forces within his jurisdiction, and as such is distinguished from Salt and Grain Taotais by the title Ping-pei Tao, " the Taotai (in charge of) military preparation." He is usually the Superintendent (colleague of the Commissioner) of the Custom House, if any, within his circuit, and is then styled Kwan Tao, " Customs Taotai " ; but this is not the case in the Kwangtung ports, where formerly the Hoppo, and since 1904 the Viceroy, is Superintendent, nor in the Fukien ports, of which the Tartar General holds the post. At

Tientsin there is a special Customs Taotai in addition to the territorial Taotai.

CHIH-FU, the " Knower of a Prefecture," commonly translated Prefect. He is supervising officer of the largest political division within a province, the Fu, of which each province has from seven to thirteen, with a total of 183 for the Eighteen Provinces. He deals more with the external relations of his Fu than with its internal administration, and is more a channel of communication than an executive officer, but acts as a court of appeal from the Hsien's court. He has no separate Fu city, but the Hsien city in which he resides is known generally by the Fu name, though on Chinese maps both the Fu and Hsien names are printed.

TUNG-CHIH, the " Joint Knower " or Deputy Prefect, is either in charge of a Chow or Chihli-ting, or exercises the delegated power of a Prefect in a branch of his functions, such as maritime defence, water communications, control of aboriginal tribes, etc.

TUNG-PAN, Assistant Deputy Prefect, holds office under the Prefect, n charge of police matters, revenue, etc.

CHIH-CHOW, " Knower of a Chow," is either in charge of a Chihli or independent Chow, with prefectural functions, and subordinated to no Prefect but reporting direct to the provincial government ; or is, like a Tung-chih of the first class, in charge of a subordinated Chow. Under this grade are also Chow-tung and Chow-pan.

CHIH-HSIEN, " Knower of the Hsien," or District Magistrate, whose functions will be described below. In the Eighteen Provinces there are 1,443 Hsien and 27 in Manchuria, making 1,470 in all. Below the Chih-hsien are subordinate officials—Deputy Magistrate, Sub-Deputy Magistrate, Superintendent of Police, Jail Warden, etc., etc., but they have no independent status.

The "Fu Chow Hsien" constitute the general administrative body of the provincial civil service. They are charged in varying degrees with the collection of revenue, the maintenance of order, and the dispensation of justice as well as with the conduct of literary examinations and of the government courier service, and in general with the exercise of all the direct functions of public administration. A specimen proclamation, given by Mr. Parker,* well illustrates the gradations of rank of the provincial officials from highest to lowest.

> " The Magistrate has had the honour to receive instructions from the Prefect, who cites the directions of the Taotai, moved.by the Treasurer and the Judge, recipients of the commands of their Excellencies the Viceroy and Governor, acting at the instance of the Foreign Board, who have been honoured with His Majesty's commands. . . . [commands end.] Respect this. Duly communicated to the Yard, or Yards [end of line], who command the *sze* [end of line], who move the *tao* [end], who instructs the *fu* [end], who sends down to The *Hsien*, etc. [Note how the *Hsien*, as imperial agent, gives himself capital letters.] We therefore enjoin and command all and several, etc."

The same gradation is also exemplified in the accompanying diagram, in which, however, the exigencies of space require the apparent subordination of the Taotai to the Sze, while he is actually " with but after " the Sze. Historically the Governor is an interloper, dating back only to the Ming Dynasty, being originally a visiting inspector delegated by the Imperial Government to supervise and report on the working of the provincial administration, but tending by degrees to become a fixture ; in some important functions of government the Pu-cheng Shih-sze, the original Governor, the present Provincial Treasurer, still in theory remains the chief. The Viceroy dates back only to the last century of Ming rule. The Taotai is still more modern, dating from the beginnings of the present dynasty. So is the Fu, but historically he is the modern representative of

* " China, Her History, etc," by E. H. Parker, 1901.

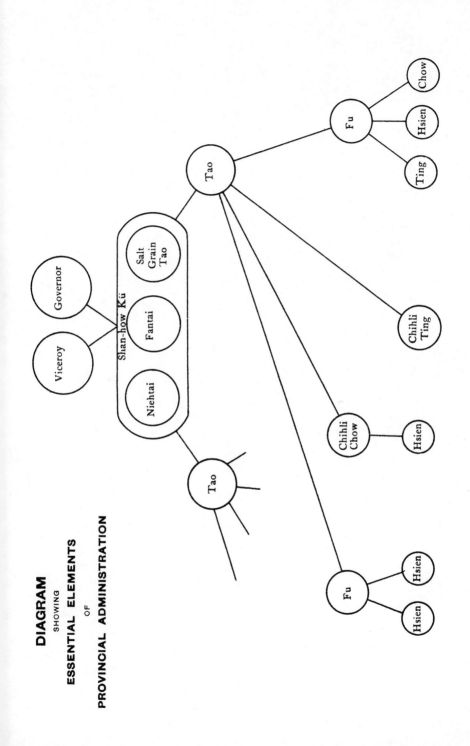

DIAGRAM
SHOWING
OF
ESSENTIAL ELEMENTS
PROVINCIAL ADMINISTRATION

Viceroy

Governor

Shan-how Kü

Niehtai

Fantai

Salt
Grain
Tao

Tao

Tao

Fu

Chow

Hsien

Ting

Chihli
Ting

Chihli
Chow

Hsien

Fu

Hsien

Hsien

the thirty-six provincial rulers of the Tsin dynasty (B.C. 221) and of the Han which followed it. The Chow is also a modern revival, representing the rulers of provincial areas (Chow) instituted B.C. 140. The Hsien is perhaps the oldest.

A few words must be said on the functions of government in the provinces which are not provided by the official hierarchy. Every Chinese official is supposed to be qualified to undertake every branch of human enterprise, from railway engineering to street scavenging, from the interpretation of the law to the execution of criminals, and to accept full responsibility for the consequences of his acts or the acts of his subordinates. In effect, however, this Jack-of-all-trades attitude is offset by the natural wish for expert aid, and by the equally natural tendency to create a gainful office whenever possible. Extra-official functions are delegated by the responsible officials, just as in Massachusetts the elected executive delegates certain of his functions to police, railway, insurance and charity commissions nominated by himself—*i.e.* by the exercise of patronage. In China this delegated employment is actually so-called, Chai-shih ; and the Director of an arsenal controlling the expenditure of millions, the officials of the likin collectorate, the Viceroy's adviser on international or on railway matters, and a deputy who does little more than carry messages, are alike in theory only the delegates *ad hoc* of the appointing power. These unofficial officials are selected from the official class, the class known as "expectant" Hsien, Fu or Tao, men qualified to serve in the posts for which they are expectant, inscribed on the register of the Board of Civil Office, but not yet nominated to a substantive post. Entry to this state of expectancy is in theory the result of examination in literature ; this is a glorious tradition ; a hundred years ago it was in the main probably true, but to-day money and political influence are the keys which open the gates of political preferment.

IV. The Township and Village

The Hsien is the civic, political, judicial and fiscal unit of Chinese life ; it comprises one walled city,* or in the case of many of the provincial capitals the half of a walled city (in the case of Soochow the third of the city), with the country immediately around it.   In it every Chinese subject is inscribed, and this inscription he does not willingly forfeit or abandon, no matter to what part of the Empire or of the outer world his vocation may call him.   Here is his ancestral temple if he is of the gentry, his ancestral home in any case ; here will he return, if permitted, in the evening of his life, and here will his bones be sent should he die abroad.   During the whole of his life he is identified with his Hsien ; it may be convenient, and may elucidate his political policy, to speak of Li Hung-chang as an Anhwei man, but to his fellow-countryman he is the Hofei(hsien) man.

The official head of this district is the Chih-hsien, who may be called Mayor, if it be understood that the municipal limits extend until they meet the territory of the adjoining municipalities.   His official salary may be from Tls.100 to Tls.300 (£15 to £50) a year, with an allowance " for the encouragement of integrity among officials " amounting to three or four times his salary ; the emoluments of his office, however, may be from a hundred to a thousand times his nominal salary, but from them he has to provide for the maintenance of his subordinates and his superiors, as is explained in Chapter IV.   He is appointed to his post generally from the list of expectants, either because he is the son of his father, or because of a sufficient contribution to what in Western countries would be the party campaign fund, or because of good work done in a Chai-shih ; occasionally, even now, a high scholar is appointed because of his scholarship, but it is seldom to a lucrative post.   To

* The cases of cities without walls, in outlying corners of the Empire, are so very few as not to affect the general statement.

the different districts of the Empire are applied, according to the facts of the case, none or one or two or three or all of the four qualifying adjectives, " busy, troublesome, wearisome, difficult." * The Hsien is duly equipped with Treasurers, Collectors, Secretaries, Clerks, Jailers, Runners, Constables, etc., many of whom hold their position by hereditary right or custom ; but an official in China, though he may delegate his functions, can never delegate or absolve himself from responsibility, and the Hsien is personally responsible for every act of what we may call the municipal government. He is everything in the municipality, and some of the most important of his functions must be described.

The judicial function is the most important. He is Police Magistrate, and decides ordinary police cases. He is Court of First Instance in all civil cases ; the penalty for taking a case first to a higher court is fifty blows with the bamboo on the naked thigh ; appeal from his court lies to the Fu, and by that time the resources of the litigants are usually exhausted. Civil cases are usually settled by the gilds in towns, and by village elders or by arbitration of friends in the country ; but they may come before the official tribunal, when the plaintiff wishes his pound of flesh and the blood of his victim as well. The Hsien is also Court of First Instance in criminal cases, though a first hearing may for convenience be held by an Assistant Magistrate ; appeal lies to the Fu, and cases involving the death penalty are reviewed by him ; death warrants are signed by the Niehtai, except in case of rebellion or of riot capable of being stigmatised as such, when summary justice is inflicted. Appeal from the death penalty may also, and in the case of officials does, go to the Hing Pu at Peking. The Hsien is also coroner, with all the duties of that office, and hears suits for divorce and breach of promise ; he is also prosecuting attorney, while a defendant may employ

* " The Office of District Magistrate in China," by Byron Brenan. *Journal, North China Branch of the Royal Asiatic Society*, 1898.

a lawyer only to draw up his plea, but not to conduct his defence ; he is also sheriff to execute all judgments of his own or a superior court ; and is jail warden, responsible for the custody and maintenance of prisoners before and after trial. If there is any part of the judicial function which has been omitted, he is that too.

The fiscal function comes next in importance. As is explained in the next chapter, the Hsien is the agent of the provincial and of the Imperial administrations in collecting the land tax and the grain tribute, but he has no concern with the special tributes or with the salt gabelle or likin ; with them his sole connection is the duty of protecting the collectors.

He is also Registrar of Land, and the system of verification is so thorough that a deed of sale certified by his seal may be accepted as a warranty of title.

He is Famine Commissioner for his district. It is his duty to see that the public granaries are kept full, and to distribute relief in time of distress. He is also Moth and Locust Commissioner to combat those plagues, and, except along the Yellow River, is solely responsible for the prevention of floods and reparation of their damage.

He is the local representative of the Kung Pu and the Provincial Treasurer in the custody of official buildings, and sees to the maintenance in order of city walls,* prisons, official temples, and all other public buildings ; and must maintain the efficiency and provide for the expenses of the Government courier service from border to border of his district. From his own funds he must execute such repairs as are ever effected to bridges and the things called roads, must see that schools are maintained, and must call upon the wealthy to contribute for public and philanthropic purposes. He maintains order, sees to the physical well-being of his district, and is the guardian of the people's morals.

---

* In cities like Soochow, divided between two or three Hsien, the maintenance of the walls is not also divided, but is entrusted to the superior officer, the Fu.

These are the principal functions of the Mayor of the Chinese municipium, and under the paternal government of this " Father and Mother of the People " the ruled might be expected to be a body of abject slaves. This is far from being the case. In most countries the people may be divided into the law-abiding and the lawless ; in China a third division must be noted—those who, though innocent of offence, come within the meshes of the law through the machinations of enemies. This, however, only serves to redress the balance, since the Chinese are essentially a law-abiding people, and, in the country at least, are guilty of few crimes below their common recreations of rebellion and brigandage. These they indulge in periodically when the harvest is in, if for any reason, such as flood or drought, the crops have been deficient ; but, apart from this and apart from the regular visits of the tax-collector, it is doubtful if the actual existence of a government is brought tangibly to the notice of a tenth, certainly not to a fifth, of the population. The remaining eighty or more per cent. live their daily life under their customs, the common law of the land, interpreted and executed by themselves. Each village is the unit for this common-law government, the fathers of the village exercising the authority vested in age, but acting under no official warrant, and interpreting the customs of their fathers as they learned them in their youth. The criminal law is national ; but, with a more or less general uniformity, each circumscription has its own local customs in civil matters. Questions of land tenure, of water rights, of corvées (when not Imperial), of temple privileges, of prescriptive rights in crops, may, in details, differ from district to district, will probably differ from Fu to Fu, and will certainly differ from province to province. Such differences are, however, immaterial ; the man of the country knows possibly only his own village and is not concerned with any district other than his own. That local custom in an adjoining district would alienate from him the foreshore accretion to his own farm concerns him but little, if the custom of his own district grants it to himself ; while the resident in the former does not think of claiming rights which were never claimed by his fathers. In matters of taxation, too, custom is the guiding principle. The government and the tax-collector are always trying to get more ; this is understood ; but the people, strong-based on custom, maintain an unending struggle to pay this year no more than they paid last year, and increment is wrung from them only after an annually renewed contest. In case of a general and marked increase the struggle is more pronounced, and may lead to riot and arson in the case of villagers, and in the case of traders to the peculiarly Chinese method of resistance, the " cessation of business," a combination of lock-out, strike, and boycott—a strong weapon against the magistrate, whose one aim is to serve his term without a disturbance sufficiently grave to come to the notice of his superiors.

The official head of the village is the Tipao, "Land Warden," nominated by the magistrate from the village elders, but dependent upon the good will of his constituents. Several small villages may be joined under one Tipao, and a large village will be divided into two or three wards, each with its Tipao ; while a village which, as is often the case, consists of the branches of one family holding its property in undivided commonalty, will have naturally as its Tipao the head of the family. The Tipao acts as constable, and is responsible for the good conduct and moral behaviour of every one of his constituents ; he is also responsible for the due payment of land tax and tribute.   He is the official land-surveyor of his village, and has the duty of verifying titles and boundaries on every transfer of land ; and the fees and gratuities from this, and the power over his fellow-villagers given by the other duties of the post, endow the Tipao with so much local importance, that the old communal theory is lost to a great extent, and the appointment is often in practice a matter of purchase.

The town is considered a collection of villages, being

divided into chia, "wards," each with its Tipao, whose duties are the same as those of his country colleague. The town has, however, its commercial questions, but these are almost, if not quite, invariably settled by the Gild concerned, in accordance with gild rules, and are seldom brought to the cognisance of the officials.

Of the relations between town and country it may be said that the interests of the countryman, peaceful and law-abiding, are sacrificed to those of the town dwellers, rowdy and competitive. The direct taxes, land tax and tribute, are assessed on rental value for farming land, and town property is subjected to no great increase from this rating. The movement of food supplies, too, is prohibited or sanctioned, not according to the interests of the producing farmer, but to meet the needs of the consuming townsman.

THE ARMY

The military organisation of the Chinese Empire is divided into two branches, the Manchu and the Chinese.

MANCHU MILITARY ORGANISATION

Dating from the time of the Manchu conquest during the first half of the seventeenth century, the Manchu "nation in arms" has been divided into eight "Banners," three superior and five inferior. The three Superior Banners are : (i) The Bordered Yellow (yellow being the colour of the Imperial family) ; (ii) The Plain Yellow ; and (iii) The Plain White. The five Inferior Banners are : (iv) The Bordered White ; (v) The Plain Red ; (vi) The Bordered Red ; (vii) The Plain Blue ; and (viii) The Bordered Blue. Each of the eight Banners is further divided into three " nations "—viz., (a) Manchu, (b) Mongol, and (c) Chinese, the last consisting of the descendants of the natives of North China who joined the Manchu invaders during the time of the conquest. Just as every Chinese is inscribed in his native district, in which he is liable (in theory) to tribute while living, and to which his bones are taken when dead, so all living Manchus and all descendants of the Mongol and Chinese soldiery of the conquest are inscribed in their proper Banners, under which they (are supposed to) fight to maintain the conquest and receive their quota of the tribute and other (theoretic) benefits of the conquest. Each Banner (Ki) has for each of its nations (Kusai) a Lieutenant-General (Tutung), a Deputy Lieutenant-General (or Brigadier), and Adjutant-Generals, two each for the Manchu and Chinese, and one for the Mongol nation of the Banner. Each Banner is divided into regiments (chala), five Manchu, five Chinese and two Mongol, each with its Colonel (Tsanling), Lieutenant-Colonel, and Adjutant. Under them are Captains (Tsoling), each charged with command and supervision over 70 to 100 households of the Banner, Lieutenants, and Corporals. The main force of the eight Banners is " encamped " in Manchuria and in and around Peking, and is provided in the capital with rations drawn from the tribute rice, of which some two million piculs (125,000 tons) are received annually. Outside Peking is the " military cordon " of twenty-five cities of Chihli, at which are settled military colonies drawn from the eight Banners. Outside these, again, are the provincial garrisons.

When the conquest was completed, the Manchus had the good sense to associate the Chinese with themselves in the government of the Empire and to hold the country by garrisons stationed at a few strategic points ; and, in the original scheme, the garrisons in the provinces made a total of half the garrison of the capital. Of the provincial garrisons about half were in a northern belt, designed partly as an outer defence to the capital, partly to look out on Mongolia ; these are the following places :

Shantung : Tsingchow and Tehchow.
Honan : Kaifeng.
Shansi : Kweihwa, Suiyuan, and Taiyuanfu.
Shensi : Sianfu.

Kansu : Ninghia, Liangchow, and Chwangliang.

The garrisons designed primarily to hold down the conquered Chinese were stationed at the following places :

Szechwan : Chengtu.

Hupeh : Kingchow (guarding the outlet of the Yangtze Gorge).

Kiangsu : Nanking, with sub-garrison at Chinkiang.

Chekiang : Hangchow, with sub-garrison at Chapu, once its seaport, now silted up.

Fukien : Foochow.

Kwangtung : Canton.

In six provinces there are no garrisons—five of them in the air strategically, Kiangsi, Hunan, Kweichow, Yunnan, and Kwangsi, and the sixth, Anhwei, being until Kanghi's time administratively part of Kiangsu.

In each of the eleven provinces thus constituting the Marches of the Manchu Empire is stationed a Warden of the Marches, the Manchu Generalissimo or Field Marshal (Tsiang Kün), commonly called Tartar-General, ranking with but before the Viceroy or Civil Governor-General, not generally interfering with the civil government, but, though now innocuous, originally able to impose his will upon his civilian colleague. Notwithstanding his high rank, he has now no more power or influence in the defence of the Empire than the Warden of the Cinque Ports has in that of England.

CHINESE MILITARY ORGANISATION

Apart from the effete Manchu army, the military forces of the Empire may be divided into two classes : (*a*) the ineffective official army under military command ; (*b*) the effective unofficial army under civilian command. The official army, constituting the provincial militia, is designated the Army of the Green Standard, and in the coast and riverine provinces is divided into land and water forces. The greater part constitutes the Ti-piao or Commander-in-Chief's force, being under his direct command ; a small

body constitutes the Fu-piao, or Governor's command ;
and, where there is a Governor-General, there is also a
Viceroy's command, Tu-piao. The army divisions are
territorial, the province being the highest unit. The
provincial Commander-in-Chief is the Titu, commonly
styled Titai and addressed as Künmen ("Gate to the
Camp "). The forces under his command are divided
into brigades, chen-piao, under the command of a Brigadier,
Tsungping, commonly styled Chentai. The brigades are
divided into territorial regiments, hieh, under a Colonel,
Futsiang, commonly styled Hiehtai ; and these again into
battalions, ying (or " camps"). Under the Hiehtai are
Lieutenant-Colonel (Tsantsiang), Major (Yuki), Senior
Captain (Tusze), Junior Captain (Showpei), Lieutenant
(Tsientsung), Sergeant (Patsung). The official hierarchy
of this army exists solely for the purpose of personal profit
and self-maintenance, the last thing they desire being to
lead their brave followers into action, even against an
unarmed mob ; while the rank and file exists mainly on
paper, but partly in the shape of gaudy uniforms to be
filled, for inspection purposes, by temporary recruits en-
listed for the day. Only at some places, such as the Kwangsi-
Tonkin frontier, the provincial Commander-in-Chief is
associated in the command of effective troops, outside his
own official organisation, for the preservation of peace and
order and the protection of his district.

The effective army is entirely, except for the possible
intervention of the Titai alone, outside the official military
organisation of the Empire or of the province. In this too
the unit is the province, and the effective armed forces of
the provinces are under the direct command of the civil
authority, the Viceroys and Governors, who themselves
lead them in chief for the suppression of serious rebellion.
This force dates from the Taiping rebellion (1850–1864), when
the official organisation was found ineffective and unwarlike, and the provincial rulers, such as Tseng Kwo-fan
in the west and Li Hung-chang in the east, were driven

to raise bodies of irregulars or volunteers, styled yung (brave), after the fashion of the volunteers of the French Revolution or of the year of Leipzig. In these the highest unit of organisation was the battalion, ying (camp), nominally of five hundred men, commanded by a battalion-chief, ying-kwan, divided into five companies, shao, commanded by a Shao-kwan. For combined action any number of battalions from two to ten or more formed a command, with no distinctive name, under a Tung-ling. This constituted the fighting army of China, such as it was, until, forty years after its first formation, its best representative, the " foreign drilled " army of the north, went down before the Japanese in 1894 ; and on this foundation is erected the " New Model " army now (1907) in process of organisation.

NOTE

The devolution of responsibility in the repression of disorder is shown in the following item of news :

PEKING, *December* 14*th*, 1906.

On December 11th, the Grand Councillors personally received an Imperial Decree to the effect that the rioters on the borders of Kiangsi and Hunan are furiously raging ¡and that Tuanfang (Viceroy at Nanking), Chang Chih-tung (Viceroy at Hankow), and Tsen Chun-ming (Governor of Kiangsi) are ordered to despatch troops to the scene of the troubles in order to suppress the same and capture the culprits and at the same time to give protection for the railway between Pingsiang and Liling as well as the mines at Pingsiang and all the foreigners there. In case of failure the said Viceroys and Governors will be held responsible.

On December 12th the Provincial Judge of Kiangsi, Ching Ping-chih, is ordered to take command of the armies from the three provinces to settle the troubles in the districts affected by rioters.

5

NANCHANG, *December 14th.*

Ching Ping-chih, Provincial Judge of Kiangsi, left Nanchang on December 14th for Pingsiang at the order of the Peking Government, and General Liu, who is the commander of the Nanchang Brigade of the Standing Army, and Admiral Hung Wei-lin, with their forces, followed the Provincial Judge.

CHAPTER III

THE GOVERNMENT—REPUBLICAN CHINA

" These two problems, each forming the counterpart of the
other, necessarily arise in the history of every nation, and in every
age : the problem of *order*, or how to found a central government
strong enough to suppress anarchy ; and the problem of *freedom*, or
how to set limits to an autocracy threatening to overshadow individual liberty."—W. S. McKechnie, " Magna Carta."

These are the problems of the West. In the East, as
exemplified by China, there has been only one problem,
that of establishing order ; and the problem of securing
individual liberty is one which has never seriously occupied
the attention of Chinese statesmen or thinkers. The
intellect of the nation has ever been drawn into the service
of the government—the agency for establishing order—
and that service has been the one channel for the accumulation of wealth ; while agitators and enthusiasts have been
driven into the ranks of the secret societies, finding all vested
interests arrayed against them.

Asiatic nations are normally satisfied with a government
which will give them order, provided that their traditional
customs are not interfered with ; and each succeeding
Chinese dynasty has satisfied the aspirations of the Chinese
people so long as it gave a strong and orderly government,
and at the same time admitted the intelligence of China to
a share in the administration. This was the case during the
reign of the first four emperors of the Tsing dynasty of the
Manchus ; but with the accession of Kiaking in 1796 corruption and weakness set in, and the discontent of the people

gave birth to many rebellions. These culminated in the
great Taiping rebellion, which, coming after the government
had been discredited by defeat in a foreign war, overspread
the country, until, in 1853, not one of the eighteen provinces
of China Proper was wholly under the dominance of the
Imperial authority. With this came defeat in another series
of conflicts with foreign Powers—England, France, and
Russia—and in 1860 the dynasty was utterly discredited,
and seemed tottering to its fall. But the Taiping dominion
was negative. Its chief characteristics were bloodshed and
devastation, and it attracted to its ranks none of the administrators of the nation; and, in 1864, the Imperial
authority was re-established in all the provinces, with the
full sympathy of the Western Powers.

An opportunity was now given to China to recover and
to regenerate herself. She did neither, and for thirty years
she slumbered. Then came the rude awakening of the war
with Japan, 1894–1895, when she was beaten to her knees
by a Power which previously she had despised; and her
people began dimly to feel that the nation's equipment for
its task was antiquated and ineffective. In 1898 Kang
Yu-wei persuaded the Emperor to institute reforms, excellent
in themselves, but too radical for the rulers of the Empire;
and reform was yet again deferred. The Boxer outbreak
in 1900 was an expression of the feelings of an ignorant
populace, dimly conscious that things were wrong, but not
knowing how to put them right ; it was a mad outburst,
and it properly failed, but it awoke the people to a sense of
nationality. Then the Russo-Japanese war, in 1903–1904,
fought on Chinese soil and resulting in the victory of the
Asiatic Power, began to show to the Chinese people great
possibilities in the future.

After 1900 education, on lines outside the limits of Confucian philosophy, was seen to be the essential condition
of progress. In 1872–1875 selected students had been sent to
America, and had there acquitted themselves with credit
in the universities. In 1881 they were recalled, and were

declared by the hide-bound statesmen of the Empire to have lost their touch with China and to be unfit for responsible posts ; they were then given employment as interpreters, telegraph operators, etc., which duties were, it was declared, all they were fitted for ; but from their number China has in recent years found some of her most capable administrators. For some years the modern education of the Chinese youth was left entirely to the American and English mission schools established in China ; but after 1900 even the rulers of the Empire realised the necessity of reforming education, and in 1903 the Ministry of Education was created. Schools were established and colleges founded, and the practice of sending selected students abroad was resumed. These students were sent principally to America and to Japan— some hundreds to the former and, owing to its proximity and the relatively lower cost, many thousands to Japan ; and it was from the Empire and not from the Republic that the students of China derived their revolutionary ideas. From Tokio came the impulse to cast off entirely the ancient civilisation of the Chinese people, and from the students educated in Japan came the agitation which was the greatest danger to a peaceful reform.

A few isolated risings against the government were easily suppressed, and order was maintained, mainly by paper reforms, during a few years ; for the national demand for reform was so pronounced that even the statesmen who had resisted it in 1898, now felt that resistance was no longer possible. Even the death of the old Empress Dowager, in November 1908, momentous as it was, seemed to make no change ; and order was still maintained and re-organisation of the government continued.

In September 1906 an Imperial edict was issued, promising reform of the official system, the laws and the finances of the Empire, and re-organisation of the army and navy, and undertaking to introduce constitutional government within a few years. On November 6th a further edict abolished the old ministries, substituting for them thirteen ministries, and creating a National Assembly of elected representatives. In September 1907 an edict placed the National Assembly on a working basis ; and in October Provincial Assemblies were created. An edict issued on December 25th, 1907, held out a promise of a future Parliament ; and on August 27th, 1908, a second edict laid down a programme for nine years, at the expiration of which a Parliament was to be summoned, and full constitutional government established ; the intervening time was, it was announced, required for the training of legislators in their duties. At the same time the draft of a proposed constitution was published, of which the first article declared that " the Tatsing dynasty shall rule over the Tatsing Empire for ever, and shall be honoured through all ages." Other articles defined the powers of the Emperor, the privileges and obligations of the subject, the rights and procedure of the Parliament, and the qualifications for the franchise.

The first Provincial Assemblies were held in October 1909. Their duties were consultative and critical, and not legislative or executive. With this limit placed on their power, they could be little more than debating societies ; and the principal result of their discussions was a collective demand that the summoning of the first national Parliament should take place within two years. This demand was rejected in an edict of January 20th, 1910.

The first National Assembly was opened by the Prince Regent at Peking on October 3rd, 1910, and its presidency was assumed by Prince Pu-Lun. It at once pressed the question of an earlier summoning of the first Parliament ; and, after some hesitation, an edict was issued fixing it for the year 1913. This did not satisfy the Assembly, which demanded that a Parliament be summoned without delay ; and it further insisted on the responsibility to it of the members of the Grand Council. The government still resisted the demand, but, after many agitated debates, the matter was compromised by an edict of December 25th, 1910, directing that an inquiry and early report on the two questions be made. The Assembly was then prorogued on January 11th.

Almost simultaneously with the second meeting of the National Assembly in October 1911 occurred the revolutionary rising at Wuchang, by which possession of that city, with Hanyang and Hankow, was secured to the forces of the party opposed to the Manchu dynasty. This rising was premature, but the plans of the revolutionaries had been well laid, and, as soon as success had crowned their efforts at Wuchang, risings occurred throughout middle and southern China, and in city after city the people renounced their allegiance to the Empire. Yuan Shih-kai, who had been driven from office three years before, was recalled to the rescue of the Imperial Court and given full powers. He was able to hold the north and even to recover Hanyang and Hankow, the latter prosperous mart being almost entirely destroyed by fire in the process ; but the united and resolute attitude of the Republicans in the centre and south, and the irresoluteness and Bourbonism of the Manchu Court and nobility combined to make impossible the task he had undertaken of preserving the dynasty as head of a constitutional monarchy. On February 12th, 1912, the Emperor abdicated and the Court withdrew to Jehol, which had been its city of refuge when the English and French occupied Peking in 1860. During the intervening fifty years the Great Tsing dynasty had been kept in power by the genius and ability of the Empress Tse-hi, the Manchus Prince Kung and Grand Secretary Wen-siang, and the Chinese Tseng Kwo-fan, Li Hung-chang and Chang Chih-tung ; but it had forgotten nothing and had learned nothing, and in the end was a mere anachronism.

The Cantonese Sun Yat-sen had been in exile, with a price on his head, since 1898, and during that time had been the moving spirit in the movement for establishing the Republic of China. On the evident success of the revolution he returned to his native land, and was, by the Provisional Assembly at Nanking, declared provisional President of the

Republic.   On the abdication of the Emperor he, with self-denying patriotism, resigned, and Yuan Shih-kai was designated as provisional President.

A National Council was also formed, and it summoned a Parliament to meet in April 1913, consisting of a Senate (Ts'an-yi Yuan) and a House of Representatives (Chung-yi Yuan).   This Parliament, sitting in joint session as a National Assembly in October 1913, elected Yuan Shih-kai as President, and Li Yuan-hung as Vice-President, for the constitutional term of five years.

A month after his election the President ejected from Parliament the members of the Kwomingtang, the party opposed to him, thereby reducing Parliament to a number below the constitutional quorum ; and in January 1914 he dissolved this Rump Parliament.   He also followed the Cromwellian precedent by substituting for Parliament a Council of State, the members of which were nominated by himself ;   and, to the end of his life, he governed the State by Presidential Mandates.   He was confronted by much opposition ;   but such as was personal and not sectional he overrode ruthlessly,   and his government gave the country the strong administration which it needed. One phase of opposition he was unable to deal with—that created by the jealousy between the North and the South. The North, with Yuan Shih-kai as its leader, would have accepted a constitutional monarchy in 1911 ;   while the South, led by the Cantonese, declared for a republic from the first outbreak of the Revolution ;   and the fissure between the two could not be bridged.

In the summer of 1915 an apparently spontaneous movement was started to re-establish the Empire, with Yuan Shih-kai as the founder of a new dynasty.   His rule was already as well established as that of Cromwell had been ;   his power in the Chinese Republic had, to all appearance, the same solidity as that of Augustus in the Roman Republic ;   but, not content with the reality, he grasped at the shadow, and announced that he would accept the throne when it should be offered to him. The time was not propitious. There were already some armed rebellions against the President's authority, and there were more when it was officially announced that there was to be a revival of the consolidated monarchy; the South pronounced against the project, and some even of the President's consistent adherents were alienated; and, at the end of February, he formally renounced his Imperial ambitions. Within four months, on June 6th, 1916, he died.

Li Yuan-hung, the Vice-President, succeeded to the Presidency. He reversed his predecessor's measures, but was compelled by the force of circumstances to adopt his methods. He summoned the Parliament which had been dissolved by Yuan Shih-kai, but within a year, in June 1917, he again dissolved it, chiefly because in it the South had more power than he was disposed to allow to it. Yuan Shih-kai had maintained his prestige because he had controlled the army; but the army controlled Li Yuan-hung, and his power in the State soon vanished. He thereupon resigned the Presidency.

The culminating event which brought him to this decision was a renewed attempt to re-establish the Empire. One military commander, Chang Hsün, had maintained himself in the south-western part of Shantung since the establishment of the Republic, not molesting it, and not molested by it. Under his leadership and with the support of his troops the Manchus now made a bid for the throne, and on July 1st, 1916, an Imperial edict was issued announcing that the Emperor Hsüantung had again mounted the throne of his ancestors. On July 7th another edict announced his second abdication. The conflict had been decided in Peking itself, and the defeated leader, Chang Hsün, had been forced to take refuge in the Netherlands Legation.

During these three years—1916, 1917 and 1918—there was much disorder in the state of China; and a detailed account, drawn from the Post-office reports, of the condition of each province, will show the difficulties created by natural causes, by personal ambition, or by the predominating rivalry between North and South—difficulties which constantly impeded all efforts to establish a strong central administration.

CHIHLI. 1916. The Peking-Chengtehfu mail time-table was rearranged to permit the couriers to pass over certain robber-infested sections during daylight.

1917. There were many impediments to postal progress due to political upheaval, flood, and famine. . . . Owing to shortage of rain the spring crops were a failure. . . . From July to October the district suffered from floods, and at one time as much as 15,000 square miles of territory were inundated to a depth of from 2 to 10 feet.

1918. Highway robbers were active in the north and south. Many villages in the south were pillaged by bandits from Shantung, causing the inhabitants of the rural areas to abandon their homes and crowd into the walled cities for protection.

SHANSI. 1916. Operations suffered much from the state of unrest in parts of the province, while in the section Outside the Wall business was more or less at a standstill all the year on account of the activities of large bands of robbers. . . . Several towns Outside the Wall were completely looted and partly destroyed by fire.

1917. Revolting troops in Shansi proper, and roving brigands in Outside the Wall, combined by their lawlessness and depredations to hamper postal operations. Besides pillaging and burning villages and hamlets, they twice looted one city, captured a second, and besieged two others. Couriers were attacked and mails lost. . . . Beginning from June martial law was declared in the provincial capital. . . . Towards the end of the year preventive measures had to be enforced to meet the outbreak of pneumonic plague.

1918. The province was not much disturbed during the year except by an epidemic of pneumonic plague.

HONAN. 1916. While the past year was a disturbed one in many parts of the country, Honan remained peaceful.

1917. In the spring and summer drought damaged the crops ; then followed abnormal rains and disastrous floods. The struggles connected with the restoration of the monarchy and other political questions tended further to disturb the tranquillity of the province. . . . Most of the native banks stopped doing business.

1918. Last year's unfavourable conditions, due to the political unrest, abnormal rains, the consequent disastrous floods, and increase of lawlessness in the country, continued during this year. Native banks closed more of their branches in the interior.

SHENSI. 1916. The northern districts of the province suffered much from roving bandits. During the year no fewer than twenty-two towns were pillaged, not to mention villages and hamlets. Further, there was much severe fighting, especially around Sianfu, consequent on the political agitation. . . . Many robberies of mails occurred ; seven couriers were killed.

1917. Bands of mounted brigands roamed through the province plundering and looting. Towards the end of the year revolting troops added to the chaos by capturing a convoy of 250 camels with guns and ammunition for Szechwan, which they proceeded to use for an attack on Sianfu. . . . After leaving Sianfu the rebels fled west, looting towns and villages as they went. . . . Trade is in many parts non-existent. . . . On almost any of the main roads can be found the walls of what used to be thriving cities, but are now merely walled enclosures of vacant ground.

1918. Continuous strife, with all its attendant miseries, has made the year one of the worst in the history of the province. Bandits have been especially active, their numbers augmented by bands of disloyal soldiers attracted by the prospect of wholesale looting. Throughout the province the tale is one of spoliation, the methods of the robbers being the same everywhere—intimidation, pillage, extortion, and even excessive cruelty to those unfortunates who fell into their clutches. . . . In most of the large cities business was entirely suspended . . . altogether 78 post offices were looted. As the bandits' sphere of operations included the whole of the province, nearly all the courier lines have been interrupted. . . . Recently Mongolian robbers have joined forces with the provincial bandits . . . in addition the country is overrun by soldiers from the neighbouring provinces. Devastation is apparent on all sides.

KANSU. 1916. The political troubles elsewhere had

little effect beyond increasing the boldness of local bands of robbers. . . . Direct postal communication was also interrupted for some time owing to bandits.

1917. Disturbances occurred in March at Kaichow, the town being looted by bandits, and in May at Kweitehting, near the Tibetan border, where the brigands had to be suppressed and the city recaptured by Mohammedan troops.

1918. The province was comparatively quiet.

SINKIANG. 1916. Peace was maintained during the year.

1917. Peace was still maintained. The province is flooded with a depreciated paper currency.

1918. The province was quiet.

MANCHURIA. 1916. Many courier lines traverse robber-infested districts and the mails are frequently endangered, but during the year only one postal courier met his death.

1917. Political changes, the Great War, the Russian revolution, highway robberies, and the unprecedented fluctuation of foreign moneys were the disquieting features that retarded postal extension in this district. . . . At Kingsingchen Mongolian insurgents raided the town.

1918. The continued unrest in Russia and Siberia rendered necessary a complete suspension of traffic for business purposes on the Siberian, Amur, and Ussuri Railways . . . all regular steamship communication on the Sungari and Amur Rivers was hampered. The usual robberies, floods, and snow-storms were encountered, and the unlimited issue of paper money did not facilitate postal work.

SHANTUNG. 1916. The tranquillity of the province was rudely broken by the political uprising, which rapidly assumed alarming proportions. Place after place along and near the Shantung Railway was attacked, seized, and looted, not excepting the two most important commercial centres in Shantung, Chowtsun and Weihsien, which became storm centres of the conflict, and ultimately the headquarters of the leaders of the uprising.

1917. The attempt to restore the monarchy in the summer and the consequent withdrawal of troops from inland places caused a recrudescence of highway robbery all over the province. . . . Drought caused the failure of the wheat crop ; then followed the overflow of the Grand Canal, resulting in the worst floods Shantung has seen for many years.

1918. Robberies have been particularly rife in the western part of the province. Five postmasters and couriers kidnapped, two couriers killed ; a large number of post offices looted. The parcel traffic has especially suffered from the unsafe condition of the roads.

SZECHWAN. 1916. Szechwan was just settling down to something like normal conditions when it became one of the centres of strife over the political changes. Then followed the invasion of Szechwan by Yunnan and Kweichow troops, severe fighting, and the restoration of the republican form of government in March, the cessation of hostilities from April to June, and, finally, the march of Northern troops on Chengtu and their defeat by the Yunnan troops. Between June and November four different provincial Governors held office. Brigandage was rife, and currency difficulties became accentuated, making business impossible. Frontier raids continued unabated. . . . There were 100 cases of loss of mails and 47 cases of loss of official funds, mainly due to brigandage ; 3 couriers were killed and some severely wounded.

1917. The incessant bid for military supremacy in this province developed during the year into the most serious crisis the province has yet faced. The invasion of Szechwan by Yunnan and Kweichow troops last year culminated in April of this year in hostilities at Chengtu between the invaders and the provincial troops, which resulted, after three days' severe fighting, in the withdrawal of the Yunnanese. Great loss of life and property occurred, and about 15,000 families were rendered homeless. . . . The environs of Chengtu were still held by the Kweichow troops, and brigandage was rife everywhere. At the beginning of July the monarchy question supplied another *casus belli*, and the twelve days' fighting which ensued between the Szechwan and Kweichow troops resulted in the destruction of one-eighth of Chengtu city and the loss of thousands of lives. Northern troops sent into Szechwan to strengthen the authority of the central government, and the revolt of certain Szechwan divisions, resolved the struggle into one between North and South. . . . The fact that the Post Office was practically the only channel by which goods could go and come with any chance of safe transport is accountable for the increase of parcels handled.

1918. The struggle in Szechwan, which had developed into one between North and South at the end of 1917, continued with renewed vigour in the opening months of the year. With their base at Chungking, the Southern troops advanced by all the routes converging on Chengtu . . . this campaign lasted for nearly two months. . . . The Tibetan revolt, minor uprisings of tribes in the Lolos' country, and brigandage throughout the province, are additional causes which impeded postal progress.

HUPEH. 1916. Parcels posted and delivered fell off, due to the disorganisation of business on account of the political troubles. Two post offices were plundered by brigands ; one courier was killed.

1917. Towards the end of the year the presence of the opposing Northern and Southern forces made itself felt, and signs of a panic were not wanting.

1918. British steamers, having been repeatedly fired upon by disaffected troops, stopped running between Hankow and Ichang from February 15th to March 6th. . . . Very few steam launches were plying between Hankow and Changsha. . . . Railway communication with the north was interrupted at various times during the summer. . . . Civil war, activities of bandits, and an epidemic of influenza interfered very considerably with postal work. Many post offices were looted by soldiers or bandits.

HUNAN. 1916. Civil war broke out at the beginning of the year and lasted for four months. Martial law was declared and censorship of mails established. Few couriers were available, and their routes became unsafe. There were numerous cases of highway robbery, and twelve cases of robbery of mails. In March the city of Yungshunfu was sacked by bandits ; a number of post offices were looted or destroyed by fire. . . . The vast amount of distress and damage, as well as the general stagnation of trade, caused by the civil war. . . .

1917. The whole province was in a state of unrest and under martial law ; this involved censorship of mails at all offices. Towards the end of October brigandage became rife, and in November lawlessness prevailed for more than a week at Changsha. Some twenty post offices were looted or destroyed, and in four cases couriers were waylaid and robbed. The parcel-boat service was suspended on account of the activities of robber bands. . . . Widespread floods in the summer ruined the rice crops, and the climax came in the depreciation of the Hunan provincial government banknotes to one-third of their face value.

1918. The year opened with the whole province in a state of unrest and under martial law, with fighting taking place in four districts. On March 25th the straggling units of a beaten army, with the local rascals joining in, began looting in Changsha, continuing it through the night. At Yochow steamers were fired on by the soldiers occupying Linsiang and Loshan. The prolonged civil war and continued activity of brigands caused extensive devastation in many parts of the province. In all 77 post offices were looted. Those at Chuchow and Liling were looted and burned in the looting and burning of the two cities.

KIANGSI. 1916. The province again suffered from floods ; currency difficulties were also felt. No disturbances were reported.

1917. Political disturbances and invasion threatened the province, but each crisis was successfully surmounted and peace maintained. The paper currency held up. . . .

1918. No acts of brigandage were reported, and the soldiers gave little trouble. . . . The paper currency was not further depreciated.

ANHWEI. 1916. During the period of political unrest censorship of mails was enforced. For a time the more important cities were under martial law. . . . The worst floods for many years . . . the number of robbers increased. Two mails were lost by highway robbery.

1917. There were local disturbances having their origin in the movements of troops in connection with the attempted restoration of the monarchy in July. Some towns were pillaged. The inhabitants of Lüchowfu and Chuchow abandoned their homes in large numbers. From July to October, when the provincial troops left for military operations in Hunan, the province from Lüchowfu northwards was in a state of anarchy. Many brigands emerged and frequent encounters took place with the troops. In September a division of soldiers mutinied.

1918. Except for the usual numerous gangs of armed bandits at large in the northern part of the province, comparative quiet prevailed. The majority of the Anhwei troops were engaged in civil warfare in Hunan.

KIANGSU. 1916. Deep political unrest in the domestic sphere and the far-extending influence of the European war combined adversely to influence postal operations. . . . For several months business between Shanghai and south and south-west China was practically suspended.

1917. The depressing atmosphere created by disorder within the nation and war without has checked postal progress. Business was practically suspended between Shanghai and all provinces to the south and west for months, while revolt and independence were declared and warlike operations were in progress. The internal disorder and unrest in other directions also had their detrimental effect.

1918. The principal hindrance to regularity of the courier service was brigandage, which was worse than ever before. . . . Large towns had to keep the city gates closed ; some were looted and burned ; kidnapping and murder were rife ; railway trains were held up by brigands, passengers being carried off for ransom.

CHEKIANG. 1916. The disturbed condition of the province during the first half-year, and in particular during April when provincial independence was declared, adversely affected postal work. . . . During the year three couriers were killed by bandits.

1917. This province has to chronicle temporary declaration of independence, local disturbances, and rebellion of troops, with the usual looting which accompanies these outbreaks. . . . Five cases of mail matter lost by highway robbery occurred.

1918. The Tuchün was determined to preserve peace in the province, and cut short any attempt at an uprising. In one attempted rising at Chüchowfu seven of the ringleaders were executed.

FUKIEN. 1916. Some couriers molested by robbers.

1917. Highway robberies were frequent. Heavy floods and typhoons caused occasional interruptions of mails.

1918. Every evil and calamity apparently concentrated in this province to strike it at one and the same time. Civil war, epidemics, floods, famine, lawlessness, and widespread brigandage, all were experienced. Not a city, and hardly a village, was spared these evils. The losses incurred as a consequence by the people throughout the province must have been as incalculable as their sufferings.

KWANGTUNG. 1916. The conditions of dull trade and general unrest which prevailed at the close of last year continued till March, when political disturbances broke out, and the province suffered the horrors of civil war till September. In June a Yunnan army, on its way to the North, turned against Kwangtung and marched on Canton by the North River. Then Kwangsi troops approached by the West River and reached within a few miles of the city, which remained in a state of siege from July 22nd till September 11th, when peace was arranged. In the meantime heavy fighting took place at several points on the East River. For six months the whole province was thus in a state of disorder. Robbers and brigands made the most of the opportunity. Business and communications almost came to a standstill. Inland offices were pillaged and burned. Postal agents were captured and held for ransom. Steam traffic with inland places was suspended, likewise the operating of many courier and boat lines. Railway traffic, for the most part, was also stopped. There were 165 cases of robbery and piracy of mails ; in other 42 cases couriers were held up and robbed of their belongings by brigands. Three couriers were killed and 4 seriously wounded.

1917. Until June the province had peace, but the events since then are now a matter of history. The establishment of the so-called Military Government ; the opening of the extraordinary parliament ; the differences of opinion between local officials and the Military Government ; the revolt of troops at Waichow, also affecting other places ; the declaration of independence against the Kwangtung Government by Defence Commissioner Mo Ching-yü of Swatow, with consequent fighting at . . . and a dozen other places ; the assumption by General Lung Chi-kwang of the Inspector-Generalship of the Liang-kwang, with the operations, naval and military, which that step entailed—all these have kept the province in a state of ferment. Mail services were suspended, commerce was at a standstill, and the whole Swatow section remained till the close of the year in a chaotic condition. There were 65 cases of brigandage and piracy of mails, besides 20 cases in which couriers were robbed of their own belongings. Thirty post offices were pillaged or burned.

1918. During the year this province suffered many calamities ; the general dissension in the country, the

6

brigandage and piracy throughout the province, devastating floods, and a disastrous earthquake, all combined. The whole south-western portion of the province, including the Island of Hainan, suffered from the ravages of the army. Luichow city was besieged for two months. Namyung city was taken by storm, and thereafter was for nearly two months accessible for mails only from Kiangsi. In the Swatow section fighting broke out early in the year, and was at its height from June to August, military operations being conducted in four districts. Besides 107 courier robberies, there were 50 robberies at post offices, and 8 post offices were burned after being plundered ; 2 postal agents were killed and 2 were captured and held for ransom.

KWANGSI. 1916. In 1915 this province was the victim of floods ; during this year it has suffered from political disturbance. The civil war, and the attack upon the neighbouring province of Kwangtung, caused a great falling off in the inter-provincial trade. . . . Forty couriers were held up by bandits, and 18 were robbed of their mails ; 1 courier was murdered.

1917. As in Kwangtung, the opening of the year seemed to promise peace and prosperity, but political unrest and two floods falsified this expectation. Trade suffered, several large business houses in Wuchow and Nanning became bankrupt. . . . Bandits held up 28 couriers, and robbed 17 of their mails ; 1 courier was murdered.

1918. The political upheaval, the activities of robber bands, and the consequent dull trade, retarded postal development. Brigandage was rife and robber bands very active. . . . Couriers were frequently molested ; 53 were held up by highwaymen, resulting in the loss of 25 mails ; 3 couriers were killed and 4 wounded.

YUNNAN. 1916. Early in the year Yunnan took the lead in the agitation against the political changes, and expeditionary forces were despatched against Szechwan and Kwangtung. An uprising of the aborigines also led to severe fighting in the south of the province. . . . The roads throughout the province continued to be infested with bandits. Thirty-five robberies occurred in which the mails were wholly or partly robbed, and the personal losses of couriers were most heavy. Five were killed and 7 wounded.

1917. The same lawless conditions as in 1916 prevailed

throughout this year also. Outlaws, who were mostly disbanded soldiers, made inland travel extremely unsafe. . . . There were 56 highway robberies in which mails were lost; 3 couriers were killed and 15 wounded. Five towns were thoroughly looted.

1918. During the year Yunnan continued to maintain its independence of the central government, and Yunnan troops stationed at strategical points in Szechwan and Kweichow dominated the political situation in those provinces. . . . The postal authorities have received the most effective and spontaneous support from the local authorities. The result has been that, notwithstanding numerous difficulties due to floods and the unsafe state of the roads owing to bandits and the turbulent Lolo tribes, postal connections were maintained with regularity. . . . Political unrest is followed everywhere in China by an aftermath of brigandage, and this has been the case in Yunnan ; 80 mails were lost by highway robbery, 1 post office plundered, 3 couriers killed, and several wounded.

KWEICHOW. 1916. On account of the transfer of all available troops for active service, robberies were numerous. There were 19 cases of mails lost by highway robbery.

1917. The year opened well, despite the activities of robber bands. In the last three months, however, when the confusion in Szechwan and Hunan was at its height, routes leading to Yangtze provinces were blocked, and Kweichow merchants practically ceased business. In 24 robberies, 13 mails were lost ; 1 courier was killed and many injured.

1918. Since the opening of hostilities in Hunan and Szechwan in 1917, the routes leading to the Yangtze provinces cannot be said to have been really open to traffic. They have been infested by robbers, hence the almost complete stoppage of trade for the entire year 1918. The deadlock in the fighting between the North and the South resulted in a recrudescence of highway robbery all over the province. Robberies of mails were frequent.

This is the record, province by province, of the state of China during three years—1916, which saw the death of Yuan Shih-kai and the short-lived attempt to restore the Ta-tsing Empire ; 1917 and 1918, in which the strife between

North and South came to the clash of arms and brought civil war to the Republic. The civil war amounted to little more than brigandage on a vast scale ; since there were no military commanders with the quality of leadership, and no disciplined troops capable of winning a decision ; but misery was caused to the people, and difficulties were created for the administration, both the central and that of the provinces.

Feng Kwo-chang had become acting President in July 1917, governing, as his predecessors had done, through a nominated Council and by means of Presidential Mandates ; but ultimately, in August 1918, a new Parliament was summoned, and on September 4th it elected Hsü Shih-chang to be President, but could not agree on a Vice-President. Meantime the fissure between the North and the South had widened, and in the spring of 1918 a rival Parliament met at Canton. It elected no rival President, but set up a government of seven " Administrative Directors," who issued a public announcement that five provinces (Kwangtung, Kwangsi, Yunnan, Kweichow, and Szechwan) had given their entire adhesion to them, and that their forces were actively engaged in seven other provinces in rescuing the administration from the control of military oligarchs, and in " fighting to make China safe for democracy."

During eight years from the establishment of the Republic it had, in theory, been administered under the Provisional Constitution drawn up in Nanking in 1911 and adopted in Peking in March 1912. The Parliament, which had by two Presidents been twice dissolved, had delegated to a convention, composed of the leaders of the nation, the task of drawing up a new and permanent Constitution. It seems hardly worth while to summarise the existing Constitution, which is only provisional, and which has not at any time been lived up to ; and below is given a summary of the proposed Constitution, which, it is hoped, may serve as the charter of a restored and regenerated Republic.

THE NEW DRAFT CONSTITUTION

" The sovereignty of the Republic of China is vested in the entire body of the people." This declaration does not exist in the constitutions of the United States of America (which is a federation of sovereign States) or of France, but it is found in those of Belgium, Chile, and the United States of Mexico. It may, however, be stated that the relations of the Chinese people to representative government are more on the level of the citizens of the Mexican Republic than of the American.

All citizens are declared equal before the law. No provision is more necessary for the Chinese nation than this, none is more disregarded, and none will be more difficult of enforcement ; but the exposition shows that the Swiss parallel —" There are neither political dependents, nor privileges of place, birth, person, or family "—served as model for China.

The citizens shall not be " arrested, imprisoned or detained in confinement, tried or punished or fined, except in accordance with the law," and, if detained, may apply for a writ of habeas corpus. The onlooker rubs his eyes. Can this be China ? This is a startling innovation for China, and, if it can be carried into effect, will constitute a revolution more far-reaching in its results than even the transformation of the Empire into a republic.

The inviolability of residence and correspondence, freedom of speech and writing, and the right of assembly for a lawful purpose are provided for—quasi-natural rights in a democratic country such as a republic must needs be ; but in China—when the governors are weak or are scared, the governed will find these rights far from secure.

The qualifications for the franchise are : adult males ; payment of direct taxes of 2 dollars per annum ; possession of immovable property of a value of 500 dollars ; being a graduate of an elementary or higher school. The alternative qualifications are sufficiently low, but even so, in a country with such masses of poverty, many millions are excluded; with a nation so utterly ignorant of the very rudiments of representative government, it is perhaps well that the franchise is thus restricted.

POWERS OF PARLIAMENT

Parliament has the following powers : to enact new laws or revise old laws ; to amend the constitution ; to pass resolutions having the force of law ; to initiate law bills, but not money bills ; to interpellate the government and make recommendations to it ; to elect the President and the Vice-President, and (the Legislature) to impeach and (the Senate) to try these officers and Cabinet ministers ; to approve money bills for levying taxes and for expenditure, and to supervise the expenditure ; and to approve declarations of war and treaties with foreign nations. In the performance of their duties members of Parliament are entitled to full freedom of speech in Parliament, and to exemption from arrest unless arrested in the act of committing a crime ; in such a case the reason for the arrest must be reported to the house of which he is a member.

Parliament is bicameral. The Senate consists of 274 senators ; 10 elected by each of 22 provincial Assemblies, 54 elected by Electoral Colleges—27 by that of Mongolia, 10 by Tibet, 3 by Chinghai (Kokonor), 8 by the Central Educational Society, 6 by Chinese resident abroad. Their term is six years, one-third retiring every two years. In the composition of the Senate the Constitution follows closely that of the American Republic, in allotting an equal number to each of the provinces, irrespective of size, population or wealth.

In one respect the Senate, in the powers it exercises, departs from the American precedent. In regulating the relations between one province and another, or between the central government and the provinces, the decision lies with the Senate, and not with the Supreme Court ; moreover, if the President's warning to a turbulent or recalcitrant province is disregarded, he may, with the approval and consent of the Senate, dismiss the Governor or dissolve the provincial Assembly.

Money bills must first be presented by the government to the Legislature (the House of Representatives). The Senate may propose amendments, but, if these are not accepted by the Legislature, they are rejected. The Legislature also controls the Board of Audit. These provisions are much closer to British practice than to American.

The Legislature consists at present of 596 members, on the basis of one member for every 800,000 of population; but no province is to send less than ten members; and the dependencies (Mongolia, Tibet and Chinghai) send the same number as to the Senate. Their term is for three years.

In its control of money bills, the Legislature is under certain restrictions; it may reduce the government proposals, but cannot increase the proposed expenditure; in this respect, again, China has followed British practice and not American. But Parliament may not abolish or curtail any of the following expenditures:

(*a*) Those belonging to the obligations of the government in accordance with the law.

(*b*) Those which are necessary for the observance of treaties.

(*c*) Those considered necessary in accordance with the provisions of law.

(*d*) Continuous expenditure.

The clauses (*a*) and (*c*) would seem to remove from the control of Parliament all payments under contracts and for the salaries of officials and government employees.

The President

In the election of the President and Vice-President the French practice is followed. The two houses of Parliament unite in national Assembly; but, instead of election by an absolute majority as in France, the Chinese rule requires

three-fourths of the number voting, with two-thirds necessary for a quorum. Under normal conditions this might
easily lead to a dead-lock; but a further excellent rule
provides that if, on the second ballot, no candidate suc-
ceeds in obtaining the required three-fourths vote, the two
names highest on that ballot shall be submitted to the third
ballot, in which a bare majority shall elect. The term of
the President and Vice-President is for five years, and
either may be re-elected. If the President vacates his
post (on impeachment and conviction, or through death
or resignation) or if he is unable to execute his powers
(through illness or absence), the Vice-President will act as
President to the end of the term or of the inability, as the
case may be.

The | theory of the Constitution is that the President
is the Chief Executive of the Republic—this is the American
practice; but at the same time he " has no initiative and
simply concurs with what Parliament or the Cabinet, as
the case may be, sees fit to decide "—this is the ceremonial
President of France. Which form may emerge in China
at any given moment depends on the strength of the President—Yuan Shih-kai was the State; under his successors
the bureaucracy has ruled, an oligarchy at Peking, other
oligarchies in the several provinces.

The President may veto bills passed by Parliament, but
a vetoed bill becomes law if again passed by a bare majority.
He convokes and dissolves Parliament; and, with the consent of the Senate, he may dissolve the House of Representatives alone. He appoints or dismisses all civil and military
officers, but a few of the highest are subject to the approval
of Parliament.

Yuan Shih-kai governed by Presidential Mandates,
which he issued under his " emergency " powers. The Constitution makers could not agree to continue these Cromwellian powers to succeeding Presidents, nor could they
agree to abolish them; but, in the disagreement, the powers
were dropped.

THE CABINET

The Cabinet, " being the actual executive [as in France and the United Kingdom], its powers are naturally large, although its acts, to be valid, must be endorsed by the President, and the Mandates appertaining thereto must needs be sealed and promulgated by him." The appointment of the Premier must be approved by the House of Representatives, but not the other ministers. The ministers of the Cabinet are not members of Parliament, but " the ministers shall have entrance to both chambers, and shall be heard when they request it," or they may send delegates in their place. The Cabinet may propose law bills, and it has the sole right to initiate money bills ; and Presidential Mandates must be countersigned by a minister, except one appointing or dismissing the Premier. So far the Cabinet finds its prototype most nearly in the late German Empire.

The Cabinet does not necessarily resign when Parliament rejects or amends its measures ; but if a vote of censure on it is passed by the House of Representatives, it must resign, unless the President, with the consent of the Senate, dissolves that House. This falls far short of the responsibility to Parliament in British and French practice, but it is a step in advance of the American.

The national Judiciary is independent alike of the legislative and of the executive branches of the government, its judges retaining their office during good behaviour, and their emoluments may not be decreased. Judges are to be appointed by the President, but the appointment of the Chief Justice of the Supreme Court (and of him alone) is subject to the approval of the Senate.

CENTRAL ADMINISTRATION

The head of the State is the President. Under him is the Vice-President, having no active duties to perform while the President exercises his functions. Under them is the

Premier, who is in theory the directing head of the administration, in so far as he is allowed by the President to perform the duties assigned to him by the Constitution. The President's office is administered by a Chief of Staff, an Assistant Chief, Heads of Departments, etc.

MINISTRIES

The names of the Ministries have been changed within a few years, and the former name is given in parenthesis after the present name. Each Ministry has its Minister, a Vice-Minister, and Councillors.

Wai-chiao Pu (Wai-wu Pu), Ministry of Foreign Affairs.
Nei-wu Pu (Min-cheng Pu), Ministry of the Interior.
Ts'ai-cheng Pu (Tu-chih Pu), Ministry of Finance.
Lu-chün Pu, Ministry of War (the Army).
Hai-ehün Pu, Ministry of the Navy.
Sze-fa Pu (Fa Pu), Ministry of Justice.
Chiao-yü Pu (Hioh Pu), Ministry of Education.
Nung-shang Pu, Ministry of Agriculture and Commerce.
Chiao-t'ung Pu (Yu-chuan Pu), Ministry of Communications.

DEPARTMENTS

Department for Mongolia and Tibet.
Sun-chi Chu, Board of Audit.
Shui-wu Chu, Board of Revenue.
Department of Telegraphs.
Department of Railways.

PROVINCIAL ADMINISTRATION

The Provincial Assemblies, which had been active before the Revolution, were suppressed by Yuan Shih-kai; but on his death they again came into being and continued their innocuous career. The administration of the provinces remained in the hands of the bureaucracy, as under the Empire. On the outbreak of the Revolution control of the administration was assumed in each province by the military commander, under the title of Tutu (the officer in supreme command). When the Republic was established the provincial governments were recast in the following form :

Civil Governor (Hsün-an-shih).
Military Governor (Tu-chün).
Administrative Departments :
General Affairs.
Interior.
Education.
Trade and Industry.
Taoyin—the old Taotai.
Hsien (Magistrate), as under the Empire.

This was the frame-work of a government which it was hoped might be set up. Most of the officials were duly appointed, but their functions have generally been exercised under the supervision of the Military Governors, who have remained in control in most of the provinces. In the latest publication * it is shown that, of twenty-two provinces, there are Military Governors alone in eight, Civil Governors alone in five ; in the remaining nine there are both Military and Civil Governors ; but it is notorious that the army dominates in all.

* "The China Year Book, 1919."

CHAPTER IV

REVENUE AND EXPENDITURE

CHINA is an Asiatic country. It seems absurd to re-state this truism, but in nothing is the fact more clearly marked than in its system of taxation and its methods of providing for the expenses of administration. The Western mind is accustomed to the system of the common purse for one administrative area, into which all receipts are covered without being ear-marked for a definite purpose, and from which all payments are made irrespective of the source from which the funds are derived ; it is also accustomed to a complete severance of the budgets of the different administrative areas—national, state and municipal in America, national and municipal in Great Britain, Imperial, Royal, and municipal in Germany—with some exceptions, such as educational expenditure in Great Britain, and those due to more centralised forms of government, as in France. This makes it difficult for the Occidental to project his mind into the system which prevails in China, and still more difficult for him to distinguish, in the mass of what appears to him gross irregularity, what is due to the system and what to administrative and financial corruption. The student of history will recall the administrative system of Europe of, say, five centuries ago, and, if he has any knowledge of China, will find many points of resemblance in matters which we to-day have come to reprobate ; but any comparison is vitiated by the real difference between the feudal organisation of Europe of that time, and the consolidated government of China, with the Son of Heaven at the top and the mass of the people at the bottom, the Emperor's representatives, the officials appointed by his centralised power, forming the link between the two. It is a matter of common knowledge that the income of the Chinese official is not in any degree measured by his official salary, that the annual profit of his office may be Tls.100,000, with an official salary not exceeding Tls.1,000. This sounds terrible to us ; and yet we do not have to go very far back to find a condition similar in kind, though perhaps not in degree, existing in Western countries.

The Chinese official is nowadays less an administrator than a tax-collector ; but an infinitesimal portion of his revenues is wasted on such heads of expenditure as police, justice, roads, education, fire-prevention, sanitation, or others of the numerous expenses falling on the official purse in the West ; so far as we, with our limited Occidental mind, can see, he exists solely for his own maintenance and that of his fellow-officials, his superiors and his subordinates. This principle he, with his superior innate capacity, has developed further than was ever done in the West ; but the West can furnish, within comparatively modern times, some similitudes which will enable present-day readers to understand more clearly the system as it is to-day in China. The revenue returnable from each administrative area in China, town, county, or province, is assessed at a certain fixed sum, which, more or less, is the minimum which must be accounted for, and in practice this minimum constitutes the maximum sum which is returned : what is this but the system which, in the seventeenth and eighteenth centuries, furnished the bloated fortunes of the farmers-general of France ? The administration of justice in China creates no charge upon the official revenues, but maintains itself from fees and exactions : Judge Jeffreys is infamous in history, but he furnished no exception to the practice of his day in swelling the revenues of his king and his country from the fees and fines of his court, and in augmenting his official income from the same source. Every Chinese official takes for himself, without question, the interest on his official balances; so did the English Paymasters of the Forces up to the time of Pitt, and probably for many years after this time ; certainly until after Fox was appointed to the post. Even modern America, with the foundations of its government freed from all feudal substructure, in some of its legitimate and legalised practices furnishes a moderate example of what in China is immoderate. Up to a very few years ago, the office of the Sheriff of the County of New York was maintained on principles inherited from the England of the eighteenth century ; he received a salary ($5,000) and fees (averaging $60,000), and himself paid the salaries of his deputies, and provided for the expenses of his office : this is the Chinese system, except that, in China, the fees are taken and the work not done. The American consular system, up to the year of Grace 1906, furnished another illustration : the income, perfectly legitimate and legal, of the Consul to Mesopotamia, let us say, would consist of his salary, $3,000, and fees ranging from $1,000 to $10,000. These instances are adduced, not in any way to belittle the (what we, with our twentieth-century views, call) administrative corruption of the Chinese Empire, but to bring home to the Western mind the underlying principle upon which the Chinese system is based.

Another distinction between the fiscal systems of the East and the West is in the " common purse." In England all national official revenue is covered into the Exchequer, in America into the Treasury. In China, theory and practice are divergent ; in theory, everything is subject to the Sovereign, land, property, and revenue ; in practice, the revenue is assigned piecemeal from certain sources of collection to certain defined heads of Imperial expenditure, and must be remitted independently for the purposes assigned. One province, for example, may be assessed Tls.500,000 as the Likin collection for the year ; instead of remitting this to the Imperial Treasury, or holding it subject to the order of the Treasury, Tls.100,000 will be remitted direct to the Shanghai Taotai for the service of the foreign debt, Tls.50,000 will be remitted to the same officer for account of Legations abroad, Tls.200,000 will be sent to Honan for Yellow River Flood Prevention account, Tls.50,000 will be retained for renewal of the provincial coast defences, Tls.50,000 will be sent to Peking for the Imperial Household, and Tls.50,000 will be assigned for the upkeep of the Imperial Mausolea. From some other source of revenue grants may be made to supplement the revenues of a poorer province ; of the eighteen provinces, thirteen forward such grants-in-aid, and nine receive them, five both granting and receiving. We may even have province A remitting to B, B in turn to C, and C remitting to A, but each one of the three will remit in full ; no attempt is ever made to strike a balance and receive or remit the difference ; to do this would deprive some hard-working official of the fruits of his industry, in the profit derivable from the mere act of remitting. To prepare a national budget of revenue and expenditure would, in Parker's phrase,* " puzzle the shrewdest firm of chartered accountants."

Another element of perplexity, sufficient to prevent the ordinary mind from penetrating the mysteries of taxation in China, is found in the question of exchange. As will be seen in a later chapter, China has no coinage except the copper " cash," of which to-day it takes about 10,000 to equal a pound sterling and 2,000 an American dollar. Her silver currency has no one uniform standard, and the hundreds of standards known in the Empire, or the dozen known in one place, vary within a range of over 10 per cent. Even the Imperial Treasury tael is an actuality only at the Imperial Treasury itself, and elsewhere in China is only a money of account. A typical case will be referred to later, where, on the tax-note, Treasury taels were converted

* " China, Past and Present," by E. H. Parker, 1903.

into cash at 2,600 and converted back at 1,105, whereby a tax of Tls.70·66 was converted into a payment of Tls.166·20. But let us take an ordinary everyday incident of revenue collected in Kiangsu and remitted as a grant-in-aid to Kansu. The tax-note will be in Treasury taels ; it will be paid in local taels ; the proceeds converted into Tsaoping taels for remittance to Shanghai, where it is converted into Shanghai taels ; again converted into Tsaoping taels for remittance to Hankow and thence to Kansu (assuming that it is remitted by draft), where it is received in local taels ; these are converted into Treasury taels for accounting with Kiangsu, and back again into local taels for deposit in a bank, and again into Treasury taels for accounting with the Imperial Treasury, and again into local taels or into cash for disbursement. This is no burlesque, but an exact account of what happens, and we have a series of ten exchange transactions, each of which will yield a profit of at least a half of one per cent. on the turn-over, apart from the rate of exchange on actual transfer from place to place, and altogether outside any question of " squeezing " the taxpayer. Moreover, as we are dealing with the past more than with the future, it is right to record that, regularly in the past and frequently in the present, the remittance is made by actually sending the silver from Kiangsu to Kansu, not reducing the exchange operations noted above by a single step, but adding enormously to the cost by the expense of transport and escort for a journey which must be counted by months and not by days.

All these considerations must be borne in mind in any study of figures * purporting to represent the revenue and expenditure of the Chinese Empire. In Western budgets the receipt side includes the entire sum taken from the taxpayer for the maintenance of the fabric of government,

* The principal authorities for the taxation and expenditure of China are E. H. Parker and George Jamieson, and any figures quoted will generally be from their writings.

and the payment side gives the entire amount expended for administrative purposes. In China this is not so. A few heads of revenue may be regarded as strictly Imperial, such as the tribute and the receipts of that new and semi-foreign institution, the Maritime Customs. Other receipts of the Imperial Treasury consist rather of surpluses handed over after providing for all costs of collection and all expenses of local administration ; they correspond somewhat to the matriculations of the German Empire ; they correspond more closely, perhaps, to the surplus remitted from Cyprus to Constantinople, after providing for the administrative expenses of the island. There are no figures available to show the enormous sums taken from the taxpayer and devoted to the maintenance of the army of officials engaged in collecting the revenue—sums the larger for being left, in the collecting, to the unregulated and uncontrolled discretion of the Collectors.

REVENUE

The heads of revenue collection may be divided into old and new. The old comprise : 1, Land Tax ; 2, Tribute ; 3, Customs ; 4, Salt ; and 5, Miscellaneous (taxes, fees, tenures and licenses) ; the new are : 6, Foreign Customs ; and 7, Likin ; with some new license fees which will fall under 5.

1. *Land Tax*

The foundation of Asiatic government is conquest, not the consent of the governed. When the various dynasties who have ruled China came into possession of the throne, they held the country in the hollow of their hand—*Dieu et mon droit* their motto—and the land and the fruit thereof became their property. Even an Asiatic government, however, does not carry all its theories into full practice, and the usufruct of the land of China is left to its occupiers, with full rights of transfer of possession ; but the rights of

7

overlordship are recognised by the payment of land tax proportioned to the (original) rental value of the land. This revenue was formerly the main dependence of the government in providing for its own needs, the amount remitted to Peking constituting, a hundred years ago, probably two-thirds of the cash receipts of the Imperial Treasury ; but a hundred years ago China had no urgent northern frontier question and no navy, and the remittances to the capital were required only for the maintenance of the Court and garrison and for the metropolitan administration. Two hundred years ago, in 1713, the Emperor, quite in keeping with the Manchu practice of considering and conciliating their Chinese subjects in every way, decreed that the land tax throughout the Empire, as shown by the records of that year, was to be fixed and immutable for all time, no increase being permitted under any circumstances. This permanent settlement endures, in theory, to this day ; the tax-note for each lot of land to-day gives the rate of assessment of 1713, and the returns of the total collection are based upon the permanent settlement, subject to authorised reductions for the effects of rebellion, drought, and flood, and to re-augmentation on recovery when reported by the provincial authorities.

The primary unit in China for fiscal, as for administrative and judicial, matters is the Hsien or township, commonly called district, constituting what in America would be called an incorporated city with the surrounding country and its villages. The Chih-hsien or Magistrate (often called simply the Hsien), in addition to his other numerous functions, is registrar of deeds and assessor and collector of taxes. All ownership and all transfers of land are, in theory, registered in his office, against a fee (see under 5, Miscellaneous taxes), and validated by his seal affixed to the deeds ; the seal being impressed in vermilion ; these regularised deeds are called " red deeds." In practice this obligation is often evaded, and the deeds, not being sealed, are then called " white deeds." This evasion is so common that the Hsien

and his officers ordinarily disregard the register of titles and
go direct to the occupant ; and so much is the payment of
land tax an incident of possession, especially in the case of
farm lands, that holding land-tax receipts for three successive
years is, in the absence of deeds, accepted as *prima facie*
proof of ownership. The tax-collector goes to the taxpayer
and delivers the tax-note itemised in accordance with law
(the permanent settlement) and precedent (the accretions
resulting from many a battle and sanctioned by the custom
of years). The amount shown as the total on the note is the
amount which must be turned into the Hsien's treasury,
and takes no account of the actual cost of collection, though
an amount is always included for it ; for the Hsien, *more
sinico*, pays his subordinates little or nothing as salary, but
compels them to scratch around for their maintenance ;
and even a tax-collector must live. The Hsien, however,
arms his collectors with power, and thus armed they are
enabled to extract their " costs of collection " from the taxpayer. The amount to be exacted is indeterminate, and
forms the subject of a battle annually renewed between
payer and payee ; but on an average it is quite safe to put
it, at the very lowest estimate, at ten per cent. on the sum
officially demanded. The official accretion is the accumu-
lated result of repeated battles. As Jamieson puts it :
" The fixing of these surcharges and the rates of commutation
appears to be left mainly with the district magistrates, with
the consent probably of the provincial treasurer. The
Imperial Government does not, so far as I know, attempt
to regulate such matters. The magistrates are mainly
bound by old custom ; what has been done before is tolerated,
but there is always a tendency to seize on every occasion to
try to obtain a little more. This, if too much, provokes a
riot, the magistrate gets into trouble with the people, and
a haggling ensues until either the extra impost is abandoned
or a *modus vivendi* is arrived at on some middle ground."

In one district, as shown in the cases given below, 44
per cent. is added for meltage fee, and 26 per cent. for an

illusory " cost of collection " : in another the amount in taels
is converted into cash at 2,600 to the tael, and converted
back into taels at 1,105, being an addition of 135 per cent.,
and then 50 per cent. is added for " cost of collection."
The latter method is the more usual, and cases are common
and well known where the conversion into cash was at the
rate of between 5,000 and 6,000, with the effect of increasing
the land tax to over five times the statutory amount.

For the province of Honan we have an illuminating
statement * by Mr. George Jamieson giving the amounts
levied on land acquired for the railway with which he was
officially connected. Land was bought in six different
hsiens through which the line ran, to the amount of 9,216
mows (the mow is roughly a sixth of an English acre).
Regular deeds of transfer were obtained, and in due course
tax-notes were presented, the correctness of the charges
being vouched for by the deputy of the Governor specially
appointed to manage, from the Chinese side, the affairs of
the railway. The tax-notes included land tax and commuted grain tax, and they are so informing that two of them
are given in full.

In Hsun Hsien the syndicate bought :

	Mows.
Land held on ordinary tenure (" min t'ien ")　　..	1,493·753
„　　„　　„ military tenure (" tun t'ien ")　　..	91·870
Total　　..　　..　　..　　..　　..	1,585·623

The taxes account presented by the magistrate of this
district translates as shown at top of next page.

The Kuping tael being a theoretical tael, the above was
paid by converting it into local currency at the rate of
103·71 local taels to 100 Kuping, giving 151·43 local taels
as the equivalent.

Here we have the land tax as settled, " fixed and im-

* " Land Taxation in the Province of Honan," 1905.

	Amount.
	Kuping taels.
Land tax proper on 1,585·623 mow at 0·0368355 tael per mow	58·407
For inferior touch or meltage fee, 44 per cent. on the above	25·690
Expenses of collection at the rate of 300 copper cash on every tael of land lax. Cash, 17,520	15·587
Grain tax at the rate of 0·005468 " shih " per mow on 1,493·75 mow (no levy on military land), equal to 8·169 " shih " or piculs at 6,400 copper cash per picul. Cash, 52,282	46·316
Total	146

mutable," in 1713, increased by accretions, as legal and as regular as any tax in any country, from Tls.58·407 to Tls.99·684, an addition of 71 per cent. ; and the commuted grain tribute, if we take the market price of grain at the very high rate of 2,000 cash a picul, increased from Tls.14·474 to Tls.46·316, an addition of 220 per cent.

In Hsin Hsiang the syndicate bought :

	Mows.
Land on ordinary tenure	1,203·512
„ „ military tenure	105·845
Total	1,309·357

The taxes account was presented as follows :

	Amount.
	Taels.
Land tax proper on 1,203·512 mow of common land at 0·0548392 tael per mow	65·9996
Land tax proper on 105·845 mow of military land at 0·044 tael per mow	4·6574
Total	70·657

	Amount.
	Kuping taels.
Payable at the rate of 2,600 copper cash per tael. Cash, 183,710	166·20
Expenses of collection at the rate of 30 copper cash per mow on common land and 25 cash on military land. Total copper cash, 38,752, equal to ..	35·06
Grain tax at the rate of 0·01255 piculs on common land (nothing on military land), total 15·1075 piculs, payable at the rate of 6,000 copper cash per picul. Total cash, 90,645, equal to	82·02
Total	283·28

NOTE.—Equivalent in local currency to Tls.293·82.

Here we have this fixed and immutable land tax increased from Tls.70·657 to Tls.201·26, an addition of 186 per cent., and the grain tribute increased from a legal maximum of Tls.27·34 to Tls.82·02, an addition of 200 per cent. The extreme accuracy of calculation also is to be noted to seven places of decimals of a unit of currency with a present value of three shillings. The two accounts give an average addition to the land tax of 128 per cent., and to the grain tribute of 210 per cent.

Mr. Jamieson goes on to show that these six districts in which land was bought are fairly representative of the soil of the whole of Honan; and after noting that the average taxation (land tax and grain tribute together) was Tls.0·1882 per mow, he proceeds to apply this average to the province.

The area of Honan province is about 60,000 square miles. Assuming that two-thirds of this is under cultivation, the taxable area would be over 25,000,000 acres, or at 6 mow to the acre, say 150,000,000 mow of ground. In the Hwei Tien, the standard, though a somewhat antiquated statistical record of the Empire, the area actually registered as cultivated is given as 63,986,185 mow. This was on the authority of the returns of the 17th year of Kiaking (1812). The amount is likely to have increased since, and may now be approximately 150,000,000 mow. But take it on the Kiaking returns, and supposing the taxation levied on the lands held by the syndicate is general, the yield of the land tax for the whole province should be Tls.12,042,200. Or if we suppose, as seems more probable, that approximately 150,000,000 mow pay taxes, the sum levied from the people would be well over Tls.28,000,000, a sum which is not very far short of what is now returned for the whole Empire of China.

Compared with the insignificant sum of less than Tls.3,000,000 now returned by the province of Honan, these figures may well seem incredible, but I simply state facts as I find them.

It will be well to proceed in another way in which we shall be on safer ground. It must be assumed that the railway corporation, a financially strong body, extraterritorialised, and officially supported by the government, pays its taxes by cheques direct to the Hsien, and is not compelled to submit to the mediation of the tax-collectors and pay them their expenses. It may further be safely assumed that the total collection reported for the province, even less in amount now than half a century ago, represents the tax of the permanent settlement. On these assumptions the land and grain tax collected in Honan may be calculated as follows:

	Taels.
Legal land tax, return of collection for year 1900	2,380,000
Accretion at the rate of 128 per cent.	3,046,400
Collectors' expenses at assumed rate of 10 per cent.	542,640
	6,969,040
Grain tribute commuted, return of 1900 ..	480,000
Accretion at the rate of 210 per cent.	1,008,000
Collectors' expenses at 10 per cent.	148,800
	1,636,800
Total land and grain taxes	8,605,840

against Mr. Jamieson's minimum estimate of Tls.12,000,000, and a possible collection of Tls.28,000,000. Every student of things Chinese knows that Mr. Jamieson's minimum estimate is well within the mark, and that, to get at the amount paid by the taxpayer, the official return of the amount collected must be at least quadrupled ; what can be said seriously is that it can be proved that the amount is trebled.

In applying the Honan figures to the rest of the Empire we are confronted by a difficulty. The permanent settlement was decreed by the second Tsing Emperor, Kanghi, and it is a matter of general knowledge that the earlier Manchu Emperors governed China with a light hand, and applied far less stringent rules to the remoter provinces than to those within easy reach of the capital. Chihli, the metropolitan province, has nearly half its area outside the Wall, under the Mongolian system, and nearly half the area within the Wall was granted in military tenure to Manchu princes and nobles, exempt from land tax ; and yet this province is third in the amount of land tax returned, collected from less than a third of its area. The three provinces (Shansi, Shantung, and Honan) immediately adjoining Chihli, and within the more direct reach of the Peking garrison, are respectively first, second, and fourth on the list ; Shansi, rated above all other provinces, is poor and exposed to climatic vicissitudes, but is attackable from Peking and from Mongolia as well. Of the remoter provinces it is sufficient to mention Kwangtung, one of the richest provinces of the Empire, rated tenth among the eighteen provinces ; and Hupeh, with great agricultural wealth, rated thirteenth. It is not for a moment to be supposed that the self-denying magnanimity of the Emperor, seated on his throne at Peking, is imitated by his representatives to-day, far removed from the control of their overlord. Of Szechwan, Mr. Parker says : " I spent a year in that province, and found that customary ratings, allowances, etc., practically made the land tax in some districts ten times its nominal charge." In Kwangtung we have regularly applied to three districts in the vicinity of Canton the phrase *shui shui, tso shui, tsou shui,* literally " sleeping in-come, sitting in-come, walking in-come," which may be thus explained : the incumbent of the first may go to sleep, while his emoluments come rolling in ; in the second he may sit still, and his emoluments come rolling in ; in the third he must trot around, but his emoluments come rolling in. It is difficult to know just what allowance to make for this diversity of treatment in applying the Honan figures to the rest of the Empire, but we shall be well within the mark if we take the reported return for the four nearer provinces, and twice the reported return for the remoter provinces, as the basis from which to calculate the amount paid by the taxpayer ; and for this purpose Mr. Parker's figures * will be taken, except for Honan, where they are increased by Tls.80,000.

Province.	Basic Collection.	Accretion 128 per cent.	Collectors' Expenses 10 per cent.	Total paid by Taxpayers.
	Tls.	Tls.	Tls.	Tls.
Chihli ..	2,600,000	3,328,000	592,800	6,520,800
Shantung ..	2,800,000	3,584,000	638,400	7,022,400
Honan ..	2,380,000	3,046,400	542,640	5,969,040
Shansi ..	3,300,000	4,224,000	752,400	8,276,400
Shensi ..	3,300,000	4,224,000	752,400	8,276,400
Kansu ..	440,000	563,200	100,320	1,103,520
Szechwan ..	4,600,000	5,888,000	1,048,800	11,536,800
Kweichow ..	220,000	281,600	50,160	551,760
Hunan ..	2,400,000	3,072,000	547,200	6,019,200
Hupeh ..	2,000,000	2,560,000	456,000	5,016,000
Kiangsi ..	2,600,000	3,328,000	592,800	6,520,800
Anhwei ..	2,614,000	3,345,920	595,992	6,555,912
Kiangsu ..	3,000,000	3,840,000	684,000	7,524,000
Chekiang ..	2,800,000	3,584,000	638,400	7,022,400
Fukien ..	2,000,000	2,560,000	456,000	5,016,000
Kwangtung ..	2,600,000	3,328,000	592,800	6,520,800
Kwangsi ..	700,000	896,000	159,600	1,755,600
Yunnan ..	500,000	640,000	114,000	1,254,000
Total ..	40,854,000†	52,293,120	9,314,712	102,461,832

* " China : Past and Present." † Amount returned, Tls.25,887,000.

Mr. Jamieson, applying the Honan average to the whole of China, says :

" In my revenue and expenditure report of 1897, I calculated there should be 650,000 square miles of cultivated land in China, equivalent to (in round numbers) 400,000,000 English acres or, at 6 mow per acre, 2,400,000,000 mow. If the average which I consider good for Honan holds good generally for the Empire, the whole amount levied from the people as land tax would amount to Tls.451,000,000.* In the paper addressed by Sir Robert Hart to the Chinese Government (printed in the *North China Herald* of April 15, 1904), recommending certain reforms in taxation, he calculated that the whole taxable land in China might amount to 4,000,000,000 mow, which, on the basis of 200 cash per mow, and taking a tael as equal to 2,000 cash, should yield a revenue of Tls.400,000,000. Sir Robert's estimate of the area under cultivation is greater than mine, but on the other hand his proposed levy of 200 cash or 10 tael cents per mow is, I should consider, much under the average actually levied. The experience of the syndicate's railway in Honan shows an average of 0·1882 tael, or nearly double the sum at which Sir Robert Hart puts it, so that if the present levy is only continued there should be Tls.400,000,000 forthcoming for Imperial purposes, and yet a very large sum left over for costs of administration and other provincial purposes."

Many good authorities, other than these two, are inclined to consider their figures as quite possible ; and a good illustration of the obscurity which veils the finances of China is furnished by the difference between the reported collection, Tls.26,000,000, the almost provable actual collection, Tls.102,000,000, and the possible collection estimated by high authorities at Tls.375,000,000 to Tls.400,000,000.

* Mr. Jamieson's " average taxation " includes both land tax and commuted grain tribute. His land tax alone for the Empire would work out to Tls.375,000,000.

The Republic has made no change in the method of assessing and collecting the land tax. In 1916 the budget showed a collection for this tax and grain tribute together, amounting to 95,972,818 dollars, or about 63,000,000 taels, nearly double the collection of the two taxes reported under the Empire as being at the disposal of the Imperial Treasury.

2. *Tribute*

Tribute is another invariable incident of an Asiatic form of government, and has formed a considerable part of the revenues of the State under all the successive dynasties which have ruled China. In the earlier dynasties the taxation took mainly the form of tribute—*i.e.* payment in kind, and generally of silk and grain, a roll of silk and a picul of grain having approximately the same value. Under the Sung dynasty, in A.D. 1004, the tribute amounted to 49,169,900 pieces and piculs ; in 1049 it was increased to 53,588,565, and in 1064 to 67,767,929 pieces and piculs.* In 1148 the grain tribute from Chekiang, Kiangsu, and Hukwang, was 2,395,000 piculs. In 1324, under the Mongol dynasty, the grain tribute amounted to 12,114,708 piculs, of which Chihli contributed 2,271,449 ; Honan 2,591,269 ; Kiangsu and Chekiang, 4,494,783 ; and Kiangsi, 1,157,448 piculs ; of this about 3,000,000 piculs were sent to Peking, the rest being retained in the provinces for the maintenance of the government and the support of the Mongol garrisons. The tribute in kind required by the ruling Manchu dynasty takes many forms, including silks from Hangchow, Soochow, and Nanking, porcelain from Kingtehchen, timber from Kiangsu, fruits from the southern coast, wax from Szechwan, etc. It also includes copper from Yunnan, the quantity required annually for coinage, before the introduction of foreign supplies, being calculated to be 85,000 piculs, of a value, by the market rates of 1906, of Tls.2,500,000. The principal tribute under the Tsing, however, as under

* " Banking and Prices in China," by J. Edkins, 1905.

previous dynasties, is grain. Before the disorganisation caused by foreign wars and rebellion, during the early years of Taokwang (1821–1850), the stipulated quantity required in an ordinary year to be sent to Peking was 2,930,000 piculs of rice and 300,000 piculs of millet. Since the Taiping rebellion, of the eight provinces liable to grain tribute, Honan, Kiangsi, Hupeh, and Hunan have commuted it for an annual money payment, leaving Kiangsu, Chekiang, Anhwei, and Shantung still to pay in kind. It is estimated that from these four provinces about 400,000 piculs continue to go by the Grand Canal, and the annual average of shipments by sea for the years 1902–1905 was 1,626,000 piculs. Besides this is the amount retained for the maintenance of the provincial forces. An illustration of the conservatism which rules Chinese finances is afforded by the continued payment by the commuting provinces to Chihli for cargo boats to convey from Tientsin to Peking the grain which they *do not* send : " A year or two ago (1895) ninety-seven cargo-boats were destroyed by a tidal wave, and Chihli has just reconstructed them at a cost of Tls.39,800 ; Hunan, Hupeh, and Kiangsi have to repay this sum between them." * There are, besides, recurring payments for " repairs " to imaginary cargo-boats.

To get at the sum received by the government from tribute is not easy, and it is still more difficult to conjecture the amounts paid by the taxpayer. One thing seems certain, that the " accretions " to the tribute payable in kind must approximate closely to those on the tribute commuted ; otherwise, with the weakness of the central government fifty years ago, it would have been to the advantage of the officials, metropolitan and provincial alike, to commute in all the provinces. We may, therefore, take Mr. Parker's figures † for the revenue from tribute and apply to them the same principle of accretion as for

* " The Chinese Revenue," by E. H. Parker. *Journal, North China Branch of the Royal Asiatic Society*, 1895–96.

† " China : Past and Present."

the land tax, but with no allowance for remoteness from the capital.

In the following table, for the province of Kiangsu, the basis collection of Tls.2,500,000 is increased to Tls.8,525,000, nearly three-and-a-half times as much.

I have been able to obtain the tax-notes for two small adjoining lots of land in the Fawangdu district near Shanghai, outside the foreign municipal juris-

Province.	Basic Collection.	Accretion 210 per cent.	Collection Expenses 10 per cent.	Total paid by Taxpayers.
	Tls.	Tls.	Tls.	Tls.
Shantung	500,000	1,050,000	155,000	1,705,000
Honan *	300,000	630,000	93,000	1,023,000
Hunan *	175,000	367,500	54,250	596,750
Hupeh *	420,000	882,000	130,200	1,432,200
Kiangsi *	800,000	1,680,000	248,000	2,728,000
Anhwei	900,000	1,890,000	279,000	3,069,000
Kiangsu	2,500,000	5,250,000	775,000	8,525,000
Chekiang	1,100,000	2,310,000	342,000	3,752,000
Kansu †	275,000	577,500	85,250	937,750
Kwangsi †	150,000	315,000	46,500	511,500
Szechwan † ..	50,000	105,000	15,500	170,500
Yunnan †	250,000	525,000	77,500	852,500
Total ..	7,420,000	15,582,000	2,300,200	25,302,200

diction, and have given them some careful study. The amounts and data filled in are written in a sprawling, running hand, difficult for a scholar, and almost illegible for a half-educated farmer ; but from them I have made out the following particulars :

First lot, area about 10 mow :

Grain tribute, 6 sheng 9 ho, taken as 7 sheng (0·070 shih = 8½ catties = 11¼ lb.), converted at 6,000 cash 420

Spring official accretion, Tl.0·095 at 2,500 cash 237

Autumn official accretion, Tl.0·095 at 2,800 cash 266

Cash .. 923

* Commuted. † Always kept for local administration.

Second lot, area about 25 mow :

Grain tribute, 1 tow 4 sheng 9 ho (0·149 shih = $17\frac{9}{10}$ catties = $23\frac{9}{10}$ lb.), converted at 7,000 cash   1,043

Spring official accretion, Tl.0·087 at 2,500 cash   229

Autumn official accretion, Tl.0·087 at 2,800 cash   247

Cash   ..   1,519

If fluctuations and the present inflated price of grain be disregarded, and the usually accepted rate of 2,000 cash per shih for grain tribute be taken as a standard, we have in this case a legal tax of 440 cash increased to an actual payment of 2,442 cash, five-and-a-half times as much ; and if the land had remained in Chinese ownership, we must assume that the increase would have been to six times. Even with the carefully digested figures given above, there are some elements of that variability which is so constant a factor in Chinese taxation. The two lots are adjoining, and apparently of the same class of land. One is assessed at the rate of 0·0069 shih of grain per mow, converted at 6,000 cash, and the other is assessed at 0·00596 shih per mow, converted at 7,000 cash. The official accretions are assessed in silver and collected in copper, but the spring accretion is converted at 2,500 cash and the autumn accretion at 2,800 cash, the actual market-rate being now about 1,100 cash ; the accretion for the smaller lot is larger in amount than that for the larger lot.

The copper from Yunnan is sent now in much reduced quantity, probably from 5,000 to 10,000 piculs a year ; and with so much of guesswork in the calculation, nothing need be added for the silks, porcelain, and other articles of tribute, though collecting and forwarding them provides honourable, but not honorary employment for many deserving officials.

3. Customs

The same veil of mystery which hangs over other branches of the revenue service covers the Customs, called the " Regular " or native Customs, to distinguish it from the newly established " Maritime " or foreign Customs. The offices of this establishment may be divided into two classes, those controlling shipping and those at land stations.

The " Regular " Customs offices within fifteen miles of a treaty port have, since November 1901, been placed under the control of the " Maritime " Customs, with the result that most of them are so far regulated that irregular exactions are suppressed and the full collection reported. The collection of the Native Customs under the Commissioners of Customs, increased from Tls.2,206,469 in 1902 to Tls.3,699,024 in 1906. Even before 1901 the income of the offices had suffered from the inevitable transfer of traffic from the junk to the safer, insurable, and speedier steamer. What can be said of them relates, therefore, more to the past than to the present.

The typical Customs post, and the fattest, was that of the " Hoppo " of Canton, abolished in 1904 as being no longer profitable. Created as soon as the Manchu supremacy had been established over Kwangtung, in order to " milk " the trade of the wealthiest trading mart in the Empire, the incumbent of the post luxuriated in an abundant supply of the richest cream during the time that Canton enjoyed its statutory and actual monopoly of foreign trade ; and even when the foreign trade had to be shared with many other ports, the local traffic of the province itself sufficed to make it a lucrative post. If Mr. Parker * is right, the amount officially reported within thirty years past cannot have exceeded 15 per cent. of the sum turned into the Hoppo's treasury, to which must be added the expense of maintaining an army of collectors, supervisors, and accountants. He

* " The Financial Capacity of China." *Journal, North China Branch of the Royal Asiatic Society,* 1895-96.

says : " Chief among them is the ' Hoppo ' of Canton, who is always a Manchu of the said ' bondsman ' class. The ' regulation sum,' which this official is bound to collect from the native Custom Houses at Canton, Swatow, Hoihow, and Pakhoi is about Tls. 157,000, and every year he goes through the farce of claiming credit for having ' by unusual zeal and industry ' collected as much as Tls.200,000, or thereabouts. But it is well known that he pays at least that sum for his appointment, and that his only chance of keeping the post for three years—the time usually granted for making his ' pile '—is to vigorously ply the palace with presents. . . . From what I could gather from members of the Viceroy's staff, at least Tls.1,000,000 a year, in fans, silks, pearls, and other presents, had to be sent to Peking at intervals (according to the nature of the present) of a fortnight, a quarter, a half-year, and a year." In 1843, with a collection exceeding ten million taels in amount, the official return was less than one million.

Of the land stations but little is known. One such post is that of the " Peking Gate," of which the regulation assessment is Tls.120,000 ; apart from the taxation of goods entering Peking, its chief function is to levy a tax on every official visiting Peking on affairs of State ; and as every high official is ordered up for Audience on appointment, or on transfer, or retirement, and as the Wardens of the Gates of Peking hold the keys, the tax is usually paid without much hesitation, amounting sometimes to Tls.50,000 and on occasion, for the incumbent of an especially lucrative post, to as much as Tls.100,000. Having secured entrance to the city, the official will then have to open his way, through quite another set of guardians, to the Palace ; and then, through the Chamberlains, to the Audience Hall. The form to be taken in expressing practical thanks to his Sovereign for the honour of an Audience, and for his appointment, is a matter of conjecture. The total collection, so far as reported, for the frontier and all other inland stations, amounts to Tls.460,000. In 1903 the Russian statistics showed an export to China exceeding the Chinese Customs import by over Tls.15,000,000, and an import from China exceeding the Chinese Customs export by over Tls.30,000,000 ; it is unlikely that this trade passed entirely untaxed, both on the inward and the outward traffic, and, at 5 per cent., the duty collected on this trade alone must amount to Tls.2,250,000.

The Republic included in the budget for the year 1916 the sum of 71,310,970 dollars from " Customs revenue." In that year the collection of the Maritime Customs, including non-Customs duties, such as Transit dues, Tonnage dues, and Opium likin, amounted to 57,700,000 dollars, leaving 13,600,000 dollars as the reported collection from other Customs offices—about 9,000,000 taels.

4. *Salt*

If the collection of the land tax is veiled by obscurity, of the grain tribute by equal obscurity, and of the " Regular " Customs by greater obscurity, the greatest obscurity covers the revenue from the salt gabelle, owing to the mixture of the official and the mercantile element in its collection. Salt is everywhere under the strictest government control, and is taxed at every stage—in its manufacture, purchase at the vats, transport, sale at the depôt, and sale to the people. For productive, administrative and descriptive purposes the Empire is divided into eleven Salt areas :

1. Shengking : sea salt, supplying Manchuria.

2. Chang-lu (Long Reed) : sea salt, supplying Chihli and the northern part of Honan.

3. Ho-tung (" East of the Yellow River ") : lake salt, supplying Shansi, the western part of Honan, and the south-eastern part of Shensi.

4. Hwa-ma-chih (" Piebald Horse Pool ") : lake salt, supplying Mongolia, Kansu, and the greater part of Shensi.

5. Shantung : sea salt, supplying Shantung and corners of Honan, Anhwei, and Kiangsu.

6. Hwai : sea salt ; for administrative and dis-tributive purposes divided into :

6a. Northern Hwai, supplying the northern part of Kiangsu north of the Yangtze, the northern part of Anhwei, and the southern part of Honan.

6b. Southern Hwai, supplying the southern part of Kiangsu north of the Yangtze, and Nanking south of the Yangtze, the southern part of Anhwei, the northern part of Kiangsi, the eastern part of Hupeh, and the greater part of Hunan.

7. Szechwan : well salt, supplying Szechwan, the north-east corner of Yunnan, nearly all of Kweichow, a corner of Hunan, and the western part of Hupeh.

8. Yunnan : well salt, supplying all Yunnan ex-cept the north-east and south-east corners.

9. Chekiang : sea salt, supplying Chekiang, Kiangsu south of the Yangtze (except Nanking), and corners of Anhwei and Kiangsi.

10. Fukien : sea salt, supplying Fukien except the south-west corner.

11. Kwangtung : sea salt, supplying Kwangtung, Kwangsi, the southern part of Kiangsi, and small corners of Fukien, Hunan, Kweichow, and Yunnan. A twelfth, self-supplying and consuming, area of small dimensions in central Hupeh need not be considered.

The Hwai Administration, supplying about 100,000,000 of the population, is the most important, and a description of its methods will suffice for all. The Viceroy at Nanking is the direct head, and under him is an army of controllers, agents, guards, etc., echelonned along and on both sides of the Yangtze, charged with control of the traffic, prevention of smuggling, and levy of taxes. Production, transport, and sale are in private hands, under licenses issued by the Administration. From the vats to the depots (the principal one being above and opposite to Chinkiang) the salt is practically in bond. At the depot the salt is bought, at a price fixed by the Administration, by the holders of licenses ; of these a fixed number, usually 300 to 400 to each province, have been issued against a capital payment which, if there were a demand for further issue now, would be Tls.10,000 to Tls.12,000 each. The licensees take their turn, which may be once in two years or twice in three years according to circumstances, and in his turn each is permitted to buy 3,750 piculs of salt. In order to evade the difficulties caused by different regulations and customs on every route, different weights at short distances, and different taxes in different provinces, it is necessary to select for consideration some one province, and Hupeh will be assumed to be the destination. The cost of production is Tls.1,130 for this quantity, in which is included the vat license fee and transport to the depot ; and the price paid at the depot is Tls.3,725, giving Tls.2,595 for government charges for storage and taxation to this point. The transport to Hupeh is controlled from point to point, and on arrival the salt is stored in one of the provincial depots, paying storage, and awaiting its turn to be sold to the licensed shops, conveyance to which is also controlled. There are numerous changes of scale, changes in the method of accounting, delays to be avoided, and difficulties to be smoothed away, which add to the cost of the salt and to the emoluments of the administration agents, and contribute nothing to the revenue, but which must all be paid for by the consumers ; and merely to enumerate the different items of taxation, and adequately describe the application of an exceedingly complicated system, would require a chapter to itself. It is sufficient to say that the regular officially recognised taxation from the depot near Chinkiang to issue from the provincial depot at Hankow is put by good authority at Tls.1·60, and a little more per picul. To get at what the people pay we need only take the retail price, which is fixed by the Salt Administration. In Hupeh, ten years ago, the average retail price so fixed was 50 cash a catty * ;

* A well-informed writer in the *China Mail*, Hongkong, 1885, gives the retail price of salt at Hankow as 64 cash a catty.

as the corresponding price in Hunan was 56 cash, and as those were the prices before the increase in taxation to meet the Boxer indemnities, this price of 50 cash may be accepted as a fair average. Converting at the same rates, the producer's cost of Tls.1,130 for the quantity, 3,750 piculs, under one license, is increased to Tls.12,545 as the price to the consumer, the difference being Tls.11,415 ; if Tls.1,415 be allowed for cost of transport and legitimate profit, the remaining Tls.10,000 (Tls.2·67 a picul) is paid by the people as tax, regular or irregular, open or covert.

The consumption of salt in the Empire can only be guessed. A hundred years ago the official " blue-books " of China put it at 20,000,000 piculs, and this was stated to be less than the amount fifty years previously ; twenty years ago a Vice-President of the Board of Revenue put it at 28,000,000 piculs. The 300,000,000 of the people of India consumed 24,300,000 piculs of salt in 1904, and it would seem a fair assumption to put the consumption of the 400,000,000 of the people of China at the same figure. On this basis, and calculating at the rates for eastern Hupeh, the people of China pay Tls.81,000,000 for their salt, of which sum Tls.64,000,000 and more is taxation in one form or another, and Tls.39,000,000 is taxation according to regularly published tariffs of charges ; the collection reported to the Imperial Government is Tls.13,050,000.* In India, in 1904, the people paid 88,000,000 rupees, of which 76,000,000 rupees was taxation actually credited to the government.

The above was written with reference to the Salt Administration under the Empire. The revenue had been more and more fully pledged for the service of foreign loans, and it was seen that a reorganisation of the supply and distribution was necessary if any surplus was to be available for the Treasury. At the end of 1913 this reorganisation was taken in hand under Chang Chun, Vice-Minister of Finance, as Chief Inspector, and Sir Richard M. Dane as Associate

* " China : Past and Present."

Chief Inspector. In the first year of working, 1914, the net revenue, after deducting the cost of production and administration, amounted to 60,409,676 dollars ; from this fund the sum of 21,106,573 dollars was paid out for the service of loans and indemnities secured on the Salt revenue, and 31,304,818 dollars were paid over to the Ministry of Finance. In 1917 the net revenue from the Salt Administration amounted to 70,627,250 dollars, and 8,858,982 dollars were received from the Maritime Customs, refunded for service of the debt ; 11,897,876 dollars were paid out for the service of loans and indemnities, and 68,613,370 dollars were paid to the Ministry of Finance. This last sum, equivalent to 45,000,000 taels, may be compared with the estimates of 39,000,000 and 64,000,000 taels given in the preceding paragraph.

5. *Miscellaneous*

Some new taxes are included under this heading, but the greater part are old ; whether new or old, they are covered by much obscurity. Many of them are of local incidence, and accordingly their collection and report depend upon the industry, the integrity, and the whim of the local officials ; others are general, but such that there is no check upon the collection such as is afforded by transit from one district to another. The principal among them are the following :

1. The reed tax, a charge upon the marshes along the Yangtze and elsewhere, producing reeds for thatching and for fuel.

2. The tea license, now probably incorporated in the likin on transit.

3. Mining royalties, insignificant in the past.

4. Fees on sales of land and houses.

5. Pawnbrokers' and other mercantile licenses, probably producing the greater part of the reported collection.

6. Lo-ti-shui, consumption and production tax, now insignificant, but capable of development on the abolition of likin.

The total proceeds of miscellaneous taxes * reported to the Imperial Government, including cash receipts from special tenures, corvées, and purveyances, is Tls.3,856,000.† This includes Tls.55,000 from Honan, for which Mr. Jamieson reports Tls.200,000 collected in 1900, and makes the following remark :

"By law there is payable on affixing the official seal to a sale or mortgage of land a fee nominally of 3 per cent. but actually of about 8 per cent. *ad valorem.* The fees which the syndicate were asked to pay came to over 10 per cent. Assuming there are 150,000,000 mow of land in Honan of an average value of Tls.10 per mow, which is well below the mark, and supposing that land on an average changes hands once in 60 years or two generations, one-sixtieth each year gives a value transferred of Tls.25,000,000 ; 8 per cent. on that should bring in an annual yield of Tls.2,000,000. And yet the returns, as given in the above balance sheet, of miscellaneous taxes from all sources (of which land transfer fees must be one) are put down as only yielding Tls.200,000 altogether."

There is, in fact, the same, or even greater, degree of accretion as in the case of the land tax and the grain tribute, and, taking the rates of increase accepted for the latter, we have the following figures :

	Tls.	Tls.
Weising Lottery	1,000,000	
Other miscellaneous taxes ..	2,856,000	
		3,856,000
Accretion, 210 per cent. on latter		5,997,600
Collectors' expenses, 10 per cent. on whole		985,360
Total amount paid by taxpayers ..		Tls.10,838,960

Included in this are the proceeds of sale of honours and titles, the amount of which cannot be exactly estimated.

* "China : Past and Present."

† Includes Tls.1,000,000 collected in Kwangtung from the Weising Lottery.

The Republic has imposed some direct taxes which were impossible to the lax administration of the Empire. Their nature and the revenue from them in the year July 1916 to June 1917 are as under :

		Dollars.
Stamp Duty	.. ..	5,864,400
Tobacco and Wine License Duty	..	2,012,852
,, ,, ,, Tax	.. .. ..	14,350,456
,, ,, ,, Income from sales	..	12,134,986
Mining Duty	.. ..	2,221,617
	Total	36,584,311

6. *Foreign Customs*

We come now to the one branch of the revenue collection of China in which the receipt and the report are in accord. In 1865 the collection was Tls.8,296,275, and in 1905 Tls.35,111,004, made up as follows :

	Tls.
Customs duty proper, Import and Export	27,817,190
Tonnage dues on shipping	1,105,350
Transit dues in commutation of provincial levy of likin	2,034,407
Convention likin on opium, properly assignable to the provinces	4,154,057
	Tls.35,111,004

The sums properly chargeable against this collection were as follows :

	Tls.
Fixed allowance to cover cost of collection and preventive service, but including considerable expenditure for Post Office (up to 1911), Marine Department, Education, and other minor services	3,168,000
Seven-tenths of tonnage dues assigned to Marine Department (Lights, Harbours, etc.)	773,745
	Tls.3,941,745

To this must be added small extras which, elsewhere than in China, would go to the national exchequer, but which in China help to maintain the purely Chinese side of the administration. There is the difference between receiving and paying rates in force at the Customs banks as at all other banks in China, which may be put at 0·5 per cent., or about Tls.180,000 ; and there is the interest on balances in hand, which, on a very safe estimate, may be put at 3 per cent. of the total, or Tls.1,050,000.

7. Likin

Up to quite recent times China, like most countries, was content to tax the movement of merchandise at the established Custom Houses only, *i.e.* practically at the seaports only, though the taxation was imposed on all movement past those fixed points, and not on the foreign trade alone. The only other tax which can be connected with the movement of goods was the Lo-ti-shui (*vide supra*). The exigencies of the government during the Taiping rebellion, however, drove the authorities to devise new forms of taxation, and likin ("contribution of a thousandth") was instituted. It was first heard of in 1853 ; and about 1861, when the active suppression of the rebellion called for largely increased expenditure, it was applied generally to all the provinces then under the control of the Imperial authorities. The original theory of the levy, one-tenth of one per cent. on the value, imposed no great burden on trade, a tax of the same amount levied as wharfage dues for the maintenance of the foreign municipalities at Shanghai, Tientsin, Hankow, and elsewhere, being scarcely felt ; but practice soon parted company with theory, and the official rates were much increased. Nor is the tax uniform in its incidence in all provinces. Hunan is proud of its independence and freedom from non-customary exactions, and in this province the payment once of the full tariff rate of likin exempts goods from further payment within the provincial limits, while the accretions and irregular exactions are less than elsewhere in China ;

Hunan is, however, exceptional. Kwangtung is more nearly typical of the Empire ; here between Canton and Wuchow, a distance of about two hundred miles on the West River, there are six likin " barriers," each constituting a barrier to the free movement of traffic, and each involving delay, vexation, and payment. Along the Grand Canal between Hangchow and Chinkiang, likin stations, alternately collecting and preventive, are established at distances averaging ten miles one from the other ; and in that part of Kiangsu lying south of the Yangtze there are over 250 stations, collecting or preventive. The route from Shanghai to Soochow presents a curious condition : the opening of Soochow as a treaty port enables foreign imports to be carried there from Shanghai without further payment of any sort, but in 1904, excluding coal and kerosene oil, the foreign products declared at the Custom House amounted only to Tls.310,000 ; for the rest of the large traffic between the two places the Chinese traders prefer to pay a composition in lieu of likin. To get their goods beyond Soochow into the " interior," they would still have to come under the cognisance of the likin authorities, and by recognising that control from Shanghai instead of Soochow, they are enabled to commute on the basis of estimated quantities, which may be made the subject of manipulation and negotiation, and not on the basis of actual quantities reported to and published by the Customs.

To get at the amount paid by the people is more difficult in the case of likin than of other taxes. The land tax and the grain tribute are assessed according to registers very strictly kept, and both are under the control of the Hsien, the " Father and Mother of the People " ; and yet, as we have seen, the regular legal accretion is, at the very lowest estimate, from 100 per cent. up to almost anything in reason. The Salt Administration is an old-established organisation ; and yet the actual receipts are threefold the reported collection, while the people pay fivefold that amount. Likin is a new levy, with its own administration independent of all other taxing agencies, and the collection is much more in the hands of the officer in charge of each barrier and his subordinates than is possible with other taxes. For the regular " accretion," a calculation may perhaps be based on the following note :

" To begin with, these are the official figures used in rendering accounts to the Superior Boards in Peking. When these same figures come to be translated to the rustic, they bear a very different meaning. A special case, for the facts of which we vouch, will perhaps best illustrate our meaning. The fees which a certain junk, chartered by a foreigner, was called upon to pay in passing a barrier, amounted to 12,000 cash. The charterer was not interested in disputing the amount, but he wished to have a receipt as a voucher for the disbursement, and for that purpose he applied to the native office, where he was tendered a receipt for Tls.4. Failing to convince the officials there that Tls.4 could not by any possibility be regarded as the equivalent of 12,000 cash when the market value of the tael was about 1,600 cash, he applied to his Consul, claiming either a refund or a receipt for what he had actually paid. In the correspondence that ensued the chief Chinese authority explicitly declared that though Tls.4 was the proper charge (which, indeed, was easily ascertainable from the tariff), yet a tael was not a tael in the ordinary sense of the word, but was such a sum as would enable the local authorities to lay down a tael of the standard weight and purity in Peking, and consequently included a meltage fee, loss on melting, freight, and costs of transmission, and general office expenses, and that all that turned into cash meant, according to old-established custom, 12,000 cash for Tls.4. Consequently a receipt for Tls.4, the legal sum, was the only receipt they could give. In other words, the procedure simply amounted to this : that the costs of collection, as far as this particular collectorate was concerned, came to nearly 100 per cent.—that is to say, they practically collected Tls.7·50, of which Tls.3·50 were the costs of collecting Tls.4." *

On this it may be remarked that, if 12,000 cash were collected in 1885, it is absolutely certain that, on general principles, 12,000 cash are collected to-day ; and further, that the likin levy has been substantially increased since 1895, and again since 1900. But, while this number of cash in 1885 was equivalent to Tls.7·50, at to-day's exchange the equivalence is Tls.10·50 ; and to the legal levy of Tls.4 there is added Tls.6·50, an " accretion " of 162 per cent. The collectors of this tax have much more opportunity to annoy traders than is possible with other taxes ; the tax is not paid at the head office either of the Likin Administration or of the traders ; the latter are anxious to get their goods to market, and will willingly pay for expedition ; and the opportunity of the collectors recurs at each barrier to be passed. Moreover, barriers on one route compete with those on another, and composition and under-declaration are recognised incidents of trade ; but, while reducing the amount collected and reported, it is not for a moment to be supposed that the collectors will permit their individual emoluments to be affected unless in a sense favourable to themselves. Students of things Chinese would promptly reject the suggestion that the addition for " collectors' expenses," the personal emoluments of the active agents, can be as low as 10 per cent. of the amount collected ; but as this rate has been taken for land tax and other levies, it will be taken for this head of revenue as well. Taking Mr. Parker's figures † for the reported collection we have, then, the following statement :

* *China Mail.* Hongkong, 1885.
† " China : Past and Present."

Tls.

Reported likin on general merchandise .. 11,930,000
Accretion at 162 per cent. 19,326,600
Collectors' charges at 10 per cent.   ..   3,125,660

Total sum paid by taxpayers   ..   Tls.34,382,260

In this is not included the collection on native opium. This product is bashful and retiring, and prefers the bye-ways to the highways, and it is absolutely certain that the difference between the sums paid and the amount reported is much greater than in the case of general merchandise ; calculating it, however, on the same basis we have :

Tls.

Reported collection from native opium * ..   2,830,000
Accretion at 162 per cent. 4,584,600
Collectors' charges at 10 per cent.   ..   741,460

Total sum paid by taxpayers   ..   Tls.8,155,060

The consumption of native opium in China is certainly † well over 300,000 piculs, and the total revenue reported as collected from it (taking the year 1904) is the above sum of Tls.2,830,000 and a sum of Tls.920,598 collected on movement by steamer through the Foreign Customs, making a total of Tls.3,750,598 ; in the same year there was collected by the Foreign Customs from 54,752 piculs of foreign opium the sum of Tls. 6,025,121.

The Republic included in its budget for the year 1917 the sum of 42,719,194 dollars (28,000,000 taels) from likin, two-and-a-third times the amount reported under the Empire.

  * Including Tls.870,000 from opium in Manchuria, which has a separate budget.
  † Written in 1906.

EXPENDITURE

When we come to consider the expenditure of the Empire we find ourselves in a labyrinth, and the difficulty is well illustrated by Mr. Parker * in the following words :

" To ascertain what is at the present day the expenditure upon each head is no easy matter, for all accounts in China seem to be so arranged as to present as many anfractuosities, callosities, and complications as possible, in clearing which obstructions the silver has, of course, all the more chance of halting piecemeal on the way to its nominal destination. Thus there are allowances on the scale for the melting-pot, for sweating, for wear and tear, for freight, for escort, for the ' rice ' of the Board officials who receive it, for local weights, stationery, cartage, haulage, porterage, etc., etc. Wherever any question comes in of turning copper cash into silver, or taels into dollars, or *vice versa*, of course there is a ' squeeze.' Then there are arrears to be dunned for, advances to be made, loans to other provinces, divertings to meet sudden or unforeseen demands, such as famines, wars, foreign loans, Imperial marriages, birthdays, funerals, etc., etc. Remissions of taxation are very troublesome, for those who have already paid their money never get it back, whilst those who receive payment have an opportunity of juggling with the date of remission, both when it begins and when it ends."

Nor is this all. As we have seen, especially in the case of the land tax, the cost of government is provided for in such a way that the greater part of the charge does not, and cannot, appear in any official account of expenditure. The basic charge on revenue account is increased by legalised and regular accretion, and this again by indeterminate charges which the collectors collect for themselves, and to a

* " The Financial Capacity of China."

great extent at their own sweet will. Both accretion and collectors' charges are stigmatised by critics of the Chinese government as " squeeze," or extortion ; but, while the method of collection opens the door to personal corruption, still this is the Chinese system. In the West, the collector is paid a fixed salary, with possibly a commission on his takings, but issued from the Treasury ; and the magistrate, the official with a fixed office, is paid by a sufficient and all-inclusive salary. This is not so in China, where both collector and magistrate must fend for themselves. The collector takes his charges, but it is a mistake to suppose that his takings are all pure profit : to maintain his position he must satisfy all in direct authority over him, thereby securing to his superiors what is considered the just Chinese equivalent of " salary." The Hsien will have received **the** basic tax plus accretion plus what may come to him as his share in collectors' charges, and from this must provide for the maintenance of all his subordinates, less the proportion which they themselves may have received as their share out of the collectors' charges ; and he must then provide for the maintenance (what we would term salary) of all in direct control over him or able to influence his appointment or his actions. On his first appointment, and annually or at more frequent periods during his tenure of office, he must give gratifications, depending in amount upon the more or less lucrative character of his post, to his immediate superiors, the Fu or Prefect, and the Taotai ; and he is the more bound to satisfy the provincial magnates, Judge, Treasurer, Governor, and Viceroy, in whose patronage lie his appointment, retention in office, and promotion ; and he must not neglect these great men's secretaries and accountants, who are in a position to slip a good or evil word into their masters' ears. So with the Fu and the Taotai. The high provincial authorities, too, must fortify their position at the capital ; and a portion of their emoluments, received from their subordinates, must be passed on, regularly and almost as assessment, to the higher metropolitan officials and Ministers of State, and to the officials of the Palace, any one of whom, if neglected, might have influence to reduce the perquisites of a self-seeking official or delay his promotion, and to put a spoke in the wheel of one who proposed measures to benefit his province. This is the Chinese system, and while a change may be brought about by the spirit of reform which is in the air, this book deals with the past alone ; but, taken as it is, the system obviously prevents any, even approximate, statement of the cost of government in China.

Even when we come to what may be called the official budget—the account of collection officially reported and transferred to the control of the Imperial Treasury—we are bewildered by the confusion resulting from the absence of the common purse. This is illustrated by a small item of expenditure, one of Tls.600,000 for the Imperial Household, which is shown in the following note by Mr. Parker *
to be drawn from eight different sources :

" Let us now descend from generalities to a few specific facts. Let us begin with the expenditure of the Emperor himself. Beginning with the year 1866, the annual sum to be sent by the various provincial Customs Stations to the Imperial Household Office was fixed at Tls.300,000 (then about £100,000, but now only equal to half that amount in gold). Two years later it was found that this amount was insufficient, and it was raised to Tls.600,000. This sum is annually 'appropriated' by the Board of Revenue before the beginning of the year in which it is due. Half has to reach Peking before the middle of July, and the balance a month before the end of the Chinese year, or, say, December. The appropriations ordered by the Board for the year 1896 are as follows :

* " The Financial Capacity of China."

	Tls.
Chekiang province, Salt dues fund ..	50,000
Kwangtung ,, ,, ,, ..	50,000
Fukien ,, Tea ,, ..	50,000
Foochow native customs receipts ..	100,000
Foochow foreign ,, ,, ..	50,000
Shanghai ,, ,, ,, ..	50,000
North Kwangtung native customs ..	100,000
Kiukiang native customs	150,000

Most of these appropriations are constant year by year, but, to take the year 1887 as an instance of change, in that year the Hupeh salt likin took the place of the Shanghai foreign customs; and the Kiangsu salt-gabelle (Tls.120,000) and native customs at Hwaian (Tls.30,000) took that of the two Foochow customs combined. It must also be explained that in 1893 the Board of Finance advanced Tls.212,390 to the Buttery Office of the Household, which sum has to be deducted and repaid in 1896."

The sum, Tls.7,000,000, allocated to the maintenance of the Manchu Bannermen at Peking, is shown to be drawn from fifty-two different sources, in sums ranging from Tls.24,000 to Tls.450,000.

Subject to full consideration of all these omissions and of all the obscurity hanging over Chinese accounts, on pages 134 and 135 is given the official budget of the province of Honan for 1900, as given by Mr. Jamieson.*

A province with a population of 21,000,000 contributes Tls.1,895,000 (£285,000) for Imperial purposes, and maintains its own provincial administration, including the expensive and burdensome Yellow River Conservancy, on an expenditure of Tls.1,678,000 (£250,000)!

Let us now abstract from Mr. Parker's figures,† the result of long and careful inquiry by a most competent inquirer, the Imperial "open" budget for the eighteen

* " Land Taxation in the Province of Honan."
† " China : Past and Present."

provinces constituting China Proper, with certain corrections to bring the actual figures up to date.

REVENUE

		Tls.
i.	Land tax reported paid in money ..	25,887,000
ii.	Tribute, whether commuted or not ..	7,420,000
iii.	Native customs	4,160,000
iv.	Salt Gabelle	12,600,000
v.	Miscellaneous taxes, old and new ..	3,856,000
vi.	Foreign customs, collection 1905 ..	35,111,000
vii.	Likin on general merchandise and native opium	13,890,000

Total .. Tls. 102,924,000

EXPENDITURE

		Tls.
i.	Cash remitted to Peking	9,131,000
ii.	Grain or its commutation sent to Peking and cost of transport ..	5,780,000
iii.	Frontier Defence	5,415,000
iv.	Admiralty general fund	1,450,000
v.	Army, Navy, and Fortifications ..	25,200,000
vi.	Arsenals	3,385,000
vii.	Yellow River and other Conservancies	1,389,000
viii.	Foreign Customs allowance and maintenance of Lights	3,942,000
ix.	Native Customs, allowance to Inspectorate	370,000
x.	Sundry Peking funds	3,842,000
xi.	Railway development fund	550,000
xii.	Imperial grants for provincial administration	34,042,000
xiii.	* Foreign loans and indemnities taken at exchange of 3s. to the tael ..	42,000,000

Total .. Tls. 136,496,000

9   * See Appendix A.

The Imperial expenditure, so far as is known or reported, exceeds the Imperial revenue, as reported, by Tls.33,572,000, indicating, as the Government is far from being bankrupt, a considerable degree of elasticity in the revenue.

The next step will be to draw up an imaginary statement of revenue according to the amounts presumed to be paid by the taxpayer; and if, in preparing this, we accept the sums recorded above for " accretion " as representing the general expenses of provincial administration, and those for " collectors' charges " as representing the local or municipal administration, the resultant figures will be readily accepted by all competent investigators as being in all cases well under the fact.

	Imperial Administration.	Provincial Administration.	Local Administration.
	Tls.	Tls.	Tls.
i. Land Tax	25,887,000	67,060,000	9,315,000
ii. Tribute	7,420,000	15,582,000	2,300,000
iii. Native Customs	3,790,000	1,290,000	249,000
iv. Salt Gabelle	13,050,000	26,000,000	25,000,000
v. Miscellaneous	3,856,000	5,998,000	985,000
vi. Foreign Customs	31,169,000	3,942,000	1,230,000
vii. Likin	13,890,000	22,502,000	3,639,000
Total	99,062,000	142,374,000	42,718,000

The grand total here shown, Tls.284,154,000, is an obviously insufficient sum on which to maintain the fabric of government of an Empire like China, but it has been reached by calculations based on a few known facts, and does not include any of those delightful exchange operations which alleviate the burden of officials charged with receiving and disbursing official funds. Such as it is, the statement is offered as throwing some light on a subject veiled in obscurity, and it may be compared with the budget for 1911 presented to the Throne—and published by authority, as given on opposite page. It may also be compared with the budget of the Republic of China for the calendar year 1916 on pages 132–133.

BUDGET FOR THE YEAR 1911

INCOME
Tls.

Land tax and grain tribute	49,669,858
Salt and tea tax	47,621,920
Customs revenue	42,139,288
Miscellaneous taxes	26,163,842
Likin	44,176,542
Rents from government property	47,228,037
Sale of official rank and titles	5,652,333
Miscellaneous	35,698,477
Sale of government bonds	3,560,000

Total .. Tls.301,910,297

EXPENDITURE
Tls.

Budget of Ministry of Foreign Affairs	2,782,288
Legations and consulates	343,727
Constabulary	4,352,040
Budget of Ministry of Finance	111,249,315
Education	2,747,477
Army	77,915,890
Navy	9,997,947
Justice	6,643,829
Communications	37,569,097
Agriculture, Industry, and Commerce	5,453,833
Dependencies	1,688,560
Grants-in-aid to provinces	37,703,362

Total .. 298,448,365

Surplus Tls.3,461,932

BUDGET FOR THE YEAR 1916

REVENUE

Ordinary :

	Dollars.	Dollars.
Land tax in money and grain	95,972,818	
Customs revenue	71,310,970	
Salt Gabelle	84,771,365	
Likin	40,271,368	
Miscellaneous taxes	32,341,704	
Miscellaneous duties	14,067,574	
Interest from government investments	2,621,261	
Miscellaneous receipts by provinces	6,927,694	
Receipts by central administration	77,942,391	
		426,237,145

Extraordinary :

	Dollars.	Dollars.
Loans	20,000,000	
Receipts by central administration	17,051,808	
Receipts under other heads as above	8,657,757	
		45,709,565
Total receipts ..		471,946,710

EXPENDITURE

Ordinary :

	Dollars.	Dollars.
Foreign Affairs	3,276,677	
Interior	49,653,982	
Finance	53,531,625	
War	135,813,986	
Marine	17,101,779	
Justice	7,665,772	
Education	12,611,583	
Agriculture and Commerce ..	3,762,244	
Communications *	1,577,408	
Mongolian and Tibetan Affairs	947,230	
		285,942,280

Extraordinary :

Finance	175,302,789	
War	6,438,727	
Expenditure under other heads as above	3,835,634	
		185,577,150
Total expenditure ..		471,519,436

* Not including Government Railways, or the Postal and Telegraph services, which are under the Ministry of Communications.

TABLE SHOWING REVENUE AND EXPENDITURE OF THE
PROVINCE OF HONAN, 26TH YEAR KWANGHSÜ, 1900

Revenue

Item.	Description.	Amount.
		Kuping Tls.
1	Land tax	2,060,000
2	,, ,, (supplementary)	320,000
3	,, grain tax commuted	480,000
4	Miscellaneous (7 categories of taxes, details not stated)	200,000
5	Economies on courier service	90,000
6	,, ,, fixed allowance for Yellow River repairs	34,000
7	Deduction of 6 per cent. on all payments (ordinary service)	60,000
8	Likin	20,000
	[NOTE.—The likin revenue is said to amount to Tls.100,000, but as Tls.80,000 are remitted direct by the Likin Administration for the service of foreign loans, the balance only is entered as provincial revenue.]	
9	Deductions from the salaries (Yanglien) of the several civil and military officials, 10 to 30 per cent.	21,000
10	Rent of public lands and various other items ..	50,000
11	Payments by the various district magistrates in respect to surplus in the collection of land tax arising from difference of scale	100,000
	Total	3,435,000

[NOTE.—Apparently there is a deficit in the Provincial Budget of Tls.38,000 even allowing for items 13 and 14 of expenditure, which are tersely marked " not paid, no funds." Moreover, items 5, 6, 7 and 9 on the revenue side are not revenue at all, but are counted as such, probably on the Skimpole principle that money not spent is money earned.]

Expenditure

Item.	Description.	Amount.
		Kuping Tls.
	Imperial or extra-provincial expenditure—	
1	Peking supply (fixed charge)	200,000
2	Kansu province, subsidy to	610,000
3	Service of foreign loans	170,000
	[NOTE.—The fixed charge for this item is Tls.390 000, of which, however, the Changlu Salt Department remits 60,000, the Grain Tax Department 80,000, and the Likin 80,000, leaving, as above, 170,000 as the charge on the general revenues of the province.]	
4	Subsidy to the I-chun army corps	173,000
5	Remittance to Board of Revenue from grain tax commutation	210,000
6	Subsidy to Sung-wu army corps in Shungtung	230,000
7	Remittance in aid of the Sungkiang-Shanghai Likin Office	20,000
8	Yunnan Copper Supply Administration	20,000
9	Remittances to Imperial Household	20,000
10	,, for upkeep of Yuen-ming-yuen Palace	2,000
11	Purchase of silks, damask, etc., for Court ..	90,000
12	Contribution to Northern Railway construction	50,000
13	Subsidy for pay of troops in three Manchurian provinces (not paid, no funds available) ..	40,000
14	Peking supplementary subsidy, termed Ku-pen (not paid, no funds available)	60,000
	Provincial expenditure—	
15	Yellow River repairs, fixed allowance	600,000
16	Pay of provincial troops : " Banner," " Green," and " River " camps	330,000
17	Provincial " drilled " force	290,000
18	River embankments in the two hsien " Ho " and " Wu "	24,000
19	Salaries (Yanglien) to civil and military officials of the province	303,000
20	Pensions, officials of hereditary rank on provincial list	20,000
21	Pay of police in eleven hsien	11,000
22	River gunboats, dockyard expenses	50,000
23	Workshops, etc., under the " Shan-hou " office	50,000
	Total	3,573,000
	Total, Imperial and extra provincial ..	1,895,000
	,, provincial	1,678,000
	Total	3,573,000

CHAPTER V

PRELIMINARY

OF the prehistoric systems of currency in China, the inscribed skins, the tortoiseshell and cowries, the axes and spades, the armlets and rings, it is not my purpose to treat, but only of those systems which lead directly to the modern currency practice of the Empire. Nearly every possible material is recorded as having served this purpose at one time or another ; but, outside the metals and paper money, we hear in historic times only of silk rolls and cowries. Silk rolls, though received for tribute at a fixed rate of conversion as late as the thirteenth century, might perhaps be considered as much a tribute in kind as currency, though it is recorded, *ad* A.D. 1206, that silver or silk could be used in payment of the salt tax. Cowries were received for taxes as late as the fourteenth century ; the records show that 1,133,119 strings of cowries were received by the Treasury in A.D. 1329. Of metals, gold seems to have been considered as currency only from the eleventh to the third century B.C., the law providing that the unit of gold in commercial transactions should be a cube of one *tsun* weighing one *kin*. In modern times gold has been a commodity pure and simple, and in the shape of jewelry or ingots or gold-leaf has been used chiefly for hoarding—for the Asiatic family reserve against times of want or of oppression. Iron has been used for coinage during the Han dynasty (B.C. 206) and by various kingdoms in West China, and in the tenth century iron coins were

136

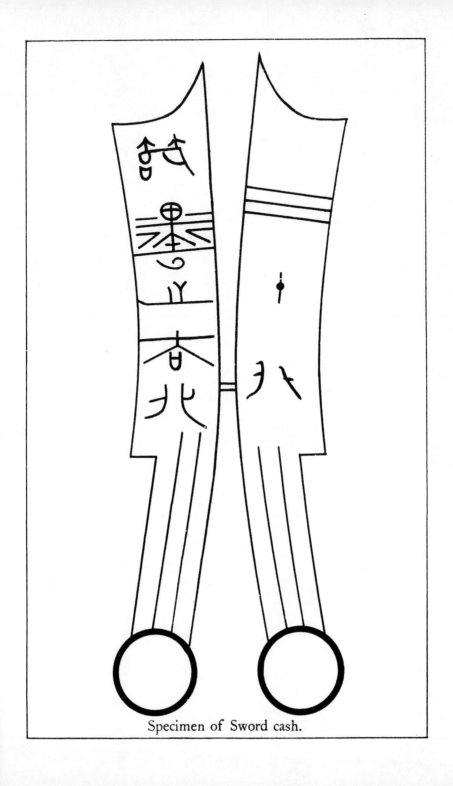

Specimen of Sword cash.

the ordinary currency in what is now Szechwan. In modern times iron was used to further depreciate the coinage of Hienfeng (A.D. 1851–1861), pieces of iron having then been issued during the time when the mints were cut off from their supplies of copper from Yunnan. These, however, are all intermittent and eccentric currencies which have not endured ; and for present-day discussion we need only consider three kinds—copper, paper, and silver.

COPPER CURRENCY

EARLY COINS

It is only in copper (or bronze) that currency and coinage are synonymous terms in China. Disregarding the archaic uninscribed tokens of rulers before the true historic period, we find the earliest recorded legislation on coinage about a century after the beginning of the Chow dynasty (*circa* B.C. 1122), the sovereign having established in B.C. 1032 certain rules for currency, and enacted that metallic pieces should henceforth be exchangeable according to their weight. Inscribed coins then came in, but for over three centuries the inscriptions contained no reference to weight or value. Then, in the first half of the seventh century B.C., the enactment of certain rules led gradually to the habit (coinage not being yet, not until B.C. 135, a government prerogative) of casting coins of regular shapes and sizes and of constant weights ; but even then the earliest known specimen inscribed with weight or value is assigned doubtfully to *circa* B.C. 375. The coins circulating from this time were of the shapes called knife and spade or *pu*, both being tokens representing for purposes of barter the implements which constituted the wealth of the people. Of these the knife coins represent a more highly developed civilisation, in that the inscriptions are more precise in giving the place of issue and in indicating that they are token currency ; the issues of the latest type, ascribed to the beginning of the first century of our era, are highly conventionalised, the blade being shortened and the ring having become a thickened copy of the round coin with a square hole which had by that time become the common coinage.

INSCRIBED ROUND COINS

Inscribed round coins came in about the seventh century B.C., the earliest known specimens being inscribed as weighing 1 liang 14 chu or $1\frac{14}{24}$ tael, having a present-day weight of 171 grains ; while others are inscribed with other weights, such as $1\frac{12}{24}$ liang, or with the place of issue and the number of *kin* or hoes they stood token for. The earlier round hole in the middle (probably a reminiscence of the armlets and rings) soon gave place to the square hole which we know to-day, and from the end of the Chow dynasty (*circa* B.C. 255) the coins are inscribed " Half a tael." The following are the approximate dates for each of the regular shapes of coins :

Knife money	B.C. 670–221
,, ,, thick and short	A.D. 7–10
Spade money (consisting of little hoes with hollow handles)	B.C. 600–350
Pu money (variant of Spade) ..	B.C. 475–221
,, ,, small and thick	A.D. 10–14
Round coins, with round holes ..	B.C. 660–336
,, ,, ,, square holes from	B.C. 221

China has had a copper coinage for twenty-five centuries, and a coinage of the shape we know to-day uninterruptedly for twenty-one centuries.

The issues of half-tael coins must have been very large, since they are in our time by no means uncommon in the trays of the petty hucksters who are found on every street of every city of the Empire. In course of time they degenerated in size and weight, and (B.C. 118) were replaced by the coins inscribed in seal character " Five chu " ($\frac{5}{24}$ tael), which remained in circulation side by side with all other issues,

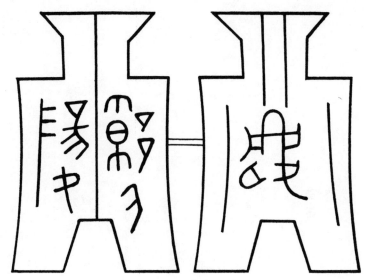

Specimen of Pu cash.

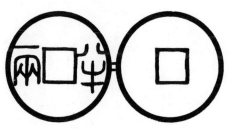

Half-tael cash.

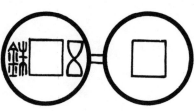

5-chu cash.

for upwards of 700 years. This coin, also easily obtainable to-day, is beautifully cast, 0·95 inch * in diameter, weighing to-day from 46 to 51 grains. Coins with other inscriptions, all in seal character and none of them dynastic, were issued from time to time, until we come to the Golden Age of China—the Tang dynasty, A.D. 618. Then began the issue of the coins inscribed in square modern character *Kai-yuan*. Coins with this inscription are recorded as having been issued by the first Tang Emperor (A.D. 618–627), by the Emperor who took those characters (Kai-yuan) for his reign title (A.D. 713–742), by the Emperor Teh Tsung (A.D. 780–785), and by the Emperor Wu Tsung (A.D. 841–847), a total of fifty-three years. The first coins to be inscribed with the title of the reigning Emperor, thus giving an exact date, were issued in the reign of Kienfeng (A.D. 666–668). This new currency, introduced by a strong and wise government in sufficient quantities for the needs of the people, supplied a type which has endured to this day. With a diameter of 0·95 inch, they were of the same approximate dimensions and weight as the coins which, until the great melting down of the past twenty years, constituted the *chih-tsien* or standard coinage of the Empire ; and thirty years ago, searching critically through hundreds of strings of cash in everyday circulation, I found among them not a few of these coins which had formed part of the ordinary currency of the people for eleven to thirteen centuries, minted before the time of Alfred of England, before Charlemagne was crowned at Rome, and long before a King of France reigned in Paris. The type persisted through the Sung dynasty (A.D. 960–1126), varied by occasional issues of coins of larger size, but generally the coinage was of standard size. These issues also were made in sufficient quantities for the needs of the people, and these, too, I have found among coins in present circulation. Speaking of thirty years ago, in every thousand coins there would be two or three of the Tang and ten or twelve of the Sung mintage. The Golden dynasty of Nüchen Tartars

* Here and later the English inch.

(A.D. 1115–1234) and their contemporaries the Southern Sung (A.D. 1127–1280) issued few coins ; and the Mongols, the Yuan dynasty (A.D. 1260–1368), ruling the China that Marco Polo knew, issued still smaller quantities, subsisting as it did mainly on fiduciary issues of paper money. The Ming dynasty then came in (A.D. 1368–1642), and found itself confronted by this financial difficulty. The early rulers were compelled for a time to continue the paper issues of their predecessors, and in addition there was during the first reign, that of Hungwu (A.D. 1368–1399), some issue of copper token coinage ; but by the time of Yunglo (A.D. 1403–1425), the reign during which the capital was moved to Peking, the finances had been restored from the condition to which they had been reduced by the unlettered and warlike Mongols, and the currency established on a sound basis. For two and a half centuries the Ming government kept the people fully supplied with circulating medium of standard size and weight, the general average of the diameter of the coins ranging from 0·90 to 1·05 inch, and the standard weight from 46 to 57 grains ; making ample allowance for the longer time that the surviving specimens of Tang and Sung coinage have been in circulation, the Ming coins must be adjudged to be superior to them, and fully equal in appearance to the coinage of the first century of the present Tsing dynasty, though less in weight. When the Manchus came to the throne, they continued the civil government of their predecessors, merely superadding the military control represented by the now innocuous Tsiang-kün (Tartar Generals) stationed at certain strategic points throughout the Empire, and creating a few milking posts, such as the Hoppo at Canton, a post abolished only in 1904 ; their rule has been in the main a government of the Chinese, by the Chinese, for the Chinese, and in nothing has this been shown more than in the continuance for nearly two centuries of the financial and monetary systems of the Mings. The earliest issues of coinage by the first Emperor to establish himself at Peking, Shunchih (A.D. 1644–1661), bore inscrip-

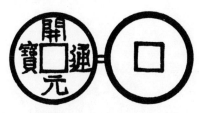

Tang, A.D. 618-906.

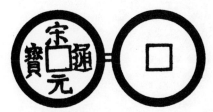

Sung, A.D. 960-1126.

Ming, A.D. 1368-1643.

Sun-chih, A.D. 1644-1661.

Kang-hi, A.D. 1662-1722.

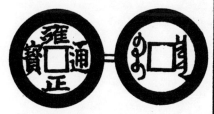

Yung-cheng, A.D. 1723-1735.

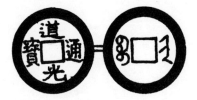

Tao-kwang, A.D. 1821-1850.

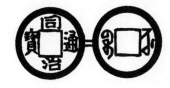

Tung-chih, A.D. 1862-1874.

tions only in Chinese, the first issues having on the reverse only the mint name, the second having in addition the value, one-thousandth of a tael (of silver) ; then, toward the end of his reign, the coins bore the mint name in Chinese and Manchu. His successor, Kanghi (A.D. 1662–1722), continued the bilingual inscriptions through the whole of his reign, but toward the end of the reign the two mints at Peking, those of the Board of Revenue (Hu-pu) and the Board of Works (Kung-pu), issued coins bearing on the reverse the mint name, and the word " currency " in Manchu only. The coins of Yungcheng (A.D. 1723–1735) are inscribed on the obverse in Chinese and on the reverse in Manchu only, and this practice has continued to this day, It is in this reign that the coinage of China may be considered to have reached its highest point, in size and weight, in quality of metal, and in elegance of inscription ; previous dynasties and previous reigns had equalled it in some one or more of these qualities, but not in the combination of all. The Shunchih coins were generally 0·95 to 1·05 inch and those of Kanghi 1·00 to 1·10 inch in diameter, and both were made of a bright yellow brass ; the Yungcheng coins were generally 1·00 to 1·10 inch in diameter, made of a rich light-brown bronze. It was from this time that the degeneration of the coinage began, and it will be well here to interpolate a note on the standard of weight and value.

Standard of Weight and Value

Leaving to one side the Half-tael and Five-chu ($\frac{5}{24}$ tael) coins, the standard introduced by the Tang dynasty and continuing in theory until to-day was a part of a bimetallic system, or even (although gold formed no part of the currency) of a trimetallic system, by which, in value, 1 gold $=$ 10 silver $=$ 1,000 copper, these being the metallic exchange equivalents in China thirteen centuries ago. The copper coin of this system was made to weigh one-tenth of a tael, making it in value one-thousandth of a tael of silver. This theory has continued to the present time, and was definitely asserted by the inscription, ten centuries later, on the coins of the first Manchu Emperor. The copper coinage being a government concern, while silver was left to the tender mercies of the bankers, the fixed exchange equivalence, or value, of the coins was treated with relative disregard, while the weight was more or less adhered to. We get into quite another question when we go into the weight of the tael ; the Five-chu coins may be assumed to have weighed 5 chu or $\frac{5}{24}$ tael when first introduced * (though this may be an erroneous assumption), and, as far as numismatics can tell us, they continued to be of the same weight down to the time when they were displaced by the Tang coins, of about the same size, and of a statutory weight of $\frac{1}{10}$ tael. Disregarding any difference of tael, this continued to be the desideratum of the mints, the actual weight of the issues varying, however, according to the laws of supply and demand, to the varying ratio between silver and copper, and to the ostensible necessity of maintaining a bimetallic proportion in the currency, but seldom falling below 0·08

* Under the Chow dynasty, on the evidence of the coins, the liang of 24 chu was probably 97·5 grains, giving 4·06 grains as the weight of the chu. The "First Emperor," Shih Hwangti, in the twenty-sixth year of his reign as Prince and the first year of his assumption of the Imperial dignity (B.C. 221), issued an edict increasing the weight and fixing the standard. On the authority of Mr. F. H. Chalfant (*Journal N.C.B.R.A.S.* 1903–4) the standard was as follows :

1 chu ..	..	..	..	0·68	gramme =	10·5 grains
24 chu = 1 liang	..	..	16·35	grammes =	252·5 grains

This standard was probably continued into the Han dynasty, which soon (B.C. 206) followed the Tsin ; and the first ruler of the Northern Tsi (A.D. 550) enacted that a hundred 5-chu coins should actually weigh 500 chu, "otherwise 1 kin 4 liang 20 chu." The actual weight (46 to 51 grains) of surviving specimens of 5-chu coins corresponds closely with the theoretic weight (52·5 grains) of this standard. When the standard was again raised is not on record ; but the first Tang coins issued seventy years later (A.D. 618) were presumably one-tenth of the modern liang of 570 to 580 grains.

tael. During the first reign of the Tsing dynasty the weight was 0·1 tael, afterwards raised to 0·125 tael, and under Kanghi, A.D. 1684, the weight was again reduced to 0·1 tael, to be again raised, A.D. 1702, to 0·14 tael, and again reduced to 0·12 tael. This continued to be the statutory weight through the reign of Yungcheng and into the beginning of that of Kienlung (A.D. 1736), when it was again made 0·1 tael. During this long reign of sixty years degeneration made progress, in appearance and in quality, and in the size and weight of the coins ; the government was still vigorous, with no sign of dry rot, and we may assume that the struggle between the mints and the illegal melter-down of too-full-weight coins had begun, and that, to keep the currency from the melting crucible, the mints were driven to reduce the intrinsic value more and more. Whatever the cause, the coinage became by degrees smaller and lighter, issues at the beginning of the reign having a diameter of 1·10 inch and weighing 0·12 tael, while at the end of the eighteenth century official issues (no account being taken of illicit coinage, so common in China) were so small as 0·85 or even 0·80 inch, and weighed no more than 0·075 tael. A memorialist just a century ago reported to the Throne that, of the coins in common circulation, from 1 to 2 per cent. weighed 0·12 tael and over, while 30 to 40 per cent. weighed the full legal 0·1 tael. The coins of the period Kiaking (A.D. 1796–1820) were of light weight, but ordinarily were still well minted ; it is in the following reign, Taokwang (A.D. 1821–1850), that the rough crude issues of the mints, which we see to-day, made their first appearance ; and the present tendency we see in a memorial from the Governor-General of Shengking, dated November 1899, in which he reports to the Throne that coins weighing 0·08 tael, such as were issued in other provinces, involve a loss, and that he is therefore minting them at 0·05 tael weight. It is safe to say that there will be no profit from melting down such coins, and that the illicit issues of counterfeiters will not be much less attractive in appearance or appreciably less in value.

Token Coinage

In the reign of Hienfeng (A.D. 1851–1861) the government fell on troubled times, with revenues reduced by wide-spread rebellion ; and, partly from this cause, partly because it was unable to get supplies of copper, recourse was had to issues of token coins. This depreciated money was issued in two forms—iron coins having the same dimensions and face value as the ordinary copper currency, and copper token coins in multiples of the ordinary cash. The iron coins had a temporary success, but within four years, in February 1857, there was a popular rising against them, and in a day they lost their currency.

The first tokens issued (in 1853) were 10-cash pieces with a diameter of 1·50 inch, but these were soon reduced to a maximum diameter of 1·20 inch and a minimum for official issues during the reign of Kwanghsü which may be put at 1·00 inch. The provinces soon followed suit and 10-cash pieces were issued by all the provincial mints except those of Hunan and Kwangtung. Other values also followed, including coins of a face value of 5, 8, 10, 20, 30, 50, 100, 200, 500, and 1,000 cash. The issues of the Fukien mint (bearing in mind that they were cast, and not rolled or stamped) are beautiful specimens of numismatology, and heavier than the contemporary coins of other mints ; and I give here the particulars of a series which lies before me.

Value.	Diameter.	Thickness.	Weight.
10-cash	1·45 inch	0·11 inch	321 grains *
20-cash	1·80 ,,	0·12 ,,	591 ,,
50-cash	2·22 ,,	0·20 ,,	1,410 ,,
100-cash	2·63 ,,	0·25 ,,	2,200 ,,

These token coins took no hold in the provinces and may be said not to have entered into the currency system of the Empire, except that, curiously enough, in Peking itself,

* Weight inscribed on rim 0·50 tael.

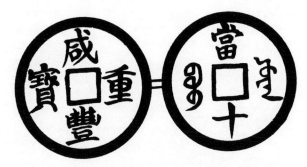

10 cash, A.D. 1853–1861.

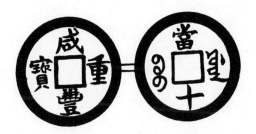

10 cash, A.D. 1853–1861.

10 cash, A.D. 1905.

though not in the province of Chihli, immediately around it, the patriotism, or the self-interest, or the timidity of the people led to their immediate adoption, and the 10-cash pieces (but none of the others) have continuously for fifty years past constituted the sole circulating medium of the capital. It must not be supposed however that, even at Peking, the 10-cash piece is considered to be worth, or is accepted for, ten cash.* The Chinese never have treated their coinage as coins, passing on their face value irrespective of their intrinsic worth, but have always looked beneath Cæsar's superscription ; and the token currency of the capital is rated closely to the value of the metal contained in it. An estimate of the true intrinsic value of a copper coinage in China must depend upon the gold exchange with silver, the gold price of copper and spelter, and the exchange between silver and the copper coinage, and the resultant of this triangular calculation will never be the same from day to day ; but taking all the conditions as they were at a certain time in 1905, I found that for one Mexican dollar I received at Shanghai 880 ordinary cash in common circulation, containing an ordinary proportion of illicit coins, of an intrinsic value of 26·4 pence ; and that for one Mexican dollar at Peking I received actually 405, being nominally † 413 pieces of 10-cash, with an actual face value ot 4,130 and a nominal ‡ face value of 8,260 cash, having an intrinsic value of 29·45 pence. The actual value in each case is somewhat, but proportionately, smaller, since I took as the basis of the fourth element in the estimate—the alloy of metal in the coins—the standard proportion of 60 parts of copper to 40 of spelter, while the proportion of copper is sometimes as low as 55.

We come now to the latest issue of token coinage, the cent. This was issued to supply a real deficiency in the circulating medium, due to extensive melting down of

* Cash, from the Sanskrit Kārsha, Kārshāpana, the translation in English of the Chinese " Copper coin."

† v. infra, page 128.   ‡ v. infra, page 131.

10

the regular coinage and the impossibility of the government supplying the wastage, both occasioned by the increasing intrinsic value of the copper contents. This coin was a close imitation of the Hongkong cent ($\frac{1}{100}$ of a silver dollar) and the issues from the Kwangtung mint are inscribed " 100 to a dollar," but those from all other mints are inscribed " represents 10 cash." While their workmanship differs, their intrinsic value is fairly uniform; with a diameter of 1·10 inch, some are of pure copper and weigh 112 grains, other contain 95 per cent. of copper and weigh 115 grains, having an intrinsic value (on the date in 1905 referred to above) of 12 pence for 100 coins or 10·5 pence for the then exchange equivalent of one dollar. There were also some limited issues of brass " cents " containing 80 per cent. of copper and 20 per cent. of spelter. At first the cents passed for their full face value of 10 cash or 88 to the silver dollar; by July 1906 they had depreciated to a value of 7 cash, or 112 to the dollar, recovering at the end of 1906 to 107 to the dollar, but in 1908 relapsing to 125 to the dollar.

MINT STATISTICS

The people of China are voracious in their consumption of cash, but it is not easy to get statistics, the only fact I can note of earlier periods being that at the beginning of the ninth century A.D. the quantity issued annually was 135,000,000. From Edkins * I give figures of the quantities of copper coins issued by the mints for certain years of the first century of the present dynasty. (See next page.)

A close correspondence in the issues of certain mints in the three columns of the second table will suggest the danger which always confronts the investigator in China, from the common habit of reporting that which should be as being that which is. Of the " cents " it is estimated that 12,500,000,000 were issued up to the end of 1906, and it appears probable that over a third of these came from the Hupeh mint.

* " Chinese Currency," by J. Edkins, Shanghai, 1901.

Shunchih 1	A.D. 1644	71,663,900	Kanghi 20	A.D. 1681	231,398,600
,, 2	,, 1645	443,751,760	,, 25	,, 1686	289,936,700
,, 3	,, 1646	624,823,960	,, 30	,, 1691	289,925,400
,, 4	,, 1647	1,333,384,194	,, 35	,, 1696	237,063,050
,, 5	,, 1648	1,449,494,200	,, 40	,, 1701	238,065,800
,, 7	,, 1650	1,682,424,510	,, 45	,, 1706	238,075,800
,, 9	,, 1652	2,097,632,850	,, 50	,, 1711	374,933,400
,, 16	,, 1653	2,521,663,740	,, 56	,, 1717	399,167,300
,, 11	,, 1654	2,488,544,460	,, 60	,, 1721	437,325,800
,, 12	,, 1655	2,413,878,080	Yungcheng 1	,, 1723	499,200
,, 17	,, 1660	280,394,280	,, 4	,, 1726	675,160
,, 18	,, 1661	291,584,600	,, 5	,, 1727	723,528,000
Kanghi 5	,, 1666	295,879,800	,, 6	,, 1728	746,304,000
,, 10	,, 1671	290,475,830	,, 8	,, 1730	757,865,000
,, 15	,, 1676	231,365,360	,, 9	,, 1731	1,048,759,660

At three periods of the nineteenth century we have figures giving the issues of each mint :

	1800–1830 Fixed quota.	1831.	1865.
Peking	899,856,000	—*	1,349,784,000
Chihli	60,666,000	60,666,000	60,756,840
Shansi	17,472,000	17,472,000	17,472,000
Shensi	87,360,000	94,584,000	94,589,040
Szechwan ..	194,127,000	194,127,000	157,733,333
Hunan	47,880,000	47,880,000	48,054,000
Hupeh	84,000,000	84,000,000	84,420,000
Kiangsi	41,928,000	41,928,000	42,037,992
Kiangsu	111,804,000	111,804,000	111,992,052
Chekiang ..	129,600,000	129,600,000	129,600,000
Fukien	43,200,000	43,200,000	43,200,000
Kwangtung ..	34,560,000	34,560,000	34,560,000
Kwangsi ..	24,000,000	24,000,000	24,000,000
Yunnan	179,784,000	5,760;000	170,569,080
Kweichow ..	94,860,000	4,464,000	89,773,200
Ili	1,122,000	1,122,000	1,122,000

VARIABILITY OF TIAO

Cash are strung on strings, in rolls of 100, of which 10 go to the string or *tiao*, or *ch'uan*, formerly called *kuan*. Nothing is ever done in China for nothing, and no oppor-

* Probably the same as in the period 1800–1830.

tunity is ever lost of making a little extra profit or lag-
niappe; and the money-changers have always charged
for their trouble in stringing, and for the cost of the string.
This charge is made by deducting one, or two, or three, or
four cash from each hundred; the deduction is more or
less (as everything in China is " more or less ") recognised
and fixed for each place, with the result that the *tiao* of
1,000 cash contains in one place 970 and in another place
980 actual coins, the full *tiao* passing however for 1,000
cash. The local quota is fixed, and the peasant who should
receive 980 but actually gets only 975, will feel that he
is not receiving his due and will enter at once upon that
war of wits which delights the heart of every Chinaman.
The following newspaper cutting * will give a clearer
picture of the situation than anything I can write, what
is said of the cent being true also of the cash.

" WUSUEH, HUPEH, *May* 1, 1906.

" This particular part of the Hupeh province has
long been distinguished for its variety of rates of
exchange. A nominal 100 cash has for a long time
been worth 97 in actual cash at Wusueh, 98 at Lungping ten miles away, 97 or 98 in different classes of
transactions at Hsingkuo ninety miles away, and
99 at Chichou, the same distance away in another
direction. To complicate matters, the only cash
bills which are popular are issued by a Wusueh bank
and are current in all these towns, but not at face
value. At Wusueh a bill equals 1,000 cash, at Lungping one has to give ten cash and a bill for a thousand,
at Chichou one must add twenty cash to the bill.
When the copper 10-cash pieces became current (and
the only currency, for cash is not now to be had at
the banks) the banks had to settle all these monetary
problems afresh. At the mint the copper pieces are

* *North-China Daily News*, May 11th, 1906.

sold at 98, *i.e.* 100 copper pieces equal 1,000 cash, reckoned at 98 to the hundred, so that when paying 100 cash one pays ten pieces, but when paying 99 or 98 cash one also pays ten pieces. At Chichou the banks decided to issue 100 copper pieces for a cash bill, thus saving money on the transaction, as they bought the pieces at Wuchang at 98 and paid them out instead of 1,000 copper cash at 99. At Lungping they had to be content without gains. At Wusueh the banks pondered, for if they bought the copper pieces at 98 and then gave 100 for a bill in a place where the rate was 97 they would lose ten cash on each hundred. They therefore decided to take one coin out of each packet they got from the mint. Had they stopped here all would have gone smoothly, for the shopkeepers would have deducted one cash from each ten copper pieces which they paid out, and no one would have lost anything. But old-time custom has allowed the banks to charge two cash for the piece of string on which the cash were threaded, and the banks did not like to yield this squeeze, so they proceeded to take a second copper piece out of each packet from the mint and put eight cash back, thus getting the two cash for the string which they no longer provided. Of course the shopkeepers objected, for they could not divide up two cash among a hundred coins. If they allowed this deduction, the loss of the two cash must inevitably fall on the man who broke the parcel of copper pieces. The result was that the matter was referred to the officials, and after plea and counter-plea, the shopkeepers have won, and by proclamation the rate in Wusueh from to-morrow will be 98 to the 100, so that the banks will hand over unbroken packets of copper coins. Does not the commercial strength of the Chinese lie just in this pertinacious struggling against the smallest losses ? "

Double Value of Cash in North China

In the north (Chihli, Shantung) one cash counts for two. The price of an article being there quoted at 100 cash, you hand over 50 coins, at 2 *tiao* you give what in the south constitutes 1 *tiao*. The same rule of deduction holds here too, and the *tiao*, nominally of 1,000 and nominally-actually of 980 cash, contains actually 490 coins. At Peking, too, the rule holds good, and the *tiao*, nominally of 1,000 cash, *i.e.* nominally of 100 and nominally-actually of 98 pieces of 10-cash, actually contains 49 pieces of 10-cash = 20-cash. In Manchuria the *tiao* consists of 160 ordinary (small) cash.

I make no excuse for devoting so much of my space to this part of my subject. The copper coinage is the currency of the people, in which the daily transactions of four hundred millions are carried on. The importer and the exporter have an exchange question ever present ; the wholesale dealer buys and sells with taels of silver bullion ; but the shopkeeper sells his commodities, and the artisan and the farmer sell the produce of their labour, for copper coins, and with these copper coins buy what will suffice for their daily needs. The basis of the currency system of the Empire is the copper cash which was originally $\frac{1}{1000}$ of a tael of silver, worth only a generation ago the third of a pound sterling ; and of this copper cash, at the exchange ruling a couple of years ago, it took approximately 10,000 to equal a pound sterling, 2,000 an American dollar, 500 a mark, and 400 a franc.

PAPER MONEY

Paper money comes to be considered next, since, speaking generally and *exceptis excipiendis*, it is in China based on copper and not on silver. There is no record to show when bank issues first began, and to-day the notes of money-changers circulate readily within a radius limited only by the credit and reputation of the issuing firm. It is not my purpose, however, to consider private issues, but only the fiduciary issues of fiat money made by the government.

Tang and Sung Notes

The first government notes of which the issue is recorded were of the Tang dynasty. The Emperor Hientsung (A.D. 806–821) on account of the scarcity of cash, issued an edict prohibiting the manufacture of copper utensils, such as basins and kettles ; and, to provide for the monetary stringency, opened offices at the capital at which merchants could deposit their coin, receiving in exchange government notes, called " bonds " or " flying money " ; the offices represented the different provinces, and the notes were redeemable at the proper provincial capital. Translated into modern terms, this means that the government began to issue paper money. These issues continued to the end of the Tang period. The first Emperor of the Sung period (A.D. 960) followed the custom of the Tang dynasty and issued government notes at large commercial centres, redeemable at other large centres. As described, these notes served rather the purpose of bills of exchange, but it is hard to believe that the government did not avail itself of the opportunity to get something for nothing, and to pay some portion of its obligations in this form. In A.D. 997 the amount of these notes outstanding was 1,700,000 strings (tiao) of cash, and in A.D. 1017 was 2,930,000 strings.

It was in the state of Shuh, the present province of Szechwan, that the true paper money was first introduced ; these were notes issued without being guaranteed by some hypothecated value. A certain *Chang Yung* introduced them to take the place of the iron money, which was inconveniently heavy and troublesome. These bills were called *chih-tsi* or *evidences*. During the reign of Chengtsung

of the Sung dynasty (A.D. 997–1022), this practice was
followed, and the notes were called *kiao-tze* or *changelings*.
They were made payable every three years ; thus in sixty-
five years they were redeemable twenty-two times ; each
note was worth a thousand cash, or a tael of pure silver.
Fifteen of the richest houses managed this financial operation ; but in course of time they were unable to fulfil their en-
gagements, and all became bankrupt, which gave rise to many
lawsuits.   The Emperor annulled the notes of this company,
and deprived his subjects of the power to issue bank-bills,
reserving it to himself to establish a bank of issue at Yihchao.
By the year 1032 there were more than 1,256,340 taels'
worth of " changelings " in circulation in China.   In 1068,
having ascertained that counterfeits were issued, the
government made a law that persons making false bills
should be punished the same as those who falsified government orders.   Later than this, and at different applications,
banks for the issue of the *kiao-tze* were established in many
provinces, and the notes of one province were not circulated
in another.   Their terms of payment and modes of circulation, too, varied at different times.*

Southern Sung Notes

For the twelfth and the first half of the thirteenth
centuries the country was divided between the Southern
Sung and the Golden dynasty of Nüchen Tartars, and both
ran a mad race in the issue of assignats.   Of the latter
government we have few records, but of the doings of the
southern kingdom Klaproth gives us the following note :

"Under the Emperor Kiotsung, in A.D. 1131, it
was attempted to make a military establishment at
Wuchow, but as the requisite funds did not come in
without great difficulty, the officers charged with
the matter proposed to the Board of Revenue to
issue *Kwan-tze* or due bills, with which they could

* Klaproth, " Mémoires relatifs à l'Asie."

pay the sutlers of the troops; and which should
be redeemable at a special office. Abuses soon
crept into the details of this plan, and the people
began to murmur. Later, and under the same reign,
similar due bills to these were put into circulation
in other provinces. During the reign of this same
monarch, the Board of Revenue issued a new sort
of paper money called *hwei-tze* or exchanges; these
were, at first, payable only in the province of
Chekiang and thereabouts, but they soon extended
to all parts of the Empire. The paper of which
they were made was originally fabricated only in
the cities of Hweichow and Kichow in Kiangnan;
subsequently, it was also manufactured in Chengtu-
fu in Szechwan, and Linan-fu in Chekiang. The
hwei-tze first issued were worth a string of a thousand cash, but under the reign of Hiao-tsung, in
1163, they were issued of the value of 500, 300, and
200 cash each. In five years, *i.e.* up to the seventh
month of the year 1166, there had already been
sent out more than 28,000,000 taels' worth of
these notes; and by the eleventh month of this
year, this sum had been increased 15,600,000 taels.
During the further sway of the Sung dynasty, the
number of the *hwei-tze* was constantly on the increase;
and besides this description of note, there were
some of the *Kiao-tze* still extant, and notes of
private individuals current in the provinces; so
that the country was inundated with paper notes,
which were daily depreciated in value in spite of all the
modifications and changes the government adopted
to augment their circulation.

"At last, under the reign of Li-tsung of the
same dynasty, in 1264, the minister Kia Sze-tau,
seeing their value so small, endeavoured to substitute
for a part of *hwei-tze* some new assignats which he
called *yin-kwan* or silver obligations. Those *hwei-tze*

which were technically named 'seventeen terms,'
were withdrawn entirely; and three of those called
'eighteen terms' were exchanged for one note of the
new currency which bore the character *kia*. But although even those bills which were torn were received
in pay for taxes, the minister was not able to get the
Treasury paper into circulation, nor to lessen the
price of commodities."

MONGOL NOTES

The Mongols then came in (A.D. 1260) and founded the
Yuan dynasty. An unlettered race of warriors, they could
devise no better means of providing for the needs of their
government than to continue the practice which they found
in vogue and issue paper money. Copper cash and silver
had been driven from their dominions; and with the chief
sources of supply of both metals in the southern provinces,
it would require a longer period of peace and a higher
development of commerce than was possible under Mongol
rule, for the ways to be opened to allow the deficiency to be
made good. From Marco Polo we hear much of the great
wealth and the high development of commerce in the Mongol
realm, but we must recall what was the state of the Europe
of that day with which alone he could make comparison;
apart from the record of history, the coinage alone would
tell us that China from the seventh to the eleventh century
was far more prosperous and more highly developed than
in the thirteenth century. To show the available resources
of the Treasury at a time a little later but during the same
(Mongol) dynasty, the following note, showing the tribute
actually received by the Imperial Treasury, in a year of
great prosperity, is illuminating:

A.D. 1329. 989 ting (= 49,450 taels) of silver *and notes*;
  1,133,119 strings of cowrie shells; 1,098,843 catties
  of raw silk; 350,530 rolls of woven silk; 72,915
  catties of cotton; 211,223 pieces of woven cloth;
  3,255,220 piculs of rice.

The first issue of Mongol government notes was made in the first year (A.D. 1260) of Kublai Khan, the title of whose reign was Chung-tung, and the successive issues in this and the following reigns must be briefly summarised.

A.D. 1260. *Kiao-chao*, representing silk, a continuation of the issues then in vogue ; fifty taels of silver would buy 1,000 taels of silk, represented by notes of the face value of 1,000 taels. (So stated by Edkins.)

A.D. 1260. November. Issue of notes *Chung-tung-chao* of 10, 20, 30, 50, 100, 200, 500, 1,000, and 2,000 cash. A note for 1,000 cash was worth a tael in *Kiao-chao* currency, and 2,000 cash in *Kiao-chao* currency represented one tael in silver.—(N.B. one cash = $\frac{1}{1000}$ tael.)

A.D. 1264. Treasury established in each province ; notes representing 12,000 ting = 600,000 taels constituted bank-note reserve.

A.D. 1275. *Li-chao* notes issued, of 2, 3, and 5 cash, but soon withdrawn.

A.D. 1287. *Chih-yuan-chao* notes issued of eleven denominations from 5 to 2,000 cash. A tael of silver exchanged for 2,000 cash and a tael of gold for 20,000 cash in these notes.

A.D. 1309. *Chih-ta-chao* notes issued of thirteen denominations from 2 cash to 2 taels of silver. One *chih-ta-chao* (tael of silver) was equivalent to 5,000 *chih-yuan-chao* cash, a depreciation in twenty-two years of 60 per cent.

A.D. 1312–1321. During the reign of Jen-tsung there was over-issue of notes, and the issue of the Chih-ta notes for silver was stopped. The Chung-tung and Chih-yuan notes continued to circulate to the end of the Mongol dynasty.

We have a record of the issues (which must include re-issues for obliterated notes) for the first seventy years from A.D. 1260, which, not including Kublai's issue of *Kiao-chao*, gives us a total issue of irredeemable paper money in sixty-four of the first seventy years of Mongol rule amounting to 47,611,276 ting or 2,380,563,800 taels nominal face value, the tael being always taken as equivalent to 1,000 cash. This is an average of over 37,000,000 taels a year ; and, as the coach gains in speed in running down hill, we may assume for the whole dynastic period of 108 years an annual average of 40,000,000 taels, at a time when the richest of the sovereigns of Europe, placed inexorably upon a cash basis, counted himself passing rich in any year in which his budget exceeded the equivalent of a million taels. How this situation struck an intelligent European, ignorant of the use of instruments of credit and bewildered by the apparent signs of wealth around him, is shown in Marco Polo's comment ; and I reproduce it here to demonstrate how changed is Europe and how unchanged is China in the six centuries which have elapsed since it was written.

　　" The Emperor's Mint then is in this same City of Cambulac, and the way it is wrought is such that you might say he hath the Secret of Alchemy in perfection, and you would be right ! For he makes his money after this fashion.

　　" He makes them take of the bark of a certain tree, in fact of the Mulberry Tree, the leaves of which are the food of the silkworms—these trees being so numerous that whole districts are full of them. What they take is a certain fine white bast or skin which lies between the wood of the tree and the thick outer bark, and this they make into something resembling sheets of paper, but black. When these sheets have been prepared they are cut up into pieces of different sizes. The smallest of these sizes is worth a half tornesel ; the next, a little larger, one tornesel ; one a little larger still is worth half a silver groat of Venice ; another a whole groat ; other yet two groats, five groats, and ten groats. There is also a kind worth one bezant of gold, and others of three bezants, and so up to ten.* All these pieces of paper are [issued with as much solemnity

* The bezant is taken to equal one tael of silver, or 1,000 cash. One bezant = 20 groats = 133⅓ tornesel.

and authority as if they were of pure gold or silver ; and on every piece a variety of officials, whose duty it is, have to write their names, and to put their seals. And, when all is prepared duly, the chief officer deputed by the Kaan smears the Seal entrusted to him with vermilion, and impresses it on the paper, so that the form of the Seal remains stamped upon it in red ; the Money is then authentic. Any one forging it would be punished with death]. And the Kaan causes every year to be made such a vast quantity of this money, which costs him nothing, that it must equal in amount all the treasure in the world.

" With these pieces of paper, made as I have described, he causes all payments on his own account to be made ; and he makes them to pass current universally over all his kingdoms and provinces and territories and whithersoever his power and sovereignty extends. And nobody, however important he may think himself, dares to refuse them on pain of death. And indeed everybody takes them readily, for wheresoever a person may go throughout the Great Kaan's dominions he shall find these pieces of paper current, and shall be able to transact all sales and purchases of goods by means of them just as well as if they were coins of pure gold. And all the while they are so light that ten bezants' worth does not weigh one golden bezant.

" Furthermore all merchants arriving from India or other countries and bringing with them gold or silver or gems and pearls, are prohibited from selling to any one but the Emperor. He has twelve experts chosen for this business, men of shrewdness and experience in such affairs ; these appraise the articles, and the Emperor then pays a liberal price for them in those pieces of paper. The merchants accept his price readily, for in the first place they would not get so good an one from anybody else, and secondly, they are paid without any delay. And with this paper-money they can buy what they like anywhere over the Empire, whilst it is also vastly lighter to carry about on their journeys. And it is a truth that the merchants will several times in the year bring wares to the amount of 400,000 bezants, and the Grand Sire pays for all in that paper. So he buys such a quantity of those precious things every year that his treasure is endless, whilst all the time the money he pays away costs him nothing at all. Moreover several times in the year proclamation is made through the city that any one who may have gold or silver or gems or pearls, by taking them to the Mint shall get a handsome price for them. And the owners are glad to do this, because they would find no other purchaser give so large a price. Thus the quantity they bring in is marvellous, though those who do not choose to do so may let it alone. Still, in this way, nearly all the valuables in the country come into the Kaan's possession.

" When any of those pieces of paper are spoilt—not that they are so very flimsy neither—the owner carries them to the Mint, and by paying 3 per cent. on the value he gets new pieces in exchange. And if any Baron, or any one else soever, hath need of gold or silver or gems or pearls, in order to make plate, or girdles or the like, he goes to the Mint and buys as much as he list, paying in this paper-money.

" Now you have heard the ways and means where-by the Great Kaan may have, and in fact has, more treasure than all the kings in the World ; and you know all about it and the reason why." *

MING NOTES

Bayonets form a poor seat for the throne of a ruler, and

* " The Book of Ser Marco Polo," translated by Col. Henry Yule. London, 1871. Book II. Chap. xxiv.

a constant diet of irredeemable assignats is not nutritious. With all the warlike prowess and rough hardihood of the Mongols, weakened though they may have been by a life of luxury, their throne, which endured for three centuries in India, fell after a single century of dominion in China before the assault of the unwarlike Chinese, driven to rebellion by the burden of heavy taxation and by the evils of an irredeemable and depreciated paper currency. The first Ming Emperor, T'ai Tsu, whose reign title was Hungwu (A.D. 1368–1398), found himself confronted by a financial situation of grave difficulty, and was compelled for a time to continue, with all its evils, the currency system of his predecessors. Government notes were therefore issued, but other steps were taken to place the Imperial finances on a sound basis, and it redounds to the credit of the government that, in a single reign and a single generation, they were able to "resume specie payments."

I have been unable to obtain a copy of a Mongol government note, which would have had a special interest as illustrating the currency, the benefits of which Ser Marco Polo described in such glowing terms to an open-mouthed and open-eared Europe. I give, however, a reduced reproduction of a note for 1,000 cash issued by the first Ming Emperor (Hungwu, A.D. 1368–1398), who may be assumed to have followed closely the procedure and copied the forms of his predecessors. This 500-year-old instrument of credit has a curious history, furnishing an absolute guarantee of its authenticity. During the foreign occupation of Peking in 1900–1901 some European soldiers had overthrown a sacred image of Buddha, in the grounds of the Summer Palace, and, deposited in the pedestal (as in the corner-stones of our public buildings), found gems and jewelry and ingots of gold and silver and a bundle of these notes. Contented with the loot having intrinsic value, the soldiers readily surrendered the bundle of notes to a bystander who was present "unofficially," Surgeon Major Louis Livingston Seaman, U.S.A., of New York, and he gave to the Museum of St. John's College at Shanghai the specimen which is here reproduced.

The note is printed on mulberry-bark paper, which now is of a dark slate colour, the " something resembling sheets of paper, but black " of Marco Polo's description. The sheet of paper is 13·5 by 8·75 inches, and the design on the face is 12·6 by 8·3 inches. The border, 1·4 inch wide, is made of extended dragons filled around with an arabesque design, and is surmounted by a panel with the inscription (from right to left) " circulating government note of the Ming Empire." The space within the border is divided into two panels. The upper has on the two sides in conventionalised square seal characters, on the right " government note of the Ming Empire," on the left " circulating for ever and ever " ; between these two inscriptions, above, in large ordinary characters " one *kwan* " (or *tiao* or string), and below a pictorial illustration representing ten hundreds of cash. The lower panel contains the following : " The Imperial Board of Revenue having memorialised the Throne has received the Imperial sanction for the issue of government notes of the Ming Empire, to circulate on the same footing as standard cash. To counterfeit is death. The informant will receive 250 taels of silver and in addition the entire property of the criminal. Hungwu........year .... month........ day." A seal 3·25 inches square is impressed in vermilion once on the upper panel, once on the lower panel, bearing in square seal characters the legend " The Seal of the Government Note Administrators." On the back of the note, above, is impressed in vermilion a seal bearing in square seal characters the legend " Seal for Circulating Government Notes " ; below, within a border 6·2 by 4·1 inches, is repeated the middle part of the upper panel of the face—one *kwan*, with a pictorial illustration representing ten hundreds of cash.

HIENFENG NOTES.

From A.D. 1403, it may be said, or at any rate from some time in the reign of Yunglo (A.D. 1403–1425), there were no fiduciary issues by the government, either of the Ming or the Tsing, until we come to the troubled times of Hienfeng (A.D. 1851–1861), when the necessities of the Treasury drove it to this method of replenishing its depleted reserves. In 1853, the year in which the issue of token coins began, the government resumed, after an interval of four and a half centuries, the issue of paper money, nominally redeemable but in practice never redeemed. The notes so issued were of two kinds, for copper cash and for taels of silver.

The cash notes were of four denominations, 500, 1,000, 1,500, and 2,000 cash, and the silver notes were for 1, 3, 5, 10, and 50 taels of the Metropolitan or Two-tael scale.* The issue of both was forced, but they rapidly depreciated in value until, in 1861, they circulated at only 3 per cent. of their face value, and soon disappeared from circulation.

For nearly forty years from the accession of Tungchih (A.D. 1862) the issue of paper instruments of credit was left entirely to private hands, banks and money-changers ; but recently some provincial governments, driven by the steady absorption of their revenues for Imperial purposes, have resumed the issue of government notes. Their re-introduction is of too recent a date to permit any extended comment upon the wisdom of the step, or upon the precautions adopted to secure their convertibility ; but the partial acceptance which they have obtained is based on reasons which carry us back eleven hundred years. The circulation of the notes of private banks is limited to the radius of credit of the issuing bank ; the Tang government notes were acceptable chiefly because they furnished a safe and convenient means of transferring funds from place to place ; and, rather to the dismay of the authorities, this

11   * See page 174.

facility of transferring funds provides the chief reason for the circulation within the limits of a given province of present issues of government notes.

SILVER CURRENCY

BIMETALLIC RATIO

There has always, for thirteen centuries at least, and in theory, been a more or less recognised correspondence and fixed ratio of convertibility between the copper and the silver currency of the Empire; and among the many facts which show this, I need only refer to the few which have been mentioned above. The Tang coinage of the seventh century A.D. was based on the trimetallic ratio of 1 gold = 10 silver = 1,000 copper; in the paper money issues of the Southern Sung and the Yuan, from the twelfth to the fourteenth centuries, the *tiao* or string, or thousand, of paper-money cash and the tael of silver are always regarded as synonymous terms (*cf.* Marco Polo, *ubi supra*), notwithstanding the fact that the paper money was much depreciated; and the first Manchu Emperor (A.D. 1644), in his desire to conform in every way to Chinese theory and practice, inscribed on his coins their theoretic silver value, $\frac{1}{1000}$ of a tael (as shown on plate facing p. 140).

SILVER COINS

Five centuries after the Tang rulers had either fixed the bimetallic ratio or had adopted that which they found in existence, silver had appreciated to double its value in its relation to copper cash, one shoe of 50 taels of silver exchanging for 100,000 cash; and about A.D. 1183, during the reign of Hiaot-sung, the second Emperor of the Southern Sung, China for the first, and (until a few years ago) last and only time, minted silver coins. There were five kinds, weighing 1, 2, 3, 5, and 10 taels respectively, each tael passing for 2,000 cash. They could be used as official and commercial currency, and served equally as metallic reserve for the paper notes. This silver coinage only lasted three years.

I am uncertain whether we should regard this as a true silver coinage of which the face and intrinsic values should correspond, or whether it was not an issue of depreciated silver token currency intended to serve mainly as metallic reserve to support the still further depreciated paper currency, the issues of which under the same dynasty had begun fifty years before ; a fair parallel, were it not for the relative credit of the two governments, might be found in the silver reserve of the Bank of France, which, being based on gold, is counted at the ratio 1 : 16. A silver coin, an exact model of the cash of the reign, was issued during the reign of the Ming Emperor Wanli (A.D. 1573–1619), but this was probably a mint sport, much like the English silver pennies issued to-day. The silver coins of the nineteenth century in the collections of Wylie and Glover can hardly be regarded as official. This, so far as is known, is the complete record of the silver coinage of China up to A.D. 1889.

CURRENCY A WEIGHT

With these insignificant exceptions, China has never had a government coin of other metal than copper ; other than copper, the currency of the country is not a coin, but a weight. This weight is the " tael," * as it is called by foreigners, the Chinese name for it being *liang* ; and when an operation in international trade, a wholesale purchase, Government indebtedness, or Customs duties have to be liquidated, payment is effected by weighing out the required number of " taels " of the stipulated quality of silver. A century ago Germany was the paradise of the money-changer with its numerous coinages, each circulating in its own principality ; but that was simplicity itself when compared with China. In China every one of the hundreds

* Tael—from the Hindu " tola " through the Malayan word " tahil."

of commercial centres not only has its own tael-weight, but in many cases has several standards side by side ; and these taels of money will be weighed out in silver which, even in one place, will be of several degrees of fineness.

VARIABILITY OF STANDARDS

One town may be taken to typify many—the town of Chungking, in the province of Szechwan, in the far west of China. Here the standard weight of the tael for silver transactions is 555·6 grains, and this is the standard for all transactions in which the scale is not specified. Frequently, however, a modification of the scale is provided for, depending in some cases upon the place from which the merchant comes or with which he trades, and in others upon the goods in which he deals. A merchant coming from Kweichow, or trading with that place, will probably, but not certainly, use a scale on which the tael weighs 548·9 grains ; a merchant from Kweifu, a town on the Yangtze, a hundred miles below Chungking, will buy and sell with a tael 562·7 grains ; and between these two extremes are at least ten topical weights of tael, all " current " at Chungking. In addition to these twelve topical " currencies," there are others connected with commodities. One of the most important products of Szechwan is salt, and dealings in this are settled by a tael of 556·4 grains, unless it is salt from the Tzeliu well, in which case the standard is 557·7 grains. A transaction in cotton cloth is settled with a tael of 555·0 grains, but for cotton yarn the tael is 556·0 grains, and for raw cotton the tael is 547·7 grains.

This seems confusion, but we are not yet at the end. Up to this point we have dealt only with the weight on the scale, but now comes in the question of the fineness of the silver with which payment is made. At Chungking three qualities of silver are in common use—" fine silver " 1,000 fine current throughout the Empire, " old silver " about 995 fine, and " trade silver " between 960 and 970 fine ; and payment may be stipulated in any one of these three qualities. Taking the score of current tael-weights in combination with the three grades of silver, we have at least sixty currencies possible in this one town.

This is characteristic of the Empire. The traveller, even a private individual, journeying from place to place in China, will be careful to take with him a small steel-yard and a string of a few selected " cash," the exact weight of which on his home scale is known to him. His first step in cashing a draft or exchanging the silver he brought with him is to ascertain the weight of his string of cash on the scales of the strange bank in the strange place ; and, having done this, he is able to work out the parity of exchange between his home and the place of his temporary sojourn. Even then, however, he is dependent on the banker in the matter of the quality of silver ; fortunately, the commercial honour of the Chinese bankers stands high, although it is hardly to be expected that they should not profit by their expert knowledge.

In China you must prove your axioms. We are accustomed to currencies in which the unit of value is a defined and accurate weight of an alloy of a precious metal (commonly gold) of an exact and known degree of fineness. In China the silver currency is an article of barter, of which neither the weight nor the quality is anywhere fixed ; and in treating of the tael of silver, we must answer two questions : What is a tael ? and What is silver ? Since " tael " connotes both a weight and a value, and since an essential element in value is the quality of the silver, we must first answer the question, What is silver ?

SILVER

Silver is most commonly current in oval ingots called " shoes," from their resemblance to a Chinese shoe ; but what may be called fractional currency is in obovoid lumps weighing up to two or three taels. At Mengtsz the sycee most commonly current is the *chieh-ting*, more commonly known as the *pai-fang* ingot ; when laid flat on a sheet of paper and traced with a pencil, it has eight curvilinear lines, a figure not unlike the brass pieces inserted in doors to protect key-holes ; in weight the pieces vary from two taels up to five taels. At Peking the Sungkiang ingot is about 10 taels. The standard ingot of China weighs about 50 taels (from 49 to 54) and, formerly called *ting*, is now called *pao* (jewel, article of value, as in the inscription on the copper cash *tung-pao* = " current coin ") and more commonly *yuan pao*, probably standing for " round ingot " from its shape, oval in plan.

The shoes of Shanghai are as shown in the accompanying plate, which represents a shoe inscribed in ink by the Assay Office of the Foreign Settlements as weighing 49·94 taels and as being of silver for the quality of which 2·75 must be added ; it is also stamped with dies at the Melting Establishment with the place (Shanghai), the name of the Establishment (Suiyuan), and a numeral (3) for the number of the furnace, of which the Establishment has six. Shanghai shoes weigh close on 50 taels each ; a lot of sixty of which I saw the weighing and touching, had fifty-four between 49·81 and 49·90 taels, five between 49·91 and 50·00 taels, and one of 50·04 taels ; other lots might have the larger proportion just over 50 taels. Hankow and other Yangtze ports also cast oval shoes close on 50 taels in weight, and Tientsin as well. The shoes of Kiangsi are rectangular, with the lip projecting at each end only half an inch, weighing also about 50 taels. The shoes ordinarily have the top of the solid part parallel to the bottom ; but in the Newchwang shoe it is inclined, so that at one end the solid part is only two-thirds the thickness of the other end ; Newchwang shoes weigh from 53 to 54 taels, and quotations for " transfer money " (*v. infra*) are per shoe of nominally 53 taels. Except to make change the small lumps of silver are seldom seen at Shanghai, and when received from other cities are sent to be cast into shoes.

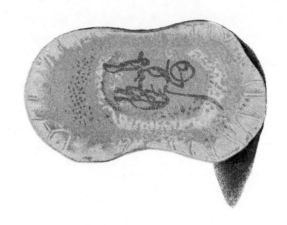

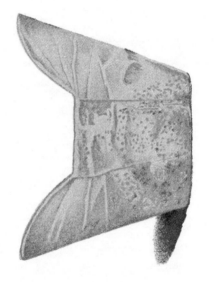

SCALE OF INCHES.

SHANGHAI SHOE OF SYCEE.

The silver contained in the shoe is called sycee, the Cantonese pronunciation of *hsi-sze*, " fine silk " ; when it is theoretically standard silver of a fineness of 1,000 it is called *tsu-seh wen-yin.*

Throughout China generally, except at Shanghai and in the country subordinated to it, silver is rated for quality by millièmes of a standard of " pure silver." Thus, at Tientsin all silver is reduced to a theoretic local standard of 992 ; at Chefoo, to one of 976 ; at Hankow, to one of 967. At Shanghai and through the greater part of Kiangsu and Anhwei silver is rated, not by millièmes of a " pure silver " standard, but by the addition, to each shoe of about 50 taels weight, of a quantity to indicate the degree of superiority of quality over a presumed standard which (subject to a certain degree of confusion between premium and discount) is 944 of the China standard of " pure silver." By this scheme of notation 2·8 silver (*i.e.* silver for the quality of which is added 2·8 per shoe, or 5·6 per 100) represents silver 1,000 fine, 2·7 silver is 998 fine, 2·4 silver is 992 fine, or thereabouts.

In Western countries the standard of 1,000 represents silver chemically pure, with no admixture of gold or of copper and lead. American quotations of bar silver are reduced to a basis of 998, and British quotations to a basis of 925 of this standard. In China the standard of 1,000 seems to refer to a silver commercially pure, as shown by the crude methods of the touchstone or of crucible assaying. This is the standard of Kuping ; it is the standard to which are referred all local millième standards, and in the Shanghai notation it is 2·8 silver. Even at Shanghai, however, super-pure silver is known in Chinese circles, and in the make-up of the Haikwan tael the requisite quality of silver is rated, not at 2·8, as for the " pure silver " of the Kuping tael, but at 3·084 (*i.e.* at 6·168 per 100 taels) to represent a higher degree of purity. Even this, however, does not graphically represent a quality of silver corresponding to what is called 1,000 fine in Western countries.

It has been ascertained in transactions in foreign bar silver that " pure silver " of the Kuping tael touch is actually 987 fine when reduced to the Western standard of chemically pure silver ; and on this basis silver of the Haikwan tael touch recognised at Shanghai is actually 992·3 fine.

Working on these figures it will be found that the Shanghai tael contains 525 grains of silver of the Kuping tael touch, 522⅛ grains of silver of the Haikwan tael touch, and about 518¼ grains of silver of the Western standard 1,000 fine.

I shall have more to say on the definition of the quality of silver when I come to treat of the Shanghai tael.

THE TAEL

It is not always possible to keep them apart in writing, but in reading it is necessary always to bear in mind the distinction between the tael of value and the tael of weight. At Tientsin, by " Tientsin tael " is meant one *Hang-ping* tael in weight of silver of the *Hwa-pao* standard 992 fine ; by " Hangping tael " is meant one Hangping tael in weight of silver or any other commodity, and, if of silver, it may be of Hwapao or any other stipulated standard ; to express fully what the foreigner calls the " Tientsin tael," the Chinese would say " Hang-ping tael of hwa-pao silver." It is not possible to use different words for the two meanings thus connoted, since they are interwoven ; and always to distinguish them otherwise would involve the use of much circumlocution.   It must be left to the reader to make the distinction, since, even without this, there will be found to be enough of " proving axioms " to break constantly the thread of thought.

THE TAEL OF WEIGHT

The tael is the " ounce " of China, of which, as in England and America, 16 make one catty,* or Chinese " pound."

* Catty or Kati—Malayan for pound.

In weighing the precious metals, however, the tael is the heaviest unit, and it has decimal subdivisions, each with its own name, down to the one thousand-million-millionth ($\frac{1}{1,000,000,000,000,000}$) part of a tael, those in daily use being the following :

> 10 Li (cash) = 1 Fên (Candarin).
> 10 Fên   = 1 Tsien (Mace).
> 10 Tsien   = 1 Liang (Tael).

Seven places of decimals (the ten-millionth part) of a tael are frequently, even regularly, seen in statements of account of revenue and expenditure submitted to the Throne. This is the tael of the arithmetics, but its actual weight will best be considered under the head of the tael of currency ; it is sufficient here to say that the weight ranges, at different places and in the same place, from 540 to 583 grains.

THE TAEL OF CURRENCY

Of the various taels of currency two may be considered to have a universal range, the Haikwan, or "Customs" tael, and the Kuping, or "Treasury" tael ; and a third, the Tsaoping, or "Tribute" tael, is current over a wide area.

Haikwan Tael

The Haikwan tael is the currency in which duties are levied by the Imperial Maritime Customs, but it is a purely fictitious and non-existent currency. Inquiry leads to no indication that it ever has been an existent currency at any time since the opening of the Inspectorate-General of Customs, and it is certain that it is not in current use at the present day. At no Custom House does any merchant tender Haikwan taels in payment of duties, and the invariable practice is to pay all Customs obligations in local currency at a rate of conversion settled on the opening of each of the several Customs Offices, now forty in number. The actual theoretic weight, apart from any question of the quality of silver, is not ascertainable with any degree of certainty. Using an official weight of 100 taels dated 1867, which had been verified at Canton by a weight of 1846, it has been found to be 581·55 grains. The result of independent tests at Canton in the same year (1905) gave a weight of 581·83 grains; while other estimates range from 581 to 589 grains. The only outside authority to which appeal can be made is in the treaties. By the Trade Regulations annexed to the British treaty of 1858 the " picul of one hundred catties is held to be equal to one hundred and thirty-three and one-third pounds, avoirdupois," giving a catty of 1⅓ lb. av. and a tael of 1⅓ oz. av., equal to 583·3 grains ; while the Regulations annexed to the French Treaty of 1858 fix the picul at 60 kilos. and 453 grammes, which gives a resultant tael of 37·783 grammes or 583·1 grains.

Taking the Haikwan tael, then, as being purely a money of account, and not an existing currency of the Empire, the place at which its value may be most conveniently found is Shanghai, at which port were paid in 1905 duties to the extent of 34 per cent. of the total Customs collection of the year. Here since the opening of the port, half a century ago, the rate of conversion has been Haikwan Tls.100 = Shanghai Tls.111·40 worked out as follows

Weight on local scale	100.0.0.0
Add for difference in weight	2.8.0.0
Add for touch	6.1.6.8
Add for expenses of melting, etc.	0.2.0.4
	——
Divide by the " Shanghai Convention," 0·98	109.1.7.2
	——
	111.4.0.0

(*N.B.*—The proper name for the Shanghai tael is " Convention Currency," referring to the convention, or understanding, by which 98 taels on the scale settle a liability of 100 taels in money of account.)

It remains to ascertain the true value of the Shanghai tael. The weight used as the basis of this is the Tsaoping tael (*v. infra*), and the equivalence is worked out as follows :

Weight on scale	100.0.0.0
Add for touch	5.6.0.0
Divide by the " Shanghai Convention," 0·98	105.6.0.0
Tsaoping taels 100 = Shanghai taels ..	107.7.5.5

The Tsaoping tael has been found to weigh 565·65 grains ; and if in 100 Tsaoping taels of pure silver there are 107.7.5.5 taels of Shanghai convention currency, then the latter will contain 525 grains of pure silver of Kuping standard. On this basis the Haikwan tael is the equivalent of 584·85 grains of pure silver ; but note has now to be taken of the quality of the silver (*v. supra*, page 167).

Introduced under the treaty of Nanking (1842), the lapse of sixty years has not sufficed to create modifications in this standard, which, moreover, is current for revenue purposes in all the ports open to foreign trade. Even with this crurency, however, this immutability has to be taken with some reservation. It seldom happens that the merchant has at hand to pay his duties the fine silver (1,000) which is, theoretically, the standard for all payments to government ; and tendering other silver, commonly the ordinary trade silver of the place, the rate at which it shall be accepted becomes a matter of arrangement with the banker ; the latter, having to account to the government for a certain weight of silver 1,000 fine, will be careful to receive an amount in other silver fully sufficient in value to cover his liability. Another element of variation, even in this currency, is the difference between the receiving and paying rates in force in all government treasuries, all banks, and with those merchants of sufficiently strong standing to make their own counting-house rules; this difference, usually between a quarter and a half of one per cent., is made not by charging a commission, but by boldly using two sets of weights, one for receiving and one for paying, and is intended to compensate for the labour of weighing ingots and lumps of silver of no fixed weight, and for the risk incurred and expert knowledge requisite for taking in silver of unknown degrees of fineness. The practice is defended on the same ground as that of the foreign exchange banks in quoting different buying and selling rates for bills of exchange.

Kuping Tael

The Kuping tael is the currency in which are collected all other dues to the government than Customs duties, excepting only those which are levied in kind (such as the grain tribute) or in copper cash. Theoretically uniform throughout the Empire, there are still differences to be observed apart from the differentiated receiving and paying rates referred to above. In one respect this tael may be considered as " bank money "—a fictitious medium of exchange from one currency to another—as when we find that (with normal exchange at 1,200 cash to the tael) 2,000 or 3,000 or 4,000 cash or more are levied where a tax, assessed in taels, is collected in cash, while the exchange is fixed at 800 cash or less where a tax, assessed in cash, is collected in silver. This, however, from another point of view, may be taken as an eccentricity of the Chinese taxing offices. The normal standard Kuping tael is 575·8 grains of silver 1,000 fine; this is the receiving rate (the paying rate being 0·2 per cent. lighter) at the Imperial Treasury, and the several provincial treasuries vary from this standard in some instances as much as one per cent.

Where the foreign obligations of the Imperial Government are concerned the equivalence of the several currencies is taken as follows :

100 Haikwan taels = 101·642335 Kuping taels.
100 Kuping taels = 109·60 Shanghai taels.

Tsaoping Tael

As the weight element of a currency tael, the Tsaoping tael is current throughout the provinces contributing tribute in kind (mainly rice) which is forwarded to the capital, either by sea or by the Grand Canal, viz. in the provinces of Kiangsi, Anhwei, Kiangsu, and Chekiang ; it is also the regular tael in use at Chefoo, on the sea route to the north, but is not known at Tientsin, the northern terminus of the Grand Canal and the port of disembarkation by the sea route. It may be stated with some degree of confidence to weigh 565·65 grains, subject always to the possibility of oscillation in the standard. While the weight is more or less constant, varying between one place and another by no more than a tenth to a half per cent. (100 Soochow Tsaoping taels = 99·90 Shanghai Tsaoping taels by weight), the tael of currency is based in different places on different standards of silver. At Chefoo the standard is 976, at Kiukiang and Wuhu 994, at Hangchow 997. In places where the standard of silver is quoted by degrees of betterness, as at Shanghai and on the lower Yangtze,* the standard for Tsaoping is 2·75 silver which, referred to a Kuping standard, is 999.

LOCAL TAELS

It may be said that every commercial place has, apart from the various government taels, its half-dozen, or dozen, or score of local taels, all generally recognised and all current ; *i.e.* each of them is a recognised currency when it

* *v. supra*, page 167).

is so stipulated, as we have seen in the case of the currencies of Chungking. Usually, however, if not generally, among these various taels there is one which is recognised as the currency of the place, in which payments would be made when there is no stipulation to the contrary, which will be commonly stipulated, and into which remittances are made from other places; for even in China the necessity is felt for some limitation on the kaleidoscopic varieties which would otherwise perplex the minds of even Chinese bankers. Sometimes, but by no means generally, this recognised local tael will extend its influence over the surrounding country within a limited radius; but ordinarily the right of even the country banker to live is fully recognised, and every place is privileged to adopt its own standards. I have notes of 170 well-recognised and different currencies, gathered mainly from the treaty ports and their immediate vicinity.

Peking Taels

The capital, Peking, is one place, it may be said the one place of importance, in which no one currency has emerged as the one local tael. Being the capital, the Kuping tael is of course much in evidence as the currency of all official government transactions. Besides this there are three standards of tael weight—the Kung-fa of 555·7 grains, the Market of 552·4 grains, and the Metropolitan or Two-tael * scale of 541·7 grains—and two recognised standards of silver, 1,000 and 980 fine respectively. Each standard of weight (except the Kuping) is expressed in each of the two standards of silver, with the result that there are at Peking seven taels all equally current. The foreign banks established there have within a few years past adopted the Kung-fa tael of 1,000 silver as their currency of account. Each of these currencies, except the Kuping

* The addition of 2 taels in the hundred, 2 per cent., will bring this to the value of the Market tael; hence probably the name.

and Kung-fa, is further subject to a difference of o·6 to o·9 per cent. according as it is " equalised " or " empty " or " mercantile " or " complete " ; thus 100 Kung-fa taels are equivalent to Metropolitan taels 102·80 if mercantile, 102·70 if empty, 102·60 if equalised, but only 102·00 if complete.

Tientsin Taels

At Tientsin I have note of nine taels generally known, and two standards to which silver is reduced. Of these, the tael which for forty years past has been recognised as " the Tientsin tael " is the Merchants tael weighing 557·4 grains of silver 992 fine. For some occult reason there has lately (since 1900) been introduced a " New Merchants " tael of 557·6 grains, differing from the old established local tael by only 0·00038 part of itself or less than $\frac{4}{100}$ of one per cent., the standard of silver remaining the same ; this new tael has not yet worked its way into general acceptance. As an illustration of the ordinary Chinese rough-and-ready methods of banking it may be noted that the true equivalence of Haikwan Tls.100 is Tientsin Tls.105·215 ; and that for fifty years, in paying Customs duties, for every 100 Haikwan taels Chinese merchants paid Tientsin Tls.106, foreign merchants in general paid Tientsin Tls.105, and Russian merchants for tea paid Tientsin Tls.104. A further complication was added in 1908, as shown by the following extract from the report on the trade of Tientsin for that year :

" Since the year 1900 the standard of the sycee current in the port has been steadily deteriorating, and the touch, supposed to be ·992, has fallen as low as ·965. Matters came to a crisis in February 1908, by the issue on the part of the Taotai of a notification to the effect that, it being stipulated by treaty that duties should be paid in pure silver, from the 1st March duties would have to be paid at the equivalent of Hangping Tls.107 for Haikwan Tls.100, instead of the Hangping Tls.105 paid theretofore. A protest from all the foreign merchants resulted, and was followed by a further notification, on the 28th September 1908, to the effect that the previous notification was cancelled and that thereafter duties could be paid at Hangping Tls.105 = Haikwan Tls.100; but that all duties must be paid in Kungku silver. This gave rise to further difficulty, as the foreign banks were possessed only of current sycee and would not honour a cheque marked ' Kungku silver.' Merchants have thus been put to great inconvenience in 'paying duty, having either to pay in sycee or purchase a native order at a premium from one of the six melting shops licensed by the Assay Office. The position is briefly this : the Chinese authorities hold that merchants are bound by treaty to pay duty in pure silver and that they must do so whatever be the standard of the local currency ; the merchants, on the other hand, claim that the authorities are responsible for the depreciation in the currency, and that they should bear the loss occasioned thereby."

Hankow Tael

At Hankow one tael stands out above the rest as " the Hankow tael " ; and, though the triple city at Hankow is a great commercial emporium not created by foreign trade, this is the " Foreign rule " tael, weighing 554·7 grains, of " Foreign rule " silver 967 fine.

Canton Tael

At Canton, and for a considerable area commercially tributary to it, extending beyond the limits of the province of Kwangtung, the standard tael is the Sze-ma tael, weighing 579·85 grains, being the heaviest mercantile tael in the Empire ; silver was originally, and is now in theory, reduced to the standard of 1,000 fine. This sounds as if we had here a departure from the prevailing diversity of currency, and could point to a tael, uniform in weight and value, not confined to one city, but current through a large commercial area. The bankers must, however, be reckoned with ; and, both in Canton and throughout the whole area, while we find the Sze-ma to be the standard of weight, it is usually varied by being subject to discounts, fixed for each sub-standard, but supplying that variability which is demanded for all transfers in China from place to place, from bank to bank, or from account to account. These sub-standards are known by the per-mill proportion to the Sze-ma standard ; and I have note of taels of the 998, 996, 995, 993, 992, 990, 988, and 986 scale, being respectively 0·2, 0·4, 0·5, 0·7, 0·8, 1·0, 1·2, and 1·4 per cent. lighter than standard Sze-ma in weight. Formerly the silver was always taken as 1,000 fine, but in the last half-century dollars, mainly Mexican, more or less battered and chopped, have entirely supplanted ingots ; for large transactions payment is always made by weight, and never by count. The result is a curious medley, it being always necessary to express clearly if the tael is of " foreign silver " (900 fine) or of " pure silver " ; in the latter case payment is effected by the rough-and-ready method of weighing out 10 per cent. additional of the dollar silver. The question is even further complicated by a practice, which has crept in of recent years, of making 20 per cent. of payments in subsidiary silver coins (800 fine), with perhaps some bargaining as to whether the proportion shall be 15 or 25 per cent. Here we have a case of degeneration within the memory of men now living. Disregarding any question of what constitutes " pure silver," a tael containing 579·85 grains of fine silver becomes one of 574·1 grains, and ultimately one of 561·4 grains ; and, as there is a tendency now (1906) to substitute 20-cent pieces entirely for dollars, the tael is on the way to become one containing 510·3 grains of fine silver. These figures are all subject to proportionate reduction for each of the various sub-standards of weight.

12

Shanghai Tael

I come now to the consideration of the currency at Shanghai, the commercial metropolis of China. Omitting the government and other exceptional taels, I must first note the exclusive use of the Canton standard (tael = 579·85 grains) for dealings in foreign bar silver ; a practice originating when foreign trade was centred at Canton and continued when the foreign banks and merchants brought Cantonese as their first compradors and shroffs to Shanghai, has been sanctified by use and by the ingrained habit of introducing, whenever possible, further elements of conversion into all dealings with the precious metals. Then the Tsaoping tael, described above, is fully current and fully recognised at Shanghai and in a large area around, and is the ordinary currency for Chinese remittances through Chinese banks to places in China, *e.g.* a remittance to Hankow is converted from " Shanghai taels " to Tsaoping taels and thence to " Hankow taels." Finally the legitimate banking and trading currency of the place is the " Shanghai tael " or " Shanghai convention currency," which is also the standard of international exchange for the trade of North China and the Yangtze basin, all other quotations in local currencies being re-conversions from the rate for Shanghai currency. The rate of the day is accepted by merchants as the rate of conversion between two fixed currencies ; and yet, if we take exchange on London as an example, one of the currencies stands for the immutable in finance, while in the other it is doubtful if many of the foreign merchants who so blindly base their operations on this exchange quotation could go into the treasury of a Chinese bank and weigh out for themselves a Shanghai tael, assuming even that they could read the inscriptions on the weights they used. The value of the Shanghai tael is made up of three elements—the weight, the quality of silver, and a convention. The weight on the scale is the Tsaoping tael of 565·65 grains, the silver is reduced to a standard of 944 fine on the Kuping basis of 1,000 fine, and the convention is that 98 taels of this weight and this silver settle a liability of 100 taels "Shanghai convention currency." In order fully to understand what is a Shanghai tael, how it may be ascertained, and what may be done with it when once ascertained, let us consider the processes to be gone through in an exchange operation under present conditions. Of course, in Shanghai as in London, the merchant will ordinarily draw his cheque, against which the bank will give him its bill of exchange ; but somewhere, and some time, there will be a cash transaction ; and thoroughly to understand the situation we must see what, in Shanghai, corresponds to the act of a London merchant who takes a thousand sovereigns to the bank and gets a draft on Paris for 25,150 *f.* or 25,175 *f.* according to the exchange. Let us assume the simple case where our Shanghai merchant wishes to remit the contents of a box full of silver (if he wishes to make up an exact sum in Shanghai currency, certain complications are added). The silver in the box will be in the shape of "shoes" of "sycee" of about 50 taels each, and of varying "touch" (degrees of fineness). If these shoes are marked, in ink, with the results of a previous assay at the Assay Office for the Foreign Settlement, the preliminary stage becomes unnecessary ; but if they have come in the course of trade from another port, or if their last previous assay was made by the Assay Office for the Chinese City, then all existing marks are washed off and the silver must be sent to the proper office. Here each shoe is weighed and the result written on one side ; it is then "touched" and the difference (usually an addition) from a certain standard, as indicated by the colour on the touchstone, is written on the other side. This difference for touch is so much for the shoe irrespective of its exact weight, which is anything between 49 and 54 taels, but an allowance of 0·05 tael is added for each tael by which the weight of the shoe exceeds 50 taels ; thus if the quality of the silver is 2·70, the addition for a shoe weighing 49·75 or one of 50·05 taels is 2·70, for one of 51·25 taels is 2·75, for one of 52·15 taels is 2·80, and so on. Let us take two such shoes weighing 50 and 51 taels and having 2·60 and 2·40 respectively added for touch, making for the two 50 + 2·60 + 51 + 2·40 = 106·00; this result, divided by 0·98 (the Shanghai " convention "), gives 108·163 as the number of Shanghai taels in our two shoes. If the transaction is one in Shanghai currency only, this ends it, the whole operation corresponding to the single action of the London merchant who takes £108 3s. 4d. from his cash to pay a bill; but we have now to connect this with foreign exchange. First, it is to be noted that at the present day no other currency is used at Shanghai, all others being actually moneys of account, which, in making payment, require first to be reduced to Shanghai taels. The government, for example, in making payments for indebtedness or indemnity, does not use the Kuping (" Treasury ") tael weights or the pure silver (1,000 fine), which make up the Kuping tael currency, but pays in Shanghai currency at the rate of 109·60, calculated as follows :

Kuping taels 100 weight = Tsaoping taels ..	101·800
Add for touch of pure silver on two shoes ..	5·600
	107·400
Divide by the " convention " 0·98	109·592
Add for meltage fee	·008
	109·600

So with Customs duties, merchants pay in Shanghai taels at the fixed rate 111·40 and never tender the " Haikwan tael-weight of pure silver " specified by treaty.

Coming now to the exchange operation, we have first to find our parity of exchange, and to do this we must get the equivalence in foreign notation. The weight used for Shanghai currency is the Tsaoping tael, and this is 565·65 grains ; for pure silver the addition for touch is 2·8 per shoe, which the Chinese treat as if it were 5·6 per cent. ; and the " convention " is 0·98. One Tsaoping tael of pure silver is, therefore, 1·07755 Shanghai tael; and one Shanghai tael contains 524·93 grains of fine silver. In one ounce of silver British Standard (0·925) are 444 grains of fine silver, or 84·6 per cent. of the amount in the Shanghai tael; and to get the parity of exchange for the latter the London price of bar silver must be divided by 0·846.* The actual rate of exchange is, of course, affected by the demand and supply of bills wanted and offered, but in the great and frequent fluctuations in the value of silver bullion we have an ever-present element of instability which must be taken into account. Our Shanghai merchant, who has once gone through such a series of manipulations and calculations, is likely to consider his time of too much value to repeat the transaction, and, as is actually the case, will leave such operations in future to his comprador, until such time as he is put on the same footing as his London brother.

Newchwang Transfer Money

One currency practice, recalling the " bank money " of the old Amsterdamsche Wisselbank, must be referred to. At Newchwang the local tael is 555·1 grains of silver 992 fine. Except of copper there is (or, as the war may have caused a change, has been) little of the metals in circulation, silver being commonly deposited at the banks, which permit withdrawal only on the first days of the third, sixth, ninth, and twelfth months, but allow transfers from account to account. This "transfer money" is exclusively used in the settlement of all mercantile transactions. On deposit, and for renewal on each quarter day, the depositor is credited with a premium which varies with the demand for money, but which, in ordinary peaceful times, ranges from 0·20 to 6 per cent. Exchange quotations also are always quoted

---

* Subject to modification by consideration of the true standard of quality of silver (*v. supra*, page 167).

in transfer money, not in hard silver.   An ordinary exchange operation would be as follows :

Silver deposited, Newchwang taels	..	100·00
Premium on deposit, 1·60 per shoe	..	3·00
Transfer money credited .. .. ,.		103·00
Exchange premium 3¼ per cent.		3·35
Shanghai taels		106·35

It may be noted that the parity of exchange is 100 Newchwang taels of silver = 104·89 Shanghai taels.   The rates of premium given above are, as has been stated, those of ordinary conditions ; the effect of the stress of war on the money market and the financial position of the bankers may be seen from the quotations of the last day of 1904 : Silver Tls.1,000 = Transfer-money Tls.1,358·50 (quoted Tls.72 per shoe) ; Transfer Tls.1,000 = Shanghai Tls.785.

These figures show the banker protecting his reserves, apparently giving 36 per cent. premium for deposits and charging 22 per cent. discount for withdrawals instead of giving a premium.   This works out to a rate of exchange for cash transactions, however, of Newchwang Tls.100 = Shanghai Tls.105·65.

INTRODUCTION OF FOREIGN COINS

A foreigner, as an individual, objects to carrying around in his pocket a 4-lb.lump of silver which he cannot subdivide, and he equally objects to carrying 6 lb. weight of coppers as the only fractional equivalent of the silver dollar to which he is accustomed ; he also objects to ignorance of the quality of the silver which he will take from his pocket to make minor payments.   All this seems axiomatic to people at home, but it is necessary to state the axiom in order to explain why foreign coins have been introduced into China.

In the north and in Mid-China these coins have remained the housekeeping currency of the foreigner, never having been admitted into the trade of the Chinese, and the foreigner is made to pay for his luxury of a coin in which he can have confidence. The same weight in a coin (the silver dollar) with the same inscription is worth at Shanghai from 3 per cent. to 5 per cent. more than at Canton, whether the value is expressed in gold, in silver taels, or in commodities ; but at Shanghai the coin remains as it came from the mint, and at Canton it is chopped. In the south the quicker-witted Cantonese and Fukienese have accepted the foreign coin, but have done so in a peculiarly Chinese manner. A coin is an officially guaranteed weight of a certain metal ; the Chinese accept that for what it is worth, but the first banker or merchant into whose hands the foreign coin comes " chops " it with an impressed ideogram about an eighth of an inch square, thereby giving the tradesman and the private individual his certificate of *bona fides* of the guaranteeing government. This is repeated by each succeeding banker, until in the end the chopped dollar resembles **a** disc, or rather a cup, of hammered silver work.

Foreign Dollars

The first dollar to be introduced was the Carolus (Spanish) dollar, also called the " Pillar " dollar from its design—the Pillars of Hercules. This for many years was the only foreign coin accepted by the Chinese ; and a curious survival of its former vogue is seen at Wuhu, on the Yangtze, where the few remaining unchopped specimens of the eighteenth and early nineteenth century, estimated not to exceed 400,000 in all, form a favourite medium of exchange and command a premium generally of 30 or even 40 per cent. over their intrinsic value. For fully eighty years the dollars of Charles IV (A.D. 1788–1808) have commanded a premium of at least 30 per cent., but not those of his predecessor or his successor, and originally over a considerable area of country from Canton to the Yangtze. On the introduction of the Mexican dollar, sixty years ago, it was readily accepted at Canton and the Carolus was " demonetised." At Shanghai, however, and in the Yangtze basin the Carolus held its own and was the sole currency of the foreign banks and merchants and for the sale of imports and purchase of exports and for exchange quotations. The ravages of the Taiping rebellion restricted the consumption of imports, and notwithstanding increased importations of Carolus dollars, collected from all parts of the world, they were soon driven to a premium, which by 1855 amounted to 50 per cent., and in 1856 to over 80 per cent. of their intrinisic value; and the curious spectacle was seen of exchange quoted at Canton at 4s. 11d. per dollar (Mexican) and on the same day at Shanghai at 7s. 9d. per dollar (Carolus). The situation became intolerable, and on a fixed day merchants' accounts at the banks were transferred, *unit for unit*, from a currency (the Carolus) containing 374½ grains of fine silver, to a currency (the Shanghai tael) containing nominally 525 grains of fine silver per unit. A Carolus dollar lies before me as I write, bought in Wuhu in 1906 for 1·40 Mexican dollar. With a diameter of 1·56 inch, it weighs 26·08 grammes = 402·5 grains, over 3 per cent. lighter than a full-weight Mexican dollar. On the obverse it bears the King's head wreathed with laurel and the inscription .1808. CAROLUS. IIII. DEI. GRATIA. On the reverse is a shield quartered with the arms of Castille and Leon, countercharged with three fleurs-de-lys, the shield surmounted by an Imperial crown and standing between two columns (the Pillars of Hercules) bearing a scroll inscribed PLUS ULTRA ; the inscription reads .HISPAN. ET IND. REX. M̊. 8 R. T.H. The milling is as usual and the reeding -o-o-o-. The obverse is stamped in black with a design having a Chinese character in the middle, constituting the guarantee of some Chinese banker. In Formosa * the chopped Carolus remained the ordinary currency at its intrin-

* Two and a quarter million of these dollars were imported at Tamsui in 1895 for the tea season.

sic valuation up to the time of the Japanese occupation in 1895. The next to be accepted was the Mexican, called by Chinese the " Eagle " dollar from its design—an eagle grasping a cactus in its talons. This has never been displaced from popular estimation, though various attempts have been made. Thirty years ago an American " trade dollar " was introduced, but the wisdom of Congress decreed that it should displace its rival by its weight—420 grains instead of the 416 grains of the Mexican ; the natural result, when these two coins were put into circulation side by side among this shrewd people, was that the heavier coin went at once into the melting-pot. The Japanese dollar (the yen) followed, and attained a moderate degree of popularity, but the establishment of a gold basis for this coin put an end to its issue as a monometallic silver coin. The later British and French trade dollars have not met with any great degree of success, except perhaps since the outbreak of the Russo-Japanese war.

CHINESE DOLLARS AND SUBSIDIARY COINAGE

The Chinese themselves have seen the utility of coins and have established large plants for minting at several of the provincial capitals. Their time-honoured copper coins, cast from moulds, are crude productions ; but the fine stamped copper cash, which were the first product of the mints, met with no favour ; and, as their issue involved a loss to the government, it was not continued. The mints then turned their attention to the dollar, and many millions of these coins were turned out. These Chinese dollars were not freely received for taxes, and when taken were accepted by weight, and not by count ; they had not the prestige of the Mexican, but had only a provincial guarantee, and outside the province of issue circulated only at a discount ; they would have disturbed, had they any vitality, the calculations of money-changers ; they gave no seigniorage to the mint ; and of late years the annual output has been thousands instead of millions. The energy of the mints has in recent years been devoted to the issue of subsidiary coinage. First 10-cent and 20-cent pieces, which, consisting of silver 800 fine, while the dollar was 900 fine, could be sold from the mint at 110 cents for the dollar and still show a profit ; these pieces became popular with the smaller money-changers because of the margin between the rate of issue and the intrinsic value, and because of the petty speculation permitted by, the margin of value. Then followed the copper cent which is now the popular coin, since it has an exchange value greater than the hundredth part of a dollar, and the money-changer, who makes his profit from the depreciated silver coinage, will make it also from appreciated copper coin. The tourist who draws on his letter of credit at a foreign bank in Shanghai, having to receive so many dollars and so many (say 74) cents, for the odd cents will be given 70 cents in depreciated silver, but for the 4 cents he will receive 3 copper cents and 2 copper cash, since by the exchange of the day 32 cash are the equivalent of four-hundredths of a dollar. I leave the last two sentences as they were written in 1905, in order to show how great has been the depreciation in this coin. Twelve months later, in July 1906, the tourist still received his 70 cents in depreciated silver, but for the 4 cents he was no longer given 3 copper cents and 2 cash, but received 4 copper cents—actually worth $0·0357.

General Considerations

In China the currency is at the top a weight pure and simple, in the middle a combination of weight and token currency, and at the bottom a coin which stands on its own feet, and neither receives support from nor absolutely gives it to any other unit in the series. At the top is the tael (call it the " ounce," and it will be better realised), in which payments are made in precisely the same way that delivery is taken of a lot of silver bars. Then comes the dollar, which, though a coin, is nowhere legal tender, and of which the specimens from the Chinese mints are inscribed, not generally dollar or "yuen," but merely 72 hundredths of a tael; though so inscribed, dollars of silver are nowhere fixed in terms of taels of silver, but are quoted at rates which vary from day to day according to the demand and supply, fluctuating within a range of six or more per cent. Then come subsidiary silver coins fractional to the dollar but subject to a fluctuating rate of exchange such that the dollar may this year change for 110 cents and next year for only 95 cents in small coin. Next comes the copper cent, inscribed at the mints of some provinces as worth " one-hundredth of a dollar," and of others as worth " ten cash," but never treated as correlated to the dollar ; whether considered in its relation to the dollar or to the cash, it is a token coin worth intrinsically less than half its nominal value. Last comes the copper cash, the currency of the people. Into this series of non-related currencies, each unit of which is in a state of unstable equilibrium, fixed neither in itself nor in relation to other units, China is now required to introduce system and uniformity and to give a legal tender character to any coin or currency which she may adopt, while the inborn disposition of her people is to accept no coin and no currency as legal tender, but to make them all accept the lowly cash the subject of barter. Where shall she begin ? Is she to take her fundamental coin, the cash, with a present-day value of the ten-thousandth part of a pound sterling, and build upon it ? This seems the natural course to those who consider first the well-being of her patient, industrious people, whose householders maintain their families on sixpence a day, and through the existence of this mite of a mite are enabled to maintain them in comfort. Or shall she consider first the broader interests of her international exchanges and of the powerful body of bankers and merchants active in the distribution of goods through the Empire ?

Multiply what has been written above a hundredfold, and some idea will be conceived of the currency question in China. To reform it would naturally appear no more difficult than

to introduce the metric system into England ; it should even
have behind it a greater weight of popular support in proportion as the simplification of the currency of four hundred
millions should give ten times greater relief than the simplification of the measures of forty millions. This presupposes
that the four hundred millions are crying for relief, but we
must first see who it is that call for currency reform. The
foreign merchant stands in the first place, with his crying
need for fixity of exchange between gold and silver, which
requires for its establishment a fixed unit of currency, which
in turn can only be attained by coinage. That he will also
be freed from bondage to his comprador does not appeal
to him, since he is unlikely to realise their relative positions,
and the activity of his advocacy will be weakened by so
much ; moreover, there are in China less than a thousand
firms of European and American nationality, even including
the protected races, such as those from British India, and
including branch firms. Then come the foreign banks,
ten in number ; they *may* consider that their profits from
rapid fluctuations in exchange, of the causes of which they
have prior knowledge, will be made good by the development
of legitimate trade resulting from certainty of exchange ;
and they *may* set against their profits from changing funds
from one standard of currency to another their newly
acquired ability to keep their own treasuries. The government of China will welcome any measure which will set a
limit to the amount which it must take from its revenues to
pay the indemnities due to the Foreign Powers ; and, as a
corporate entity, may be willing to have a uniform currency
in which the revenue may be paid and received. No other
element of support can be brought in by any flight of the
imagination. All the vested interests in China will be against
the change. The members of the Government as individuals,
from the highest Minister of State in Peking to the humblest
assistant-deputy sub-district magistrate, will give it their
tacit, if not openly-expressed opposition. The tax-collector,
with his assistants and his servants, and backed by his family

in all its many branches, will fight strenuously against any obligation to pay into the Treasury the exact coin which he has received from the taxpayer. The powerful body of Chinese bankers, organised as such when Europe did not yet know the science, will accept the change only if they are shown the possibility of greater profits than under existing conditions. The compradors and shroffs may be trusted to do their best to resist any attempt to curtail their privileges and profits. Even the native merchants and tradesmen, who will benefit enormously by simplification of the currency, will also oppose a change from the present system, in which each man counts confidently on getting the better in the encounter of wits. Ordinarily the proletariat remains neutral in such a question; but in China the merest coolie, earning sixpence by a long day of hard work, will spend an hour of his time to gain on exchange the equivalent of ten minutes' work.

CHAPTER VI

WEIGHTS AND MEASURES

WHILE the currency of the Empire is in a state of confusion, it is at the same time regulated by, and in the interest of, the bankers and money-changers, trained in their profession for many centuries. The state of the weights and measures is, however, chaos itself, and the amount of regulation applied to it is infinitesimal. In this country of weak application of the governmental function and of widely democratic organisation, the trader uses as a matter of course the differentiated measures which are illegal in modernised countries, buying with a long or heavy measure and selling with a short or light measure ; and the only interference by government takes the form of an Imperial edict at an interval of perhaps a century, or an occasional proclamation which is disregarded as soon as the rain has washed the ink. The gilds make some attempt to preserve a local uniformity in the measures accepted by themselves, but they have no official function, and their efforts are mainly directed to secure open dealing between their own members, their motto being that of the New York statesman, "The public be damned." In this chaos, however, some conventions must be recognised if trade is to go on, and fixed theoretic standards can be found ; but it may be said at once that in any place every trade has its own standard, and that the trade standards of one place are not the same as those of other places.

The English peoples are in a position to understand, better than any others, the theoretic system—the tables of weights and measures—prevailing in China, having themselves a system in which the various measures have no common inter-relation, and of which the tables in use in the United Kingdom and the United States proceed on no one notation, but skip lightly from dozens to scores, from sevens to fours, from a decimal to a duodecimal notation. In this last respect the Chinese are wiser, and with two exceptions base their tables on a purely decimal notation ; but in their disregard of any common relation between the different measures, they are on the same footing as ourselves.

While in theory their tables are based generally on a decimal notation, the Chinese would not be Chinese if, in applying this theory to practice, they did not make some differences, perfectly recognised and accepted as the custom of the trade and place. Thus the table gives 100 kin (catty) as making 1 tan (picul) ; but at Amoy the picul of indigo is 110 catties, of white sugar 95 catties, and of brown sugar 94 catties ; of rice the picul at Shanghai is 100 catties, at Amoy 140 catties, and at Foochow 180 catties ; for tribute rice the stipulated picul is 120 catties, but at Nanking it is 140 catties. These are enough to illustrate this form of irregularity ; but generally the purpose of this chapter is to consider only the standards accepted at each place by the gilds concerned.

WEIGHT

As in England and America 16· ounces make 1 pound, in China 16 liang (tael) make 1 kin (catty), constituting one of the two exceptions to the purely decimal system ; then 100 catties make 1 picul. In practice quantities of ordinary commodities are usually, and in exact accounts invariably, stated in the single unit of catty, even when the amount is millions ; and for valuable articles, such as musk, in taels, even to the amount of thousands. The catty generally known to foreigners is that imposed by treaty as the weight to be used for levy of Customs duty, 21⅓ ounces avoirdupois, as stipulated by the British treaty, 604·53 grammes as stipulated by the French treaty, the two differing by 0·4 gramme or 6 grains. This is a purely arbitrary standard imposed by, or on, the foreign merchant, and accepted because it was a round figure approximating closely to the merchants' standard prevailing at Canton, actually weighing 21·21 ounces avoirdupois, with which the English trader first came in touch, and which a hundred years ago he used in buying his tea and silk. At Canton and in its vicinity there are other standards, by which the catty ranges from 19·68 to 22·06 ounces. In the trade area of Shanghai there is a standard for the use of Chinese in their foreign dealings by which the catty is 20·4 ounces, while the regular gild catty is 18·6 ounces ; the Soochow gild catty is 19·7 ounces, that for rice paid as Imperial tribute is 20·6 ounces, while that for the sale of oil is 23·2 ounces and for sugar is 27·25 ounces. At Hangchow there are seventeen different standards, ranging from 16 to 24 ounces, all equally recognised in their respective trades ; and throughout the Empire catties are known, ranging from 12 to 42·5 ounces.

CAPACITY

The Chinese table of capacity gives sixteen decimal divisions, down to $\frac{1}{1,000,000,000,000,000}$th part, of the shih ; those in common use are the tow ($\frac{1}{10}$), sheng ($\frac{1}{100}$), and ko ($\frac{1}{1000}$). Measures of capacity are seldom used except for rice and grain, and these are ordinarily sold wholesale by weight ; fluids, such as oil, spirits, molasses, etc., are almost invariably sold by weight. Grain tribute is assessed on the tax note by measures of capacity, but is generally collected by weight at a rate of conversion fixed by the collectors, when it is not collected in money at rates also fixed by the collectors. The tow (which we may call peck) for tribute contains 629 cubic inches (10·31 litres), but in different parts of the Empire different standards of tow exist ranging from 176 all the way to 1,800 cubic inches.

LENGTH

The table of length is divided decimally down to the $\frac{1}{10,000,000}$th part of a foot, and goes up to 10 feet = 1 chang. The foreign merchant knows as the unit of length the chih, commonly called "foot," imposed by treaty, accepted by the Customs for the measurement of cloth, and measuring 14·1 English inches ; this finds no exact counterpart at Canton, where the carpenter's foot is 13·8 inches and the tailor's foot is 14·8 inches. Land is sometimes measured by a special standard, but usually throughout China by the carpenter's foot : Canton is divided into two magistracies (hsien) by a line running through the middle of the city ; on the west of this line, land is measured by a foot of 14·7 inches, and on the east by a foot of 14·8 inches, which is the tailor's foot of Canton. At Shanghai the tailor's foot is 13·85 inches and the carpenter's foot is 11·1 inches ; the official land foot is 12·1 inches, but the foot in ordinary use for transfers of land is 13·2 inches. At Nanking the carpenter's foot is 12·6 inches, but the foot for measurement of timber is 13·5 inches. At Soochow the tailor's foot is 13·45 inches, but that used for the measurement of cloth is 11·1 inches. At Shiuhing carpenters use a foot of 14 inches, but masons working on the same building use a foot of 13·6 inches, and flooring tiles are made by a foot of 11·1 inches. These instances of inconsistency might be amplified indefinitely ; suffice it to say that in China local standards of the foot range from 8·6 to 27·8 inches.

DISTANCE

The Chinese do not much trouble themselves with the accurate measurement of distance, and would sympathise fully with the Dutch measurement of canalboat-runs by the number of pipes smoked. A theoretic unit exists, the li, measuring 1,800 of the land foot ; but, as the latter varies throughout the Empire, so would the li vary, if any

13

one cared to measure it. Based on a foot of 14·1 English inches it would measure 705 yards, or four-tenths of a statute mile. In practice it is one-hundredth of the distance a laden porter will cover in a day of ten hours marching ; on the plain this would represent a third of a mile, a half-kilometre, more or less, but in hilly country it varies considerably. By Chinese reckoning, if it is 50 li to the top of Mount Washington, returning by the same road to the same point the distance may be 25 li ; and similarly a mountain may be spoken of as 100 miles high—by road.

AREA

The table of area is purely decimal, the unit, the mow, being divided down to the $\frac{1}{10,000,000}$th part ; 100 mow make a ching. In the calculation of the mow occurs the second of the two departures from the decimal system in China : it is 240 square " paces " or " bows," each bow being 5 feet long, and is therefore 6,000 square land feet ; but as the land foot varies, so does the mow vary. The " customary " mow at Shanghai is exactly one-sixth of an English acre (7,260 square feet, English) ; but throughout the Empire the mow varies from 3,840 to 9,964, with one standard of 18,148 English square feet.

To give further details of all the vagaries of the measures of China would take a volume, but enough has been written to indicate in some degree the variability of what are held to be standards, and the mental attitude of those on whom it is sought to impose uniformity. The example of other countries may be cited, where order has been evolved from chaos and uniformity from diversity, but it must be remembered that China is not one country, it is a dozen ; it is a continent, with the population and the diversity of a continent, with the inborn habit of centuries to stereotype the minds of the people, and with the natural stubbornness of an old civilisation to resist all change.

CHAPTER VII

EXTRATERRITORIALITY

THE privilege of extraterritoriality was, thirty years ago, and even less, more commonly referred to as exterritoriality. Of these terms Sir Francis Piggott * says :

" The words ' exterritoriality ' and ' extraterritoriality ' are treated by some writers as identical ; by others as indicating, the first the privilege of Ambassadors and their suites, the second the Treaty privilege under which Consular jurisdiction has been established in the East. Both these privileges are, however, more correctly described as ' exterritorial ' ; the condition of those to whom they are accorded as ' exterritoriality.' On the other hand the government of the privileged persons by their own authorities from home is ' extraterritorial.' "

Notwithstanding this dictum the orotund forms extra-territorial-ity-ised have prevailed and are now applied to governors and governed alike. This chapter is intended to explain how the exceptional privilege originated, and the manner of its working.

In the earliest times the traveller was protected by no law ; the Tyrian voyager along the coasts of the Mediterranean secured only such rights as he could buy or enforce, but he neither carried with him his own law nor was he entitled to claim the protection of the law of those among whom he sojourned. With the extension of the Roman dominion the *pax Romana* spread, and every citizen travelling

* " Exterritoriality," by F. T. Piggott, 1892.

195

was under the ægis of the *jus Romanum* ; the principle
established was that the Roman elsewhere than in Rome was
extraterritorialised—he was not required to submit to the
territorial laws of the " foreign " country, but remained
outside them and continued to enjoy the protection of his
own laws.   As an echo of this privilege we find that in the
Constitution of A.D. 824 imposed upon the people of Rome
by Lothair, acting as vicegerent for his father, Lewis the
Pious, each inhabitant of the city was required to choose the
code—Roman, Frankish, or Lombard—by which he wished
to live, and was then judged according to the law selected.
The underlying principle is obvious.   It was recognised as
inequitable that, for example, the Frank, who was entitled
by his native law to compound for a homicide by payment
of weregeld, should by the accident of residence in what,
though the capital of the Empire, was still to him a foreign
city, be compelled to submit to what would appear to him
the cruel and vindictive penalty of death ; and while he
wished to preserve for himself his own law, he did not wish
to impose it on the Roman people or on the Lombards who
less than a century before had been masters of the city.
The Frank in Rome was fully extraterritorialised. but of
Rome the Frank was titular sovereign.

Edward I of England in 1303 granted his Carta
Mercatoria to foreign merchants resident in London, assign-
ing to them, in exchange for an increase in customs duties,
many valuable privileges for the furtherance of their trade.
Among them one clause provided that, in any suit between
a foreigner and a native, the jury should be drawn, six from
the men of London, and six from the men of the same
town as the foreigner party to the suit.

When the West first met the East on equal terms at
shorter range than a lance's length, it was found that their
laws were incompatible : that no Venetian or Genoese, the
pioneers in commerce in those days, would willingly or could
in reason be expected to submit himself to Moslem law,
based on the stern requirements of the Koran ; and that no

follower of the Prophet could yield obedience to a code whose leading exponent was the Pope. There was no thought of requiring either to conform to the law of the other ; as between one country of Europe and another the *lex loci* might be applied, but to assimilate the legal procedure of two diverse civilisations was the mingling of oil and vinegar. The question was one-sided, since no Moslem ever strayed from the fold, and the Padishah settled it off-hand by bidding the Giaours judge, control, and protect their own nationals according to their own customs. While the trading states were weak and the Moslem power strong, the *imperium in imperio* thus created caused no more trouble than the old protection which the Roman citizen carried with him everywhere ; but in the course of years the Turkish realm lost its old-time force, the more powerfully organised nations of Europe entered the field, and the obligation of extraterritoriality became a right, claimed by all strong enough to enforce it, enjoyed by all in the comity of nations, and duly sanctioned by the Capitulations signed with each Power. These are the Charter of extraterritoriality in the Turkish Empire and in the states now or formerly vassal to it.

At first the natural assumption was that the traveller carried his law with him, in so far as he was entitled to the protection of any law ; but by degrees, in the history of those countries whose government is based on law and not on the will of the governors, law became paramount, and the law of the locality was never set aside to pleasure a chance visitor. This is now the rule, the Capitulations in Turkey being merely survivals of the Middle Ages. When the European first came to the Far East, he had no thought that he was entitled to carry his law with him, and submission to the *lex loci* was merely an incident in his adventurous career, duly provided for in his profit and loss account. The Black Hole of Calcutta was typical of the treatment likely to be accorded to the English anywhere in India at the time, when once removed from the protection of the British flag ; the Portuguese in China enjoyed life, liberty, and the pursuit of happiness only on condition of remaining safely in the tiny peninsula of Macao ; and the Dutch in Japan, cooped up in Desima, were allowed to monopolise a profitable trade, but were otherwise subject to the whims of the Japanese. At the opening of the nineteenth century the English and Americans resident in China were restricted to the " Factory " or trading post of Canton, privileged for exercise to walk a hundred paces in one direction and then a hundred paces in the other. They were in general well treated, since the trade so profitable to them was equally profitable to the Chinese, and were not molested so long as they were law-abiding—but law-abiding in the sense of abiding by the law of China. It was irksome to them to have no lawyer to instruct them in the law of the land, to have no fixed and certain law to appeal to, to be doubtful of the application of the law to any particular case, and to have no doubt whatever on the course likely to be followed by the administrators of the law ; but this was all an incident of their position, and the rapid accumulation of fortune enabled them to shake the dust of the country from their shoes after a very short stay. So the position was endured, and the *lex loci* submitted to, probably, from what we know of the English and American character, with many murmurs but without overt opposition.

It is no part of my purpose to describe the state of the prisons of China or the methods by which testimony and confession are elicited, nor to demonstrate the insistent need to the Chinese people of the article in King John's Magna Carta, " To no man will we deny or sell justice." The incompatibility of laws based on diverse civilisations is nowhere more marked than in China. There no bankruptcy law is possible : if a debtor's own estate will not suffice to pay his debts, the deficiency must be made good by his father, brothers, or uncles ; if a debtor absconds, his immediate family are promptly imprisoned ; if the debtor returns, he is put in prison and kept there indefinitely, so long as he can find money for his daily food, until released by payment in full or by death : this is the law. When in 1895 Admiral Ting found himself forced to surrender Weihaiwei and his fleet, he committed suicide ; by this courageous step, technically dying before surrender, he saved his immediate family—father, mother, sons, and daughters—from decapitation, and their property from confiscation, the penalty when a commander surrenders an Imperial fortress : this is the law. When in the old days an English gunner caused the death of a Chinese by firing a salute from a cannon from which, by oversight, the ball had not been removed, he was seized, tried, and executed ; and in 1839, when in the course of a disturbance with English and American sailors at Canton a Chinese was killed, the authorities demanded that, if the guilty person could not be detected and executed, the whole party should be handed over for execution : this is the law. Intention is never taken into account. A dollar for a dollar, an eye for an eye, a life for a life, and all for the Emperor and his representatives : this is the law of China. The feeling against continued submission to this law and to its arbitrary and inequitable application had been growing ; and when the Chinese authorities committed an overt act of aggression in seizing and destroying the property of the foreign merchants of all nationalities at Canton, burning their " Factory," in which alone, as in a Ghetto, they were permitted to reside, and forcibly expelling them from Chinese soil, the British took up the cudgels and the war of 1842 followed. The movable property destroyed consisted of opium, and consequently the war is in common parlance called the " Opium War " ; this is an ill-chosen designation for the Americans as for the English, since, as the direct result of the war, the American Government secured a treaty containing even more favourable terms than the British treaty. In fact, the direct cause of the war was the growing sense of the need for better protection to life and property, though behind this was the ground cause of the need for better relations generally. John Quincy Adams gave it as his opinion that the Kotow was the cause of the war. In the words of Dr. Hawks Pott's " Sketch of Chinese History "—" The first war with China was but the beginning of a struggle between the extreme East and the West, the East refusing to treat on terms of equality, diplomatically or commercially, with Western nations, and the West insisting on its right to be so treated." As has been the rule from the outset, England bore the brunt of the battle in securing the rights of the West, and the privileges secured to her as the result of the war, became the heritage of all the Western Powers coming later into the field. Equality of treatment was conceded in 1842 on paper, but the execution of the concession in practice left much to be desired, and friction continued. There were, of course, faults on both sides, as is always the case where a bold aggressive race comes, especially in matters of trade, in contact with a weaker race given to supplement its want of strength by methods of chicanery and indirectness ; but underlying everything were the demand for equality of treatment and extraterritorial rights on the one side, and on the other a stubborn disinclination to yield either. A second war became necessary in which the French joined hands with the English, and a second time America and other interested Powers came in and secured treaties simultaneous and identical with those signed by the British and French Envoys. These treaties, signed independently by Great Britain, France, Russia, and the United States in 1858, by Prussia and the North German Confederation in 1861, and by other Powers in later years, are still the charter of liberty of the foreigner resident in China ; and in each of them, in addition to a " most favoured nation " clause, is contained the stipulation of extraterritoriality.

The earliest treaties with China were made by Russia, whose Envoys came by the Siberian route, and whose colonists and armed forces were in constant conflict with the Manchus and the sons of Han on the long frontier of the Amur and in Central Asia. The earliest of these treaties, that of Nipchu (or Nerchinsk) signed in 1689, contains (Art. VI.) the following provision :

" If hereafter any of the subjects of either nation pass the frontier and commit crimes of violence against property or life, they are at once to be arrested and sent to the frontier of their own country and handed over to the chief local authority, who will inflict on them the death penalty as a punishment of their crimes."

The Treaty of the Frontier (called also the Treaty of Kiakhta, at which place the ratifications were exchanged) signed in 1727, contains (Art. X.) the following provision :

" Those who pass the frontier and steal camels or cattle shall be handed over to their natural judges (*leurs juges naturels*), who will condemn them to pay ten times, and for a second offence twenty times, the value of the property stolen ; for a third offence, they shall be punished by death."

The supplementary treaty of Kiakhta, signed in 1768, contained minute stipulations for the arrest and extradition of criminals, but includes this provision :

" The subjects of the Middle Kingdom (China) who shall have committed acts of brigandage shall be delivered, without distinction of persons, to the tribunal which governs the outer provinces and punished with death ; the subjects of the Oros (Russia) shall be delivered to their senate, to undergo the same penalty."

Here then, from one to two centuries before the first of the treaties with any of the maritime Powers, we have the principle of extraterritoriality accepted : the penalties are prescribed by negotiation between the two Powers concerned, but the culprits are to be handed over to their own natural authorities—are to be judged and condemned according to the legal procedure of their native land.

The British treaty of Nanking, signed in 1842, as the

result of the war of that year, contained provisions for uniformity of Customs duties and equality of treatment for British officials ; but the only reference to Consular jurisdiction is found in Art. II., to the effect that Consuls are

> " to be the medium of communication between the Chinese authorities and the said merchants, and to see that the just duties and other dues of the Chinese Government as hereafter provided for are duly discharged by Her Britannic Majesty's subjects."

The supplementary treaty of Hoomunchai (1843) contains provisions for extradition, and annexed to it are some " General Regulations under which British trade is to be conducted at the five ports of Canton, Amoy, Foochow, Ningpo, and Shanghai " which had been published at Hongkong by a proclamation issued on July 22nd, 1843, by Sir Henry Pottinger, Minister Plenipotentiary and Superintendent of Trade. Of these Regulations, No. XIII., after stipulating that " disputes shall be arranged amicably," *i.e.* by arbitration or by diplomatic procedure, makes the following provision :

> " Regarding the punishment of English criminals, the English Government will enact the laws necessary to attain that end, and the Consul will be empowered to put them in force ; and regarding the punishment of Chinese criminals, these will be tried and punished by their own laws, in the way provided for by the correspondence which took place at Nanking after the concluding of the peace."

This regulation was in its form a concession to the Chinese, designed to control the unruly members of the crews of foreign ships. It was reserved for the United States of America, peacefully following on the sound of the British cannon, to step into the breach, and to express more clearly the one condition which renders it possible for American, English, German, or other merchants to enjoy in quiet the fruits of their trading activity, or for their missionaries to peacefully pursue their holy calling, subject to the laws of the land of their allegiance and not of the land of their sojourn. In the Treaty of Wanghia, signed in July 1844, Art. XXI. reads as follows :

"Subjects of China who may be guilty of any criminal act towards citizens of the United States shall be arrested and punished by the Chinese authorities according to the laws of China, and citizens of the United States who may commit any crime in China shall be subject to be tried and punished only by the Consul or other public functionary of the United States thereto authorised according to the laws of the United States ; and in order to the prevention of all controversy and disaffection, justice shall be equitably and impartially administered on both sides."

The French Treaty of Whampoa, signed in October 1844, contained a similar provision that French subjects accused of any crime should be " livrés à l'action régulière des lois françaises," adding, however, an enunciation of the principle of extraterritoriality :

" Il en sera de même en toute circonstance analogue et non prévue dans la présente Convention, le principe étant que, pour la répression des crimes et délits commis par eux dans les cinq ports, les Français seront constamment régis par la loi française."

The underlying principle was more clearly expressed in the Chefoo Convention (1876) between Great Britain and China, and again in the American Supplemental Treaty of Peking (1880) ; in the latter, Article IV. reads as follows :

" When controversies arise in the Chinese Empire between citizens of the United States and subjects of His Imperial Majesty which need to be examined and decided by the public officers of the two nations, it is agreed between the Governments of the United States and China that such cases shall be tried by the proper official of the nationality of the defendant. The properly authorised official of the plaintiff's nationality shall be freely permitted to attend the trial, and shall be treated with the courtesy due to his position. He shall be granted all proper facilities for watching the proceedings in the interests of justice. If he so desires, he shall have the right to present, to examine, and to cross-examine witnesses. If he is dissatisfied with the proceedings, he shall be permitted to protest against them in detail. The law administered will be the law of the nationality of the officer trying the case."

This is the principle adopted since that time in all treaty negotiations entered into with China by each one of the treaty Powers, which, in the order of the dates of the first treaty with each, are Russia, Great Britain, the United States, France, Belgium, Sweden and Norway, Germany, Denmark, the Netherlands, Spain, Italy, Austria-Hungary, Japan, Peru, Brazil, Portugal, and Mexico.

This is extraterritoriality, secured by two wars and by treaties with seventeen Powers, each one of which must consent to its abrogation or modification. By it the foreigner resident in China is subject to no one provision of the law of China, either as to his person or to his property,* but at all times and in all places is entitled to the protection of his own national law administered by his own national officials. There are no two voices as to the necessity for this right among those resident in China, and the right has been recognised by the various governments as supplying the one condition under which their nationals can remain in that country. We have now to consider the application of this right by, and to, the Consul, the merchant, and the missionary ; and, as different national laws, regulations, and customs cannot be treated on one common footing, the application of extraterritoriality to the American will be taken as typical of all.

THE CONSUL

We all know, or think we know, the ordinary functions

* Except that in the tenure of land the *lex loci* must apply.

of the ordinary Consul. Practically they may be reduced to three. He is the commercial agent of his government, and in that capacity must study the commercial possibilities for American traders and manufacturers in the country to which he is accredited, and inform the nation by the reports which he writes. He is a notary public, certifying invoices for the U.S. Customs, and attesting documents signed before him for use in the United States. Finally he is the adviser to Americans sojourning abroad, supplementing their ignorance of foreign laws and customs, and indicating to them the means by which they may be in the position, as to knowledge, which they would occupy in their own country. Coming to China, we find the Consul performing these functions, and many more besides, all of which add to his cares and his responsibilities.

First, by the direct action of the principle of extraterritoriality, he is a police magistrate to try offences committed by American citizens, civil judge for suits brought against Americans by Chinese, by other Americans, or by foreigners of other nationalities, and criminal judge for more serious crimes committed by Americans, even up to murder in the first degree. He is also coroner, probate judge, and registrar of deeds. From his decisions appeal is difficult. His judgment may be reviewed by the U.S. Minister at Peking, but this is in no sense a re-trial ; and in certain cases an appeal may be taken to the U.S. (federal) Circuit Court of California, six thousand miles away. His position is the more difficult from the fact that he has to administer, not the law of Massachusetts or of New York, or even of California, the nearest state, but "American law," and this often without the aid of trained lawyers ; he must administer the common law unelucidated by any statutes of later date than 1776, and must often give judgments which Solomon would have envied. Besides American law he must have a sufficient knowledge of the *lex loci*, as in the case of a land suit to which an American is defendant, and instances have been known when his judgment has depended upon the right interpretation of the tenets of the Buddhist religion.* With all this complexity he has still another element of difficulty : his instructions from the State Department require him first to bring two suitors to common terms of settlement, and having attempted this without giving one party a clue to the case of the other, and having failed, he must then erase from his mind all he has learned in the matter and go on the bench to sit as judge.†

Besides requiring him to act as judge, the extraterri-torialised position of the foreigner in China places on the Consul's shoulders still another burden of responsibility. Beyond the protection of American law, the American in China is safeguarded by the stipulations of the treaties. These specify, to select a few among the many instances, that Customs duties shall be uniform, that inland transit dues (akin to octroi) may be compounded, that Americans may freely rent or charter houses, boats, etc., that they shall not be prevented from preaching the gospel, that the U.S. Minister may freely and safely reside in Peking. While sitting as judge when an American is defendant, when an American has a plaint against a Chinese defendant the Consul is by law the official advocate in the case (a position presenting some embarrassment in cross-suits) ; when the plaint is against the Chinese Government, the Consul is the more necessarily an advocate from the need of interpreting and applying the stipulations of the treaties—not only of the American treaties, but, under the " most favoured nation " clause, of all the treaties made with China. This

* See Appendix B.

† The opening on January 2nd, 1907, of a United States District Court for China will remove cases of a certain class from the Consul's jurisdiction, and to this extent will modify what has been said in this paragraph ; but this description still applies, more or less exactly, to the Consuls of other Powers, such as France, Germany, etc. Only Great Britain and the United States have thought it necessary to establish separate courts. Appeal from a French Court is taken to Saigon, from a Russian Court to Vladivostock, from a German Court to Leipzic.

makes of him a diplomatic representative, not merely a representative of the Minister at Peking, but of the State Department at Washington ; and in this capacity he has to present arguments and bring pressure to bear on the Chinese officials to an extent not sanctioned by procedure in European countries.

In cases of riot and disturbance in a country of weak government, the foreign military and naval forces must be called in to give due protection to their nationals. The Consul is the natural diplomatic intermediary with the Chinese officials, and all representations, by way of persuasion or of ultimatum, must pass through him. It is for him alone to judge when the toga must yield to arms ; and, added to all his other responsibilities, he is the resident civil authority in control of the armed forces of his own country.

By virtue of extraterritoriality direct action against a foreigner's person or estate can only be taken through his own Consul, and in the case of an arrest for contravention of municipal regulations it is by him that the prisoner must be tried. The foreign communities are little self-governing and self-taxing republics, each in its square mile or two of territory, but even against their own members those communities cannot act through their own courts, which do not exist. If the municipal police arrest gamblers, let us say, among whom are men of six different nationalities, plaint must be made before six different Consular courts, with, incidentally, the result that one culprit may be fined a dollar and another a hundred dollars on the same day for the same offence. The Municipal Council governing such a community is subject to no legally constituted tribunal, since none such exists of competent jurisdiction ; and, being after all only a body of private gentlemen of many nationalities with no official status, can only communicate with the Chinese officials, with whom they have constant and important dealings, through " their own " Consuls. To meet these varying needs of the regularly constituted governing body of these little republics, the Consuls take united action, holding deliberative meetings for that purpose, and act by the voice and pen of the " Senior Consul "—the Consul longest in residence ; and they appoint certain of their number to constitute a Consular Court, a tribunal before which the Municipal Council may be sued.* This gives the Consul an important part in the municipal control, not only of his own nationals, but of all foreigners in the community.

THE MERCHANT

The position of the merchant in the days of the old trade has been indicated in this chapter, and is further described in Chapter IX. ; and in giving some details of his exceptional position under extraterritoriality, it is necessary from point to point to contrast it with what would be his normal condition.

On the entry of a ship in the ante-treaty days she became a chattel in the hands of the Chinese authorities and of monopolists licensed by them, and was the subject of " milking " limited in amount only by what the trade could stand. The sums extracted were not all capable of being put into a detailed statement, but one authentic official account (given in Chapter IX.) shows that to the constituted authorities, over and above irregular exactions, one ship, which for the same charges would to-day pay £25, paid what was then equivalent to £900. To-day a ship's papeis are deposited with her Consul, and the Chinese authorities can exercise control only through him, while all attendance and supplies may be obtained in the open market.

The cargo could formerly be sold only to licensed monopolist dealers, while now an importer may find his own buyers and make his own terms ; and for exports the same monopoly has been exchanged for the same freedom.

The merchant formerly lived and stored his goods in

* Jurisdiction over the municipality of a "Concession" is in the hands of the Consul of the controlling Power, as explained in Chapter VIII.

the Factory, in which he was the tenant and guest of the monopolists who alone could buy his imports and sell him his exports, and which he could not leave even to inquire the market prices of commodities. Now he is privileged to rent or build his own premises, subject only to the condition that they shall be at one of the treaty ports, now over forty in number, and usually within a circumscribed area at those ports ; but in any case he now has free access, without intermediaries, to his ships and to his market.

Formerly the merchants had no knowledge of the amount of taxation levied, inwards and outwards, on his goods, but it was none the lighter for that. Now the tax is strictly limited to the rates, based on a uniform 5 per cent. levy, specified in a revenue (non-protective) tariff, which forms an integral part of the treaty under which he lives and trades. From the inland taxation, too, which presses so heavily on Chinese traders who are subject to the levy of likin, his goods are exempted by payment of " transit dues " not exceeding a nominal 2½ per cent. *ad valorem.*

No Chinese authority has a right to claim any municipal taxes from foreign premises ; and within the " areas reserved for foreign residence and trade," all taxes levied are solely for the benefit of such reserved area. The foreign resident is equally free from the incidence of benevolences, or from the necessity of contributing to public charities and patriotic funds, or from inducement to buy official honours and titles, to all which the Chinese merchant is liable.

No capitation fee may be imposed, or right of deportation exercised on foreigners by the Chinese officials, as was the case in the old days.

No foreign merchant is now liable for any but his own criminal offences, and for those with which he may be charged he is judged according to the provisions of his own laws.

In civil cases he is held accountable for the requirements of the commercial code of his own country ; and in suits against Chinese he is aided by the advocacy of his own official representative, the Consul.

14

Finally, in at least ten of the treaty ports, the foreign merchants collectively are privileged to form their own municipal government, subject only to the oversight of the Consuls, to tax themselves and administer the proceeds of the taxes, to construct their own roads, and to control their own measures of police and sanitation.

Others could be added, but these constitute a formidable list of exceptional privileges, enjoyed by the foreigner and denied to the Chinese. It is no part of my purpose to inquire if these privileges are equitable or not ; it is enough to say that they will be maintained so long as foreign nations are strong enough to insist on their maintenance. Protection is thus given to foreigners in their daily business such as Chinese do not enjoy ; and it would be unreasonable to expect that no foreigner would be found ready, for a consideration, to lend a corner of his flag to cover the nakedness of the poor Chinaman. Among the foreigners resident in China there is the same proportion of good, bad, and indifferent as among the same class in the home lands, and the malpractice is common ; but while the abuse of the flag provides a decent income to many among them, it causes great injury to the legitimate commerce of the countries from which they come, and disorganises the methods of administration, right or wrong, just or unjust, of the land in which they live. Because an American can take certain goods from one place to another for a hundred dollars in taxes, while it would cost a Chinese twice that sum, provides no reason good in the eyes of the American nation, the American manufacturer, or the legitimate American trader, why the Chinese should be allowed to save half his outgo by the misuse of the American flag ; the differential taxation is a matter between the Chinaman and his own government and is no concern of the American nation, and yet, if an American has lent his name to the transaction, the American Consul is bound to intervene to protect the Chinaman's goods. This is only one example of many in which extraterritoriality is abused to give to Chinese a protection from their own officials to which they could otherwise lay no claim. Instances have been known where a foreigner with no capital—not a penny —opened branch firms in several places and ran steamers in his name and under his flag, but had no share in the working of the business and was never heard of, except when it became necessary to call a case out of the Chinese magistrate's yamen to the foreign Consular court. In one instance a small steamer was transferred within a few months first to the British, then to the French, then to the American, then to the Italian flag, in order to keep her out of the Chinese court to which both the claimants to her ownership were subject ; the transfers were frequent because the case was too notorious to be upheld even by the lax methods of China, but the legal machinery was there and was used. Each Power professes to wish to stop these abuses, but nothing can be done except by unanimous consent of all the seventeen treaty Powers ; one recalcitrant Power would provide for its nationals a rich harvest from the traffic denied to other foreigners ; and it is unlikely that anything will be done, unless the great commercial nations take the matter in hand and decide it by themselves.

The Missionary

While the merchant may live at the treaty port, and even within the reserved area at the port, and find his customers come to him readily, provided the wares he offers are wanted, the missionary must go to the people and offer them his evangel ; they will not hunt him up. To reach their hearts, he must go into the highways and byways to preach the gospel ; and to shut him up in the treaty port is to neutralise all the facilities for his work which have been secured by treaty. China is no exception to the rule that the heathen are quite content with their existing religious state, and have no desire for a " new religion " ; and the history of missionary work in this country is as much marked by the martyrdom of the saints, allowance being made for the general ethical progress of the world, as ever in any country in which the Cross has been advanced. The Chinese government has never for long actively encouraged the Christian propaganda. St. Francis Xavier, the proto-missionary, was denied access to the mainland, and died in 1555 on its threshold, on the island now called St. John. Matteo Ricci first arrived at Nanking in 1595, but secured the right of living in the city only after four years more.

Robert Morrison, the first Protestant missionary, was for some years unable even to obtain a teacher from the bigotedly conservative literati, and finally secured the instruction he desired by virtue of his connection, as interpreter, with the East India Company, and even then by stealth. The Russian Orthodox religion was, however, protected from the first, for the reason that little or no attempt has ever been made to proselytise. The treaty of 1727 provided for the maintenance in Peking of four priests of the Orthodox Church, and of six others, students of the language ; this, be it observed, during the continuance of the great persecution of the Roman Catholics decreed by Yungcheng (1723–1735). The treaty of 1851 provided that the Chinese government would interpose no obstacle to " Russian subjects celebrating in their factories divine service according to the ritual of their own religion " ; and the Russian Treaty of Tientsin, 1858, granted facilities to " la mission ecclésiastique russe."

The first reference to missionaries, otherwise than as citizens of their respective states, in the treaties of other Powers was in those of 1858. The British and American were almost identical, Article XXIX. of the American treaty being as follows :

"The principles of the Christian religion, as professed by the Protestant and Roman Catholic Churches, are recognised as teaching men to do good, and to do to others as they would have others do to them. Hereafter, those who quietly profess and teach these doctrines shall not be harassed or persecuted on account of their faith. Any persons, whether citizens of the United States or Chinese converts, who according to these tenets peaceably teach and practise the principles of Christianity shall in no case be interfered with or molested."

To the French the question was more material. That government had for centuries been recognised as protector of all Roman Catholic missions in the Orient, and its principal *casus belli* was the murder of the missionary Auguste Chapdelaine in Kwangsi ; and Article XIII. of the French treaty was as follows :

" La religion Chrétienne ayant pour objet essentiel de porter les hommes à la vertu, les membres de toutes les communions Chrétiennes jouiront d'une entière sécurité pour leurs personnes, leurs propriétés et le libre exercice de leurs pratiques religieuses, et une protection efficace sera donnée aux missionnaires qui se rendront pacifiquement dans l'intérieur du pays, munis des passeports réguliers dont il est parlé dans l'Article huit. Aucune entrave ne sera apportée par les autorités de l'Empire chinois au droit qui est reconnu à tout individu en Chine d'embrasser, s'il le veut, le Christianisme et d'en suivre les pratiques sans être passible d'aucune peine infligée pour ce fait.

" Tout ce qui a été précédemment écrit, proclamé ou publié en Chine par ordre du Gouvernement contre le culte Chrétien est complètement abrogé et reste sans valeur dans toutes les provinces de l'Empire."

When the allied forces reached Peking and had again to impose terms on the Chinese Government, Article VI. of the French Convention of Peking, 1860, stipulated as follows :

" Conformément à l'édit impérial rendu le vingt mars mil huit cent quarante-six par l'auguste Empereur Tao-Kouang, les établissements religieux et de bienfaisance qui ont été confisqués aux Chrétiens pendant les persécutions dont ils ont été les victimes seront rendus à leurs propriétaires par l'entremise du Ministre de France en Chine, auquel le Gouvernement Impérial les fera délivrer avec les cimetières et les autres édifices qui en dépendaient."

To the Chinese, but not to the French, text of this article was added, surreptitiously as the Chinese government has always declared, the following clause :

" And it shall be lawful for French missionaries in any of the provinces to lease or buy land and build houses."

As cognate to the same subject it will be well to give here for reference the much debated wording of Article XII. of the British treaty of 1858 :

" British subjects, whether at the Ports or at other places, desiring to build or open Houses, Warehouses, Churches, Hospitals, or Burial-grounds, shall make their agreement for the land or buildings they require, at the rates prevailing among the people, equitably and without exaction on either side."

There are two points which have been raised in connection with missionary work under the treaties—the right of residence in the interior, and the protection to be accorded to converts.

The right of residence in the interior depends upon the application to a pre-existing practice of a liberal interpretation of the treaty provisions given above. When the Roman Catholic missionaries entered on the mission field in the sixteenth and seventeenth centuries, there were no treaty ports, and, except later at Canton, no place at which foreigners were privileged to reside, and they spread over the Empire wherever they found a centre suitable for their propaganda. When the Emperor Kanghi was confronted by the infallible decision of the Pope, contrary to his own, on the correct rendering into Chinese of the name of the Deity, he and his successor Yungcheng decreed the exclusion from his dominions of this alien power, and all teachers of the gospel were banished and their churches closed ; in the

Liangkiang viceroyalty alone a hundred prosperous churches were so closed, and even in the extreme west, in Szechwan, there were churches not a few. Upon the resumption of a policy of toleration the pastors returned to their flocks, and the nineteenth century again found them in every province of the Empire. The edict of the Emperor Taokwang in 1846 restored to the missions all the property of which they had been deprived " during the persecutions " ; and, even without the interpolated clause, the year 1860 found the Roman Catholic missions owning and occupying, by right, churches and houses at important centres in all parts of the Empire. Apart from special treaty privilege, they have had a right of user, dating back three centuries with interruptions, and uninterrupted, except by massacre and arson, for over seventy years ; this right was confirmed by treaty in 1860, and upon this right, sanctioned by acceptance for that period and strengthened by the interpolated clause, is based the further right to acquire new property now secured by the later commercial treaties, the British of 1902 and the American of 1903.

What is permitted to one nation is *ipso facto* granted in China to all nations, the privileges of one Church may be claimed by other Churches, and what is conceded to the Roman Church becomes at once the right of the Protestant Churches of Great Britain and America. The earlier Protestant missionaries clung to the ports ; but, compelled to seek their hearers, they went into the Chinese cities and the densely populated suburbs, away from the " areas reserved for foreign residence," and in principle as much in " the interior " as places a hundred miles away. When the foreign Legations were established at Peking, the Protestant missionaries accompanied them, and joined the Roman Catholics who had been there for three centuries, in what was not then and is not now a treaty port ; and in the sixties and seventies they too spread over the country, wherever they could find men to listen to their words. But besides the **prescriptive right derived through the Roman Catholic** missions, they claimed under Article XII. of the British treaty, given above, by the terms of which they were permitted to own property " whether at the ports or at other places " ; it was not intended by the negotiators on either side that the right of residence in the interior should be granted by these words, but, strictly interpreted, they certainly carry on the rights claimed and continued by their Roman Catholic colleagues.

Of German missions there are both Protestant and Catholic, though neither are numerous, but they attract attention because of the terms of the German treaty of 1861, of which Article X. reads as follows :

> " Die Bekenner und Lehrer der christlichen Religion sollen in China volle Sicherheit für ihre Personen, ihr Eigenthum und die Ausübung ihrer Religions-Gebräuche geniessen."

Thus to Germany, and therefore to all nations, by this curt clause is guaranteed full security to the persons *and property* of missionaries *and their converts* ; and this brings us to the second debated question in connection with missionaries, the degree of protection to be accorded to Chinese subjects who have become Christians.*

The German treaty, in its brevity, seems to remove the convert from the jurisdiction of his own laws and to extraterritorialise him ; but is it for a moment to be supposed that this was the intention of the negotiators, even on the German side ? The convert remains a Chinese subject, and is under the jurisdiction of his own laws and entitled to such justice as they will give him, as much after his conversion as before, subject only to the proviso that he shall not be persecuted because of his faith ; and in this respect the same right of user cannot be claimed as in the case of mission property and residence in the interior, since the Chinese government has always, even in the time of its greatest weakness, resisted the idea that its subjects could change their status. With the reservation of the case of persecu-

* See Appendix C.

tion, most missionaries, certainly most Protestant missionaries, generally accept this position; but they cannot
always be trusted to temper zeal with discretion and to
distinguish what is right from what is lawful.   In this lies
an element of danger to the missionary and to his cause.
Not only in the treaty ports, the sole authorised places for
foreign trade, is the Westerner covered by his extraterritorialised position, but in every corner of this vast Empire
in which he may put his foot.   When the missionary far in
the interior, many miles from the observing eyes of his
Consul, transfers a corner of his protecting cloak to his poor
Chinese convert, he may be doing what is right, but it is
not lawful; and this is the naked fact underlying many an
episode leading to a riot.   You cannot eradicate from a
missionary's mind the belief that a convert is entitled to
justice of a quality superior to that doled out to his un-
converted brother: it could not be got out of your mind, or
out of mine, in a similar case.   None of us could endure that
a protégé of ours should be haled away to a filthy prison for
a debt he did not owe, and kept there until he had satisfied,
not perhaps the fictitious creditor, but at least his custodians
who were responsible for his safe keeping.   The case is
particularly hard when the claim is not for a debt, but for
a contribution to the upkeep of the village temple—the
throne of heathendom—or of the recurring friendly village
feasts held in connection with the temple—counterparts of
Fast Day and Thanksgiving; and when conversion drives
its subject to break off all his family ties by refusing to contribute to the maintenance of family ancestral worship and
the ancestral shrine, the hardship is felt on all sides—by
the missionary, who cannot decline to support his weaker
brother in his struggle against the snares of the devil; by the
convert, who is divided between his allegiance to his new
faith and the old beliefs which made all that was holy in his
former life; by the family, who not only regard their re-
creant member as an apostate but are also compelled to maintain the old worship with reduced assessments from reduced

numbers ; and by the people and governors of the land, who may find in such a situation a spark to initiate a great conflagration. No missionary, none of ourselves, could refuse his support in such a case ; and yet few missionaries consider that the support should be given : almost to a man they think that they must regard, in such matters, what is lawful and not necessarily what is right ; and almost to a man it is always " the other fellow " who does these things. With all this self-abnegation, direct interference and direct representations to the judges of the land, in cases of " religious persecution," in suits for debt, in land suits, and even in criminal cases, are only too common ; and in some parts of the country, notably in Chekiang, Catholic and Protestant converts frequently engage in clan fights, while the missionaries on either side charge those on the other with fomenting the trouble and with enlisting the aid of the officials to support their side.* The strength of a chain is that of its weakest link, and the rights of the missionary in the interior may some day have to be tested, not by the conduct of the decent majority, but by that of an aggressive minority bent, for one reason or another, on extending their own extraordinary rights to Chinese converts, who otherwise must share such justice as is meted out to their fellow-subjects.

There are, however, two sides to this question. There are numerous cases, susceptible of proof to the man on the spot but of which it would be difficult to carry conviction to the minds of those at a distance, where the missionary undoubtedly intervenes to make capital for his mission, and to secure for his followers some tangible advantage from their acceptance of his propaganda. At the other extremity there is the manifest tendency, clearly recognised by all, even the most impartial, but quite incapable of legal demonstration, for the judges of the land, in cases where the right is not obviously on one side or the other, to decide *ex motu suo* against the convert ; ostensibly such decisions are given

* See Appendix D.

on as good legal grounds as any case in China is ever decided, but practically the underlying reason is the convert's
religion—not the judge's antipathy to the religion itself, but
his ingrained feeling that the convert has become less Chinese
than the non-convert, that he has received that foreign taint
which, in 1900, sent missionary and convert alike to one
common sacrifice on the altar of nationalism.   When cases
fall under one or other of these extremes, and either the
proof is forthcoming or the decision has to be taken by one
capable of feeling where lies the right and where the wrong,
there can be no question on the course to be followed.   The
great majority of cases, however, are such as to be insus-
ceptible of proof, or fall into the wide field between these
two extremes ; and in them the missionary must be held
bound to exercise the greatest discrimination, in the interests of his mission work, of his own national government,
and, not least, of his converts themselves.

Mixed Courts

The law applicable to Mixed Courts in China at the
present day is that prescribed by the Chefoo Convention of
1876 with Great Britain, and in Article IV. of the American
treaty of 1880, given above, but they merely regularised
what had been the practice since foreign nations undertook
the task of enforcing justice on and for their nationals.
There is not anywhere a special tribunal, as in Egypt, for
the trial of all mixed cases ; but the court is, in each instance, a court of the defendant's nationality, giving its
decision under the supervision of a competent representative of the plaintiff's nationality.   This is the theory.   In
practice the Chinese have seldom sent representatives to
sit on the bench in the foreign courts, since it has generally
been recognised that the judgments rendered there are based
on the law and the evidence ; on the other hand, the foreign
Powers have never felt the same confidence in Chinese decisions, and no suit is brought in China by a foreign plaintiff

against a Chinese defendant and left to the sole decision of the Chinese judge, without the presence of an assessor of the plaintiff's nationality or acceptable to him.

In a " concession," such as those at Tientsin, Hankow, or Canton, this Chinese court for mixed cases sits at the Consulate of the lessee Power, and the assessor is invariably the Consul of that Power or his representative, irrespective of the actual nationality of the plaintiff. To allow any other assessor would admit an *imperium in imperio*, subsidiary to the foreign *imperium* already interjected into the Chinese *imperium* ; besides, as Chinese, other than employés of the foreign residents, are not permitted to live on the " concession " of the old type, the cases appearing before such a court are generally only police cases, and defendants in civil suits must ordinarily be sought on Chinese soil.

Shanghai has a problem all its own. There, living within common municipal limits, and those the limits of the " area reserved for foreign residence and trade," are (in 1905) 12,328 treaty-power foreigners, and 535,500 Chinese, in addition to somewhat over 100,000 Chinese living in the city or its suburbs under purely Chinese jurisdiction ; and legal action against one of the half-million Chinese is taken before the nineteenth of the courts of competent jurisdiction existing in Shanghai. This Mixed Court is presided over by an official with the rank of Deputy Prefect (the present incumbent has lately received the substantive rank of Prefect), with two Assistant Magistrates to relieve him. The foreign assessors are an essential part of this court, and are supplied in rotation by the American, British, and German Consulates; when a person of other nationality than that of the sitting assessor appears as plaintiff or is interested in a police case, the case is remanded until an assessor of his own nationality ean sit, either (if one of the three) in due rotation, or (if of another Power) until an assessor can be supplied from his own Consulate.

In criminal cases, in which by Chinese law the death penalty is, or might be, inflicted—such as homicide, rebellion, counterfeiting, rape, etc.—the proceedings take the form of a demand for extradition ; and, upon a *prima facie* case being made out, the defendant is remitted to the custody and judgment of the Shanghai city magistrate (Hsien), who, though of nominally lower rank than the President of the Mixed Court, is yet an Imperial representative, qualified to administer the criminal law of China. In criminal cases of lesser magnitude the judgment is rendered by the President of the Court, but subject to the approval of the foreign assessor sitting with him. This course is· followed also in police cases for contravention of municipal regulations ; but as it is not required that these regulations should have the prior approval of the Chinese authorities, and as Occidental and Oriental ideas are not always in harmony in such matters as sanitation, nuisances, control of traffic, incidence of license fees, etc., there is here an opening for a judicial review of alien legislation which is not always lost, and it happens occasionally that the opinions of the judge and the assessor do not agree.

Civil cases in China are commonly settled by gild action, and are seldom brought before the official tribunals, but the relative uniformity of justice secured by foreign supervision has caused a greater resort to the Shanghai Mixed Court. When the plaintiff is a foreigner, the ordinary course is followed, and the approval of the assessor is held necessary to the judgment of the court. Not infrequently it happens that a case with plaintiff and defendant both Chinese becomes a mixed case by the interjection of a foreigner into the plaintiff's claim ; the Chinese authorities have always tried to distinguish these pseudo-claims, but it is generally held that on them lies the onus of proof of non-interest, not an easy thing to prove. These cases then generally follow the usual course, unless it can be definitely proved that the foreign interest was introduced at the eleventh hour in order to divert the course of justice.

Suits which are admittedly between Chinese on both sides are a bone of contention. One side maintains that, being purely Chinese, they are no concern of the foreign Powers, and are therefore not subject to the decision of the foreign assessor; the other side holds that every judicial question arising within the " area reserved for foreign residence and trade" concerns the foreign Powers, and that the foreign assessor of the day is bound to exercise an oversight. On both sides it is felt, but not generally admitted, that there is some reason in the contention of the other; and the assessor is generally passive unless there are evidences of extortion and flagrant injustice, while the magistrate generally puts himself into agreement with the assessor when a municipal regulation comes into the case, neither being too desirous of crystallising the differences and precipitating a conflict. Occasionally, however, when the incompatibility of view cannot be compromised, a sharply defined issue is made.*

The Chinese official view is unimpeachable; appeal is made to the letter of the treaty stipulations granting to foreign Powers the right of oversight in cases in which a foreign interest is involved, and only in those cases. The foreign official view is equally unimpeachable. When in the years 1853–1864 the Taiping rebels devastated the country for hundreds of miles around Shanghai, many thousands of refugees found there under the foreign flags the protection to life denied them under their own flag. In the ten years which elapsed before the restoration of order these thousands were sheltered within the area reserved for foreign residence, from which it would have been inhuman barbarity to expel them; and while there police and sanitary measures were necessarily adopted to protect the foreign residents from them, and them from each other. The impetus thus given, Chinese continued to flock to the foreign settlement of Shanghai, within the limits of which there are to-day over half a million. There has thus grown up a foreign interest in real estate valued at over two hundred million taels, and a foreign interest in the main-

* See Appendix E.

tenance of order and the administration of justice among the half-million Chinese living under the same jurisdiction as the foreign residents ; and the foreign official view is that foreign supervision is necessary over foreign and Chinese residents alike in the interest of foreigners ; and, further, that two independent police and justiciary administrations cannot be allowed to function within the same area, and that, if there is to be one administration, it shall be the foreign.

To the ordinary functions of a Consul, the foreign representative in China adds those of judge, diplomatic agent, civil authority in control of the military, and has a potent voice in municipal administration. The foreign merchant is entirely removed from the jurisdiction of the laws of China, and is entitled to the protection—for life, liberty, and property—of his own national laws. The foreign missionary carries the protection of his own flag to the remotest corner of the Empire. All this arises from extraterritoriality. This remedy for the intolerable situation of the first half of the nineteenth century has now been in force for seventy years, and through it life in China has been rendered possible for all foreigners ; without it, during those seventy years the contention of the Chinese government that none of the outer barbarians should abide on the sacred soil of the Middle Kingdom would have worked its own accomplishment. It is based on force, as was the first occupation of Massachusetts Bay and the progress of the Union from the Atlantic westward to the Pacific, or as was the settlement of New Zealand and of Canada ; and on manifest destiny so long as its beneficiaries can compel destiny. It has no logical or moral argument to uphold it ; and yet it is a necessity of the case, if the foreign merchant and the foreign missionary are to remain in the country ; and so long as their stay there is legitimate, so long will extraterritoriality provide them with a buckler in following their lawful occupations. The right will not, and cannot, be abrogated until all the foreign Powers concerned are unanimous in their opinion that residence in China will be as safe, and protected by guarantees as sound, as in other countries; or until the growing strength and improved administration of China herself enable her to claim and to maintain the right of governing all within her borders.

CHAPTER VIII

THE PROVINCES AND THE TREATY PORTS

CHINA Proper is divided into eighteen provinces, and to distinguish it from the rest of the Empire this part is commonly, and even officially, referred to by the Chinese as " The Eighteen Provinces." The events of the last few years, since 1894, have brought into commercial and political prominence the region which we call collectively Manchuria, divided for administrative purposes into three provinces ; these are called by the Chinese " The Three Eastern Provinces," lying east of the eastern end of the Great Wall, where it comes to the sea at Shanhaikwan, built to protect the Eighteen Provinces forever from invading hordes from the north, whether Mongol or Manchu. The estimated area of the Empire, based not on any cadastral survey but on the simple process of multiplying degrees of longitude by degrees of latitude, may be put as follows :

China Proper	1,535,000	Eng. sq. miles
Manchuria	365,000	,, ,,
Mongolia, Tibet, Turkestan, etc.	2,400,000	,, ,,
Total	4,300,000	,, ,,

The population is variously estimated from 270,000,000 (Hippisley 1876, and Rockhill 1904) to 421,800,000 (Popoff 1894) ; Parker's estimate * of 385,000,000 is probably the safest to follow. For China " outside the Wall " the safest estimates are 16,000,000 for Manchuria and 10,000,000 for

* " China : Past and Present " (1903).

Mongolia, Tibet, etc., making, with Parker's estimate for China Proper, a total of 411,000,000. An official census taken in 1910 gives a total of 311,374,000 for China Proper, 14,917,000 for Manchuria, which, with 10,000,000 added for the dependencies, gives a total of 336,291,000.

The Eighteen Provinces extend roughly from latitude 20° to 40° N. and from longitude 98° to 122° E., comprising the seventh and eighth hours of Zone time east of Greenwich. The western part is mountainous, filled with the spurs of the Central Asian plateau ; while on the east are the great plains formed by the outfall of the Yellow River and the Yangtze ; and in the south is the small, but incredibly rich, plain of the Pearl (or West River) delta, lying around Canton. Of the nineteen provinces (treating Manchuria as an undivided area), treaty ports have been opened in fourteen—coast, riverine, and frontier—while five (Shansi, Shensi, Kansu, Honan, and Kweichow) find their outlet through extra-provincial ports.

Treaty Ports

Treaty port is almost synonymous with " port of entry," but it is something more. The first men of the West, Portuguese, Dutch, English, or American, to come to China conducted their trade mainly at Canton. The Portuguese in their enterprising days had traded at Ningpo and Foochow as well, but under such circumstances that in 1557 they obtained a lease of Macao, 88 miles from Canton, and there they settled—and stagnated. In the eighteenth century the traders of that day, the English and Dutch, visited both Canton and Macao ; but the traders of the early part of the nineteenth century, the English and Americans, made Canton their commercial centre. Here, cooped up in their factory, or trading post, they had the privilege of residing, and here they bought and sold—much of the former and little of the latter. The conditions, both of residence and of trade, were unsatisfactory, and the British Treaty of Nan-

king (1842) opened the first " treaty ports," five in number :
Canton, Amoy, Foochow, Ningpo, and Shanghai. These five
ports have now grown to over forty, including some that have
been opened voluntarily by China, not under the obligation
of any treaty, but on the same footing and under the same
trade regulations as the regular treaty ports. At these
ports foreign nations are privileged to establish Consulates,
foreign merchants are permitted to live and trade, and on
the trade at these ports are levied dues and duties according
to a tariff settled by both parties by treaty. At some ports
are national concessions, as at Tientsin, on which municipal
and police administration is under the control of the Consul
of the lessee Power ; at others are settlements or " reserved
areas for residence," as at Shanghai, with municipal organisation, but at which the Power which issues the title-deeds is
China ; at others, including most of the newer ports, there
is neither concession nor reserved area, excepting " International Settlements " established at a few places by the
Chinese authorities. At all the treaty ports, however, there
is one common right, the privilege of exempting goods by
one payment from all further taxation on movement. On
a bale of sheetings imported at Shanghai, a treaty port,
the importer will pay once duty at the tariff rate ; it may
then, perhaps a year later, be shipped to Hankow, a treaty
port, without further payment ; it may then be shipped to
Ichang, a treaty port, without further payment; it may
then be shipped to Chungking, having the privileges of a
treaty port, without further payment ; but if it then goes
on fifty miles farther, or if, instead of taking the journey
of 1,400 miles in three stages to Chungking, it goes " inland "
to a place which is not a treaty port thirty miles from
Shanghai, the bale is liable to the taxation which is levied
in China on all movement of commodities not exempted by
special privilege. A treaty port may be miles away from
the nearest navigable water, it may be the most inland of
inland marts, but in matters of taxation and of privilege
a broad distinction is drawn between these forty ports

and all the rest of China, which, even on the coast, is " inland." This is the one reason underlying the constant demand for the opening of new treaty ports, with all the expense for administrative and preventive work imposed on China, and for the enforcement of extraterritorial rights imposed on the foreign Powers.

MANCHURIA.

Of the three eastern provinces, two, Heilungkiang and Kirin, may be dismissed with few words. The chief interest in them attaches to the Amur (or Heilungkiang, Black Dragon River) and the Sungari and their degree of navigability, and to the great wheat production of Kirin and the flouring mills established by the Russians at Harbin. This town is important as the junction between the railway north from Port Arthur, Talien (Dairen or Dalny), Newchwang and Moukden, and the Russian main line from Irkutsk and Lake Baikal to Vladivostock. The southern province, Shengking, is the most important, and contains, probably, nine-tenths of the total population of Manchuria; of this population it is estimated that less than a fourth, and possibly not more than a tenth, consists of the original stock of the conquering Manchus, the great majority being immigrants from Shantung and Chihli, and their descendants. The western part of this province is made up of the plain of the Liao and the valleys of its tributaries, and grows wheat and durra for food, and beans from which are made an esculent and illuminating oil, and bean-cake shipped to restore exhausted fertility to the fields of Japan and of Kwangtung. The eastern part is mountainous and hostile to the husbandman and the soldier, and its principal products of value are opium and silk. The latter product China supplies from as far south as latitude 22° N., in its highest excellence from latitude 30° N., and, in the shape of " wild " silk or tussore from worms feeding on the oak, from beyond latitude 40° N. In minerals Manchuria is sufficiently rich to call for development, gold, silver, copper, lead, iron, and coal being known to exist. In the province of Shengking are three treaty ports, and in addition there is the territory of Port Arthur and Dalny (Talien in Chinese, Dairen in Japanese), granted in 1898 to Russia on a lease, which was subsequently, in 1905, transferred to Japan. In Heilung-kiang and Kirin are seven ports.

NEWCHWANG. (40° 41′ N., 122° 16′ E.) This port, situated 13 miles above the mouth of the Liao, was opened officially in 1861, but actually in 1864, at Yingtze or Ying-kow, 30 miles below the unimportant city of Newchwang. Recently the port has been distinguished as Yingkow, but Newchwang is and has been the name officially given to the Treaty Port, the Custom House, and the Post Office. A British concession was laid out, and through the long years of waiting for trade the little clump of buildings on this— dingy, dirty, and dusty—sufficed for all the requirements of the port. Now there are, on the left bank, the remains, not yet eroded out of existence, of the old British concession, and a new Russian concession, with 6,000 feet frontage, at the terminus of the branch line connecting the port with the main line of railway at Tashihkiao, which presumably goes with the railway to the Japanese ; and, on the right bank, a new British concession with 3,000 feet frontage and a Japanese concession with 3,000 feet frontage, have been staked out, but not yet agreed to by China, and, next down stream, the "Imperial Chinese Railway Reserve," with 13,000 feet frontage. The Chinese population at the port is estimated at 75,000, and on December 31st, 1905, there were within the district 291 resident civilian foreigners, of European and American nationality, and 7,408 Japanese reported by the Consulate. The slow development of trade at New-chwang will be judged from the following figures, which in this case, as in the case of all the other ports to be described, show the value of the traffic in " foreign-type vessels " (*i.e.* nowadays mainly steamers) under the cognisance of the Imperial Maritime Customs, and do not include the junk traffic under the cognisance of the Native Customs.

	IMPORTS. Tls.	EXPORTS. Tls.	TOTAL. Tls.*
1864	709,738	1,710,398	2,420,136
1874	2,433,135	1,753,543	4,186,678
1884	3,690,410	4,123,084	7,813,494
1894	7,886,161	8,532,443	16,418,604
1904	29,358,392	12,159,486	41,517,878
1911	31,359,794	26,722,737	58,082,531
1918 (war)	20,437,165	9,550,996	29,988,161

During 1904 the junk trade amounted, in addition, to Tls.6,365,261 for imports, and Tls.4,313,861 for exports, a total of Tls.10,679,122. This gives a total of Tls.52,197,000 as the value in 1904 of the water-borne trade of the district, of which Newchwang has been until 1906 the sole official and legal port of entry, and does not include any trade which may have been carried by rail across the land frontier or through Dalny. Among imports the principal items are cotton woven fabrics (value in 1904 Tls.10,050,000 for foreign, and Tls.7,815,000 for native weaving), cotton yarn (value Tls.3,946,000), hemp and gunny bags (Tls.315,400), cigarettes (Tls.428,890), flour (Tls.837,000, supplies from Harbin being shut off), matches (Tls.428,500), paper (Tls.1,705,000), kerosene oil (Tls.1,087,000), sugar (Tls.1,497,000), rice (Tls.962,000), and wheat (Tls.603,000). Of products of the district finding their outlet at Newchwang the principal are beans (value in 1904 Tls.6,577,000), bean-cake (Tls.4,589,000), bean-oil (Tls.2,133,000), silk (Tls.2,005,000), and such opium as was declared for assessment of duty (Tls.289,000).

MOUKDEN (41° 51′ N., 123° 26′ E.) is the Manchu name of what in Chinese is known as Shengking (the Sacred Capital), and administratively was from A.D. 1625 called Shenyang, and is now officially termed Fengtien. The old capital of the Manchus before they marched to the conquest

* The tael (Tls.) of silver had an exchange value of 6s. 8d. in 1864, of 6s. 4d. in 1874, of 5s. 7d. in 1884, of 3s. 2d. in 1894, of 2s. 10d. in 1904, of 2s. 8¼d. in 1911, and of 5s. 3½d. in 1918 (under war conditions).

of China and migrated to Peking, it still * remains a sleeping capital, with a complete equipment of Ministries, duly provided with Presidents, Vice-Presidents, and Secretaries, whose most important functions have for two-and-a-half centuries been those connected with pay-day. The practical administration is in the hands of a Governor-General, who is at the same time Military Governor (Tsiang-kün, Tartar General), and of a Civil Governor, who is assimilated to the Governors of the Eighteen Provinces. Situated at a distance of one hundred miles from Newchwang, in the heart of the plain of the Liao valley, it is admirably placed to serve as a distributing centre. It is connected by rail with Dairen and Newchwang, and, when the line from Sinmingfu is extended, will also find direct outlets at Chinwangtao and Tientsin. Outlets may also be found through Vladivostock and Irkutsk. The population is estimated at 250,000.

ANTUNG (40° 8' N., 124° 14' E.) and Tatungkow, 23 miles below, at the mouth of the Yalu River, which separates Manchuria from Korea, were opened as treaty ports in March 1907, and tap the wealth of timber standing on the mountains flanking the river, providing also an outlet for the silk of eastern Shengking, which formerly went by junk to Chefoo and Dairen. Antung is a station on the line of railway connecting Korea with Manchuria. In 1911 the trade of the two ports was valued at Tls.5,662,412 for imports, Tls.4,810,194 for exports, total Tls.10,472,606. In 1918, under war conditions, the net combined trade was valued at Tls.24,545,679 for imports, Tls.15,684,124 for exports, total Tls.40,229,803.

HARBIN, the junction of the railways from Irkutsk to Vladivostock, and from Harbin to Kwanchengtze, where it joins the Japanese line to Dairen, has been made the seat of a Custom House to control the railway traffic. In 1911 the trade passing through the offices at Harbin and the other points in Heilungkiang and Kirin at which offices have been opened (Aigun, Sansing, Manchuli, Suifenho,

* In 1906.

Hunchun, and Lungchingtsun) was valued at Tls.18,395,860 for imports, Tls.27,190,536 for exports, a total of Tls. 45,586,396. In 1918, under war conditions, the corresponding figures were: Tls.17,303,501 for imports, Tls. 13,857,929 for exports, total Tls.31,161,430, an indication of the disorganised state of the trade with Russian territory.

DAIREN has been under the control of Japan since 1905, and a Chinese Custom House controls its trade under regulations similar to those in force at Tsingtau (*q.v.*). In 1911 the value of the trade passing through this office was Tls.28,331,120 for imports, Tls.33,730,976 for exports, a total of Tls.62,062,096. In 1918 the trade passing through Dairen was valued at Tls.79,811,474 for imports, Tls. 86,012,733 for exports, a total of Tls.165,824,207. The figures for Dairen and Antung together, contrasted with those for Newchwang, indicate the strong hold, further strengthened by war conditions, which Japan has taken on the trade of Manchuria.

CHIHLI

The metropolitan province of Chihli, with an estimated area of 115,000 square miles, and a population* of which the estimates range from 21,000,000 to 29,000,000, may be roughly divided into a northern half, mountainous and thinly peopled, lying mainly outside the Great Wall, and a southern part, densely populated, of flat alluvial plain, robbed in the course of ages from the waters of the Gulf of Pechihli by the detritus carried down by the Yellow River, and the loess borne on the winds. The hill country contains much mineral wealth, of which the bituminous coal mined at Tongshan and the anthracite of the hills west of Peking are conspicuous examples. The plain is a vast hive of human industry on which, as everywhere on the plains of China, man is pitted against the forces of nature,

* Census of 1910 gives 32,571,000.

and, with no other appliances than those possessed by their remote ancestors, the men of the hive win out. This is a part of the country running from Tientsin to Chinkiang through seven degrees of latitude, and traversed by the various courses followed during the centuries by the erratic Yellow River, where man is at a peculiar disadvantage from the friable nature of the soil, the aggressive character of the water when in flood, and the fact that at such times the level of the waters is higher than that of the land. One grand scheme of reclamation is recorded in the time of Yung-cheng, A.D. 1723–1735, when 120,000 acres of marsh were converted into good arable land, and the canals, weirs, and bridges by which this work was carried out can be shown to-day after 175 years ; but in recent times little has been done on any extensive scale. The products of Chihli are those of the farm and farm-yard, the usual crops being millet, durra, and wheat. The treaty ports opened in the province are two in number, Tientsin and Chinwang-tao ; but the exceptional position of Peking calls for a description of that city.

PEKING (39° 54′ N., 116° 27′ E.). The capital of the Empire was first established at Peking (the Northern Capital) by Kublai Khan, when he initiated the Yuan Dynasty, A.D. 1260 ; the first Ming Emperor, A.D. 1368, established himself at Nanking (the Southern Capital), but the third of that line transferred the capital in 1421 to Peking, which has remained the seat of government continuously since then. Peking is a quite unofficial and quasi-foreign designation, the Imperial name being King-shih (The Capital) and its name, as a unit of the provincial administration, being Shuntien. In the same way it may be observed that the Empire has no name ; it is designated as " The Empire " or " (All within) The Four Seas," or " (All beneath) The Canopy of Heaven," or, quite unofficially, " The Middle Kingdom " ; it is true that the Republic has adopted the name Chung-hwa, " Middle Flowery," but the name " China " is an old Buddhist name which has dropped out of use in the country which is designated by it, and is to-day, of all the countries using the Chinese ideograms, employed only by the Japanese. Peking is a camp, with the head-quarters of the commander-in-chief in the middle, and the army encamped around ; then to the south, outside the walls but protected by their own walls, are the camp sutlers— the Chinese traders purveying to the Manchu garrison. The Chinese estimate of the population is 1,300,000. Considered commercially, Pekin is a mouth, fed by the provinces, and having no industrial output ; and yet the foreign purveyors and hotel-keepers who have gathered around the Legations have found it to their advantage to act as if the city had the status of a treaty port—not one with the duty-exemption privilege, but a place in which they are permitted to reside, to buy and sell, and to act as general traders. Against this assumption the Chinese government has repeatedly protested.

TIENTSIN (39° 9′ N., 117° 11′ E.), " The Ford of Heaven," is situated at the junction of the Grand Canal, which, starting from Hangchow, finds here the end of its long course, of the Peiho (North River) leading north to Peking, and of the Haiho (Sea River) emptying into the Gulf of Pechihli. The city is distant from the sea 35 miles by road, but 56 miles by the original corkscrew windings of the river, a distance since reduced to 40 miles by the work of the Haiho Conservancy, and in time to be reduced to 36½ miles. Even after all the improvement that has been effected, there are few cities in the world of equal commercial importance or supplying so rich a hinterland, which have such poor shipping facilities. A bar on which certain conditions of wind and tide will reduce the high-water depth to three or four feet, a channel in which the summer floods will cause the mud bottom to rise faster than the water surface, a river of many bends and restricted width, all combine to impose a limit on the carrying capacity of steamers entering the port. The eternal struggle of the enterprising merchants, foreign and native alike, of Tientsin can only be compared

to the fight of the farmers of the province against the
forces of nature, both having the same problem to solve.
Tientsin is, with a few insignificant exceptions, the one
official city of the Empire, of the rank of district city, which
is to-day without the protection of walls. It was in the
reign of Yung-lo (A.D. 1403–1425) that it was permitted
the privilege of walls ; these endured until the rule of the
foreign Provisional Government which followed on the
Boxer movement of 1900, when the walls were razed and
the official city was left naked to the winds. Apart from
the humiliation, the loss was a gain ; the walls afforded
no protection to the wealthy commercial quarter, which,
as is invariably the case in China, was in the suburb lying
between the city and the river, and they have been well
replaced by the broad avenues made on their site and
providing thoroughfares unknown to other Chinese cities.
Tientsin is rich in " concessions " for residence and foreign
trade, having no less than thirteen—viz. British (1860),
British Extension (1897), British Extra-mural Extension
(1900), French (1861), French Extension (1900), American
(granted in 1861, but at once abandoned and in 1902 added
to the British Concession), German (1895), German Extension (1901), Japanese (1896), Japanese Extension (1900),
Austro-Hungarian (1902), Italian (1901), Russian (1900), and
Belgian (1902). The last four and the various extensions,
except the British, date from 1900 and later. The original
concession, the British, dating from 1860, is held under a
lease in perpetuity to the British government, a small
ground-rent being reserved to show the ultimate sovereignty
of China. The area was divided into lots, the leases of
which were sold to provide for roads and bunding, and
which are held under a ninety-nine years' lease granted by
the British government, the annual rental being the due
proportion of the reserved ground - rent. The Consul is
ex officio the ruling functionary ; all actions of the Municipal
Council, elected by vote of the "land-renters," being
submitted for his approval, and the annual " town meet-

ing " or any special meeting being held under his presidency. The residence of Chinese on the concession being prohibited, otherwise than as servants of the foreign residents, the Consul has jurisdiction over all questions of landed property, and over all other questions in which a non-British European is not defendant. The Consul, as representative of his government, is *de jure* ruler of the concession ; but, in conformity with English practice, he actively intervenes only in a crisis, and ordinarily the duly-elected Municipal Councillors are *de facto* rulers of a self-constituted little republic. In the other concessions nomination, and not selection, decides the choice of Councillors. For the French concession the Municipal Council consists of the Consul as *ex officio* President, the six land-owners paying the highest taxes, and the three tenants paying the highest rent. Germany in 1897 contracted with a commercial syndicate to develop and administer her concession ; and in 1905 the Reichstag passed an enabling Act to allow self-government when desired. On the Japanese, Russian, Belgian, and Italian concessions the Consul is sole administrator. On the Austro-Hungarian concession there is little if any Austrian or Hungarian interest, the land-owners and inhabitants being Chinese ; and here the power is vested in an Administrative Secretary, nominated by the Consul, and in six of the leading Chinese residents, also nominated. Of the extensions, the French, German, and Japanese are merely extensions of the original concessions, held in the same way under lease in perpetuity to the foreign Power. In the British Extension, which was the first, a different principle was followed. The soil remains Chinese, and title-deeds are sealed and issued by the Chinese authorities as at Shanghai, and as at Shanghai it is only administrative functions—taxing, works, and police—which are delegated by the sovereign power. The Municipal Council, in its corporate capacity, and the " land-renters " of the British Concession own a considerable portion of the land in its extension, and the Municipal Council of the extension is composed of the members elected to the Municipal Council of the concession, *ex officio*, and four others elected *ad hoc* ; this makes it possible, while having separate budgets, to carry on the administrative work of the two areas with a staff common to both. In 1918 it was decided to abolish the two forms of government in the British territory, and to amalgamate all three areas into one British Concession, as had been originally done with the French, German and Japanese. In the foreign residential section of Tientsin, with a total area of 3,550 acres, of which 28 per cent. is in the Russian Concession, we have thus six distinct forms of government under eight European Powers. At Tientsin and in its consular district live (December 31, 1905) a total of 3,770 civilian foreigners, including 679 British, 387 American, 465 German, 244 French, 115 Russian, 60 Austro-Hungarian, 100 Belgian, 34 Italian, 1,538 Japanese, and 148 others. Formerly the population of the city and its suburbs was estimated at a million, but, with all its development, recent and more careful estimates put it at 750,000. The development of trade is shown by the following figures of the value of merchandise (not including treasure) carried in foreign bottoms :

	IMPORTS. Tls.	EXPORTS. Tls.	TOTAL. Tls.
1864	7,645,422	1,730,786	9,376,208
1874	17,682,684	1,144,893	18,827,577
1884	20,328,981	3,610,076	23,939,057
1894	37,412,806	6,864,248	44,277,054
1904	54,059,315	14,895,375	68,954,694
1905	81,826,313	14,739,359	96,565,672
1911	77,241,699	39,294,949	116,536,648
1918	101,958,588	51,180,055	153,138,643

In addition, during 1905, produce to a value of Tls.8,018,223 was exported by junk. Among imports the principal items are cotton woven fabrics (value in 1905 Tls.21,314,000 for foreign, and Tls.440,000 for native weavings), cotton yarn (Tls.6,514,570 for foreign, and Tls.574,100 for native spinnings), copper (Tls.3,119,000 for foreign, and Tls.460,840 for Chinese), cigarettes (Tls.1,287,000), tobacco (Tls.422,600), kerosene oil (Tls.2,268,600), railway plant and machinery in general (Tls.3,995,000), sugar (Tls.3,286,000), timber (Tls.1,445,000), paper (Tls.2,290,000), rice (Tls.10,592,000), silks (Tls.1,840,000), tea (for local consumption Tls.1,132,000, for transit to Russia by land Tls.2,861,600). The principal among the articles of export were bristles (Tls.831,713), spirits (Tls.666,500), skins and furs (Tls.5,210,000), strawbraid (Tls.858,600), and wool of camel, goat, and sheep (Tls.3,326,400).

CHINWANGTAO (39° 55′ N., 119° 38′ E.) is a comparatively ice-free port on a frozen coast, affording an outlet when Tientsin (December to February) and Newchwang (November to March) are frozen up. Originally opened as a coal-shipping port for the output of the Kaiping mines, and utilised as a winter landing for passengers and mails, it proved of great value in enabling the foreign garrisons at Peking and Tientsin to maintain communication with the outer world during the winter 1900–1901; and when the military forces were withdrawn to Tientsin, a Chinese Custom House was established there in 1902. The trade of the port developed at once, and in 1905 amounted to Tls.18,817,120 for imports, and Tls.3,033,959 for exports, a total of Tls.21,851,079, but in 1911 had fallen to Tls. 6,130,449 for imports, and Tls.3,372,308 for exports, a total of Tls.9,502,757, the greater part of which should be added to the trade of Tientsin, of which Chinwangtao is the "winter jetty." Of its special export, coal, 168,576 tons were shipped in 1905, in addition to 25,183 tons shipped from Tientsin. On the opposite side of the bay is the seaside resort of Peitaiho, frequented during the summer by residents of Peking, Tientsin, and Shanghai, and by missionaries from the interior of North China.

SHANTUNG

Shantung, the " Mountains of the East," the home of Confucius, has an area estimated at 56,000 square miles and a population * estimated at 37,000,000. It is divided sharply into two halves, the mountainous country to the east and the plain to the west. The eastern part, with a width of 80 miles at the base and 30 miles at the tip, projects boldly for a length of 150 miles into the sea, separating the waters of the Yellow Sea to the south from the Gulf of Pechihli to the north, and is rich in minerals, notably coal, iron, and gold. The western part is a portion of the plain formed by China's Sorrow, the Yellow River. This river has changed its course many times, finding its outlet into the sea at several places within a range of eight degrees of latitude ; prior to the sixth century before Christ, it formed a delta with its northern mouth at Tientsin, latitude 39° N., and its southern mouth near the present outlet, latitude 38° N. ; from the seventh century A.D. it emptied by one mouth about latitude 38° 30' N. ; toward the end of the twelfth century it plunged south-east from a point midway between Kaifeng and Tsinan, and emptied into the Yellow Sea south of Shantung, at about latitude 34° N. ; toward the end of the thirteenth century it broke away to the south-east from Kaifeng, and emptied partly through the last mentioned mouth and partly into the Yangtze, the southern mouth of which is at latitude 31° N. ; in 1324 it broke away lower down below Kaifeng, and flowed south-east to the mouth at latitude 34° N. ; this course it kept until 1853, when it resumed its north-easterly course, flowing close to the north of Tsinan to a mouth in the Gulf of Pechihli, north of Shantung, at latitude 38° N. These are what may be termed the " official " channels, the courses which the river condescends to recognise at seasons of low water. In times of flood it breaks out where it wills, and, even at the present time, finds an

* Census of 1910 gives 29,600,000.

outlet for its waters where it can, some falling at times into the Yangtze, some into the Yellow Sea, some as far north as Tientsin, and some by its present legitimate mouth. In 1887, for example, it broke out above Kaifeng, just below the spot where the Peking-Hankow Railway now crosses the river, and formed a temporary channel to the south-east through Honan and Anhwei. Coming from the treeless plateau of Central Asia, and flowing through a treeless country, the River (Ho, *i.e.* Hwang-ho, as the Chinese call it) brings down the melting snows and falling rains in sudden flood laden heavily with detritus from the loess formation of the west and north-west ; and this detritus, checked in its speed, is deposited so rapidly that the river bed is filled by degrees until everywhere its bottom is higher than the surrounding plain. Were is not for the vast sums of money and vast amount of work spent upon it every year and through the whole year, the Yellow River would have no fixed channel, but, with every recurring summer and its attendant flood, would spread over the plain which extends from longitude 114° E. to the sea, and from the Yangtze latitude 32° N. to Tientsin. Nor do these floods enrich the soil, as do those of the Yangtze and the Nile, but they deposit an infertile sand which is prevented from being rendered fertile by the combined action of wind, sun and rain, through its lightness and friability, which expose it to the destructive independent action of each element. This, too, is the only soil on which to raise protecting dykes, and catastrophic floods from breaches in the banks are of almost annual occurrence, being recorded in seven of the ten years 1882–1891, and in seven of the years 1892–1901. With all this, or because of all this, Shantung, though rich in products, is richer still in its men, and richest of all in having produced Confucius. The Master was born B.C. 551 (dying B.C. 479) in what is now the district of Chow-hsien, and his Memorial Hall is still standing at Chüchow in the prefecture of Yinchow, in the western part of the province ; and through all the vicissitudes of revolutions, rebellions, and falling dynasties, his memory has been kept green and his name honoured by the perpetually hereditary rank of Kung (Duke) bestowed upon his family. His seventy-sixth lineal descendant to-day divides his time between Peking and his ancestral home : this, it may be noted, gives an average of 31·4 years for a generation.

Shantung produces coal, iron, and gold, and its farm products are beans, opium, silk, wheat, millet, and tree-fruits. Within its limits are the treaty port of Chefoo and the foreign " leased territories " of Kiaochow and Weihaiwei.

CHEFOO (37° 33′ N., 121° 22′ E.) : the treaty port, opened in 1863, is not at Chefoo, which is on the north side of its harbour, but at Yentai on the south side. The road-stead provides a commodious anchorage, safe for vessels at all times with some selection of a berth, but so far exposed to certain winds, north and east, as to render the discharge of cargo difficult at times. Here there is neither concession nor settlement, in the sense of an administrative munici-pality ; but since the opening of the port the entire promon-tory of Yentai, which projects into the harbour, has been, more or less ·tacitly, and without any formal agreement, reserved for occupation as a foreign quarter. The residents have bought their own land, have made their own winding roads, and have maintained cleanliness and order mainly through the force of public opinion. They have assessed themselves and have expended their assessments through a headless committee, but have no official status as a self-governing administrative body ; and Chefoo represents the third of the four types of municipal government to be found operating at the treaty ports, of which the first is seen in the " concession," as at Tientsin already described, the second in the " settlement," as at Shanghai, and the fourth in a special form of government which will be de-scribed under Yochow. For many years, until about ten years ago, Chefoo was the sole summer resort available in China, and is still frequented by many, attracted by its sea bathing and sea breezes, and by the summer visits of

16

many of the foreign war-ships on the station. The resident foreign population of the port and district in 1905 was 1,431, including 433 British, 221 American, and 547 Japanese. For trade purposes the port is not well situated, being in the middle of the northern side of the mountainous section, and connected with the plain country only by such routes as are called roads in China, or by junk to the harbourless ports of the north coast; and yet, as an outlet and supply depot for the province, its development has been marked. A portion of its trade is with the coast of eastern Shengking lying opposite across the Gulf of Pechihli. The value of its trade during the past fifty years has been as follows, treasure not included :

		IMPORTS. Tls.	EXPORTS. Tls.	TOTAL. Tls.
1864	..	2,766,669	2,758,547	5,525,216
1874	..	5,851,159	1,960,402	7,811,561
1884	..	5,922,202	4,138,314	10,060,516
1894	..	8,208,938	6,569,738	14,778,676
1904	..	21,569,021	12,686,154	34,255,175
1905	..	27,179,259	11,952,125	39,131,384
1911	..	16,654,026	13,916,518	30,570,544
1918	..	14,730,966	16,094,919	30,835,885

To this has to be added for 1905 the value of the junk trade, imports Tls.11,531,033, exports Tls.2,311,260, total Tls. 13,842,293. Among the imports the principal were cotton fabrics (value in 1904 Tls.3,120,000 for foreign, and Tls.155,000 for native weaving) cotton yarn (Tls.1,728,000 for foreign, and Tls.80,355 for native spinning), cigarettes (Tls.674,000), coal (Tls.510,000), flour (Tls.1,332,000), matches (Tls.578,000), kerosene oil (Tls.1,917,000), sugar (Tls.1,732,000), and rice (Tls.3,415,000). Among exports the principal articles were beans and bean-cake (Tls.2,794,000), wild silk (Tls.4,803,000), straw-braid (Tls. 1,413,000), vermicelli (Tls.1,573,213).

LUNGKOW (37° 41′ N., 120° 17′ E.). A newly opened port west of Chefoo. In 1918 its trade was valued at Tls.2,553,126 for imports, Tls.676,549 for exports, total Tls.3,229,675.

WEIHAIWEI (37° 30′ N., 122° 9′ E.) was occupied by Great Britain under a lease from China in 1898, as an answer to the Russian occupation of Port Arthur and Talien, which followed on the German occupation of Kiaochow. The government is by a Commissioner. There is no resident foreign population to form an electorate, and the Chinese are ruled *more Sinico* through the village elders. The port is a summer station, but not a base, for the British East Asiatic squadron, and an hotel and a school have been established there. Considering the meagreness of the population and that it is supposed, while being a free port, to have no legitimate traffic with its hinterland, its sea-borne trade is surprisingly large.

KIAOCHOW is and remains a Chinese city at the head of its wide shallow bay, with good anchorage only at its mouth. Here lies Tsingtau (36° 4′ N., 120° 18′ E.), the port and seat of government of the German "Territory of Kiaochow." Possession of this port and its environs was taken on November 14, 1897, as reprisal for the murder of two German missionaries, and subsequently, in March 1898, a lease for ninety-nine years was obtained from the Chinese government. The local administration is controlled by a Governor, assisted by a Council composed of the heads of departments, eight in number, to whom are added three unofficial members. The town and port have been developed by subsidies provided by the German government ; the town has been laid out with broad streets and provided with fine buildings, while the port is an artificial creation with its moles and breakwaters, and equipped with all needed European appliances ; and fifty million marks is a moderate estimate of the sum expended on their creation. As a summer resort Tsingtau is growing in popularity with the residents of Shanghai. The bay of Kiaochow lies at the junction of the plain and the mountain, and from its inner end Kublai Khan (A.D. 1260) made a canal to the north shore at Laichow, which, until the restoration and completion of the Grand Canal provided a safer route, enabled the tribute-laden junks to make their journey to the north without encountering the perils of the stormy passage around the Shantung Promontory. The canal has long since been unavailable for transport, but its modern substitute, the railway from Tsingtau to Tsinan, 450 kilometres, taps the wealth of production of the plain part of Shantung, and the trade of the western, the richer, portion of the province is destined more and more to gravitate to Tsingtau. This is a German port, but the authorities have had the wisdom to invite the fiscal co-operation of the Chinese government, and in July 1899 the Chinese Kiaochow Customs Office was opened and functioned at the port itself. The fiscal arrangement then made was tentative, and has since been improved. Beginning from January 1, 1906, the Kiaochow Customs took entire control of the movement of merchandise inward and outward, at the same time conceding to Tsingtau all the trade privileges of a Chinese treaty port ; the harbour with its moles, and the railway terminus with the area around them, were declared a " Freibezirk," much like a huge bonded warehouse, into which movement is unrestricted, and in which bonded manufacturing may be carried on ; the Chinese Customs tariff duty is levied on exports when shipped by sea, and on imports when leaving the free zone ; every facility is to be granted to the Chinese Customs as if on Chinese soil ; and 20 per cent. of the collection from imports is to be handed over to the German authorities as a contribution to the maintenance of the port. With this arrangement, if it is found to work, and the railway communication with its hinterland, the future of the port is assured, the more that the ordinary bureaucratic methods of German administration are not so much in evidence in the " Kiautschau-gebiet " as in other German colonies. Though through railway traffic to Tsinan was initiated only in 1905, the trade of the port has already made considerable progress, as evidenced by the following figures, in which the unimportant junk traffic is included :

		IMPORTS (Tls).	EXPORTS (Tls.).	TOTAL (Tls.).
1900	..	2,852,576	1,104,574	3,957,150
1902	..	8,075,250	2,269,392	10,344,642
1905	..	15,097,422	7,225,258	22,322,680
1911	..	26,287,988	19,853,669	46,141,657
1918	..	33,912,790	29,534,540	63,447,330

The tendency of the trade of western Shantung to gravitate to Kiaochow to the detriment of Chefoo, formerly the only treaty port outlet for the province, is signally evidenced by the case of straw-braid ; of the total export of this product of home industry from the two Shantung ports in 1903 Chefoo contributed 70 per cent. and Kiaochow 30 per cent., while in 1904 the Chefoo contribution fell to 40 per cent., and in 1905 fell further to 21 per cent. ; in 1911 the export from Kiaochow was 88,002 piculs, and from Chefoo only 4 piculs. Other important products exported from Kiaochow are yellow silk, bean-oil, and ground-nut oil. In November 1914 the port and forts of Tsingtau were surrendered to a force of Japanese, with whom was a British contingent. Japan remained in occupation of the port and leased territory, but, at the time of the surrender, announced her intention of restoring them to China after the war, on conditions to be settled between Japan and China. At the date of writing (December, 1919) the conditions have not yet been settled. The Customs arrangement made with Germany, and adopted also at Dairen, has necessarily been continued. The result of the Japanese occupation, combined with the effect of war on industry throughout the world, has been to divert to Japan a large part of the trade of Tsingtau, both import and export.

OTHER NORTHERN PROVINCES

On the latitude of Shantung is a string of inland provinces with no direct outlet on sea or river, the one river common to and running through them all, the Yellow River, not being generally navigable in any part of its course.

HONAN, " South of the Ho " (Yellow River), is hilly in its western part, where it borders on Shansi, Shensi, and Hupeh, and a plain to the east where it borders on Shantung, Kiangsu, and Anhwei. The estimated area is 68,000 square miles, and population* 21,000,000. A rich country with no navigable rivers, it is destined to be recreated by railways ; and its produce, which formerly found outlets at Tientsin in the north or at Chinkiang in the south, is beginning to find its way to Hankow by the Peking-Hankow line, which bisects the province from north to south.

SHANSI, the " Mountains of the West," lies between Chihli and Shensi. With practically no rivers intersecting it, and skirted on the west and south by the unnavigable Yellow River, it occupies a high plateau with a steep escarpment on its eastern side. Any failure of rain brings drought and almost unrelievable famine, and the difficulties of transport are such as to be overcome only by the construction of railways. A line connects the capital, Taiyuan-fu, with the Peking-Hankow line at Chentow. The estimated area is 82,000 square miles, and population 10,000,000.

SHENSI lies between Shansi, Honan, and Hupeh on the east, Szechwan on the south, and Kansu on the west. Its produce finds an outlet partly through Honan and partly over the mountains and down the Han River to Hankow. At or near Sianfu was the ancient capital of what then constituted the Empire, in the third century before Christ and again in the sixth century after Christ ; and at Sianfu, to which the Court fled for refuge from the troubles of 1900, are maintained simulacra of Ministries, as at Moukden, but without staffs. The area of the province is estimated at 75,000 square miles, and its population at 8,800,000. The name of this province affords an instance of the difficulties of the Chinese language and its dependence on tones or inflexion of the voice. In spelling there is properly no distinction between Shansi and this province, and to distinguish correctly the sound as spoken, the former should

* Census of 1910 gives 25,600,000.

be Shànsi and the latter Shānsi : Shensi is only a convenient conventionalised mode of distinguishing the two provinces.

KANSU forms the extreme north-west corner of the Eighteen Provinces, and has an area estimated at 125,000 square miles and a population of 5,000,000. Traversed by the Yellow River, it is restricted to land transport ; and its produce, mainly wool of sheep and camel, finds its outlet through Mongolia, thence down from the north-west to Tientsin.

KWEICHOW lies far to the south, but is more conveniently mentioned here, as the only other province not having treaty ports. It lies between Szechwan to the north, Yunnan to the west, Kwangsi to the south, and Hunan to the east, and has an area estimated at 67,000 square miles, and population at 11,300,000. It is rich in minerals, especially of the less common kinds, and its products, of which opium is the most important, find their outlet through Hunan and Kwangsi.

SZECHWAN

Szechwan, the " Four Streams," has an area calculated to be 218,500 square miles. Nothing better illustrates the uncertainty impending over everything statistical in China than the variability of the estimates of its population. The estimates made within the last twenty years have ranged from 35,000,000 (Hobson, 1892) to 79,500,000 (Popoff, 1894) ; but the general tendency of investigators has been to put it between 50,000,000 and 65,000,000; Parker (1903) is inclined, however, to doubt all the high estimates ; and Hosie (1904), than whom few have studied the province more carefully, puts it at 45,000,000. The official census of 1910 gives it as no more than 23,000,000, but this is probably an underestimate. The surface of the province is made up of masses of mountains, through which the Yangtze has cut its deep and narrow channel, and which is everywhere cut up by steep-sided valleys and ravines. In the whole province there is but one extensive plain, that of Chengtu, the capital, on which the irrigation system is among the wonders of the world. Among the minerals found are gold, silver, cinnabar, copper, iron, coal, and petroleum, and among its natural products the chief are opium, hemp, white wax, yellow silk, and some hundreds of products of its hills and valleys included in the Chinese pharmacopœia. Chief among the products of this rich province is salt, obtained from artesian borings, some of which extend 2,500 feet below the surface, and from which for centuries the brine has been laboriously raised by windlass and water buffalo power. The one outlet for Szechwan, except at the cost of toilsome mountain journeys, is by The Great River (Kiang) or The Long River or simply " The Kiang "— the river otherwise without a name, the spinal cord of China, which foreigners have united to call by the name given to it by the Chinese only for the last hundred miles of its course of thousands of miles : Yangtze. Flowing from the extreme west of China to the extreme east, it is only within the borders of Szechwan that this route presents any difficulties, and these are occasioned by the rapids over which the stream pours tumultuously in its passage through the famous Yangtze Gorges. Down stream the inherited and trained skill of the boatmen carries their frail craft safely past dangers with the current rushing, in places and at times, as much as fifteen miles an hour ; but up stream this skill is called into full play, and the boats, of about twenty-five tons capacity, pulled by a struggling, shouting, sweating crowd of a hundred trackers, more or less, frequently meet with accident in the passage of the rapids. Repairs are effected and damaged cargo is dried promptly on the way, but it is estimated that, apart from total losses, a full tenth of the boats upward-bound arrive with their cargo more or less damaged by water. Near each of these rapids is maintained an efficient life-saving boat service, one of the few public services in China of which nothing but good is said. The province contains two treaty ports,

CHUNGKING (29° 34′ N., 106° 31′ E.) is situated at the confluence of the Great River (or the River of Golden Sand, as it is sometimes called in parts of its course through Szechwan) and the Small (or Kialing) River.   In the Chefoo Convention (1876) it was stipulated that Chungking should be an outpost for watching trade, but that " (British) merchants will not be allowed to reside at Chungking, or to open establishments or warehouses there, so long as no steamers have access to the port." The first " steamer " to reach Chungking was a small steam-launch in March 1898, and the first cargo-carrying steamer was the *Pioneer* in June 1900, both taken up by the developer of Szechwan, Mr. Archibald J. Little ; but, in fact, the place had been opened as a treaty port, with all its privileges, in March 1891. It is improbable that, under existing conditions, steam traffic can advantageously engage in the Szechwan carrying trade ; and the trade passing through the " Maritime Customs " is carried by junk, as is that passing through the Likin Stations, the latter offering the advantage of a flexible tariff and complaisant officials, the former based on its treaty port privilege by which the single import duty paid at Shanghai carries goods without additional taxation 1,400 miles farther into the heart of China.   The city, with a population of 300,000, occupies a rocky promontory on which mountain paths and flights of stone steps take the place of streets.   The river rises here in summer normally 70 feet above its winter level, frequently more, and in 1905 rose to a height of 108 feet.   The few foreign residents are scattered over the city and on the opposite shore and have no municipal organisation.   In considering the volume of trade it must be remembered that it is optional with merchants to pass their cargo at the Maritime Customs or at the Likin Stations, and that the latter publish no statistics.   The value of the trade passing the Customs has been as follows :

	IMPORTS. Tls.	EXPORTS. Tls.	TOTAL. Tls.
1894 ..	5,782,701	4,997,688	10,780,389
1904 ..	18,451,938	10,952,028	29,403,966
1911 ..	19,069,597	10,069,575	29,139,172
1918 ..	15,227,128	14,872,629	30,099,757

Of the imports five-sixths are made up of cotton manufactures, viz. cotton piece goods (in 1904 Tls.3,777,600, all
foreign weaving), and cotton yarn (Tls.8,993,700 foreign,
and Tls.2,681,500 native spinning). Among exports the
principal items were bristles (Tls.477,000), hides (Tls.458,000),
medicines (Tls.974,000), musk (Tls.983,000), opium (Tls.
4,084,000), silk (Tls.1,813,000), goat-skins (Tls.450,000),
white wax (Tls.332,000), and sheep's wool (Tls.315,000).
Much of the opium sent from the province takes various
land routes to escape too rigid a scale of taxation, but the
quantity sent down the river through both taxing offices
in 1904 was 36,856 piculs, and in 1905 was 36,311 piculs,
valued at Ichang, after passing the dangers of the river,
at about Tls.16,000,000, in each year.

WANHSIEN, the opening of which is provided for in the
British commercial treaty of 1902, is situated on the Yangtze,
midway between Chungking and Ichang. The port was
opened to trade in 1917. For the year 1918 the trade was
valued at Tls.2,921,238 for imports, Tls.2,665,304 for exports, total Tls.5,586,542.

HUNAN

Hunan, "South of the Lake" (Tungting), consists of
mountains to the south and west, with the Tungting Lake
and its surrounding alluvium occupying the north-eastern
quarter. Its area is estimated at 83,400 square miles, and
its population at 23,600,000. Its people are the sturdiest
and most straightforward of the provincials of China, and
they have never allowed the Empire to forget that to them
was due its salvation during the period 1853-1863, when the

Hunan levies under Tseng Kwo-fan arrested and turned back the advancing wave of the Taiping rebellion ; from that time, until the recent formation of the " New Model " army, the Chinese army was largely composed of Hunanese " braves." Anthracite coal is mined in the south-east, bituminous coal in the south and west, and from the west come antimony and others of the uncommon metals. The alluvial lands and valleys produce rice with an exportable surplus of over a million piculs annually, tea of which 300,000 piculs are forwarded annually to Hankow, and sub-temperate products in general ; and large rafts of timber are floated down the Yuan River, the value of annual floats to Hankow being estimated at upwards of ten million taels. Formerly a vast trade between Canton and Hankow passed from Kwangtung over the Cheling Pass and down the Siang River through Hunan, and Siangtan was then, in consequence, one of the principal trade marts of China ; but, since the advent of steam traffic, this trade now takes the sea and Yangtze route via Shanghai. In Hunan two places have been opened to trade as " treaty ports."

YOCHOW (29° 20′ N., 113° E.) was opened voluntarily by China in 1899. Situated at the point where the Tungting Lake empties into the Yangtze, it was expected that this port would tap the entire trade of Hunan, owing to the presumed necessity of transhipping from the deeper vessels possible on the Yangtze to the lighter draft boats of the inner waters, but this expectation has not been realised, and the later opening of Changsha has effectively killed whatever prospect of trade Yochow may have had. The municipal plan adopted at Yochow is one which has been introduced at some other ports. The Chinese government expropriated the land required for an " international settlement," laid out roads and sold the lots by auction, reserving an annual ground-rent of a substantial amount ; wharfage dues, moderate in amount, are levied ; municipal work and police are under the joint control of the Yochow territorial Taotai and the Commissioner of Customs ; all expenses are at the charge of the Chinese government, and the community is burdened neither with further taxation nor with the task of governing ; in the event of further taxation becoming necessary, it will be under the control of a representative body. The population of Yochow is 20,000, and the " treaty port " is five miles distant, at a point where alone a safe anchorage could be found.

CHANGSHA (28° 12' N., 112° 47' E.), the capital of the province, on the Siang River, was opened as a treaty port in 1904. The city is a centre of learning and culture, encouraged by the wealth remitted to their homes by the many eminent officials of Hunan birth, and protected by the independent character of the people ; and it marks the extreme western limit of the advance of the Taipings, who were repulsed from its walls, though gaining numerous victories in nine provinces. Its population is stated at 230,000. Thirty miles farther up river is Siangtan, the population of which was formerly stated to be 700,000, but is now supposed not to exceed half that number. The depth of water up to Changsha in summer may be put at fully ten feet, but in winter is reduced in places to three feet. The trade passing the Customs of Yochow and Changsha combined was valued in 1905 at Tls.4,447,058 for imports, and Tls.1,938,830 for exports, a total of Tls.6,385,888, and in 1911 at Tls. 10,119,265 for imports, Tls.11,027,060 for exports, a total of Tls.21,146,325. In 1918 the combined values were : Tls.16,903,284 for imports, Tls.16,350,861 for exports, total Tls.33,254,145. Considering that the export of Hunan tea alone must be worth Tls.10,000,000, these figures show that the trade of this rich province continues to be carried in the small Yangtze junks.

CHANGTEH (29° 1' N., 111° 27' E.), on the Yuan River west of the Tungting Lake, was in 1906 on the point of being voluntarily opened by China, but the intention was not carried out. The so-called lake is to-day a lake in summer only, and in winter is a series of wide, shallow channels in a waste of mud ; and, summer and winter, traffic to Changteh passes by the sinuous channels of the deltaic land lying south of the lake between the mouths of the Siang and Yuan. During the winter the greatest draft of water which can go through to Changteh does not exceed two feet. Changteh is a city of 150,000 inhabitants, and its chief value as an open port lies in the fact that imports are carried free of duty so much the farther inland.

HUPEH

Hupeh, " North of the Lake," has an area estimated at 71,400 square miles, and a population of 24,900,000, and forms with Hunan the Viceroyalty of Hukwang, " The Lake District." Mountainous to the north and west, its centre is covered by an extensive plain forming a triangle, with its base well north of the line Hankow-Ichang, and its legs formed by the Yangtze in its course from Ichang south-east to Yochow, thence north-east to Hankow. This plain, dotted with lakes and intersected by canals, is much of it depressed, some of it covered by floods every summer, and most of it protected from repeated summer flooding only by a vast system of embankments, admirably designed and constructed, and kept in continual repair ; and its principal product is cotton. In this province are three treaty ports.

ICHANG (30° 42′ N., 111° 16′ E.), a city of 40,000 people, is situated at the head of steam navigation on the Yangtze, at the throat of the main outlet from Szechwan, and at the point where the mountains of Szechwan and western Hupeh meet the central plain of Hupeh. Here a great emporium might have been expected to spring up at which the men of the mountains should meet the men of the plains, and the inland men should meet the men from the sea, for the mutual exchange of products. The course of trade has, however, undergone no change, and Ichang, opened as a treaty port in 1876, has done no more than use its advantage of steamer traffic and take from Shasi a portion, and the major portion, of the work of transhipping the Szechwan trade from the deep-draft lower-river boats to the light upper-river boats and *vice versa* ; while the emporia for the exchange of products are still at Hankow and Shanghai. The character of the trade of Ichang may be judged from the following figures for the traffic which, between Ichang and Chungking, went by " chartered junk," subject to the control of the Maritime Customs, and, between Ichang and Hankow, went by steamer, competing with the lower-river junk, the value of the traffic by which is not included ·

	GROSS IMPORTS.	RE-EXPORTS (*i.e.* transhipped).	NET IMPORTS.
	Tls.	Tls.	Tls.
1894 ..	10,373,903	9,427,920	945,983
1904 ..	35,559,841	34,129,018	1,430,823
1911 ..	7,345,258	4,047,163	3,298,095
1918 ..	6,300,675	4,544,036	1,756,639

SHASI (30° 17′ N., 112° 17′ E.), a city of 80,000 people, was opened as a treaty port in 1896. Originally, before the opening of Ichang, it was the ordinary place of transhipment for the Szechwan trade ; and in itself should be a good distributing centre, placed in the heart of the Hupeh plain, with canals radiating from it through the plain and into Hunan. One such canal connects it directly with Hankow by a much shorter route than that taken by steamers on the Yangtze ; and to this canal facility must be attributed its failure to develop as a steamer port. The value of the trade has been as follows :

	IMPORTS.	EXPORTS.	TOTAL.
	Tls.	Tls.	Tls.
1897 ..	135,292	181,220	316,512
1904 ..	1,334,328	622,043	1,956,371
1911 ..	1,968,847	979,809	2,948,656
1918 ..	4,192,521	2,169,971	6,362,492

HANKOW (30° 35′ N., 114° 17′ E.), " Han-mouth," is situated at the junction of the Han River and the Yangtze ; across the Han is Hanyang, containing extensive iron and steel works ; and opposite both, across the Yangtze, is Wuchang, the provincial capital : the combined population of the triple mart is estimated at 870,000. This was an important commercial centre before the foreign trader put in an appearance ; was further developed when it constituted the head of steam navigation ; still further developed since the opening of the upper reaches of the Yangtze to steamers ; and its recent start as a railway centre can only add to its importance. Opened as a treaty port in 1861, an area of 62 acres was granted to the British government as a concession, governed on the same plan as that of Tientsin ; here for thirty-five years merchants of all nations lived and traded, content with their modest area and its half-mile of river frontage. In 1896 this concession was extended by an additional area of 53 acres, on the same footing as the original grant. Next below the British concession is the Russian. A French concession was granted in 1861, but was not taken up, and was re-granted in 1896. Next below the French comes the German concession, granted in 1895, with an area of 108 acres ; and below the German is the Japanese concession of 31 acres. Including the Peking-Hankow Railway reservation, still farther down stream, there is, starting from the Chinese business quarter of Hankow, a frontage of 6,000 yards under foreign control, most of it well bunded. The foreign population of Hankow, in December 1905, was 2,151, including 504 British, 500 American, 162 German, 68 French, 89 Russian, 84 Belgian, 134 Italian, 537 Japanese, and 73 others. When present plans are carried out, Hankow will be at the intersection of a cross, formed by the Yangtze from east to west, and the trunk railway Peking-Hankow-Canton from north to south, and it is difficult to set any moderate limit to its prospect of development. In the past the value of its trade has been as follows :

| | IMPORTS. | EXPORTS. | TOTAL. |
	Tls.	Tls.	Tls.
1864 ..	7,935,558	13,453,425	21,388,983
1874 ..	14,885,471	18,276,094	33,161,565
1884 ..	17,467,883	16,403,998	33,871,881
1894 ..	15,915,966	23,218,827	39,134,793
1904 ..	44,364,324	63,085,050	107,449,374
1905 ..	53,837,696	57,205,350	111,043,046
1911 ..	43,882,937	74,074,547	117,957,484
1918 ..	62,336,980	102,825,328	165,162,308

To enumerate the principal imports would be to give a
list of the principal imports into China. Among exports
originating in Hankow, and not, as in the case of Kiukiang tea, first originating elsewhere, the principal were
in 1905 tea (Tls.9,729,000), cotton yarn (Tls.1,829,000),
beans (Tls.7,089,000), bean-cake (Tls.868,000), wood-oil
(from seeds of *Aleurites cordata*, Tls.3,320,000), cotton
(Tls.3,910,000), jute (Tls.1,704,000), hides (Tls.3,177,000),
pig iron (Tls.987,000), rice (Tls.2,130,000), sesamum seed
(Tls.3,172,900), skins and furs (Tls.2,050,000), vegetable
tallow (Tls. 1,403,000), tobacco (Tls. 2,184,000). Of the
steamers entered and cleared at Hankow during 1905, a
total of 3,715,710 tons, 50 per cent. was under the British
flag, 17 per cent. under the Chinese, 16 per cent. under the
Japanese, and 13 per cent. under the German.

KIANGSI

The province of Kiangsi, with an area estimated at
69,500 square miles and a population of 14,500,000, is
mountainous over much of its surface, but has the general
appearance of a trough trending to the northern border.
The basin of the trough is the Poyang Lake, into which
flow rivers from the east, south, and west, and which finds
its outlet to the north, emptying into the Yangtze at Hukow,
some twenty miles below Kiukiang. The Poyang Lake
and the Tungting Lake in Hunan act as reservoirs to take
the first rush of flood waters coming down the Yangtze

every summer, and reduce their catastrophic effects.   The lake and its affluents, accessible through the portal of Hukow, furnish the channels of transportation through the province.   From Kiangsi over the Meiling Pass to Canton runs a main trade route, by which formerly a considerable traffic passed, and by which even now goes much of the porcelain sent from Kingtehchen to Canton, to be there painted with the florid Cantonese designs.   Kingtehchen itself, a town of no official status, *i.e.* with no official head or government, with a population estimated a century ago by Abbé Huc at a million, destroyed in the Taiping rebellion, and revived so as to support a present population of 150,000, is the centre of production of Chinese porcelain. Formerly unapproachable in quality and inimitable in the colouring of its designs, this porcelain rapidly deteriorated from the end of the eighteenth century, and received its death-blow on the destruction of the ovens by the Taipings ; and since the revival of the industry the product has been coarse and heavy in material, and crude in the colouring and design of what is painted at the place.   Other products of the province are tea, tobacco, paper, hemp, and wood-oil. In the province is one treaty port.

KIUKIANG (29° 44′ N., 116° 8′ E.), a city of 55,000 people, opened as a treaty port in 1861, is situated near the outlet of the Poyang Lake.   In this year a British concession was granted, with municipal government like that of Tientsin, and this constitutes to-day the residential quarter for the foreign community.   Thirteen miles from Kiukiang is the mountain resort of Kuling, " Bull Ridge," where, at an altitude of 3,500 feet, the foreign residents of Shanghai and the Yangtze valley have established a " summer cottage " colony, comprising, with no hotels, by the census of September 1906, a summer population of 1,100.   The intended function of the port, to serve as a tea market, was maintained for a few years, but by degrees the control of the business was transferred to Hankow, and to-day most of the tea prepared for the foreign market remains

17

in Chinese hands until it is sold at Hankow. The progress
of trade at the port is shown by the following figures, the
shipments of tea in thousands of piculs being shown in
parentheses after the export values :

		IMPORTS.	EXPORTS.	TOTAL.
		Tls.	Tls.	Tls.
1864	..	2,622,319	4,070,948 (137)	6,693,267
1874	..	3,932,987	9,921,679 (245)	13,854,666
1884	..	2,852,825	6,351,800 (279)	9,204,625
1894	..	4,911,997	6,705,479 (211)	11,617,476
1904	..	12,045,395	12,302,165 (186)	24,347,560
1911	..	15,601,240	19,071,686 (245)	34,672,926
1918	..	18,863,631	21,180,299 (154)	40,043,930

Among the imports in 1904, cotton yarn was valued
at Tls.4,327,000, kerosene oil at Tls.859,000, sugar at
Tls.767,000 ; among exports the principal were tea
(Tls.4,945,000), porcelain (Tls.714,300), cotton (Tls.502,300),
hemp (Tls.926,000), paper (Tls.1,443,000), and tobacco
(Tls.645,000).

ANHWEI

The province of Anhwei, with an area estimated at
54,800 square miles and a population variously at from
25,000,000 to 35,000,000, but given in the official census of
1910 as only 17,300,000, was formerly a part of the province
of Kiangsu, from which it was separated administratively
in the reign of Kang-hi, A.D. 1662–1723. The portion north
of the Yangtze, except for some part of the extreme west
bordering on Hupeh, is plain, and may be termed the
granary of the Empire, annually producing a greater exportable surplus of rice than any other rice-growing district.
South of the Yangtze, except for plains bordering the river,
is mainly hilly. The principal products are rice, tea,
opium, hemp, cotton, and paper. Anhwei is the country
of Li Hung-chang, who supplemented the work of the
Hunanese Tseng Kwo-fan in suppressing the Taiping re-

bellion, and who from 1870 until near his death in 1901
was Grand Secretary, Viceroy of Chihli, Imperial Commissioner for Foreign Trade, Generalissimo of the military
and naval forces in the north, and principal negotiator for
the Imperial Government of its treaties and conventions ;
through his agency the men of Anhwei were brought forward
in official life and in recruiting for the army, thus preventing
the Empire from becoming the exclusive pasturage of the
men of Hunan ; and his family have for many years dominated the rice trade of his native province.   The provincial
capital, Anking, is a port of call for Yangtze steamers,
and at Tatung is the Superintendency of the Salt Likin
Collectorate, the revenues of which are pledged for foreign
loans.   In the province is one treaty port.

WUHU (31° 20′ N., 118° 21′ E.), a city of 137,000 inhabitants, was opened to foreign trade in 1877.   For
twenty-eight years there was no concession, settlement,
or reserved area for foreign residence ; but in 1905 an area
was marked off for an international settlement, to be
administered on the Yochow plan.   The following figures
show the development of trade :

		IMPORTS.	EXPORTS.	TOTAL.
		Tls.	Tls.	Tls.
1884	..	2,681,697	1,206,793	3,888,490
1894	..	5,068,450	5,156,090	10,224,540
1904	..	9,916,453	13,306,930	23,223,383
1911	..	10,796,055	10,636,102	21,432,157
1918	..	15,902,901	12,972,728	28,875,629

The imports in 1904 included cotton woven fabrics
(Tls.1,750,000 for foreign, and Tls.274,000 for native weavings), cotton yarn (Tls.818,000), gunny bags (Tls.426,000),
kerosene oil (Tls.718,000), and sugar (Tls.1,209,000) ;
the exports included few articles of much importance
except rice, of which the shipments, ranging generally from
2,000,000 to 4,000,000 piculs, amounted to 5,621,143 piculs
in 1904, and 8,438,093 piculs (502,250 tons) in 1905 ; but in
1911 the export was only 2,665,151 piculs (158,630 tons)

KIANGSU

The province of Kiangsu is essentially a country of the plain, comprising nearly the entire area of the alluvial deposit of the mouth of the Yangtze, and the coast strip, as far up as Shantung, of the Yellow River deposit. Its area is estimated at 38,600 square miles, and its population variously at from 14,000,000 to 39,000,000, but given in the census of 1910 as 17,300,000. It is a province in which, through its whole extent, every inch of ground is utilised, even the otherwise barren wastes of the low coast supplying the salt for the Hwai Administration, which provides officially for the needs of six provinces or parts of provinces, with a probable total of a hundred million consumers. The natural products are rich in quality and infinite in variety, including silk, by nature the finest in the world, rice, the choicest of any in China, cotton, of short staple but fine fibre, besides opium, wheat, beans, etc. ; while the products of its hand-looms, of the silk weavers of Soochow and Nanking, and of the cotton weavers of every farmstead in the province, have been renowned for centuries. Trade is an instinct of the province, facilitated by the canals which everywhere and in all directions intersect its surface, the Grand Canal being only *primus inter pares*. The ruined bridges, temples, and houses of this smiling land, devastated by the Taiping rebels (1853–1864), were a marked characteristic of Kiangsu thirty years ago, and are still observable in many places. Kiangsu, Kiangsi, and Anhwei form the Viceroyalty of Liangkiang, " The Two River (provinces)." In the province are four treaty ports, Nanking, Chinkiang, Soochow, and Shanghai.

NANKING (32° 13' N., 119° 25' E.), the " Southern Capital," the official name being Kiangning, " River Rest," was the capital of the Empire at several periods of its history, the last occasion being under the two first Ming Emperors, 1368–1402. Remains of some of the old walls are still discernible, one of the time of the Six Dynasties, A.D.

221–587, and another of the city under the Southern Sung (A.D. 1127–1280), and Mongol (A.D. 1280–1368) Dynasties. The present wall, substantially that of the Ming Hung-wu (A.D. 1368), but renovated after its capture by the Taipings in 1853 and its recapture after a siege of eleven years in 1864, has a circuit of twenty-five miles, and encloses an area sufficient rather for the possible population of the capital of an Empire than for the present population of 275,000. The walls and city, and the tombs of the early Ming Emperors attract visitors ; but the pride of Nanking, the famous porcelain pagoda erected by Yung-lo (A.D. 1403–1424), was destroyed by the Taipings. Nanking is the capital of the Viceroyalty of the Two Kiang, but the Governor of Kiangsu has his seat at Soochow. The first treaty made by China with any of the maritime Powers was the British treaty of 1842, signed at Nanking. The French treaty of 1858 provided for the opening of Nanking, then in the hands of the Taipings ; but when, in 1865, the British and French Commissioners visited the place, they decided that the trade prospects were too unpromising, and it was actually opened as a treaty port only in 1899. The principal industry is silk-weaving, which, however, has not fully recovered from the dislocation caused by the disorders of the Taiping occupation, the number of looms being said to have been 50,000 in the city and its immediate vicinity before the rebellion, and to be only 5,000 now. The development of trade is shown by the following figures :

	IMPORTS.	EXPORTS.	TOTAL.
	Tls.	Tls.	Tls.
1900	.. 2,158,311	1,710,284	3,868,595
1904	.. 5,296,119	3,529,929	8,826,048
1911	.. 6,092,015	2,970,523	9,062,539
1918	.. 14,920,284	8,075,482	22,995,766

The imports comprised the usual requirements of a distributing centre, and of exports nearly two-thirds of the value consisted of satin (Tls.2,335,000 in 1904).

CHINKIANG (32° 13' N., 119° 25' E.) occupies an important position near to the point where the Yangtze leaves the old geologic formation and becomes more or less deltaic in character, and at the point where the Grand Canal is intersected by the Yangtze. By means of the Grand Canal it is a distributing and collecting centre for a large area, extending into Shantung, Honan, Anhwei, and even into Chihli. The city, with a population of 170,000, was opened to foreign trade in 1861, and the foreign residential quarter is on the British concession, administered in the same way as the British concession at Tientsin. The course of trade is shown by the following figures :

	IMPORTS. Tls.	EXPORTS. Tls.	TOTAL. Tls.
1864	4,673,294	1,208,486	5,881,780
1874	11,439,133	1,029,008	12,468,141
1884	11,108,506	976,425	12,084,931
1894	15,165,088	4,127,403	19,292,491
1904	23,941,579	8,381,625	32,323,204
1911	18,237,184	5,242,502	23,479,686
1918	15,735,616	3,382,730	19,118,346

The principal imports in 1904 were cotton woven fabrics (Tls.3,866,000), cotton yarn (Tls.3,693,000), matches (Tls.572,000), kerosene oil (Tls.1,786,000), sandal-wood (Tls.325,000), sugar (Tls.3,681,000), wood-oil (Tls.1,058,000), and tobacco (Tls.594,000). The principal exports were beans (Tls.535,000), bean-cake (Tls.781,000), ground nuts (Tls.1,804,000), ground nut-oil (Tls.911,000), sesamum oil (Tls.876,000) and satin (Tls.759,000). Of the total import of foreign goods, excluding opium, in 1904 (Tls.15,185,682), 78 per cent. went inland under transit pass, 38 per cent. going to destinations in the home province, and 40 per cent. into other provinces, Anhwei, Shantung, Honan, etc.

SOOCHOW (31° 25' N., 120° 34' E.), the provincial capital, has for centuries been famous for its wealth and its magnificence, and is the subject of two well-known proverbial expressions :

> Shang yu tien tang,
> Hsia yu Soo Hang.
> (Above is heaven's blue,
> Below are Hang and Soo.)

The other is more cryptic, and is expressed in three words " Hang Soo Lin," which may be explained as follows : " Be born at (Hang-) chow, because there the men are handsomest and most learned ; marry at (Soo-) chow, because there the women are most beautiful ; die at (Lin-) chow, because there may be found the finest wood for coffins." Poets have sung the city in many another phrase, and Western poets may there find keen enjoyment, provided that, as elsewhere in China, they have no olfactory nerves. The population, estimated before the rebellion at a million, is now about 500,000 ; the walls are about ten miles in circuit, and, as is usual with Chinese cities, the greater part of the trade is carried on in the suburbs, outside the walls, more especially to the north-west. The one important industry is silk—reeling, spinning, and weaving. Soochow was opened as a treaty port in 1896, and an international settlement was laid out, to be administered on the plan afterwards adopted for Yochow, situated outside the south wall, at the greatest possible distance from the business quarter and from the railway station, opened to traffic in 1906. The opening of the port has produced but little effect on the course of trade, which continues to follow old channels to Shanghai ; the total value in 1904 was Tls.1,247,668 for imports, of which. tobacco contributed nearly a fourth, and Tls.1,886,194 for exports, of which silk contributed four-fifths. The figures for the trade in 1918 show that it had begun to adopt the new facilities provided : Tls.3,910,722 for imports, Tls.14,134,154 for exports, total Tls.18,044,876.

SHANGHAI (31° 14′ N., 121° 29′ E.), " By-the-Sea," is now far removed from salt water, but is the first point on entering the Yangtze at which a port can be established.

At a distance of 60 miles from the North Saddle light, on an outlier to the entrance, and at 32 miles from the Tungsha lightship, marking the outer bar of the southern entrance to the Yangtze, at the village of Wusung, is the first affluent of the Yangtze, the Hwangpu, draining an extensive area of canal-intersected plain between Chinkiang and Hangchow. The Hwangpu, a tidal river emptying into a tidal river, has an outer and an inner bar, the latter originally with only a general depth of 19 feet at high water, spring tides, though at times this is increased to 23 feet. This sufficed for the vessels engaged in the carrying trade in the early days, but, with the increase in carrying capacity of steamers in recent times, many ocean steamers are now compelled to discharge outside Wusung, and in 1906 a Conservancy Board was established by the Chinese Government, under the stipulations of the International Protocol of September 8th, 1901, which has much improved the condition of the river. Twelve miles up the Hwangpu is the city of Shanghai, with excellent anchorage and discharging facilities. The anchorage had thirty to forty years ago a general width of 1,800 feet, but, by the agency of natural causes acting mainly upon the works of man, this is now reduced to about two-thirds of the former available width, but with unaltered depth. At Shanghai is the junction with the Soochow Creek, which provides water communication with the country to the west, and which, almost entirely through human agency, is now reduced to less than a hundred yards in width. The approaches from the sea are lighted by seventeen lights.

Shanghai is mentioned in history 2,150 years ago, and 900 years ago was a mart of sufficient importance to be made a Customs Station. It was occupied in 1842 by the British forces on their way to Nanking, and, having been declared a treaty port by the treaty of Nanking, was formally opened to trade on November 17th, 1843. The first district to be occupied for foreign residence was selected by the British authorities, bounded on the south by the Yangkingpang, a ditch running east and west about a quarter-mile north of the Chinese city, on the north by the Soochow Creek, on the east by the Hwangpu, and on the west by Defence Creek dug at one mile distance from the Hwangpu, enclosing an area of 470 acres with a river frontage of three-fourths of a mile. In 1849 the French authorities delimited an area between the Yangkingpang and the city, and in 1853 obtained in extension the narrow strip lying between the city and the river, having, with narrow depth, a river frontage of nearly three-fourths of a mile. The Americans occupied the district called Hong-kew, lying north of the Soochow Creek, with frontage on that creek and on the river, including the most valuable part of the wharfage of Shanghai. This American Settlement was in 1863 amalgamated with the British Settlement, both governments waiving their exclusive rights and thereby creating the self-governing republic styled " The Foreign Community of Shanghai, North of the Yangking-pang," the French Government having refused to surrender its jurisdiction over the so-called " Concession Française." In 1899 these various settlements were extended, and the authority of the Municipal Council of the " International Settlement," as it is called for short, now extends over 5,584 acres, while the present area of the " Concession Française " is 358 acres. The resident population of the International Settlement at different periods and of the whole of Shanghai and district for 1910 are shown on next page.

The resident population under the French Municipality in 1905 was 831 foreigners (including 274 French, 109 British, 47 German, 73 Japanese) and 84,792 Chinese. By whatever name they are called, and whatever the minor differences in their form of government, the several " reserved areas " at Shanghai, whether British, French, American, or International, are not concessions such as exist at Tientsin. Hankow, and Canton, where a grant has been made by a lease in perpetuity from the government of China to the foreign Power, and where the " land-renter " holds under a title-deed issued by the foreign lessee Power, and regis-

	1880.	1885.	1890.	1895.	1900.	1910.	
	Int. Sett.	Int. Sett.	Int. Sett.	Int. Sett.	Int. Sett.	Int. Sett.	All Shai.*
British	1,061	1,511	1,663	2,055	2,987	5,269	5,569
American	230	274	323	328	562	940	961
French	41	66	114	138	176	330	862
German	159	216	244	314	525	811	886
Japanese	168	595	386	250	736	3,361	5,535
Portuguese	285	457	564	731	978	1,495	2,199
Russian	3	5	7	28	47	317	377
Austro-Hungarian	31	44	38	39	83	102	107
Italian	9	31	22	83	60	124	131
Spanish	76	232	229	154	111	140	140
Danish	32	51	69	86	76	113	123
Other foreign	102	191	162	478	433	534	665
Total	2,197	3,673	3,821	4,684	6,774	13,536	17,555
Chinese	107,812	125,665	168,129	240,995	345,276	488,005	690,000

tered only at the Consulate of that Power. They are
" Settlements," reserved areas within which foreigners are
permitted to acquire land, in which Chinese may continue
to hold land, in which foreigners acquire land by direct
negotiation with the original owners—for such land a bill
of sale is not issued, but it is held under " perpetual lease,"
sealed and issued by the Chinese territorial authority ;
and this title-deed may be registered at any Consulate,
ordinarily that of the land-renter, and not compulsorily at
that of the titular controlling Power. The Settlement has
complete self-governing power, including the power of
taxation and police ; but the systems on the two sides of
the Yangkingpang differ. They are alike only in not
granting the franchise to Chinese, who are considered to
be residents of the Foreign Settlements by sufferance, a
sufferance dating from the time when they came by thousands as refugees from the Taipings, and found under the
foreign flags the safety they could not find under their own.

The first Land Regulations for the British Settlement
were drawn up in 1845, with a " Committee of Roads and

* The figures included for the population outside the International Settlement are those for 1905.

Jetties " nominated by the Consul. These, as amended in 1854 and approved by the Chinese authorities, extended the privilege of acquiring land within the Settlement to all foreigners ; and when in 1863 the British and American Settlements were united, the Municipal Council, first elected in 1855, became the Municipal Council of the Settlement with the long name mentioned before. The Land Regulations were last amended in 1898, and, having received the assent of the foreign Ministers at Peking, are now the governing charter of the community. The electorate consists of all householders who pay rates on an assessed rental of Tls.500 a year, and owners of land valued at Tls.500. The French Municipality was organised in 1862 ; the electorate consists of all owners of land, occupants paying a rental of 1,000 francs a year, and residents having an income of 4,000 francs a year ; and the Municipal Council is under the presidency of the French Consul-General, whose assent is necessary for the validity of its decisions. Under these forms of government the place has grown in wealth, the International Settlement, built up by British, American, and German enterprise, naturally more rapidly than the French. In the International Settlement in 1905 the assessed value of the 5,584 acres contained therein was Tls.83,000,000,* representing a market value well over Tls.100,000,000 ; on 2,471 foreign and 45,328 Chinese houses the assessed annual rental was Tls.8,350,000, representing an additional capital value of over Tls.100,000,000. The assessed value of the 358 acres of land under the French Municipality in 1905 was Tls.8,500,000, and the assessed rental of houses was Tls.1,145,000. The soil on which the Settlement is built is described by a competent authority as consisting of " a water-logged highly micaceous sand of extreme fineness and of alluvial deposit and generally, under pressure, with no more consistency than a quicksand " ; and it says much for the enterprise of the com-

* Shanghai tael, worth less by 10 per cent. than the Haikwan tael in which the values of trade are expressed.

munity that a modest beginning has been made in sky-scrapers of six storeys in height.

When the foreign trader advanced his outpost from Canton to Shanghai, this, the chief mart of Central China, was to him North China, a fact preserved for posterity in the name of its oldest newspaper, the *North-China Herald*, with its daily edition, the *North-China Daily News*; and the absence of good deep-water ports in the north has continued to Shanghai its old-time function of distributing centre for North China as well as for the Yangtze basin. The commercial history of the port can be shown by figures better than by any narrative.

TONNAGE OF SHIPPING ENTERED AND CLEARED.

	1864.	1884.	1904.	1911.
British	991,786	2,306,036	6,524,801	7,311,167
American	548,175	544,032	394,659	454,467
German	116,945	105,458	1,614,027	1,600,051
Japanese	756	206,473	495,292*	3,986,523
Other foreign ..	130,397	158,060	1,143,970	1,754,010
Chinese steam ..	—	704,439	2,009,049	3,073,254
Total ..	1,788,059	4,024,498	12,181,798	18,179,472

It is important to show the distributing trade of Shanghai rather than its purely local trade, and this is brought out in the following figures :

FOREIGN PRODUCTS IMPORTED

	GROSS IMPORTS. Tls.	RE-EXPORTS. Tls.	NET IMPORTS. Tls.
1859 ..	32,429,232	2,609,603	29,819,629†
1864 ..	30,522,183	17,723,355	12,798,828
1874 ..	52,902,102	43,764,978	9,137,124
1884 ..	47,158,013	39,690,117	7,467,896
1894 ..	96,920,931	66,435,217	30,485,714
1904 ..	196,905,998	151,617,898	45,288,100
1911 ..	220,279,867	139,160,662	81,119,205
1918 ..	220,900,052	132,515,864	88,384,188

* Japanese tonnage in 1904 reduced from 1,744,249 tons in 1903, owing to Russo-Japanese war.

† The Yangtze and northern ports not having been opened to foreign shipping, re-exports thither did not pass through the Customs in 1859.

CHINESE PRODUCE IMPORTED

	GROSS IMPORTS. Tls.	RE-EXPORTS. Tls.	NET IMPORTS. Tls.
1859	.. —	—	—
1864	.. 27,542,065	17,062,865	10,479,200
1874	.. 36,734,241	29,946,189	6,788,052
1884	.. 39,454,313	32,576,102	6,878,211
1894	.. 53,361,347	47,092,163	6,269,184
1904	.. 127,970,828	107,966,192	20,004,636
1911	.. 173,806,469	147,781,070	26,025,399
1918	.. 231,104,855	170,580,017	60,524,838

CHINESE PRODUCE EXPORTED

	ORIGINAL EXPORTS. Tls.	RE-EXPORTS. Tls.	TOTAL. Tls.
1859	.. 33,003,545	—	33,003,545
1864	.. 20,137,038	17,062,865	37,199,903
1874	.. 27,541,834	29,946,189	57,488,023
1884	.. 26,603,194	32,576,102	59,179,296
1894	.. 45,340,093	47,092,163	92,432,256
1904	.. 80,187,434	107,966,192	188,153,626
1911	.. 90,115,886	147,781,070	237,896,956
1918	.. 175,089,475	170,580,017	345,669,492

TOTAL TRADE

	INWARD. Tls.	OUTWARD. Tls.	TOTAL. Tls.
1859	.. 32,429,232	35,613,148	68,042,380
1864	.. 58,064,248	54,923,258	112,987,506
1874	.. 89,636,343	101,253,001	190,889,344
1884	.. 86,612,326	98,869,413	185,481,739
1894	.. 150,282,278	158,867,473	309,149,751
1904	.. 324,876,826	339,771,524	664,648,350
1911	.. 394,086,336	377,057,618	771,143,954
1918	.. 452,004,907	478,185,356	930,190,263

In the original exports from Shanghai in 1904, silk and its products figured for Tls.33,411,000, raw cotton for Tls.16,000,000, cotton cloth from steam factories Tls.747,000, and from hand-looms Tls.5,920,000, factory-spun cotton yarn Tls.4,150,000, and rice Tls.5,100,000.

CHEKIANG

Chekiang, with an area of 36,700 square miles and a population estimated at 17,000,000, formed the northern end of the ancient Kingdom of Yueh, which extended along the coast from Canton to Shanghai. It is divided by the Tsientang River, emptying into the sea between Hangchow and Shaohing, into a large southern section, generally mountainous, but with some considerable plains in its northern part, and a smaller northern section, almost entirely plain, deposited by the Yangtze. The plains of the northern section and of the northern part of the southern section are protected from incursions of the sea by well-built sea walls, starting from Hangchow and skirting both sides of the estuary of the Tsientang, with a total length of about 250 miles. The Hangchow or Tsientang bore or eger, seen at its best opposite Haining, is among the wonders of the world, presenting the sight of a solid and almost perpendicular wall of water, 12 to 15 feet high, rushing into the estuary and up the river at a speed of 12 to 15 miles an hour. The plain country, especially north of the Tsientang, is intersected by canals, including the Grand Canal, the southern starting-point of which is Hangchow; all are on the same level, and freely intercommunicating, except those from Hangchow along the coast to Haining and intersecting the city of Hangchow, which are on a higher level. Being in China, where so much is topsy-turvy, the high-level canals adjoin the estuary of the Tsientang, in which the range of spring tides is 25–35 feet, and the low-level canals are inland. The principal products of the province are silk, tea, and cotton, and it contains three treaty ports.

HANGCHOW (30° 12′ N., 120° 12′ E.), the provincial capital, and for a time the capital of the Southern Sung

Empire (A.D. 1129–1280), was opened as a treaty port in 1896. A centre of the silk industry, in which it surpassed Soochow, it shared the fate of other cities of the Yangtze plain during the Taiping rebellion, and has not yet fully recovered from the devastation it suffered at that time. Its present population is estimated at 350,000. As at Soochow, opened at the same time, an International Settlement with an area of 182 acres was set aside by the Chinese authorities and retained under their control, and alongside it was granted a Japanese concession of 120 acres. Some fifty miles from Hangchow is the mountain resort of Mokanshan, with many summer cottages built by residents of Shanghai and other places. Trade communication outside the district is entirely with Shanghai, by a route following the Grand Canal and other inland waterways, and is maintained by " trains " made up of passenger and cargo-boats towed by steam-launches. A considerable trade ends and originates in Hangchow, as shown by the following figures :

	IMPORTS. Tls.	EXPORTS. Tls.	TOTAL. Tls.
1898	2,960,234	5,033,245	7,993,479
1904	8,702,249	9,158,519	17,760,768 ·
1911	8,065,977	9,632,054	17,698,031
1918	9,418,301	9,269,781	18,688,082

Among the imports of 1904 cotton manufactures figured but little, the principal being tin (Tls.197,000), kerosene oil (Tls.699,000), matches (Tls.97,000), sugar (Tls.1,710,000), beans (Tls.795,000), bean-cake (Tls.275,000), bean-oil (Tls.134,000), wood-oil (Tls.135,000), rape-seed (Tls.111,000), and tobacco (Tls.418,000). Among exports the principal were cotton (Tls.306,000), fans (Tls.800,000), silk and its products (Tls.3,182,000), and tea (Tls.4,245,000).

NINGPO (29° 53′ N., 121° 33′ E.) was visited by the Portuguese in 1522, but their traders were expelled in 1542. It was occupied by the British forces in 1841, and in 1842 was declared a treaty port. Its population is estimated at 260,000. There is no foreign concession or reserved area, and the police and roads are maintained at the cost and under the control of the Chinese authorities. There was in the early days some question whether Ningpo or Shanghai should become the commercial centre for trade at the mouth of the Yangtze, but the strong organisation of the Ningpo merchants in the gilds kept the trade of the port in their own hands, with the result that Shanghai took metropolitan rank. Ningpo is, and for fifty years has been, commercially subsidiary to Shanghai, with which almost alone trade is carried on, communication being maintained by a daily steamer. The opening first of Wuhu, then of Hangchow, diverted a part of the trade from Ningpo. The course of trade is seen from the following figures :

	IMPORTS. Tls.	EXPORTS. Tls.	TOTAL. Tls.
1864	10,264,616	6,250,306	16,514,922
1874	7,532,465	7,013,845	14,546,310
1884	6,649,117	4,773,272	11,422,389
1894	8,984,676	5,615,081	14,599,757
1904	13,296,271	8,001,141	21,297,412
1911	14,357,411	7,863,141	22,220,552
1918	15,820,957	14,141,813	29,962,770

With so slight an expansion of values expressed in silver, obviously a non-progressive port. Among the imports of 1904 the principal were cotton fabrics (Tls.2,950,000), cotton yarn (Tls.533,000), tin (Tls.1,300,000), kerosene oil (Tls.561,000), sugar (Tls.1,529,000), and tobacco, including cigarettes (Tls.312,000). The chief exports were cotton (Tls.1,972,000), rush mats (Tls.290,000), tea (Tls.3,409,000), and fishery products (Tls.339,000).

WENCHOW (28° 1′ N., 120° 40′ E.), a city of 80,000 inhabitants, is situated toward the south of Chekiang. A fairly clean and very picturesque city, intersected by canals, it reminds the visitor somewhat of Venice. It has no foreign settlement, and few foreign residents. It was opened as a treaty port in 1877, and has failed to develop a trade. In 1904 imports were valued at Tls.1,523,480, including kerosene oil (Tls.189,000) and sugar (Tls.137,000) ; and exports at Tls.866,905, including tea (Tls.505,000) ; making a total trade of Tls.2,390,385. The trade of 1911 and 1918 was only a little more.

FUKIEN

Fukien, with an area of 46,300 square miles and a population variously estimated from 8,000,000 (Ross, 1891) to 25,000,000 (Popoff, 1894), but given by the census of 1910 at 13,100,000, is essentially a mountainous province. The principal river is the Min, which, with its many branches, drains the greater part of the province, and has its mouth at Foochow. The valleys and foot-hills produce tea, sugar, opium, and food for the inhabitants, while from the mountains come timber, bamboos, and, in recent years, camphor. One of the most important industries is fishing, and the passenger on the mail steamer, out of sight of land or seeing only projecting headlands, will pass through fleets of thousands of fishing-boats, cockle-shells riding buoyantly on the waves of the stormiest piece of water in the world, the Formosa Channel. Supported mainly by the sea, with a rough and not particularly fertile hinterland, the people of the province are driven to emigrate in great numbers, and from Amoy, it is estimated, at least 200,000 able-bodied men go every year to the Southern Seas, usually on arrival indentured for terms of three to five years. In Fukien are three treaty ports.

SANTUAO (26° 40′ N., 119° 40′ E.), the " Haven of the Three Marts," has one of the finest harbours in the world, eminently suitable for a naval station ; and this, with the desire to protect it by quasi-neutralisation, led to its voluntary opening in 1899. The port is shut off by mountains from all except a small distributing area, and the opening has produced but small effect on trade, the only visible result being that a quantity of tea, which formerly was

18

carried by porters over the mountains to Foochow, now originates in Santuao, is shipped to Foochow for its old market, and is re-exported thence. In 1904 the imports by steamer were valued at Tls.53,723 ; to exports, tea (110,772 piculs) contributed Tls.1,936,000, and all other goods Tls.5,359.

FOOCHOW (25° 59′ N., 119° 27′ E.), the " City of Happiness," the provincial capital, has a population estimated at 625,000. It is situated on the Min River at a distance of thirty-four miles from the sea, and nine miles above Pagoda Anchorage, the highest point reached by steamers. At Pagoda is the Foochow Arsenal, a government dock and ship-building yard, partly destroyed by the French in 1884. Foochow was opened as a treaty port under the British treaty of 1842, but nothing was done to develop its trade until ten years later, when traders went there to secure the teas of Fukien, Kiangsi, and Anhwei, coming over the mountains to the port ; even after the opening of the Yangtze ports in 1861, tea continued to go to Foochow from the southern part of Anhwei. Foochow was opened before the period of residential concessions (1861), nor has it a settlement such as those of Shanghai, opened under the same treaty. The residential quarter is on the south side of the river, opposite the city, and its municipal organisation is of the inchoate form described under Chefoo. The resident foreign population of the district in 1905 was 841, including 194 British, 163 American, and 349 Japanese. Foochow is an instance of a port which, as far as foreign interests are concerned, is decadent ; it depended mainly on one industry, tea, and, with a diminishing tea trade, its former prosperity has departed. In the following figures, after the export value are given in parentheses the quantities (in thousands of piculs) of shipments of tea, including in 1904 and 1911 re-shipments of tea received from Santuao.

	IMPORTS. Tls.	EXPORTS. Tls.	TOTAL. Tls.
1864 ..	7,134,000	13,124,000 (487)	20,258,000
1874 ..	4,668,220	15,406,672 (683)	20,074,892
1884 ..	5,038,689	8,508,752 (680)	13,547,441
1894 ..	6,425,919	7,025,013 (487)	13,450,932
1904 ..	10,048,966	7,217,002 (293)	17,265,968
1911 ..	8,437,141	8,859,075 (307)	17,296,216
1918 ..	8,253,811	7,388,408 (214)	15,642,219

Those are the figures for the trade by steamer, to which in 1904, to get the total trade of the port, must be added the value of the junk trade, imports Tls.3,134,173, exports Tls.8,316,932, total Tls.11,451,105. During the year 1904 the principal imports, by steamer and junk, were cotton fabrics (Tls.810,000 for foreign, and Tls.584,000 for native weaving), cotton yarn (Tls.1,011,000), tin (Tls.159,000), kerosene oil (Tls.747,000), sugar (Tls.309,000), beans (Tls.516,000), bean- and tea-oil (Tls.475,000), and wheat (Tls.485,000). The principal exports were tea (value, including Santuao tea, Tls.7,117,000), soft-wood timber (Tls.4,736,000), edible bamboo shoots (Tls.919,000), paper (Tls.3,612,000) ; among other noted products of the port are lacquered ware and ornaments carved from soapstone.

AMOY (24° 27′ N., 118° 5′ E.), a city of 300,000 inhabitants on an island of the same name, serves as steamer port for the prefectures of Chuanchow (Chinchew) and Changchow. The outer anchorage offers good holding-ground, but is exposed to the south-west, while the inner harbour affords perfect shelter, except from typhoons which, getting in, are unable to find their way out. The inner harbour, with a width of a third to a half-mile, lies between Amoy, on which are the business offices, and the rocky island of Kulangsu, which constitutes the foreign residential quarter. The municipal organisation was of the headless and unsanctioned kind until 1903, when Kulangsu was made an International Settlement with powers of self-government, much on the Shanghai model. In 1899 a

Japanese concession was marked out on the Amoy side, but has not been developed. At the upper end of the inner harbour is a graving dock, 300 feet long and 60 feet wide. The resident foreign population of the district in 1905 was 1,912, including 364 British, 35 American, and 1,426 Japanese. Amoy is one of the tea markets of China, the earlier shipments begin mainly of Amoy Oolong ; this soon deteriorated in quality, and, as the export fell off, its place was taken by Formosa Oolong, the culture and preparation of which were introduced by Amoy tea-men, and which, even since the Japanese occupation of Formosa (1895), has continued to find its way to Amoy to be there blended, packed, and matted. The history of the trade in Oolongs is interesting, and may be read in the following figures of the quantities in piculs shipped from Amoy and from Tamsui respectively, the Tamsui output being entirely re-shipped to foreign countries, chiefly the United States :

	AMOY TEAS.	FORMOSA TEAS.	
		via Amoy.	Direct.
1864	37,217	—	—
1874	71,560	24,610	—
1884	42,923	98,754	—
1894	29,312	137,245	—
1904	3,065	100,683	63,630
1906	2,450	59,005	67,717
1911	1,741	337	

The following figures show the course of trade at Amoy, the value of exports including that of Formosa tea imported and re-exported :

	IMPORTS. Tls.	EXPORTS. Tls.	TOTAL. Tls.
1864	7,064,720	2,830,359	9,895,079
1874	5,692,781	4,617,061	10,309,842
1884	8,745,061	4,831,021	13,576,082
1894	10,043,128	7,771,091	17,814,219
1904	14,522,053	6,604,634	21,126,687
1911	16,671,785	3,741,554	20,413,339
1918	11,431,407	2,494,876	13,926,283

Among imports in 1904 the principal were cotton fabrics (Tls.797,000), cotton yarn (Tls.1,509,000), tin (Tls.208,000), bicho de mar (Tls.138,000), flour (Tls.505,000), matches (Tls.130,000), kerosene oil (Tls.589,000), rice (Tls.1,907,000), beans (Tls.964,000), and bean-cake (Tls.1,192,000). Among exports tea from Formosa (Tls.4,025,000) constituted three-fifths of the whole ; other exports were paper (Tls.884,000), sugar (Tls.441,000), and tobacco (Tls.324,000).

KWANGTUNG

Kwangtung, the " Eastern Broad," forms with Kwangsi, the " Western Broad," the Viceroyalty of Liang Kwang, the " Two Broads." Kwangtung is in the main a mountainous province, with two rich plains, one lying around Chaochow (of which the port is Swatow), the other being the delta of the Pearl River, formed by the junction of the West River, flowing from Kwangsi, the North River, which flows from the watershed separating Kwangtung to the south from Kiangsi and Hunan to the north, and enters the West River at Samshui, and the East River, flowing from eastern Kwangtung and entering the deltaic system near Whampoa, the deep-water anchorage of Canton. Including the island of Hainan, administratively only a prefecture of Kwangtung, the area of the province is estimated at 100,000 square miles, and its population at 27,700,000. The people are sturdy and industrious, differing in this from other sub-tropical peoples, and are aggressive and independent. They are of two distinct races, the punti or indigenous, and the hakka or immigrants, intermingled but never coalescing or intermarrying, speaking dialects mutually unintelligible to each other, and frequently engaging in clan fights. From the eastern to the western extremity of its coast, a sailing course from headland to headland, not entering the inlets and not including Hainan, would measure nearly 700 nautical miles. The people of this coast are hardy fishermen, and, when occasion serves, bold pirates. The inland people of the country are industrious husbandmen, and in the cities is a laborious industrial population. The province produces great quantities of rice, and imports annually some half-million tons additional to supply the deficiency for its needs; it also produces silk, good but inferior to that of Kiangsu and Chekiang; tea, far inferior to its former quality; matting, from a rush grown on the low islands of the delta coast; cassia, from Loting; ginger, from the north-west; sugar from the eastern parts of the province, from Leichow, and from Hainan; fruits, from all parts; and sub-tropical produce generally. The industries carried on in the cities are literally innumerable, but all such as can be carried on by one man and his immediate family working in his own shop or in his own home. In the province are six treaty ports, Swatow, Canton, Samshui, Kongmoon, Kiungchow, and Pakhoi; two Customs Stations, Kowloon and Lappa, to supervise the junk trade between China and Hongkong and Macao respectively; and two ceded and one leased territories, Hongkong, Macao, and Kwangchowwan.

SWATOW (23° 22′ N., 116° 40′ E.), an unofficial town with a present population of 60,000, the port of Chaochowfu, the easternmost prefecture of Kwangtung, was opened to trade in 1860. The anchorage is good, four miles up stream from Double Island, which lies as a breakwater across the mouth of the Han River. The foreign community lives partly on the north, and partly on the south side of the river, with the business offices on the north side, and they have no municipal organisation. The people of the Chaochow prefecture, commonly called the Swatow men, are very clannish, holding themselves apart even from their co-provincials the Cantonese, and are well organised and closely united in every place in the Empire to which trade has called them; and on many occasions they have successfully resisted attempts to impose more stringent conditions upon them (such as lower prices for their products, higher freights, special clauses in a bill of lading, etc.) by united gild action, proceeding even on occasion to the extreme measure of a boycott or of abstention from all trade. The district is a large importer of beans and bean-cake, and, though rice-producing, of rice as well; its staple exports are sugar and tobacco. The following figures show the course of trade:

	IMPORTS.	EXPORTS.	TOTAL.
	Tls.	Tls.	Tls.
1864	6,399,786	3,700,165	10,099,951
1874	11,057,659	4,367,739	15,425,398
1884	12,385,969	7,386,349	19,772,318
1894	19,424,841	6,483,667	25,908,508
1904	34,615,923	14,664,863	49,280,786
1911	36,095,506	15,320,190	51,415,696
1918	35,048,206	15,134,731	50,182,937

The large excess of imports introduced into this self-contained district is striking, and is explained by the value of an export not recorded in ordinary statistics of trade, that of the hardy and industrious coolies who emigrate in thousands for short-term service in the islands of the Malay Archipelago. Among imports in 1904 the principal were cotton fabrics (Tls.2,146,000), cotton yarn (Tls.3,699,000), tin (Tls.645,000), flour (Tls.312,000), matches (Tls.256,000), kerosene oil (Tls.738,000), rice (Tls.7,422,000), beans (Tls.2,525,000), bean-cake(Tls.5,432,000), hemp (Tls.696,000), and wheat (Tls.343,000). The principal exports were sugar (Tls.6,050,000), tobacco (Tls.866,000), grass-cloth (Tls.837,000), and paper (Tls.1,749,000).

CANTON (23° 7′ N., 113° 16′ E.), the provincial capital, is styled the "City of Rams," from the legend of the five Immortals who rode into the city on five rams in the time of the Chow dynasty (B.C. 1122–255); the rams were turned into stone and are there to-day as visible evidence of the truth of the tale. The name of the city is Kwangchow, Canton being the Portuguese rendering of the name of the province, Kwangtung. The estimates of the population have ranged from 500,000 to 2,500,000, the figure now generally accepted being 900,000. The foreign residents in the district in 1905 were 1,437, including 225 British, 484 American, 65 German, 158 French, 140 Japanese, and 334 Portuguese. In the early years of trade the merchants lived in the " Factories," surrounded by unsavoury Chinese streets, and this continued after Canton was made a treaty port in 1842 ; they were driven away in 1856, and on their return in 1857 found their houses in ruins. The head houses of the firms were then generally established in Hongkong, and, in foreign trade, Canton became a mere commercial dependency of the British colony. At Canton the " factory " sites were abandoned, and in 1859, a new residential quarter was created by embanking and reclaiming Shameen, a mud flat about half a mile long and a fifth of a mile wide in its widest part, situated at the south-west corner of the city. Of this reclamation four-fifths were assigned as the British concession and one-fifth as the French concession ; and here, surrounded by a wide moat with guarded bridges, the foreign community lives, somewhat restricted for space, but self-governing on the model of the corresponding concessions at Tientsin. This completes the list of the old-time foreign concessions, all dating from 1859–1861—Newchwang, Tientsin, Hankow, Kiukiang, Chinkiang and Canton. The city and suburbs of Canton form a buzzing hive of workers, and few sights in the world are more instructive, to the sociologist and ethnologist, than a mere cursory trip in a sedan-chair through the narrow, crowded, reeking, and malodorous streets, in which the busy throng, hustling, shouting, and pushing, yet manages to disentangle itself by some rule of the road imperceptible to the insight of the mere Westerner, and where a shop, filled with priceless treasures of antiquity or with the dainty work of ivory-carvers and silk-embroiderers, stands cheek by jowl with a shop in which an artisan carries on some primitive handicraft with the implements and by the methods employed by his progenitors a thousand years ago. Even the hasty globe-trotter, who allots from his tour three days to India

and three hours to the Empire of China, may profitably
employ those three hours in such a trip, and feel that his
time has not been wasted ; and as he steams back to Hongkong he will have the history of half a century of foreign
relations recalled to his mind by the sight of the stately
Roman Catholic cathedral erected by the French on the
site of the Viceroy's Palace, destroyed in 1857 by the
allied forces, who then occupied Canton, as a reminder of
the wanton destruction of foreign property in the preceding
year. The early history of the trade of Canton is the
history of the foreign trade of China, and is treated in that
chapter. In 1842, by the British treaty of Nanking, Canton
lost its monopoly of trade, and the produce of the country
was allowed to find its outlet where best it could by any
one of the four other ports—Shanghai, Ningpo, Foochow,
and Amoy—then opened to trade ; and when, in 1860,
the Yangtze ports and Swatow were thrown open, Canton
was absolutely restricted to its own producing and supply
district. Since that time the course of trade is shown by
the following figures, the value of silk and its products (in
millions of taels) being put in parentheses after the value
of the export trade :

	IMPORTS. Tls.	EXPORTS. Tls.	TOTAL. Tls.
1860 ..	13,061,230	11,516,815 (3·7)	24,578,045
1864 ..	2,393,085	9,860,220 (4·0)	12,253,305
1874 ..	6,626,441	16,287,633 (9·1)	22,914,074
1884 ..	11,886,781	13,853,243 (8·0)	25,740,024
1894 ..	27,385,876	18,031,721 (12·6)	45,417,597
1904 ..	52,885,637	43,361,439 (29·5)	96,247,076
1911 ..	47,597,577	54,627,044 (33·6)	102,224,621
1918 ..	45,205,295	58,020,793 (38·8)	103,226,078

It will be convenient to consider here the status of the
two supervising stations for the junk trade with Hongkong
and Macao, the stations of KOWLOON and LAPPA.

The foreign colonies of Hongkong and Macao being
free ports, with no Customs duties or supervision to trammel

their trade, the preventive measures necessary to check smuggling were obviously imposed on the Chinese authorities alone. Smuggling was easy, and, easy or difficult, the habit is ingrained in the Chinese character. Macao was on the mainland, Hongkong (the original cession) was separated by a short half-mile of water from Chinese territory, and smugglers by water from either had their choice of a score of routes by which to reach a profitable market. Opium and salt were the principal subjects of the traffic, opium because of the great value and high duty attaching to a small bulk, and salt because of the strictness with which the government monopoly is preserved in China; but smugglers do not in China despise the profits from evading the incidence of a tariff based upon a 5 per cent. levy, and smuggling was universal. The Chinese authorities were driven to adopt some preventive measures, and the result was the so-called "blockade of Hongkong," a preventive cordon instituted in 1868 and maintained by cruisers under the control of the native authorities of Canton. The situation, with lax native control, became intolerable in the eyes of those who would maintain the absolute freedom of those free ports; and in the Additional Article of 1885 to the Chefoo Agreement of 1876 between Great Britain and China, it was provided that the measures for the repression of the smuggling, stipulated in the Agreement, should be considered at once. The Chinese Customs Stations of Kowloon and Lappa then, in 1887, came into existence, and, to avoid the irregularities which had marked the old régime, were placed under the control of the Inspectorate-General of Customs. These establishments have their head offices in the respective colonies, Hongkong and Macao, for the mutual convenience of all concerned; but the supervising and collecting stations and the preventive cruisers are echelonned outside; when the boundaries of the British colony were enlarged in 1899, the Kowloon Customs Stations were pushed further out, so as to be in Chinese waters and on Chinese soil. These offices control the junk traffic from Chinese ports, mainly in the **Canton** district, to Hongkong and Macao ; and the value of the trade passing their stations, added to the value of the trade passing the Canton Customs, given above, may fairly represent the collective trade of the Canton delta. This collective trade has been as follows :

		IMPORTS. Tls.	EXPORTS. Tls.	TOTAL. Tls.
1887	..	29,186,636	31,656,019	60,842,655
1894	..	53,792,843	41,607,808	95,400,651
1904	..	92,650,896	65,102,878	157,753,774
1911	..	90,961,424	73,760,559	164,721,983
1918	..	94,472,676	77,894,438	172,367,114

The principal imports into the delta through the three offices in 1904 were cotton yarn (Tls.4,171,000), flour (Tls.1,133,000), kerosene oil (Tls.3,834,000), rice (Tls.11,423,000), sesamum seed (Tls.2,763,000), and sugar (Tls.1,276,000). The principal exports were silk and its products (Tls.31,420,000), cassia (Tls.1,233,000), eggs (Tls.509,000), fans (Tls.572,000), leather (Tls.601,000), straw mats (Tls.929,000), matting (Tls.3,369,000), paper (Tls.1,234,000), and tobacco (Tls. 1,605,000). Tea, which in 1860 with shipment of 263,264 piculs, contributed 50 per cent. to the value of the export trade of Canton in that year, in 1904 contributed (53,250 piculs) less than 2 per cent. to the value of the exports passing the three offices.

SAMSHUI (23° 6′ N., 112° 53′ E.), " Three Waters," an unimportant city of 5,000 inhabitants, situated at the junction of the West and North Rivers, was opened as a treaty port in 1897. It was expected to tap all the North River trade and much of that by the West River, but the hopes entertained have not been realised. In 1904 imports were valued at Tls.1,828,935 and exports at Tls.1,217,873, a total of Tls.3,046,808. In 1911 the figures were Tls. 4,370,103, Tls.1,315,146, and Tls.5,685,249.

KONGMOON (22° 35′ N., 113° 9′ E.), " River-mouth," a city of 35,000 inhabitants, situated on a side creek of the delta near the mouth of the westernmost branch of the network of rivers, distant 70 miles steaming from Canton, 87 miles from Hongkong, and 45 miles from Macao, was opened as a treaty port in 1904. The object of its opening was to tap the trade of the western part of the delta and of the district lying west of it, and a measurable degree of success has been obtained. Not including the trade by junk to and from Hongkong and Macao, which is included in the statistics of the Kowloon and Lappa stations, the value of the trade by steamer and junk in 1905, the year following the opening, was—imports Tls.3,082,954, exports Tls.3,794,676, total Tls.6,877,630. In 1911 the figures were—imports Tls.4,191,990, exports Tls.1,309,902, total Tls.5,501,892. The principal exports are palm-leaf fans, straw mats, and poultry.

KIUNGCHOW (20° 1′ N., 110° 16′ E.), the prefectural city of the island of Hainan, contains a population of 35,000, and is situated 3 miles inland from Hoihow ("Seaport") its port. Its opening as a treaty port was stipulated in the treaties of 1858, but, as none of the mercantile community had any interest in it, the actual opening was deferred until 1876. The port serves the trade of Hainan and of the prefecture of Luichow on the mainland, across the Straits of Hainan, 12 miles wide. Hoihow, the port, has a population of 25,000, and the anchorage is a roadstead open to the Straits from north-east around to north-west, and accessible to cargo-boats loading and discharging only at high water of the one daily tide which rises here as in the whole of the Gulf of Tonkin. The course of trade has been as follows :

		IMPORTS.	EXPORTS.	TOTAL.
		Tls.	Tls.	Tls.
1884	..	1,326,499	1,119,682	2,446,181
1894	..	1,817,398	1,283,821	3,101,219
1904	..	2,548,725	2,469,878	5,020,509
1911	..	3,308,601	2,106,679	5,415,280
1918	..	2,347,013	2,195,662	4,542,675

The principal exports in 1904 were pigs (65,306 valued at Tls.881,631), sugar (Tls.507,000) and betel-nuts (Tls.120,000).

PAKHOI (21° 29' N., 109° 7' E.), " North of the Sea," a dirty, insanitary town of 20,000 inhabitants, situated at the head of the Gulf of Tonkin, is the seaport of Limchowfu, 13 miles distant, and was opened as a treaty port in 1877. In common with other ports on the Gulf it has but one tide in the twenty-four hours. The district directly served by it is poor and sandy, producing sugar, indigo, and ground-nuts, with fishing and piracy as bye industries ; and the chief hope for any development of trade lay in the use of the port as a side door through which to evade the fiscal obstructions imposed on the natural routes to Yunnan and Western Kwangsi, viz. the Red River through Tonkin and the West River through Kwangsi. The figures for the trade of Pakhoi given below are for years which have been selected to show the paralysing effect of the Chinese system of internal taxation, driving trade from natural water routes to a channel by which expensive transport over hill roads must be substituted ; and they must be considered with reference to the following dates :

1884 (seven years after opening of port), French occupation of Tonkin transformed the frontier from an internal to an external boundary.

1889, the opening of Mengtsz and relaxation of fiscal restrictions in Tonkin restored the Red River to its natural use as a trade route to Yunnan.

1897, the opening of Wuchow as a treaty port, carrying the one-duty privilege into Kwangsi and neutralising the likin barriers of Kwangtung, made the West River available through its entire course as a route to Yunnan and Western Kwangsi. (For table see next page.)

The value of the trade of Pakhoi in 1904 was—imports Tls.1,892,235, exports Tls.1,122,423, total Tls.3,014,658. The exports included sugar (Tls.296,000) and indigo (Tls.257,000).

Goods.	Annual Average in			
	1881–83.	1888–90.	1894–96.	1898–1900.
Shirtings Yards	36,120	4,081,600	3,127,160	1,488,120
T.-Cloths „	1,337,950	2,987,875	1,357,050	499,250
Fine cottons „	14,600	1,315,660	790,920	576,900
Cotton yarn, Piculs	11,323	91,481	76,090	45,654
Long Ells Pieces	5,306	20,109	13,171	6,434
Total value of all cotton and woollen goods Tls.	357,899	2,454,334	1,922,160	1,221,749

CESSIONS IN KWANGTUNG

There are no less than three areas in Kwangtung ceded to foreign Powers under different conditions—Macao to Portugal, Hongkong to Great Britain, and Kwangchowwan to France.

MACAO (22° 11′ N., 113° 33′ E.) was first occupied by the Portuguese in 1557, after their traders and trading ships had been driven away from Ningpo and Foochow. Here for three centuries they held under conditions which were never clearly defined, one side contending that it was by right of conquest and occupation, the other disputing this and maintaining Chinese taxing stations within the colony itself: one indisputable fact being that the Portuguese government paid to the Viceroy at Canton a rent of Tls.500 in every year up to 1848. In that year the Portuguese authorities refused to continue to pay the rent, and expelled from the colony the Chinese taxing stations and all other signs of Chinese authority. The sovereignty of Portugal was recognised finally by China in the treaty of 1887. The Portuguese and Dutch trading ships frequented the port in the seventeenth century, the English came there in the eighteenth century, and the English and American in the first half of the nineteenth century, making usually their final departure from Macao; and when, in 1839 and again in 1856, the merchants were driven from their factories at Canton, it was in Macao that they found refuge. The cession of Hongkong to the British in 1842 and its development from 1856 gave a final blow to the decadent legitimate trade of Macao, and from that time its prosperity depended mainly upon the coolie traffic, until the Portuguese government suppressed it in 1874. The Chinese Customs Station of Lappa (*vide antea*) was established in 1887 to control the trade by junk between Macao and Chinese ports. Macao occupies a small peninsula connected by a narrow isthmus with Chinese territory, and the cession includes two islands, Taipa and Kolowan, dominating the harbour. The population on December 31, 1899, was 63,991, composed of 3,780 Portuguese, 154 other foreigners, and 60,057 Chinese.

HONGKONG (22° 18′ N., 114° 10′ E.), " Fair Haven," was formally occupied by the British authorities by a notification published on May 1, 1841, and its cession was recognised by China in the treaty of Nanking, the ratifications of which were exchanged at Hongkong on June 26, 1843. The Royal Charter creating the colony was dated April 5, 1843. The original cession included only the island of Hongkong, with an area of 29 square miles. North of this, between it and the mainland, is the fair haven of Hongkong, one of the few harbours in the world which may be called perfect, the eastern entrance being 600 yards wide, and the western entrance full wide, but protected by outlying islands, while the anchorage has a general width of a mile. The Kowloon peninsula, with an area of about two square miles, projecting towards the harbour on its north side, was added to the cession in 1860. The northern side of the harbour was dominated through its whole extent, except for the Kowloon peninsula, by Chinese territory; and in 1899 the " Kowloon Extension," with 376 square miles on the mainland, was added to the colony by a lease from the Chinese government for ninety-nine years, the lease including also the large island of Lantao and the waters to the farther shores of Mirs Bay and Deep Bay. Hongkong has been a busy mart, especially since 1856, and has filled for the ports of South China the function of distributing centre, filled for North China and the Yangtze basin by Shanghai ; of the collective foreign trade of the whole of China it may, with a fair degree of certainty, be said that one-fourth of the imports and one-third of the exports are financed and distributed through Hongkong, the balance being handled by Shanghai or, to a small extent, directly by subsidiary ports. This cannot be supported by reference to the statistics of Hongkong, since the colony publishes no statistics of trade ; and the only statistics it publishes—those of shipping—are misleading, since they include in the foreign trade shipping actually engaged in the coasting trade to places often only a few miles away. Hongkong was formally declared a free port on February 6, 1842, and a free port it has remained ever since, subject only to the aid it has given, since 1887, to the Chinese government in the prevention of smuggling in opium. The Chinese Customs Station of Kowloon (*vide antea*) was established in 1887 to control the trade by junk between Hongkong and Chinese ports. A garrison of about 4,000 is maintained in the colony, and the resident civilian population in 1906 was 319,803, composed of 307,388 Chinese, 6,085 British and other Europeans and Americans, and 5,902 other foreigners, mainly Asiatics. Of the Chinese 216,240 were males and 91,148 were females.

KWANGCHOWWAN (21° 1′ N., 110° 25′ E.) is one of the four cessions on lease made in the period after the China-Japan war, the four, with dates of first occupation, being Kiaochow (Germany, November 14, 1897), Port Arthur and Talien (Russia, March 27, 1898), Kwangchowwan (France, April 22, 1898) and Weihaiwei (Great Britain, May 24, 1898). The Bay of Kwangchow has a good anchorage, but with a difficult entrance through sand-banks ; and access to Kwangsi by rail will be possible over a not too difficult country. The French authorities have taken no steps to develop the legitimate trade of the colony, and, apart from the smuggling incidental to a free port, the chief use of the cession has, so far, been to advance the French flag so much the farther to the east and the nearer to the mouth of the Canton river.

KWANGSI

Kwangsi, with an area of 78,000 square miles and a population of 6,500,000, is in its central and eastern part at a general altitude of 500 to 800 feet above the sea, and slopes upward towards the mountains of the north and west, heights of 6,000 to 8,000 feet. It includes the drainage basin of the West River, the affluents of which converge, as the fingers of the hand converge to the wrist, to their outlet at Wuchow, the waters then flowing for a short distance in one channel through Kwangtung until, at Samshui, they again diverge to form the channels of the Canton delta. Proceeding up the West River, to the west, it is known by that name as far as Sünchow (Tamchow in local dialect), where it is bifurcated into the North and South Rivers. The North River receives several important affluents, but slightly navigable, and is itself navigable for some distance by boats of 20 tons capacity. The South River is often also called the West River (constituting, as it does, the main trade route) up to a point 30 miles above Nanning, where it is bifurcated into the Left Branch leading to Lungchow, and the Right Branch leading to Poseh, whence is a main trade route into Yunnan, by which the trade with Hongkong and Canton via Wuchow and via Pakhoi finds its way ; Poseh is accessible to large native craft, of perhaps 30 tons capacity, navigated through the many rapids with great skill. The fall of the river from Poseh to Wuchow, about 500 miles, is 800 feet. Entering the system at Wuchow is the Cassia River, running south from the provincial capital, Kweilin, from the head waters of which a small canal gives access to the head waters of the Hsiang River, flowing through Hunan into the Yangtze. The people are a riotous lot, considering brigandage and rebellion the natural con-

19

comitants of a bad harvest ; it was in Kwangsi that the Taiping rebellion took its rise, and the latest of the rebellions of China was that of Kwangsi 1902–1905. Its natural products are not important, with the exception of aniseed, of which the province has almost a world monopoly ; it comes from two districts, one lying around Poseh, the other, giving oil of better quality, lying across the Tonkin frontier between Lungchow and Langson. In minerals the province offers great, but as yet unproved, possibilities. A geologist has stated, though not with the sense of responsibility attaching to a report, that within one square mile he found by boring coal, iron, copper, and lead, a richness probably unsurpassed by many individual square miles in the world. These minerals are all known to exist, as well as gold, silver, antimony, asbestos, bismuth, etc. Timber is cut on the mountains of the north-west. In the province are three treaty ports.

WUCHOW (23° 29′ N., 111° 20′ E.), a city of 65,000 inhabitants, opened as a treaty port in 1897, is well placed for its purpose. Its treaty port status enables the trader to carry his goods, import or export, past the numerous and vexatious likin barriers of Kwangtung ; and at Wuchow he commands the waterways of the province, all of which converge to that point. The development of the steamer traffic is shown by the following figures :

	IMPORTS.	EXPORTS.	TOTAL.
	Tls.	Tls.	Tls.
1898	2,976,807	1,244,951	4,221,758
1904	7,806,436	3,277,791	11,084,227
1911	6,849,795	3,807,867	10,657,662

In addition the value of the trade by junk was—

	IMPORTS.	EXPORTS.	TOTAL.
	Tls.	Tls.	Tls.
1911	1,659,880	14,750,024	16,409,904

making the total trade of the port in

1911 amount to 27,067,566

Of the total foreign import by steamer in 1904 entitled to them, with a value of Tls.7,487,289, no less than 80 per cent. was sent inland under transit passes, thereby escaping likin taxation, 13 per cent. within the province, 59 per cent. into Kweichow, and 8 per cent. into Yunnan. In 1904 the principal exports were aniseed and aniseed-oil (Tls.410,000), cattle (11,126 valued at Tls.251,000), poultry (Tls.351,000), and hides (Tls.591,000).

LUNGCHOW (22° 22′ N., 106° 45′ E.), "Dragon City," is of the type of frontier port which will be described under Mengtsz. It was opened to foreign trade in 1889 in the hope that the trade of Western Kwangsi might pass through it to Tonkin, by the railway which it was the intention of the French government to promote. The railway, built in Tonkin, has not been extended beyond the frontier over the 40 miles of much accidented country which intervene between it and Lungchow, and the trade which it was to attract continues to find its way to Canton, by a river journey of 800 miles. The Customs officials stationed there find little to do except to admire the picturesque scenery, the value of the trade in 1905 being—imports Tls.163,330, exports Tls.67,122, total Tls.230,452. In 1911 the total was Tls.257,196, and in 1918 Tls.99,601. The principal imports were timber and dye-yams, and the principal export, other than opium, was American kerosene oil which had come up the river from Canton.

NANNING (22° 48′ N., 108° 15′ E.), a city of about 100,000 inhabitants, situated about 30 miles below the junction of the Right and Left Branches of the main (southern) stream of the West River, is the commercial centre for south-western Kwangsi, and a forwarding depot for the West River route to Yunnan. That portion of the Yunnan and Kwangsi traffic which passes through Pakhoi converges on this point. The opening of Nanning to foreign trade has been under consideration for some time, and it was opened voluntarily by China, on January 1, 1907. The Municipal Government will, it is announced, be of the type adopted at Yochow. In 1911 the trade was valued at—imports Tls.2,124,928, exports Tls.2,575,589, total Tls. 4,700,517 ; in 1918 the total was Tls.6,930,736.

YUNNAN

Yunnan, " South of the Clouds," is an elevated plateau of bright sunshine, lying south of cloud-covered and foggy Szechwan. It was the last of the Eighteen Provinces to be assimilated by the Empire, its direct government by China dating only from the time of Kublai Khan (A.D.1260), through whose conquest Yunnan was annexed and his suzerainty over Burma, Annam, and Cambodia reaffirmed. The area is put at about 145,000 square miles, and the population at 8,500,000. The Panthay rebellion in 1867, occasioned by an attempt on the part of the Mohammedan population to set up a government of their own, was suppressed with great difficulty and with ruthless slaughter ; and this brought in its train the bubonic plague, which was for many years endemic in Yunnan (at Mengtsz, with a resident population of 12,000, nearly 1,000 deaths are said to have occurred in each of the years 1892 to 1896), was first seen by the European surgeons at Pakhoi in 1882, and reached Hongkong and the outer world in 1894. These causes for a reduction in the population, combined with the ungrateful nature of the soil, explain the small density of population for the province. Yunnan is decidedly mountainous. The western part is covered with mountain chains rising to heights through which the passes are over 8,000 feet in altitude, with steep slopes running north and south, the valleys containing rivers with great volumes of water, formed by the rains and melted snows of Himalayan ranges, rushing down through rocky beds which themselves are several thousand feet above the level of the sea. The greater part of the eastern portion has been described as " an elevated broken plateau, having an average height of 5,000 feet " ; but this " plateau " is so broken up that the plains cannot be discerned, and the mountains are the most distinguishing feature. The waterways are unavailable for transport within the province, acting with their deep valleys rather as barriers to trade ; and the paucity of the population forbids the use of human porters, making the pack-mule and horse, supplemented on emergency by pack-cattle, the only agency of transportation. The water outlets from the province begin only on its borders, and those available for the major operations of trade are three : the Red River from the southern border into Tonkin, supplemented by the railway to Yunnanfu, the provincial capital; the West River from the eastern border, leading to Canton and Hongkong ; and the Yangtze from the northern border, leading down to Hankow and Shanghai. Of the agricultural products of the province, the only one deserving attention is opium, which is considered in the chapter on that drug, and which is the principal means by which Yunnan pays for the imports which it consumes. The chief wealth of the province is in its minerals, of which there are known to exist cinnabar, coal, copper, gold, iron, lead, orpiment, salt, silver, tin, and zinc. The mining industry was severely crippled by the Panthay rebellion, but prior to that date, though iron ore is the most abundant, copper was mined on a much larger scale in order to provide for the requirements of the mints of the Empire, which formerly were almost entirely dependent upon the Yunnan mines for their needs, which may be put at about 6,000 tons annually. Argentiferous lead ranks next in importance, of which over twenty mines were known. Tin comes from Kochiu, about 20 miles from Mengtsz, from which port 4,500 tons were exported in 1905. Coal, though known to exist, has not been mined to any considerable extent. The salt produced in the province supplies its own population. Along the southern and western frontier of the province are three treaty ports.

MENGTSZ (23° 24′ N., 103° 22′ E.), population 12,000, may be taken to illustrate the frontier port, and is the only one of the four now open which has developed a trade worthy of consideration. Situated at an altitude of 4,500 feet, it is 40 miles distant from its junk port, Manhao (altitude 900 feet) on the Red River, which again is six days' junk journey above Hokow; this last place on the Yunnan side, opposite to Laokay on the Tonkin side of the frontier, was in 1895 made the first sub-port of entry for the Mengtsz district. Before the building of railways, the course for imports from Haiphong during the summer floods was by steamer to Laokay, and during the winter by steamer to Yenbay, thence by native craft up the rapids to Laokay; thence by native craft to Manhao; thence by pack-animal to Mengtsz, and so on for distribution through the province, each pack-animal taking an average load of 160 lb. Mengtsz was opened as a treaty port in 1889, with the special stipulation, not applying to coast and riverine ports, that imports should pay only seven-tenths and exports only six-tenths of the tariff duty; moreover, when the revised Import Tariff was put in force in 1902, it was held that the old tariff, with its lower duties, was still to be applied to the frontier ports. Transit dues, being half the tariff duty, are, however, based on the un-diminished rate, and it is chiefly to avoid the Chinese inland taxation that the trade of Mengtsz, in particular, has been developed; of the imports in 1904 nearly 74 per cent. continued their journey under transit pass, one-sixth of this transit trade adopting this roundabout way for Kweichow. The opening of Wuchow (1897) produced no effect on the trade of Mengtsz, as shown by the following figures, the percentage of imports going inland under transit pass being given in parentheses after the import values:

		IMPORTS.	EXPORTS.	TOTAL.
		Tls.	Tls.	Tls.
1894	..	1,241,879 (92)	943,321	2,185,200
1899	..	3,373,641 (85)	1,883,297	5,256,938
1904	..	6,063,777 (74)	4,683,522	10,747,299
1911	..	4,644,758 (77)	6,750,304	11,395,062
1918	..	9,474,225 (70)	11,398,818	20,873,043

The principal import in 1904 was cotton yarn (Tls.3,732,000), and the principal exports were opium (Tls.1,332,000) and tin (Tls.3,187,000). Of the imports 86 per cent. were declared from Hongkong in bond through Tonkin, and 14 per cent. from Tonkin ; of the exports 70 per cent. were declared for Hongkong, and 30 per cent. (including opium Tls.1,332,000 out of Tls.1,404,000) for Tonkin.

SZEMAO (22° 47' N., 101° 2' E.), also called Esmok, with a population of 15,000, at an altitude of 4,700 feet, is situated in the south-west corner of Yunnan at a distance of eighteen days' pack-animal journey from Mengtsz and from Yunnanfu six days from the French Laos frontier, and twelve days from the British Shan frontier. The transport is solely by pack-animals. The port was opened in 1896, and the value of its trade in 1904 was—imports Tls.221,753, exports Tls.45,230, total Tls.266,983. The principal import was cotton, and there were no exports distinguished above others. In 1911 the total was Tls.235,208.

TENGYUEH (24° 45' N., 98° 15' E.), with a population of 10,000, lies at an altitude of 5,500 feet. Situated on the western border of Yunnan, it is seven days' pack-animal journey from Bhamo in Burma, and twenty-four days' from Yunnanfu, by a road crossing a succession of mountain passes rising at times to 8,000 feet, and dipping into valleys some as low as 2,500 feet above the sea. The opening of Tengyueh, attempted in 1900, was accomplished in 1902, and in 1904 its trade was—imports Tls.1,747,820, exports Tls.337,684, total Tls.2,085,504. In 1911 the total was Tls.1,684,213, and in 1918 Tls.3,952,883. The principal imports in 1904 were cotton fabrics (Tls.393,000), cotton yarn (Tls.849,000), and raw cotton (Tls.184,000) ; the principal export was yellow silk (Tls.224,000). Of the imports 74 per cent. in 1904 and 69 per cent. in 1911 went inland under transit pass, three-fourths to Yunnan points, and one-fourth across the whole width of Yunnan in Szechwan and Kwei-chow.

TIBET

Tibet contains one treaty port, YATUNG (28° N., 89° E.), with no inhabitants and collecting no revenue. The value of the trade passing there in 1903 (before trade was interrupted by the advance of the British Mission of 1904) was—imports Tls.343,020, exports Tls.343,662, total Tls. 686,682.

CHAPTER IX

FOREIGN TRADE

THE records of the foreign trade of China in olden time are obscure, and the proper elucidation of that trade would require a special treatise to discuss the routes by which the silks of China reached the Roman Empire, following the Central Asian caravan routes which were later followed by the Polo brothers and their nephew Marco Polo ; the routes by which the Arabs came by sea to trade during the Tang (A.D. 618–907) and Sung (A.D. 960–1127) dynasties ; and the routes followed by the Chinese themselves in trading with the islands of the Southern Sea, to which the north-east monsoon of winter carried their junks laden with the products of their own land, while the south-west monsoon of summer brought them back in surety with the spices of the tropics. It is sufficient for the purpose of this chapter to trace the progressive steps by which the trade of China was developed by European nations.

The PORTUGUESE were the discoverers of the East, as the Spanish were of the West, and the first recorded arrival of a European ship in China was that of Raphael Perestrello, who sailed from Malacca in 1516. In 1517, Fernando Perez de Andrade entered Canton waters with a squadron of four Portuguese and four Malay ships, and was well received by the local officials, then as ever quite ready to encourage trade, and was allowed to proceed in person to Peking. His brother Simon arrived in the following year, and so conducted himself that he was driven off the coast, while Fernando was put in prison in Peking, ultimately losing his life. Other ships arrived and initiated trade at Ningpo (where a regular "factory," or trading-post, was established), Foochow, and Amoy, while three posts were established near Canton, one being at Macao. The general conduct of the Portuguese was in keeping with the attitude maintained at that time by all Christian nations toward the heathen, probably intensified by the difficulty of getting the better of Chinese traders in a bargain, and the Imperial order went out to slay them. This was done effectively in the north, 800 losing their lives at Ningpo, and the Portuguese concentrated at Macao, where they were allowed to settle in 1557 on payment of Tls.500 annually as rent ; in 1573 the Chinese shut in the settlement by a wall, and in 1587 established a civil magistracy to rule the Chinese inhabitants and collect all dues of the government : both endured until 1848. Several Portuguese embassies went, or attempted to go, to Peking : the first, accompanying de Andrade in 1517, was stopped at Canton ; the second, in 1552, was stopped by the Portuguese Governor at Malacca ; a third in 1667 reached Peking, but accomplished nothing ; a fourth in 1727 was graciously received at Court, but secured no tangible advantages ; and the same result attended a fifth in 1753. After the assertion of the independence of Macao in 1848, political relations became strained, and with one exception (Mexico), Portugal was the last of the Western Powers to secure (in 1887) a treaty of amity and commerce with the Imperial Government.

The SPANISH were the next to enter into the foreign trade of China. They had entered the East from the West through the Philippines in 1543, by reason of the decision of the Borgian court of delimitation; and their first visit to China was in 1575, when they were well received at Canton. A diplomatic mission started for Peking in 1580, but was detained at Canton and sent back to Manila ; this was the last embassy until 1847, and the first treaty was made in 1864. The development of the Spanish trade with

China was left to the Chinese trading between Manila and Fukien ports (Amoy, Chinchew, etc.), and the Chinese population of Manila increased so fast, became so influential, and showed so much independence, that in 1602 the Spaniards instituted a general massacre, and killed most of the 20,000 Chinese immigrants. Thus, up to the beginning of the seventeenth century, the Chinese could only judge that European traders based their trade on cannon and the sword.

The DUTCH first arrived in 1604, and next in 1622, when a fleet of seventeen vessels appeared off Macao. Portugal was then a part of the Spanish dominion, and Macao was fair spoil of war and was attacked ; the Dutch were, however, driven off and proceeded to the Pescadores, from which they were driven by the Chinese, partly by force of arms, partly by negotiation ; they then settled in Formosa, over which at that time China had no right of government. Here they built two massive brick blockhouses (tradition says they brought the bricks from Holland !) with walls six to eight feet thick and thirty feet high, one in 1624, Fort Zealandia, at Taiwanfu in the south, one at Tamsui in the north. Their first embassy to Peking was in 1655, where it was received and had the distinction of being, except its own successor, the only European embassy, from first to last, to perform the kotow. In 1662, after a siege in Fort Zealandia of nine months, the Dutch were driven from Formosa by Koxinga, an independent partisan. In 1663 they occupied Amoy, and in 1664 sent a trading expedition to Foochow ; but after that were content to trade at Canton on the same footing as others. A special embassy went to Peking in 1665, and their last was in 1795. Their treaty, on the same terms as those of other nations, was made in 1863.

The ENGLISH made several attempts to reach China after the date, 1596, when Elizabeth wrote a letter to the Emperor, which was not delivered ; but the first to arrive in China was Weddell, who reached Macao in June 1637. The policy of every nation in that day was to restrict the trade of others, in the belief that trade was a stagnant reservoir, the abstraction of a portion of the contents of which by others would leave so much the less for themselves ; and the Portuguese interposed obstacles and misrepresented matters to the Chinese authorities in such a way, that Weddell's fleet was fired on from the Bogue Forts. A good answer was made, and in the end Weddell was allowed to obtain a cargo. The next attempt was in 1664, when one ship was sent to Macao, but returned without a cargo. Trade was opened with Formosa, not then under the Imperial authority, and in 1677 one small ship was sent to Amoy. In 1678 the ships took " trading goods " valued at £4,000 and £6,000 in specie, and brought back silks, rhubarb, and spelter. The Amoy post was abandoned in 1681 and re-established for a short time in 1685. The English were unable to obtain a footing at Canton before 1684, and even then could do little trade owing to the opposition of the Portuguese, an important item in the budget of the colony of Macao consisting of presents to the Chinese officials, given to secure a monopoly. The trade prospered, however, little by little, until in 1701 the " investment " for Canton amounted to £40,800, while that for Amoy was £34,400. In 1701 an unprofitable attempt was made to trade at Ningpo. At Canton in 1702 a beginning was made of what afterward developed into the " Hong " or " Factory " system. The English trade with China was in the hands of the East India Company until the abolition of its monopoly in 1834, all other English merchants trading under the Company's license. The first British embassy to Peking was that of Lord Macartney in 1793, which was well and honourably received, but produced no practical result ; and the second was that of Lord Amherst in 1816, who did not secure an audience, owing to regrettable misunderstanding. The third was that of Lord Napier in 1834, whose necessary assertion of the sovereignty and dignity of his country led, in the natural sequence of events, to the first war between

China and a Western Power, and to the first British treaty of 1842.

The RUSSIANS approached China first by land, their first, unsuccessful, embassy reaching Peking in 1567 ; others, also unsuccessful, reaching Peking in 1619 and 1653. Their earliest trading caravans reached Peking in 1658, 1672, and 1677. The first treaty was signed in 1689, partly to regulate land trade, but chiefly to recover from Russia ground she had occupied in farther Manchuria. Other diplomatic missions followed in 1692, 1719, 1727, 1755, and others up to the mission which signed the treaty of 1858. In 1806 the Russians sent two ships to open up the sea trade with Canton ; they obtained cargoes, but the only result was that the Chinese prohibited all trade to nations not already established in the Canton factories.

The FRENCH first made touch with China, other than by missionary enterprise, by a letter written by Louis XIV. to Kanghi in 1688. The first commercial attempt was in 1728, but it was followed up only by private enterprise. The French flag was again hoisted at Canton in 1802, but was hauled down on the resumption of hostilities with the English, and was not again raised until 1829. Their first diplomatic mission was in 1844, and by it the first treaty was signed.

The AMERICANS first made direct entry into the China trade in 1784, their previous connection with it having been solely through the East India Company, which was especially insistent that they should buy its tea. Though now an independent nation, they crept in under the wing of the English, but with the friendly support of the French, and joined in the " factory " life of the day. The only political event especially concerning them was the suspension of American trading in 1821 owing to what the Americans believed was the accidental killing of a Chinese by an American sailor ; when the American was given up and had been strangled, trade was resumed. The first American embassy was in 1844, when the first treaty was signed.

By this time the Americans had attained a position in the trade of Canton second only to the English, a development fostered by their position as neutrals during the Napoleonic wars and as free-traders in a world of monopoly, but furthered by the Yankee trading instinct.

Other nations had come at various dates to share in the China trade, and there had been established among the factories at Canton the Swedish, Danish, and Imperial ; the memory of the Danes is still preserved in Dane Island at Whampoa, and the Imperial factory provided chiefly for what is now Belgian trade and, possibly, for that of the Hanseatic towns. Others, without separate factories, came also under British protection from India, as if in anticipation of their future absorption. The Portuguese remained solely at Macao, but otherwise Canton was a microcosm with (in the order from east to west) its Dutch, East India Company's, general English, Swedish, Imperial, American, French, Spanish, and Danish factories, with four others let out in apartments.

Factory and Hong System

In the old Canton régime, the " factory " (which must be understood in the old sense of the residence or station of the " factor " or agent of the home company) represented the purely foreign side, being the counting-house, warehouse, treasury, and residence of the foreign trader during such time of the year as he was allowed to remain at Canton. The Hong, or Co-Hong, or Gild was the sole medium through which the foreign trader could enter into trade relations with the Chinese Empire. The first steps in this direction were taken in 1702, when one man was appointed to be the sole broker through whom all foreigners should buy and sell. In 1720 the Co-Hong was established as a body corporate, and in 1745 their position was reaffirmed, they were given an absolute monopoly of all dealings with foreigners, and were held responsible for their debts and good behaviour ; in the latter days the number of members was thirteen. In 1760 more stringent regulations were drawn up to the following effect :

I. All vessels of war are prohibited from entering the Bogue. Vessels of war acting as convoy to merchantmen must anchor outside at sea until their merchant ships are ready to depart, and must then sail away with them.

II. Neither women, guns, spears, nor arms of any kind can be brought to the factories.

III. All river pilots and ships' compradors * must be registered at the office of the Chinese magistrate at Macao, who will furnish each with a license or badge which must be worn at the waist. No boatmen or other people must hold communication with foreign ships unless under the immediate control of the ship's comprador, and the latter will be punished if any smuggling occurs on the ship to which he is attached.

IV. Each factory is restricted to employ eight Chinese (their functions enumerated).

V. Foreigners are prohibited from going on the river at their own will. By a relaxation made in 1819, they were allowed on the 8th, 18th, and 28th of each month to go to the Flower Gardens (about a mile away), but not in droves of over ten. If they stayed out overnight, their exeat would be refused for the next holiday. They must always be accompanied by a " linguist," and he is punished for any breach of rule.

VI. Foreigners are not allowed to address the officials directly ; if they have any representations to make, it must be done through the Hong merchants.

VII. Hong merchants are not to owe money to foreigners. Smuggling goods to and from the city is prohibited.

VIII. Foreign ships arriving with merchandise must not loiter about outside the river ; they must come direct

* Ship chandlers.

to Whampoa and must not engage in clandestine trade elsewhere.

These and others of the older regulations remained in full force up to the very last of the factory days. In 1830, for example, no less than three ladies, wives of some of the staff of the E.I.C. factory, ventured to come from Macao to Canton, where their arrival caused great commotion ; they left after a few days, but not until the officials threatened to stop all trade ! By this system the foreign trader, living ordinarily at Macao, came to Canton to attend to the business of his ship, and while there lived in his factory ; when his ship's business was finished, he was supposed to return to Macao, or to any other place in the outside world, obtaining for his exit, but not for his entrance, a permit (or rather four documents : 1st, a guarantee by several of the Hong merchants ; 2nd, the Hoppo's *laissez passer* ; 3rd, a formal pass to be countersigned by each fort and taxing station *en route* ; 4th, a permit for the effects and property taken along), for which he paid a fee which, on occasion, would rise as high as Tls.300 (£100). This was the theory ; in practice the ships arrived in fleets, or at fixed periods, aiming at reaching Canton as soon after the north-east monsoon had set in as possible (October), and at leaving before the south-west monsoon had developed force (say March) to prevent a good passage down the China Sea ; and the foreigners usually came and went in a body. During the summer one or two members would be left in Canton, not, ostensibly, to protect the factory, which was under the absolutely trustworthy protection of the Co-Hong, or rather of that member specifically assigned to the factory, but on the pretext, always accepted for an annually recurring consideration, that an out-of-season ship was, or might be, expected, or that their import cargoes had not been sold. When a ship arrived, its first duty was to obtain a licensed pilot at Macao, and a ship's comprador first at Macao, later at Whampoa, the anchorage, ten miles below Canton : these, especially the latter, monopolised all dealings with the ship, as ship, fixing their own prices. On arrival at the Bogue (Boca Tigris, Hoomunchai, Tiger's Gullet), the one narrow entrance for laden ships, a permit to enter had to be taken out, for which fees had to be paid. An authentic account * of the fees paid for a ship entering in 1830 shows the extreme elasticity of the official tariff, over and above the gratifications paid to numerous subordinates to facilitate the smooth running of the machinery.

	Tls.
Tonnage dues calculated according to measurement of length and breadth	842·285
Loss in converting into bullion	75·806
Shroffage	15·161
Official gratuity	810·691
Hoppo's " fee for opening the barrier " ..	480·420
Transport to Peking and weighing in Government scales	150·145
To the Superintendent of the Treasury ..	116·424
Add 1$\frac{1}{10}$ per cent. converting into bullion ..	1·212
	2,492·212
Difference in weights between Canton and Peking, 7 per cent.†	174·455
Total	Tls.2,666·667

equivalent at the ordinary exchange of the day to about £900, but evidently not including " all the old charges of measurement, entrance, and port-clearance fees, daily and monthly fees, etc.," which, according to the special Regulation of July 1843, " are to be abolished." Under present regulations, which have been in force since 1858, the total

* " The 'Fan Kwae' at Canton," by W. C. Hunter.

† The actual difference in weights is under 1 per cent., but the other way around, the Canton scale being the heavier.

sum payable on the above account for this ship of 420 tons is Tls.168, equivalent at to-day's exchange to £25. When the ship arrived at Whampoa, she continued to be a source of daily profit to the ship's comprador, to the officials from daily and monthly fees, from payments to subordinates, and from some uncertain gratuities to expedite her departure. Her agent in Canton took her manifest, giving full particulars of the cargo, and handed it to that member of the Co-Hong who was responsible, and the Co-Hong took all the necessary steps and paid all the necessary sums to have the cargo discharged into privileged (monopoly) lighters and brought to the factory. The specie, which formed a great part of the inward lading, was then deposited in the treasury of the factory, and the cargo might be sold to the factory's member of the Co-Hong and to no one else. Outside these limitations there was no compulsion ; the importer could hold for a better market, or he could send his goods back whence they came (thereby materially reducing the space available for tea), but he need not sell unless he wished. For export cargo the main staple was tea, which was almost invariably contracted for a year ahead ; here again the foreign trader had his option ; he could fix both quantity and price at time of contracting, or he could fix the quantity only, leaving the price to be settled according to the rates ruling for quality on the opening of next season's tea market. Shipments of silk could not exceed a certain limit (140 piculs = 167 cwt.) for any one ship—except on paying for the privilege, not according to a tariff, but enough to secure the permit. " Chow-chow " cargo (as it was then termed, the " muck and truck " of to-day's jargon, " sundries " other than tea and silk) could be shipped apparently without special limit, but a special permit—paid for—was required for shipments of bullion, the export of which was actually prohibited. When the export cargo, taken down in privileged lighters, was duly laden on board, the Co-Hong obtained the " Grand Chop " or clearance permit—paid for ; provided with which the ship could proceed to sea. This was a system which worked without friction. Every one was pleased : the foreign merchant enjoyed his practical monopoly, and had nothing of the extortion thrust under his eyes, while the annoyances of his daily life were as nothing to the prospects of rapid fortune ; the Co-Hong paid, one way and another, its millions, but could recoup itself many times ; and the officials were quite contented. The best commentary on its commercial aspect is the admitted fact that there grew up side by side, during a century of joint working, a body of Chinese and of foreign merchants than whom there has never, at any time or at any place, been a more honourable ; with never a written contract, with many an occasion of help in time of difficulty, and with much sympathy and friendliness from one to the other. When the East India Company was thrust from its high estate in 1834 and the British government sent a Royal Envoy to assume, for the first time, the control of trade, then the full light of day was thrown on the system, and it was seen to be, from its governmental side, a system not of taxation but of milking. From first to last the foreign trade was milked. From the time a ship entered port until she left, she and her equipment and her cargo and her agents were solely in the hands of men who were under the authority and direct control of the Co-Hong or the officials. Disregarding the smaller fry— the licensed and monopolist pilots, ship chandlers, stevedores, lighterers, brokers, shroffs, linguists, guides—all of whom dipped their hands into the pot, we need only consider the relations between those most friendly of rivals, the foreign traders and the Co-Hong merchants. The foreigner was surrounded by an impenetrable veil ; he had no access to markets, he could not even walk down a street of shops, he could send no independent and trustworthy agent out to inquire prices, but must in all cases accept without criticism the prices offered by his broker, a member of the Co-Hong. This applied equally to imports and to exports ; and that the Chinese system allowed the foreigner not only to make a living but to accumulate a modest fortune, that a member of the Co-Hong would, when occasion called for it, wipe out the debt of a foreign merchant who had fallen into difficulties, says much for the generosity and the business capacity and foresight of the Chinese merchants, but it emphasises also the fact that there must have been a wide margin of profit to allow of such liberality. For the Co-Hong was the milker, milking the foreign trade for all it was worth, and paying heavily for the privilege. Its members paid for their appointment, Tls.200,000 (over £60,000) being reported as the sum so paid by one ; they were frequently called upon for special contributions, say Tls.100,000, for a Yellow River flood or some other catastrophe ; they had to maintain their position (their " pull ") at the capital ; they had to keep well with the officials at Canton, especially their over-lord, the Hoppo ; and every one who knows China knows that they had to gain and keep the good will of every subordinate of every official, down to the humblest gate-keeper. When Canton submitted in 1841 to pay a ransom of $6,000,000, the Hong merchants contributed from their private means $2,000,000. And yet the best known among them, Howqua, himself stated in 1834, nine years before his death, that his estate was valued at $26,000,000, a great fortune for those days, probably the largest mercantile fortune in the world.

Up to 1834 China was the admitted master of the situation. China it was that laid down the terms on which alone foreign trade was permitted, and foreign nations, represented by the trading interests alone, accepted those terms and submitted to them without a murmur ; while the traders themselves were quite content, at Canton as at Nagasaki, to accept a position of recognised inferiority so long as their trade was profitable. The arrival of Lord Napier as British Envoy introduced another question, that of equality between sovereign Powers, and on this the

Chinese were stubborn ; and a further element was thrown into the crucible by the suddenly revived but undoubtedly honest prohibition sentiment of the Imperial Court towards opium. The contest lasted for twenty-six years, from 1834 to 1860, and had behind it four main elements of strife—

1st, The claim for equality of treatment as between nations : this was settled by the British treaty of 1842, and finally settled in 1860.

2nd, The opium question: this, in their treaty of 1842, imposed at the cannon's mouth, the British left alone, and it was finally settled incidentally by the inclusion of opium in the tariffs annexed simultaneously to all the treaties of 1858.

3rd, The monopoly of the Co-Hong and the irregular incidence of taxation : this was settled in 1842.

4th, Security to foreigners for life, limb, and property from the principles of Chinese law and their inequitable application : this the British treaty of 1842 left unsettled, and it was first introduced into the British supplementary treaty of Hoomunchai (1843) and the American treaty of 1844.

The position was now reversed, and from 1860, partly by the action of Great Britain and later of Great Britain and France, partly through the weakness caused to China by rebellion and disorder, the foreign Powers have been masters of the situation, and foreign trade has been conducted on conditions laid down by them and not by China.

The component elements of the old trade are not well known, and will some day be elucidated by a study of the East India Company's archives for the period. All that is known is that China wanted very little that the West could supply. Cotton manufactures in 1905 constituted 44 per cent. of the value (excluding opium) of all foreign imports ; but in this industry the West could compete with cheap Asiatic labour only after the development springing from the inventions of Richard Arkwright and Eli Whitney, and

in the eighteenth and early nineteenth centuries the movement of cotton cloth was from China to the West, in the
shape of nankeens to provide small-clothes for our grand-
fathers. Woollens were wanted, but only in small quantities,
the Chinese preferring their own silks, and even now the
import of woollens does not exceed 1 per cent. of the
total import trade. Quicksilver and lead were wanted,
but in no great quantities; and the goods introduced consisted to a great extent of those articles which were objects
of curiosity to the Chinese, corresponding to the lacquered
boxes and carved ivories, the painted fans and quaint
Buddhas, which went to the West in exchange. Apart
from opium, to be considered in another chapter, and raw
cotton, imported into a cotton-producing country, the trade
was on a cash basis. It was before the day of extended
bank facilities, by which an excess of exports from one
country is paid for by the imports into another country,
and at Canton there were no banks, each factory and each
merchant having a treasury which must always be kept
stocked with specie, an individual factory having frequently
over a million dollars on hand ; only the East India Company
worked its India and its China trade one into the other,
and drew or gave bills on Bombay or Calcutta, receiving
or shipping treasure only when funds were not sufficient
to cover its bills. To some extent the Dutch India Company could do the same, but generally the movement of
merchandise from the Dutch Indies was outward, as it was
from China. This course was not open to others, and the
lading of a ship of 498 tons which left New York for Canton
in 1824 may probably be taken as more or less typical ;
it consisted of furs (coal to Newcastle !), bar and scrap
iron (probably as ballast), lead (required for packing tea,
but also mined in China), quicksilver (in demand, import
779,600 lbs. in 1868 and 156,000 lbs. in 1905), and 350,000
Spanish dollars in kegs. That veracious historian, J.
Fenimore Cooper,* writing in 1847 of a trade of which

* " The Crater."

he had some knowledge, describes two voyages of the good ship *Rancocus* in 1796 and 1798. In the first she sailed from Philadelphia to Europe, and there engaged in trade, profitable to neutrals, " until a certain sum in Spanish dollars (specie was scarce in America at that time) could be collected, when she was to . . . make the best of her way to Canton," and load tea. In the second she sailed for the South Pacific islands with " trade goods " and axes to pick up a cargo of sandalwood (with some misgivings in the minds of her owners as to its employment for idolatrous purposes), and, after an interrupted voyage, arrived in Canton, sold her sandalwood at good prices, bought tea, and had some thousands of dollars surplus, also spent in Canton, but for another purpose. In the year 1831, so Hunter informs us, three ships, arriving from New York, brought with them $1,100,000 in coin. Even as late as 1859, a year in which the imports and exports of merchandise at Shanghai about balanced, the import of treasure at that port through foreign channels was Tls.10,483,550 and the export Tls.4,246,067 ; and in 1860, with exports exceeding imports in value, the movement of treasure at Shanghai was Tls.15,201,277 inwards and Tls.1,742,510 outwards. After that date banking facilities were more fully developed in the East, and in 1905 was seen the spectacle of a Chinese import trade (Tls.447,000,000) valued at nearly double the value of the export trade (Tls.228,000,000) and financed with only a comparatively trifling movement of treasure, about ten million taels on balance for the year, and that inwards, in the same direction as the merchandise. The truth is that China has for centuries levied tribute, commercially, on the outside world in a way which will be referred to later.

The new trade of China, based on conditions laid down by the foreign Powers, has been conducted since 1860 on lines similar in many ways to those followed in other parts of the world, and practically identical up to the moment when foreign imports are sold to the Chinese distributor, and from the moment when Chinese produce is bought for shipment ; but one fact must be borne in mind, that Customs duty is levied in China on exports as well as on imports, both being assessed at rates based on a nominal five per cent. levy. The development of trade in the past forty-five years cannot be fully gauged by a mere statement of the total value inwards and outwards, since a much more important factor is the increase in the number of articles demanded from the West and of those supplied for export. The Chinese Customs statistics, issued from 1860, assumed their present shape in 1867, and that year is taken for comparison with 1905 in order to show the progress made in the exchange of commodities during thirty-nine years of the new dispensation.

SHIPPING

During the sixteenth century the only ships trading to China were the Portuguese. During the seventeenth century Portuguese ships traded to Canton, Dutch to Formosa and Amoy, and English to Amoy and, from 1684, to Canton. In the eighteenth century trade was rigidly restricted to Canton, and at this port the flags of the principal maritime commercial nations were shown in greater or less numbers, including, from 1784, the American. In the first part of the nineteenth century, in the days of the " old trade," restricted as before to Canton, the principal part of the carrying trade fell to the British flag, and, next to that, to the American. The fifth and sixth decades of the century were a period of scramble, and since that time the development of the carrying trade under the principal flags is shown in the table on opposite page.

IMPORTS

Imports generally (net, after deduction of re-exports to foreign countries) were valued in 1867 at Tls.69,329,741 (£23,109,914) and in 1905 at Tls.447,100,791 (£67,065,119).

	1864.	1874.	1884.	1894.	1903.*	1911.
	Tons.	Tons.	Tons.	Tons.	Tons.	Tons.
British ..	2,862,214	4,738,793	12,152,949	20,496,347	28,122,987	34,712,440
American ..	2,609,390	3,184,360	2,140,741	129,127	559,686	712,161
French ..	93,099	137,253	93,963	348,291	1,178,200	3,154,157
German ..	580,570	530,377	939,765	1,983,605	7,310,427	6,849,069
Japanese ..	756	480	215,105	379,044	7,965,358	19,172,727
Norwegian ..	38,195	22,507	10,455	288,051	1,136,056	1,246,304
Other Foreign	396,673	197,784	460,197	458,290	1,106,466	2,043,573
Chinese † ..	64,588	494,237	2,993,613	5,539,246	9,911,209	17,881,542
Total ..	6,635,485	9,305,801	18,806,788	29,622,001	57,290,389	85,771,973

Opium was imported in 1867 to the amount of 60,948 piculs, of which 26,297 piculs was Bengal (government monopoly) opium, and 34,651 piculs from Malwa (independent Indian states) and Persia; the value was Tls.31,994,576, being 46 per cent. of the value of all foreign imports in that year. In 1905 the import of foreign opium was 51,890 piculs, of which 34,235 piculs were Bengal and 17,655 Malwa and Persian; the value was Tls.34,070,021, being 7½ per cent. of all foreign imports.

Cotton Manufactures in 1867 were valued at Tls.14,617,268, being 21 per cent. of the total, and in 1905 at Tls.181,452,953, being 40 per cent. of the total; the imports of 1905 were above the normal, but the increase was maintained in 1906. Of plain fabrics (grey and white shirtings, sheetings, drills, jeans, and T-cloths) the import in 1867 was 3,738,965 pieces, about 118,875,000 square yards, of which 130,000 pieces came from the United States and the rest mainly from England; the value of these plain fabrics was Tls. 10,537,427, which was 72 per cent. of all cotton imports. Of these same plain fabrics the importation in 1905 was 28,702,693 pieces, about 1,167,600,000 square yards, of which the country of origin was as follows:

* Japanese carrying trade in 1904 affected by Russo-Japanese War, 1904–1905.

† Steamers and sailing vessels engaging in trade under the regulations of the Inspectorate General of Customs.

	PIECES.	SQ. YARDS.	VALUE, TLS.
English ..	14,393,846	589,200,000	43,480,144
American ..	12,693,793	519,770,000	42,977,175
Japanese ..	789,290	30,530,000	2,079,313
Indian ..	651,011	22,330,000	1,461,369
All others ..	174,753	5,770,000	486,884
Total ..	28,702,693	1,167,600,000	90,484,885

This value was 48 per cent. of the value of all cotton products imported in 1905. Fine cotton fabrics were imported in 1867 to the extent of 781,359 pieces, about 15,860,000 square yards, composed more than half of figured (white and dyed) shirting and chintzes, almost entirely of English weaving ; the value was Tls.2,464,075, being 17 per cent. of all cotton imports. In 1905 fine cotton imports were 10,821,885 pieces,· about 220,195,000 square yards, which may be divided approximately between the countries of origin as follows :

	PIECES.	SQ. YARDS.	VALUE, TLS.
English ..	7,634,054	186,304,000	23,135,583
American ..	541,977	16,253,000	2,006,350
Japanese ..	1,813,480	11,368,000	1,446,054
All others ..	832,374	6,271,000	921,432
Total ..	10,821,885	220,195,000	27,509,419

This value was fifteen per cent. of the value of all cotton products in 1905. The kinds which were prominent in 1867 have lost their prominence in 1905, and in the latter year the great bulk is made up by " imitations," by cheap cotton substitutes for a more expensive woollen fabric, by an appeal to the eye ; of the Tls.27,509,419, the value of all fine cottons, no less than Tls.19,240,889 are supplied by cotton Italians, cotton lastings, cotton Spanish stripes, cotton flannel, and cotton blankets. The import of cotton yarn in 1867 was 33,274 piculs, entirely of English spinning ; it was of the finer counts, with an average value of Tls.48·20

(£16) a picul; and the total value, Tls.1,603,807, was 11 per cent. of all cotton products. In 1905 the cotton yarn imported was 2,577,748 piculs, of which 22,075 piculs were English spinning, 1,867,309 Indian, 684,671 Japanese, and 3,693 from all other sources; this import was mainly of the coarser counts (12's to 24's), with an average value of Tls.26 (£3 18s.) a picul, and the total value, Tls.66,892,485, was 36 per cent. of all cotton imports: in 1903 and 1904 the percentage of yarn to the total had been 52 and 48 respectively. If we add Tls.20,000,000, the value of the 750,000 piculs of yarn machine-spun annually in the factories of Shanghai and other ports, it may be declared that normally and on the average a full half of all foreign cotton products is now in the shape of the semi-finished product yarn. This yarn is imported to give a strong warp, on which the people in their homes weave a coarse durable fabric, filling in with a hand-spun weft of Chinese cotton; it penetrates to every corner of the Empire, and in every village street may be seen the long white stretches arranged by the women in preparation for their labour at the loom. In Western countries the cheapness of the machine-woven cotton fabric has driven out the home-spun of our grandmothers, whose descendants may now more profitably employ their time and energy in other occupations; in China the machine has only succeeded in partially supplanting the spinning-wheel, but the hand-loom is still unconquered.

Woollens were imported in 1867 of a value of Tls.7,391,236, constituting 10 per cent. of all foreign imports. In 1905 the value was Tls.4,414,713, being less than 1 per cent. of all imports. Those Chinese who can afford woollens prefer silks and furs, and the wearers of sheep-skins and cotton-wadded garments cannot afford woollens; while the demands of fashion are met by cotton imitations.

Metals were valued in 1867 at Tls.1,630,351, a little over 2 per cent. of all imports, and in 1905 at Tls.46,318,231, being 10 per cent. of the whole; but this requires some explanation. The import of copper in 1867 was 11,150 piculs, valued at Tls.198,017, and in 1905 was 985,287 piculs, valued at Tls.31,762,337 : almost the entire import in the latter year was for the mints of China, which were then engaged in wild orgies of issues of copper token coinage. Lead (57,780 and 143,652 piculs) is chiefly wanted for packing tea, and tin (31,758 and 54,193 piculs) chiefly for making tin-foil and those paper simulacra of silver bullion which are offered so profusely in religious worship, specially at the ancestral tombs. Tinned plates in 1867 amounted to 1,744 piculs, and in 1905 to 182,188 piculs, in addition to a considerable quantity of second-hand plate coming as lining to cases containing piece-goods, kerosene oil, and other commodities, every foot of which is utilised in this land of poverty and thrift, and the quantity of which is estimated at not less than 500,000 piculs a year. The consumption of iron and steel is in all countries the index of industrial progress ; the import into China in 1867 was 117,381 piculs (7,000 tons) ; in 1905 this had increased to 2,713,113 piculs (161,500 tons). This is satisfactory, but another indication of the poverty and thrift of the people is found in the fact that of the import of 1905 close on a half (1,323,593 piculs) consisted of old iron, plate cuttings, etc., the discards of Western markets, coming mainly from England.

Sundries, i.e. all goods other than opium, cottons, woollens, and metals, were valued in 1867 at Tls.13.636,376, just under 20 per cent. of the whole ; in 1905 their value was Tls.186,338,096, just over 40 per cent. of the whole. Nothing but a brief summary of the more important articles can be attempted. Fish and products of the sea in general imported from foreign ports in 1867 were valued at Tls.1,358,716, and in 1905 at Tls.11,820,686. Cigarettes were unknown in 1867, and in 1905 their value was Tls.4,427,171, imported half from the United States, a fourth from England, and a fourth from Japan. In 1867 the import of coal was 113,430 tons ; in 1905 China produced some 400,000 tons, coming under Customs cognisance, and

imported a further quantity of 1,314,032 tons. Aniline
dyes were not an article of commerce in 1867 ; in 1905 the
value was Tls.2,626,545 for aniline dyes in general, not
including Tls,1,726,950 for synthetic indigo to displace
the natural product of the country. The taste for foreign
luxuries has been introduced by returned emigrants, and
flour, unknown in 1867, was imported in 1905 to the extent
of 2,635,000 bags of 50 lbs. Window glass and glassware were
valued in 1867 at Tls.25,182, and in 1905 at Tls.1,554,832.
Matches in 1867 figured for 79,236 gross of boxes, valued
at one tael a gross ; in 1905 the import was 26,057,221
gross, valued at Tls.0·215 a gross, nearly ten boxes for
each one of the 400,000,000 of men, women, and children
in the Empire. Kerosene oil was not an article of general
commerce in 1867, the import amounting only to 29,842
gallons for the foreign community ; the trade began to
expand in 1878, when the import was 4,161,100 gallons,
entirely American ; Russian oil was introduced in 1889,
Sumatran in 1894, and Borneo oil in 1901 ; in 1905 the
total import was 156,948,040 gallons, of which 52 per cent.
was American, 8 per cent. Russian, 32 per cent. Sumatran,
and 7 per cent. from Borneo. Rice is always wanted for
the people of China, but of the 713,494 piculs imported in
1867 a large part went to Ningpo, while the 2,227,916 piculs
in 1905 were mainly for Kwangtung. Of sugar the import
in 1867 was 186,176 piculs, entirely Chinese sugar re-
imported from Hongkong ; in 1905 the import was 4,644,315
piculs, of which no more than 365,000 piculs could have
been Chinese sugar re-imported, the greater part being
Java sugar, with some quantity from the Philippines,
shipped to Hongkong and imported thence either in its
original state or, to the extent of 1,322,000 piculs, refined.
Timber, hard and soft, was imported in 1867 to the value
of Tls.205,168, and in 1905 of Tls.3,121,841 ; in the latter
year the quantity of soft-wood planks was 90,432,396 super-
ficial feet, of which 61 per cent. came from the United
States and 38 per cent. from Japan.

Raw Cotton occupies a peculiar position in China, being both exported and imported. In 1867 the export (from Shanghai) was 29,391 piculs, and the import from India (chiefly into Canton) was 336,072 piculs, its value constituting a third of the foreign "sundries" imported. In 1904 the export was 1,228,588 piculs, and the import 60,057 piculs. China is a great cotton-growing country, and the proportions for 1905 (export 789,273 piculs, import 90,581 piculs) represent the normal movement.

EXPORTS

Exported goods were valued in 1867 at Tls.57,895,713 (£19,298,571), and in 1905 at Tls.227,888,197 (£34,183,230), a much smaller development than is shown in the case of imports. The export trade of China is in three broad divisions—silk, tea, and "sundries," the last being the official designation of what was called by merchants in the old trade "chow-chow," and to-day is called "muck and truck." In 1867, of the whole export trade, silk and its products accounted for 34 per cent., tea for 59 per cent., and sundries for 7 per cent. ; in 1905 the proportions were —silk 31 per cent., tea 11 per cent., and sundries 58 per cent.

Tea * constituted the main staple of the old trade of China. As has been stated, the fragrant leaf formed the main part of the outward lading of ships, vessels which could take a thousand tons or more of tea being restricted, in theory and by law, to 140 piculs, less than ten tons in weight, of the other staple export, silk. This preponderance

* The English and Dutch obtained their first tea at Amoy, and consequently called the leaf tea (rhyming with obey), the name in the Amoy dialect ; French, Germans, Americans, and others first obtained the leaf, and with it the name, through England or Holland. The Portuguese and Spanish obtained it from Canton, and consequently called it by the Cantonese name cha. The Russians, obtaining it by the northern frontier, called it tchai, from the northern Chinese name cha-yeh, "tea-leaf."

continued in the new régime, and, as we have seen, in 1867 tea contributed three-fifths of the value of all exports. In the two seasons 1848–1849 and 1849–1850 the average of shipments of tea to England was 335,920 piculs, of which 249,660 piculs were shipped from Canton and 87,260 piculs from Shanghai; and shipments to the United States averaged 26,600 piculs, from Shanghai. Tea shipments from China increased in actual volume until the culminating year, 1886, when, with a quantity the highest on record, the value contributed but 43 per cent. of all exports ; thereafter both quantity and price fell off, until in 1905 tea gave little over a tenth of the value of all exports. With a reduction in quantity there has been a still greater decline in value, notwithstanding the reduced exchange value of the unit, the tael of silver ; and, with a restricted market for tea of the finer qualities, there is a distinct falling off in the proportion of tea leaf to brick tea, made of refuse leaf, dust, and stalks, as shown in the following table :

		TEA LEAF.		BRICK TEA.	
		Quantity.	Value.	Quantity.	Value.
		Piculs.	Tls.	Piculs.	Tls.
1867	..	1,248,256	33,838,423	65,311	717,665
1886	..	1,846,989	31,246,063	370,212	2,258,757
1905	..	839,173	21,013,687	530,125	4,431,965

This change is the more significant when it is remembered that tea leaf goes to Europe and America to be infused and provide the beverage we know, while the brick tea is for the inhabitants of Siberia and Central Asia, who make of it a soup. The decline in the China tea trade has come from the competition with India, which learned its lesson from China and has improved upon the instruction given. The first experiments were made in India in 1838, in which year 500 lbs. were shipped to England ; it took over twenty years for shipments to reach a million pounds, but then the trade advanced by leaps and bounds. In 1867, when

China shipments were one and a quarter million piculs, the export from India was 40,000 piculs ; in 1886, shipments of all kinds from China were 2,217,201 piculs, and from India 565,690 piculs. Ceylon came into the market in 1883, and under the influence of heavy shipments from Ceylon and from India, the English market was gradually lost to China tea, until in 1905 the quantities withdrawn from bond for consumption within the United Kingdom were as follows :

China	6,658,966 lbs.	=	49,142 piculs
India	150,530,446 ,,	=	1,128,978 ,,
Ceylon	89,385,901 ,,	=	670,394 ,,
Other countries	12,513,284 ,,	=	93,850 ,,

Fifty years ago China supplied practically all the tea infused in the United Kingdom, and to-day she supplies just one-fortieth. The United States is not one of the great tea-drinking nations, its per capita consumption being about one-fifth that of the British, and since the opening of Japan the American tea-drinkers have taken rather to tea from that country ; in 1867 shipments to the United States from China amounted to 194,153 piculs, being 65 per cent. of the American import of that year. In 1905 the corresponding quantity was 182,123 piculs, which was 23½ per cent. of the American consumption. Russia has always been an important customer for Chinese tea. Sea-borne tea for Russia in early years cannot be distinguished, since so much was bought on the London market. Direct shipments declared for Russia have been as follows : in 1867, leaf, 13,251 piculs, brick, 53,123 piculs ; in 1886, leaf, 239,086 piculs, brick, 360,091 piculs ; in 1903 (before the dislocation of trade occasioned by the Russo-Japanese war), leaf, 401,087 piculs, brick, 618,458 piculs, the total being 60 per cent. of all exports of tea from China during the year. The English market and that of Australia, with the largest per capita consumption in the world, have been lost to China, chiefly for the reason that the Indian and Ceylon teas give a strong infusion, and are as strong in that second drawing which is so dear to the housekeeper's heart. The English taste has become so thoroughly perverted and insensible of the delicacy and cleanness of flavour characteristic of China tea, that the market can never be recovered even by reduced price ; and in the contest, China is handicapped by several factors. Indian tea is prepared and fired by mechanical appliances, the use of which is possible only where, as in India, large plantations, of a thousand or more acres, are under one management ; in China all is done by hand, and no change can be made in a country where the individual cultivator has only a small patch of a very few acres, ten acres being a large plantation. In twenty years of a declining market the tea shrubs have been left un-pruned and uncultivated, and it is doubtful if they can ever recover their old-time condition. Finally, the Chinese fiscal system is to tax everything in sight. In India there is no tax on the production or export of tea ; in China not only was there for forty-five years an export duty of Tls.2·50 a picul, reduced only in 1903 to Tls.1·25 (equivalent at present exchange to $\frac{1}{3}d$. per lb.), but on the way from the producing district to the shipping port there is levied a series of taxes, amounting on the average to more than Tls.2·50 a picul for official tax, with something to be added for irregular levy and delay and loss of interest. No in-dustry thus burdened could compete with a rival free of all burden.

Silk is the product for which China has been noted for two thousand years, and it is now the product which in-dividually contributes the greatest proportion of the value of the export trade. By the nineteenth century the supplies obtained from China had developed to a considerable quantity, the average annual shipments to England in the last five years of the East India Company's monopoly, 1828–1833, being 5,393 bales (4,314 piculs). During the next four years of open trade, 1833–1837, shipments increased

21

to an annual average of 12,497 bales (9,998 piculs). Then followed a period of war and interrupted trade, and in the five years 1839–1844 the annual shipments fell to 2,080 bales (1,664 piculs). Upon the restoration of peace and the opening of the five treaty ports, the annual export to England rose again in the five years 1845–1850 to 18,654 bales (14,923 piculs). In 1860 Japanese silk found its outlet through Shanghai to the amount of 6,248 piculs. Apart from this the export of white and yellow raw silk from Canton and Shanghai respectively has been as follows :

			CANTON.	SHANGHAI.	TOTAL, ALL PORTS.
			Piculs.	Piculs.	Piculs.
1860	..	..	5,571	61,552	67,123
1867	..	..	9,259	30,358	39,627
1886	..	..	19,406	44,967	64,488
1905	..	..	34,231	44,303	80,335

In addition, wild silk, the product of silkworms feeding on the oak, was exported as follows: 5,127 piculs in 1860, 5,363 piculs in 1867, 12,555 piculs in 1886, and 25,584 piculs in 1905. The value of the export of each category of silk products—cocoons, raw silk (white, yellow, and wild), waste silk, and woven silk goods—has been as follows :

		COCOONS.	RAW SILK.	WASTE SILK.	WOVEN SILK.
1860	..	53,845	23,804,284	16,807	2,166,481
1867	..	39,598	16,372,518	113,924	2,234,887
1886	..	350,482	19,210,052	2,271,996	6,753,939
1905	..	1,344,286	53,425,473	4,844,343	9,938,750

In 1905 the raw white originated almost entirely in Shanghai and Canton ; yellow silk came chiefly from Szechwan, a smaller quantity being also produced in Shantung ; wild silk came chiefly from Manchuria, with secondary sources of supply in Szechwan and Kwangtung ; waste silk came from many quarters ; and woven silks were produced chiefly in the vicinity of Nanking, Soochow, Hangchow,

Shanghai, and Canton, and, in the shape of pongees woven from wild silk, at Chefoo. Of all these products raw white silk is the most important, and this is mainly produced within a radius of 150 miles around Shanghai, and in a smaller district around Canton ; of the two the Shanghai silk is of the finer quality. In this district the silkworm is by nature the best in the world, producing naturally from the best mulberry the largest quantity of the finest silk ; and formerly, in silk as in tea, China set the standard for the world. In the course of years the silkworm all over the world was attacked by disease. In Europe, and later in Japan, scientific remedial measures were evolved by patient study, with the result that the disease can make no headway there, and with the further result that their silk is much improved in quality. China had for centuries adopted a method of eliminating the weaklings from the eggs by exposure to frost and snow, a method more effective than any adopted in Europe, and fully effective so long as no disease attacked the eggs or the worms ; but her failure to adopt the scientific remedy of microscopic examination is by degrees putting her behind in the race. Of 1,000 eggs passed as healthy by this test it may be said that 700 will survive through all the stages of moulting and development, and will spin strong full-sized cocoons, of which it will take 3 to 4 lbs. to reel 1 lb. of silk ; of 1,000 eggs passed by the test of frost alone, 700 may hatch out, and of these 700, fully 400 will die during the successive moults, having meantime eaten leaf to waste, and the surviving 300 will spin weak under-sized cocoons, of which it will take 6 to 7 lbs. to reel 1 lb. of silk. The proportion between the producing capacity of the Italian and the Chinese silkworm may be put at 100 to 25, apart from the waste of leaf. Once upon a time China was the sole source of supply of silk for the West, and within a half-century she supplied a full half ; on the basis of the average output of the three years 1902–1904, and not including the home weaving of China and Japan, the West was supplied with silk, 27 per cent. from China, 28 per cent. from Japan, 25 per cent from Italy, and 20 per cent. from all other countries ; and China's proportion in 1905 was reduced to less than 25 per cent. Owing to the improved methods introduced in Japan that country has now become China's most important competitor, and the export of raw white silk from the two countries has been as follows, 1899 having been the year in which China's export reached its highest figure :

	1899.	1904.	1905.
	Piculs.	Piculs.	Piculs.
China	109,279	81,511	69,617
Japan	59,069	96,586	72,419

Can it be that silk, which furnishes a third of China's exports, is going the way of her tea ?

Sundries furnish the evident line of advance for China in providing commodities for shipment abroad, their value having risen from Tls.4,487,414, being 7 per cent. of the total of all exports, in 1867, to Tls.132,008,712, or 58 per cent. of the whole, in 1905. In the earlier year the only noticeable items were cassia (Tls.325,686), cotton (Tls.458,424), mats and matting (Tls.384,542), and sugar (Tls.462,157). Those commodities which were of importance in 1905 are considered below.

Beans are used to make an oil for cooking and, prior to the introduction of kerosene, for illuminating purposes ; the bye-product of this process, bean-cake, is used to fertilise the fields chiefly of Kwangtung and Japan. The foreign export of beans is first recorded in 1870 with shipment of 578,209 piculs, and of bean-cake in 1890 with 96,297 piculs ; in 1905 the export of beans was 2,665,523 piculs, of which 80 per cent. went to Japan, and of bean-cake 2,897,948, entirely for Japan ; in addition, over two million piculs of beans and two and a half million piculs of bean-cake were imported into Kwangtung ports. The chief source of production is Manchuria, next to that Shantung, Hupeh, and the lower Yangtze; and from those provinces a large export to Europe has been developed.

Bristles must always be an important export from a land in which the pig provides the principal meat for the table. Their export is first recorded in 1894, with 18,378 piculs, increased in 1905 to 39,588 piculs. They come chiefly from Tientsin, Chungking, Hankow, and Canton.

Cotton has been referred to before. In 1864, owing to the American Civil War, shipments to Europe were made amounting to 391,287 piculs, while the import was 4,528 piculs; in 1867 the export was 29,391 piculs, and the import (from India into the southern ports) 336,072 piculs; in 1902 the export was 774,536 piculs, and the import 251,219 piculs, introduced from India into the chief cotton-producing centre in order to regulate prices; in 1904, with high prices ruling in the Western markets, exports rose to 1,228,588 piculs, and imports fell to 65,129 piculs; in 1905 exports were 789,273 piculs, and imports 94,243 piculs. The cotton is produced in the entire Yangtze basin from Hupeh to Chekiang, Shanghai being the chief centre; and fully 90 per cent. of all shipments go to Japan.

Fire-crackers and fireworks, almost entirely to help young America in celebrating the Glorious Fourth, were exported to the extent of 16,186 piculs in 1867, and 128,245 piculs in 1905; nearly the whole export came from Canton.

Fibres, hemp, jute, and ramie, are first recorded as an export in 1879 with 10,456 piculs; the export in 1905 was 262,443 piculs, coming chiefly from Hupeh and Kiangsi, and going chiefly to Japan.

Hides were exported in 1867 to the extent of 146 piculs, and of 279,976 piculs in 1904, which was about normal; the export in 1905 was only 189,446 piculs. About half came from Hupeh, and next in importance were Szechwan and Kwangsi: their destination was fairly divided between the principal countries of Europe.

Matting, entirely the product of the Canton district, and almost entirely destined for the United States, was shipped in 1867 to the extent of 89,908 rolls of 40 yards ; in 1905 the export was 438,009 rolls.

Minerals make but a poor showing. With all her vast mineral wealth China provides but a small surplus for shipment abroad. China is a coal country, and the total foreign export in 1905 (11,534 tons) was less than 1 per cent. of the quantity imported ; it has large fields of iron ore, and the export in 1905 (24,600 tons) was less than a sixth of the import ; it is a copper country, and, with no export in 1905, it drew from abroad 57,000 tons to supply the demands of the mints ; it is a tin country, and in 1905 imported 54,193 piculs, while its export, entirely from Yunnan to Hongkong, was 75,302 piculs, this being the first year in which the export exceeded the import. Antimony is the only other mineral deserving notice ; the export of ore, regulus and refined, coming from Hunan, in 1905 was 94,327 piculs.

Provisions were shipped in 1905, chiefly for consumption at Hongkong, to a value of Tls.7,239,410, including cattle, sheep, pigs, and goats, valued at Tls.3,210,100, and eggs valued at Tls.1,554,607.

Oil seeds (cotton, rape, and sesamum) have only recently entered into the foreign trade. In 1888 the export of rape-seed was 873 piculs, and of sesamum-seed 3,027 piculs ; in 1898 the export was—rape-seed 212 piculs, sesamum-seed 47,388 piculs, and cotton-seed 566,105 piculs ; in 1905, rape-seed 19,751 piculs (from Hupeh and Anhwei), sesamum-seed 575,721 piculs (from Hupeh and Kiangsu), and cotton-seed 659,705 piculs. The rape-seed and cotton-seed go entirely to Japan, the sesamum-seed chiefly to Germany and Japan.

Skins, consisting mainly of goat, kid, and lamb, coming from the Mongolian plateau, chiefly through Tientsin, to a secondary degree through Hankow, form an increasing industry. The export in 1867 was valued at Tls.5,501 in 1887 at Tls.652,174, in 1897 at Tls.3,083,517, and in 1905 at Tls.9,684,286. Of the export of 1905 the United States took 42 per cent., Great Britain 30 per cent., with Japan, Italy, and Germany next.

Straw braid is one of the few home industries introduced expressly for the foreign trade. The seat of the industry is in the plain bordering the Yellow River in western Shantung and southern Chihli, producing a wheat with long straw. The export was 1,361 piculs in 1867 ; 25,930 piculs in 1877 ; 82,413 piculs in 1886 ; 100,184 piculs in 1896 ; and 110,222 piculs in 1905. The principal demand is for Great Britain, which in 1905 took 44 per cent., with France, the United States, and Germany next.

Wool comes mainly from Kansu and Mongolia through Tientsin, and to some extent from Tibet through Chungking, and, notwithstanding the long caravan journeys, finds an increasing market. The export in 1867 was 1,097 piculs ; in 1887 this had increased to 56,261 piculs, and in 1897 to 232,343 piculs. In 1905 the export was 281,294 piculs, viz. 35,331 piculs of camels' wool (entirely for England) and 245,963 piculs of sheep's wool (mainly to the United States).

BALANCE OF TRADE

An essential part of any study of the foreign trade of China is the consideration of the means by which the balance of indebtedness between China and the outer world is struck. Up to 1895 the Empire had practically no foreign debt. As the result of the war with Japan which ended in that year a foreign debt of over £50,000,000 was incurred ; and the indemnities to be paid to foreign Powers in settlement of the military operations necessitated by the Boxer movement of 1900 added to the foreign obligations a further sum of £67,500,000 ; the annual charge for obligations incurred since 1895 is, according to the exchange, between Tls.42,000,000 and Tls.45,000,000. The natural commercial effect on the trade of the country would be to increase the quantity of commodities required to be exported to maintain commercial equilibrium ; but, in fact, the tendency has been in the direction of an increase of imports. Considering merchandise only, passing through the various Custom Houses, imports exceeded exports in 1901 by 27 per cent., in 1902 by 28 per cent., and in 1903 by 31 per cent. ; in 1904 the excess increased to 43 per cent., and in 1905 to no less than 97 per cent., but in these two years the greatly increased import trade, apart from any question of increased absorptive power by the people, was largely financed by remittances to maintain the Russian and Japanese armies in the field, rendering the conditions of trade abnormal. The year 1903 must then be taken as the last normal year. Outside the maritime Customs, statistics are unknown in China, and all that can be done in seeking information is to adopt a reasonable working hypothesis, and on it to base a conjecture. With this serious limitation, an attempt * has been made to investigate the different liabilities and assets of international indebtedness as for 1903.

Liabilities.—The first is the visible liability of merchandise imported, valued at Tls.310,453,428, to which must be added bullion and coin imported, Tls.37,000,000 ; in the last is included an estimated sum of Tls.10,000,000 brought back in cash in the pockets of returning emigrants, but the treasure movement is obscured by the fact that China must return as foreign all movement to and from Hongkong, the financial centre for South China. Then we have Tls.44,210,000, the annual charge for loans and indemnities for 1903 at the exchange of that year. For invisible liabilities it is estimated that Tls.4,320,000 were spent for the maintenance of Chinese legations, consulates, and students abroad ; and that the net profits of foreign residents, merchants, and others, and of foreign shipping and insurance companies amounted to Tls.22,750,000. A

* " An Inquiry into the Commercial Liabilities and Assets of China in International Trade," by H. B. Morse.

further sum of Tls.5,000,000 is added as the possible value of war material not included in merchandise. The total so estimated is Tls.423,733,428.

Assets.—The merchandise exported was Tls.236,205,162, and bullion and coin Tls.33,046,000, including as before shipments to Hongkong. Then there is an item of un-recorded trade across the land frontier, which, on the authority of the Russian statistics of trade with China, must be put at over Tls.20,000,000 excess of exports. The money and material provided from abroad for the development of railways and mines, a future but not a present liability of China, is estimated at Tls.27,000,000. The sums required to be remitted for the maintenance of foreign legations and consulates, foreign garrisons and navies, for the maintenance and repairs of foreign shipping. for the upkeep of foreign missions, hospitals, and schools, and for the expenditure by foreign travellers, were con-sidered in the light of all the information obtainable, and were estimated at Tls.51,500,000. Finally, there remains China's most important invisible asset, her export of brawn and brains in the emigration of a portion of her redundant population, whether as traders or as labourers, remitting to their homes the fruit of their labour in an annual sum which, on the lowest possible estimate, is Tls.73,000,000. The total assets so estimated amount to Tls.440,741,162.

CHAPTER X

CHINA is a continent, mountains and deserts replacing on the west the seas which circumscribe it on the east and south; and no study of its trade conditions would be complete which was restricted to its maritime traffic. Prior to the application in Europe of the magnetic needle to the mariner's compass in the twelfth century, the only traders by sea to the land of Sinim were the venturous Arabs; but centuries before that date the *Serica vestis* had reached the West by land transport over the mountains, plateaux, and deserts of Central Asia, through the hundred degrees of longitude which separated the silkworm from the European wearer of its product. These routes were mainly in the north. From the north-east the routes taken in the seventeenth century, and those taken to-day by the Russian tea caravans, outflanked the deserts and struck well north until they emerged in what is now Siberia. The main trade routes, however, struck north-west through the province of Kansu, following those lines which appeared on the school maps of the middle of the nineteenth century with the mysterious designations Tien Shan Pei Lu and Tien Shan Nan Lu, which, being interpreted, mean the Routes North and South, respectively, of the Mountains of Heaven. This is no longer a through trade route. Another such route is that taken to-day in supplying tea and salt to Tibet from Szechwan by Tatsienlu, with an alternative route by Sungpan; and another is the now unimportant route from Yunnan by Szemao into Burma.

The same enterprise which built up a foreign trade by land, was applied also to the development of internal trade between provinces of the size of kingdoms, passing by routes many hundreds of miles in length. At times of falling dynasties this traffic would become insecure ; but as each succeeding dynasty became established in power the ways were opened, and a *pax Romana* allowed the free interchange of commodities between the different parts of the Empire. In the competition between the coasting trade by sea and the internal trade, the latter had many advantages, more than compensating for the economic gain from water transport in large bulk. On the internal route there were no " Rhine Barons " or others to levy illegal toll, while the danger from bandits was more than counterbalanced by the risk of piracy on the sea ; until less than fifty years ago there was no likin or other tax on transit in general ; and, while generally water transport could be utilised through the whole or the greater part of the distance on most of the routes, the cheapness of human labour minimised the cost of transport by land. By sea, the clumsy junks were at the mercy of the monsoon, making good speed to the north during the summer, and to the south in autumn and winter, but unable to make commercially profitable voyages against the prevailing winds ; while the Custom Houses were established at the seaports alone, and, moreover, taxed all movement, to home as well as to foreign ports, and repeated the tax whenever goods came again under their cognisance, as if all previous levy had been made by alien, as it was by independent authority.

There are no records of this internal trade, and its component parts can be studied only by the light of the coasting trade by steamer which to-day has taken its place on many routes. The routes themselves are innumerable, but a selection will be made for description of a few of the most important, viz. :

1. The West River route, west from Canton.
2. The Cheling Pass route, north-west from Canton.
3. The Meiling Pass route, north from Canton.
4. The Min River route, north-west from Foochow.
5. The Lower Yangtze route, as far west as Hupeh and Hunan.
6. The Upper Yangtze route, from Ichang into Szechwan.
7. The Kweichow route.
8. The Han River route, from Hankow into Shensi.
9. The Grand Canal, from Hangchow to Tientsin.
10. The Shansi route.
11. The Kiakhta route.
12. The Manchurian route.

1. The *West River* route from Canton commands the whole of the trade of Kwangsi, and penetrates into Yunnan and Kweichow. At Wuchow the Cassia River provides a water-way, interrupted by rapids but navigable by small boats, to the provincial capital, Kweilin. Farther up, at Tamchow, the route again divides, the river coming in from the north-west providing a route, interrupted by rapids and shallows, but navigable by boats of 15 tons dead-weight capacity, and penetrating to the north-western part of Kwangsi and, via Liuchow and Kingyuan, into Kweichow. The southern of the two branches at Tamchow continues the name of West River until, some 30 miles above Nanning, it divides into the Left Branch continuing west to Lungchow, and the Right Branch leading north-west to Poseh: to these points boats of 25 tons dead-weight capacity can safely pass the rapids. From Poseh runs the main trade route for traffic by pack-animal into western and central Yunnan. There are no statistics of the Chinese produce brought down and sent inland, and the only gauge of the volume of traffic on this route is in the quantity of foreign goods sent inland under transit pass, which, from Canton and Wuchow in 1905, was as follows :

The West River at Lungchow.

	No. of Passes.	Value of Goods.
		Tls.
To Kwangsi	22,275	860,803
„ Kweichow ..	83,228	4,856,903
„ Yunnan	5,114	340,086

Before the development of traffic by Mengtsz the Yunnan trade by the West River route was very much greater than at the present time. From Yunnan and Kweichow comes opium, and the tin of Yunnan, which now finds its outlet by Mengtsz, formerly followed this route. Great rafts of timber are floated down from the mountains of north-western Kwangsi.

2. The *Cheling Pass* route follows the North River up from Canton, and a branch which falls into it from the north-west at Shaochow; thence by porters over the pass to the water-ways of Hunan. This pass, of less than 1,500 feet altitude, offers but slight impediment to the sturdy coolies of South China ; but the surveys of the American engineers, prospecting for the line of the Hankow-Canton railway, have revealed the fact that the true pass is not on the line of the old highway, and that for many centuries millions of tons of merchandise passing over this route have been laboriously carried on men's shoulders to a height 150 feet higher than nature demanded. The water-ways of Hunan are reached at Chenchow, on an affluent of the Siang River, and thence traffic passes by small boats down into the Siang. At Siangtan, once a place of great import-ance with a population estimated at 700,000, transhipment was ordinarily effected into the larger deep-draft junks plying down the Siang and into the Yangtze. Descending the Siang, the traffic then reached the Tungting Lake, a lake in summer with vast uncharted shoals, but in winter a congeries of wide and shallow channels meandering between broad islands of alluvial deposit, and neither in summer nor in winter available for commercial use. The main stream of traffic skirted the eastern side of the lake and,

entering the Yangtze at Yochow, descended that stream 125 miles north-east to Hankow. The lesser part of the traffic passed through the crooked channels of the alluvial delta of the Siang and the Yuan, forming the south shore of the lake, and then, skirting the western shore, passed into the Yangtze near Shasi by the canals which were the work of the Great Yü in times long gone by ; thence the Yangtze furnished a route west into Szechwan. By the Cheling Pass route came the teas of Hunan and Hupeh for shipment abroad from Canton in the old factory days, and a conservative trade calls those teas to-day, in the land of their origin, by the old-time Cantonese names Oonam and Oopack (Hunan and Hupeh). By this route, too, passed an enormous traffic, of which to-day the only remnant is the amount required for local trade by the way. Not a single package is now carried through between Canton and Hankow, for, even in this land of cheap transport, the cheapness and security offered by steam carriage have prevailed, and this trade now passes around, via Shanghai, by the sea and the Yangtze. The railway taking the Cheling Pass route from Canton by Hankow to Peking will adhere closely to the air line between the two termini.

3. The *Meiling Pass* route follows the North River up from Canton, and at Shaochow goes north-east to the Meiling (Plum Ridge) Pass. This ridge has an elevation of 2,000 feet, and the route is through a notch, at an altitude of only 1,000 feet, over which a land portage of 24 miles carries the trader to the waters of the Kan River. This river has the ordinary winter shallows of a stream running through a deforested country, but has few dangerous rapids ; and it leads through the channels of the shallow Poyang Lake into the Yangtze near Kiukiang. By this route passed, in the old factory days, the teas of Kiangsi and Anhwei ; and by this route passed then, and passes now, the porcelain of Kingtehchen. The porcelain of to-day, however, consists of plain ware sent to Canton to be painted with the florid and multicoloured designs peculiar to that

market. A curious instance of the conservatism of Chinese trade was shown in 1903. In that year, in the general search for additional sources of revenue, an increase was made in the rate of likin levied at Canton on porcelain from Kiangsi. The trade resented this ; but, instead of resorting to steam traffic by the Yangtze and the sea, and thereby escaping the likin levied on the inland route, the traders adopted the time-honoured Chinese method of cessation of all business until their grievance was removed, and the export of porcelain from Canton, from an average of 105,142 piculs in the two preceding years, fell to 59,010 piculs in 1904. The Meiling is the route taken for centuries by Chinese officials proceeding to their posts in the south, and was followed by the various foreign embassies going to Peking in the seventeenth and eighteenth centuries ; and its continued use as a trade route to-day is due to the short length of land portage and the slight rise over the pass.

4. The *Min River* route serves mainly its own province, Fukien. The Min, emptying into the sea at Foochow, waters with its ramifications the greater part of the province ; but its chief interest for us lies in the fact that the teas of Kiangsi, following this route, found their way to Foochow in the interval after Canton lost its monopoly of foreign trade, and before Hankow established its firm grasp on the market for teas from the Yangtze basin. Down this river come to-day the rafts of timber from the mountains in, and on the western border of, Fukien, and the paper made from their forests and bamboo groves,

5. The *Lower Yangtze* is to-day, except for wayside traffic, given up to steam. From Shanghai to Hankow the winter provides a way for river steamers of from one to two thousand tons register, while in summer full-sized ocean steamers proceed to Hankow, and at least two battleships of 12,000 tons have ascended the river to that point. The myriads of junks of former days, whose sails of matting reflected the sun in golden patches, have yielded the main thoroughfare to their quicker and handier rivals, and have

been driven to the byways of trade ; but to this general statement there are some exceptions. Salt, owing to the government connection with the traffic, continues to go solely by junk ; and steamer preponderance is manifest only as far up the river as Hankow. The Hunan trade with Hankow has not yet taken to steam ; the huge timber rafts continue to float down to Hankow and below ; the coal continues to come to Hankow in roughly constructed barges, which are there broken up ; and the tea and rice continue to be carried in the old-time junks, which take back from Hankow their freights of the products of foreign countries and of the southern provinces. Nor on the Middle Yangtze, from Hankow to Ichang, has steam entirely conquered. The trade of central Hupeh, which, if steamer-borne, would pass through the port of Shasi, continues to follow the canals which subtend the arc formed there by the Yangtze ; and the traffic of West China continues to pass over this portion of the route in as great volume by junk as by steamer. The trade by the Yangtze route may be gauged by the figures for the value of the net import and original export by steamer alone at the ports from Chinkiang up, which in 1905 were as follows :

					Tls.
Net Imports ..	..	..	..		129,407,753
Original Exports	..	..	..		118,104,228
	Total	..	..		247,511,981

A moderate estimate for the junk trade would carry this total well over Tls.300,000,000.

6. The *Upper Yangtze* route is one continuous struggle of man against the forces of nature. The Yangtze, flowing for the upper two-thirds of its course through a valley nowhere wider than the river bed,* emerges from this narrow channel at Ichang after passing the famous Yangtze Gorges. The flow of the river past Ichang is 560,000 cubic

* " The Far East," by Archibald Little,

feet per second as an average for the whole year round ; and this volume of water, in passing through the Ichang Gorge, flows through a channel contracted to a width nowhere exceeding 250 yards and in places diminished to 100 yards, hemmed in by precipitous cliffs on either hand ; in the Fengsiang (Wind-box) Gorge, 100 miles farther up stream, the channel is even more restricted and the cliffs more precipitous. The average speed of the current throughout the year is not less than five knots an hour, and at times, especially during the summer floods, and in places, this speed rises to twelve knots and even more. The swift current drives the boatmen to tracking on their upward journey, and the trackers find but scanty foothold on the steep hill-sides, and in many places are driven to follow paths which are little more than goat tracks, traced on the sides of the cliffs, up to a hundred feet or more above the level of the water. This is the least of their difficulties. From the upper end of the Ichang Gorge to Fengtu, a distance of 300 miles, the river is strewn with rapids, full forty being considered worthy of enumeration in that distance, not including mere whirlpools and races. Of the difficulties apart from the rapids the following episode, occurring before the lowest rapid was reached, furnishes an illustration :

> " October 6th. The boats under way 6 a.m., tracking up the right bank. At 8.30 a.m. the track-ing-line of No. 1 boat broke, and in less than fifteen minutes we had drifted back nearly to last night's anchorage." *

The tracking-lines are made of long strips of bamboo plaited together into a cable as thick as a man's arm. Of the ascent of the rapids Mr. Hobson says—

> " More dangerous navigation it is impossible to conceive ; double tracking-lines having been paid out, extra breastlines provided, and extra trackers engaged, we started from under the lee of the rocks, outside which the mighty torrent poured. Inch by

* " Ichang to Chungking," 1890, by H. E. Hobson.
22

inch only did the boats advance, until by nightfall we reached the shelter of a small bay beyond."

At several rapids he records that the trackers of three boats were put on to haul one. From Mr. Little's account * we gather some illuminating sentences describing the difficulty.

" We had a tough job to get round the point which forms the western limit of the gorge, the boatmen clinging on to the crevices in the rock, with long bamboos armed with small steel hooks. . . . Half of our crew then drag the boat by main force around the point, those remaining on board fending her off the rocks, the water meanwhile boiling and foaming under the bows and threatening to swamp her. . . . The hookers have to be mighty careful never to lose their hold, as that involves drifting back into the current . . . losing in a minute or two the fruits of hours of work. . . . The boat heeled over, threatening to capsize on the instant ; fortunately our trackers promptly cast off the tow-line in the nick of time, and we incurred no other danger than being swept violently down-stream in the eight-knot current."

The stream thus characterised furnishes the only water outlet for the trade of one of the richest provinces of China, the alternative routes being mountain roads over a much accidented country intersected by deep ravines, feasible only for light packages carried on men's shoulders. By this route the traffic is carried in junks of varying size. The largest are of a dead-weight carrying capacity of 60 to 70 tons, with a regular crew of 24 and a force of 85 trackers (re-enforced at the worst rapids), engaged for the upward voyage ; junks of medium size carry 30 to 40 tons, with a crew of 18, and 45 trackers ; small junks carry 14 to 20 tons, with a crew of 10 and 20 trackers. The upward journey takes about four weeks at the most favourable season, while in the summer, against the full strength of the Yangtze in flood, the voyage may be extended to three

* " Through the Yangtze Gorges," by Archibald J. Little.

or even four months : under the most favourable conditions the average rate of progress does not exceed 15 miles a day, and it may fall as low as 3 miles a day through the whole of the course of 420 miles from Ichang to Chungking. It is on the upward journey that most of the accidents occur, and a full tenth of the junks arriving at Chungking arrive with their cargo more or less damaged by water, while total loss is not uncommon. Down stream sails are furled and masts struck, and the junks, driven by oars to give sufficient speed for steerage way, are taken down in charge of the skilled pilots working the route, and seldom meet with accident : the downward journey may take from three or four days to a week. By this route merchants may elect to pass their goods through the maritime Customs or to pay likin on the way, each offering certain advantages for Chinese produce upward or downward. In 1905 the value of the trade passing the maritime Customs was, upward Tls.16,562,371, downward Tls.11,169,256, total Tls.27,731,627 ; a fair allowance for the goods passing the likin offices would bring the total value of the waterborne traffic of Szechwan to Tls.40,000,000.

7. The *Kweichow* route up the Yuan River from Changteh and the Tungting Lake, is barred by numerous rapids and available only for small boats. The downward traffic consists of timber, opium, and mining products ; the officially declared value of the timber is Tls.6,000,000 a year, from which, in China, a true value of Tls.10,000,000 and more may be inferred. The upward traffic is not great. The only index to its volume is the value of the foreign goods sent under transit pass from Hankow into Kweichow, valued in 1904 at Tls.1,207,695, and in 1905 at Tls.835,277 ; by other routes in 1905 Kweichow received foreign goods under transit pass to the value of Tls.4,856,903 by the West River, Tls.598,432 from Mengtsz, and Tls.30,636 from Tengyueh by land route crossing the whole width of Yunnan.

8. The *Han River* route from Hankow into Shensi

presents few difficulties to navigation, beyond the gradually
diminishing depth of water, as far up as Sichwanting in the
south-west corner of Honan, and for small boats as far as
Shangnan in Shensi, a distance of 1,730 li (nominally 575
miles) from Hankow. From that point, land transport
for 320 li (nominally 100 miles) over the rugged Tsingling
mountains, carries goods to Sianfu, the capital of Shensi.
Beyond Sianfu land transport alone is available to other
parts of the province, and on to Kansu, Mongolia, and
Siberia. Tea, less in amount than by Tientsin and Kiakhta
but still in considerable quantity, goes by this route overland to Russia ; the quantity fluctuates, and has been
small in the past few years, but in 1896 was valued at
Tls.1,617,401, and in 1900 at Tls.1,032,471 ; in the former
year the greater part was tea leaf, 78,297 piculs, and in
the latter year brick tea, 70,905 piculs. The foreign
goods going from Hankow under transit pass in 1905 into
Shensi were valued at Tls.825,540, and into Kansu at
Tls.26,319.

9. The *Grand Canal* furnishes an inland water route
from Hangchow to Tientsin, a distance of 900 miles, cutting
through the flat alluvial plains and intersecting the provinces
of Chekiang, Kiangsu, Shantung, and Chihli. The oldest
section, from the Yangtze to the Hwai, was opened for
traffic B.C. 486, and is therefore 2,400 years old. The next
section to be made was that from the Yangtze at Chinkiang
to Hangchow, which was constructed between A.D. 605
and 617, and this section was much improved by the
Southern Sung Emperors, who had their capital at Hangchow. Kublai Khan (A.D. 1260–1295), besides beginning
(but not completing) the canal from Kiaochow intended
to cut off the mountain mass of Shantung, improved,
deepened, straightened, widened, and extended the Grand
Canal under the supervision of the famous mathematician
Kwo Show-king as engineer ; by him, the capital having
for the first time been established at Peking, the water-way
was extended to the north from the then course of the

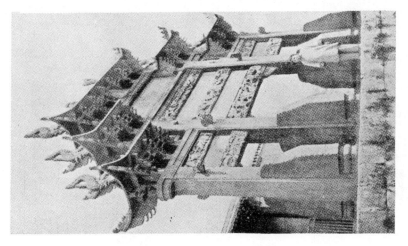

Monumental Arch at Wusih on Grand Canal.

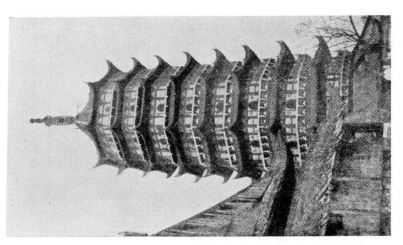

Pagoda at Wusih on Grand Canal.

Bridge over Grand Canal at Wusih.

Grand Canal passing through Wusih.

Yellow River, where it was joined by the Grand Canal at Tsingkiangpu, over the summit level skirting the higher land of Shantung, until it joined the Wei River, which, improved, became then the Grand Canal to Tientsin. Succeeding Emperors of the Ming and Tsing Dynasties, until within the past fifty years of material national decadence, have spared no effort to maintain the canal as a navigable water-way ; even when, in 1853, the Yellow River took its last plunge to the north-east and cut the canal farther to the north, the crisis was met and the intersection of the two streams duly provided for. Starting from Hangchow the canal goes by Kashing to Soochow, a distance of 100 miles, and thence by Wusih and Changchow through long straight stretches to Chinkiang, another 100 miles. It is here unlike our preconceived ideas of a canal—a current-less water-way barely wide enough to allow two streams of boats to pass each other—and has often a width of over a hundred feet between its sides, faced in many parts of its course with cut stone bunding. Many of its picturesque accessories were destroyed by the Vandals of China, the Taiping rebels, but much still remains to attest its past magnificence ; here and there are fine stone bridges spanning the main canal, some with their three arches, graceful to an extreme, others with a single arch, lofty and imposing, and well adapted for a country with no wheeled traffic ; along the banks are numerous specimens of single-span hump-backed bridges by which the tow-path is carried over side canals connecting with the system of canals which intersect the country for many miles ; and from the canal are to be seen on both sides many memorial arches of stone and lofty tapering pagodas. In these 200 miles there is no difference of level, and therefore no locks ; and after all these years of neglect there is everywhere a safe depth of 5 feet of water at the lowest stage, the depth at the Hangchow end being ordinarily 7 feet at low-water stage, rising after prolonged rains to 11 and at times to 13 and more feet ; only at Tanyang, some 20 miles south from Chinkiang, the depth is frequently too little for the larger boats during the season of low water. In this section boats up to forty tons dead-weight capacity ply regularly. At Chinkiang the traffic crosses the Yangtze and enters the oldest section of the canal, which, passing Yangchow, goes to Tsingkiangpu, 130 miles from Chinkiang ; in this section there is a constant depth of water sufficient for boats of 30 to 40 tons capacity. Of this part of the country it is that Mr. Parker says :

> " The Chinese engineers who manipulate the complicated system of lakes and levels forming the network about the Grand Canal and Hungtseh Marsh, are almost as expert in an empirical sense as the wary Dutchmen who keep an ever-watchful eye on the Zuider Zee and the intricate system of Netherlands dykes. The supply of water and the sacrifice of land are carefully measured and jealously watched with a view to keeping open the canal and preventing disasters of great magnitude."

The next section is the worst : it starts from Tsingkiangpu and, passing Tsining, debouches on the present course of the Yellow River near Tungping, full 450 miles from Chinkiang. This section was made by improving and connecting existing rivers, and follows all their original meanderings. Though the country is flat, there are still some differences of level—of 20 or 30 feet at most—and these are provided for, not by locks, which do not exist in China, but by barrages across the canal, over which the boats, after discharging their cargo, are hauled by windlasses. The whole of this part is much neglected and silted up, and is only available generally for navigation during the summer, and even then is generally traversed only by the tribute rice boats which go together in fleets. North of the Yellow River the newest part of the canal—made by Kublai Khan—continues until it strikes the Wei River, cut in places to a depth 60 or 70 feet below the level of the surrounding

Types of Bridges on and near Grand Canal.

country, and prolongs the route for another 250 miles to its northern end at Tientsin ; water transport continues for another 120 miles by the winding course of the Peiho to Tungchow, and thence, for tribute rice only, for 13 miles by an artificial canal to the government granaries on the eastern side of Peking. This is the Grand Canal, from Hangchow by Chinkiang to Tientsin, and thence to Peking, a main artery of trade traversing a network of water-ways which provide means of transport for a country incredibly rich in material resources. No estimate can be formed of the number of millions in which the value of the traffic on its surface must be stated ; its chief value to the Empire lies in the fact that it provides a safe inland route for a thousand miles from south to north in a country in which, in the past, time has had no value, and that thereby trade was enabled to escape the perils of the sea passage. One small indication of the extent of traffic is found in the value of the transit pass trade with Shantung passing the Chinkiang Customs, traversing a distance along the Grand Canal of 250 miles, a part of it the worst portion of the route, to the nearest markets in Shantung, valued in 1904 at Tls.3,646,000, and in 1905 at Tls.3,331,000.

10. The *Shansi* route is mentioned to illustrate the mediæval conditions prevailing in China wherever transport by water is not available. The province may be described either as an accidented plateau or an unaccidented mountain region, with a steep escarpment on the east, where it rises some 4,000 feet from the plain of Chihli. The route followed by the railway in course of construction from Chentow, near Chengtingfu, in Chihli, to Taiyuanfu, the capital of Shansi, affords the direct route from the lowland into the heart of the province ; but this is what may be termed an express package route, short and direct, but too difficult for ordinary purposes of trade. When the great famine of 1877, which more than decimated the province, made it necessary to send supplies of food to Shansi, this route was naturally selected to meet the urgency of the

case ; and the result was visible in the piles of grain in bags, the broken carts, and the foundered mules which strewed the road leading up to the plateau. Another route available for access to Shansi passes from Kaifeng in Honan up the valley of the Yellow River to the south-western corner of Shansi, thence up the valley of the Fenho toward Taiyuanfu ; neither the Yellow River nor its tributaries are generally navigable, and this circuitous route is in the main available only for land transport. A third route, and the one generally adopted for the transport of merchandise into Shansi, follows in its beginning the next route to be mentioned, the Kiakhta route, leaving it at Kalgan (Changkiakow), entering Shansi as its northern end, and preceding by Tatungfu south to Taiyuanfu. The length of land transport from the nearest navigable water-way by this route is not less than 400 miles, and by the road from Chengtingfu is only 150 miles, yet this is the best and cheapest and the most frequented route into Shansi.

11. The *Kiakhta* route is, and has been for more than two centuries, one of the most important trade routes in the Empire. North of the Yangtze communication from east to west is blocked by steep mountain slopes, the Yellow River acts as a barrier to trade, and north of the Yellow River the elevated mass of Shansi interposes a further barrier. It is only when the elevated but generally traversable plains of Mongolia are reached, that a way is found available for traffic from the eastern shore to the extreme west. The main route from Tientsin and Peking goes by Kalgan across Mongolia to Kiakhta, and, branching off at Kalgan, the traffic goes also west to Shensi, and, farther west, to Kansu ; camels and mule carts furnish the means of transport. By this route go the caravan tea for Russia and brick tea for Siberia, and by this route and its branches Mongolia, Shansi, northern Shensi, and Kansu obtain their supplies and forward their products, making Tientsin the shipping port for a hinterland extending considerably over

a thousand miles to the west and north-west. Statistics give us but a slight indication of the volume of this traffic, burdened by the cost of land transport over long distances, but a few items may be noted. In 1905 tea with a net weight of 357,265 piculs, valued at Tls.2,861,660, crossed the Mongolian frontier by this route ; and in the same year foreign products were forwarded from Tientsin, under transit pass, to Shansi valued at Tls.5,664,950, to Shensi Tls.74,509, to Kansu and Turkestan Tls.679,575, and to Mongolia Tls.217,300. Certain articles of Chinese produce shipped from Tientsin can be identified as probably originating in Mongolia or in Kansu ; among these are wool (of camel, goat, and sheep), of which the Tientsin export in 1905 was 186,918 piculs valued at Tls.3,326,000, and skins (goat and sheep), valued at Tls.3,725,000.

12. The *Manchurian* route is important because of the construction of the railway from Talien (Dairen or Dalny) to Harbin, and thence east to Vladivostock and north-west into Russian territory ; and by this railway in 1903 went 378,739 piculs of Chinese tea. My present concern is, however, with the internal trade of China. This route, proceeding east from Peking and north-east from Tientsin, passes through the narrow defile between the mountains and the sea at Shanhaikwan, where the Great Wall ends on the shore, and then goes on to Ningyuan, where three hundred years ago the Manchu invaders met their only serious check. By this route came the Manchus, and by this route have come tribute and ginseng from Korea, until, in 1894, the tribute ceased. With the development of steam traffic, trade between Chihli and Manchuria by this portal fell away, until the exigencies of war shut out the merchants of Newchwang from their hinterland and drove its trade temporarily to Tientsin, from which port the foreign goods sent by railway into Manchuria under transit pass in 1905 were valued at Tls.4,925,000. From Newchwang the Liao River in summer and the frozen plain of Manchuria in winter furnish the means of distributing

a trade which, import and export, was in 1905 valued at more than Tls.70,000,000.

These are the principal internal trade routes of the Chinese Empire, thronged with boats or with the carts and pack-animals engaged in the interchange of commodities between a race of traders developed through the course of many centuries. By these routes comes the Chinese produce intended for export from the shipping ports, and by these routes foreign products are distributed for consumption in the marts of the interior ; but there are no statistics to show the volume of the enormous traffic which originates and ends within the limits of the Empire. Some slight indication is given by the quantities of a few articles of the purely domestic trade conveyed by the steamers which, on some routes, have now displaced, wholly or partially, the old primitive means of conveyance ; and a few brief notes are given on the more important commodities.

Rice, shipped from producing to non-producing, from agricultural to industrial districts, has always been an important item in the domestic trade of China, shipment to foreign countries being prohibited. From Hunan it is estimated that an average annual surplus of 1,000,000 piculs is available for shipment to Hankow. Anhwei is the principal rice-field of the Empire, and from its port, Wuhu, were shipped 5,621,143 piculs in 1904, and 8,438,093 piculs in 1905. From Chinkiang the export in 1905 was 619,190 piculs, and from Shanghai 1,706,845 piculs. Of these shipments 2,804,164 piculs were sent to Tientsin, 1,553,894 piculs being tribute rice and the rest in merchants' hands, and 1,337,479 piculs to Chefoo ; except some small shipments to other southern ports, the balance went to the industrial centres of Kwangtung, in addition to 2,227,916 piculs of foreign rice, to supplement the produce of the rich rice fields of that province.

Beans were shipped in 1903 (much of the trade was diverted from Manchuria during the Russo-Japanese war) to the extent of 3,423,766 piculs from Newchwang, 1,928,543 piculs from Hankow, 404,063 piculs from Chinkiang, and enough from other ports to make a total of 6,327,080 piculs ; of this quantity 1,836,707 piculs were shipped to Japan, some 72,000 piculs to other foreign destinations, and the balance, except 590,000 piculs for Amoy, went to the Kwangtung ports, Canton and Swatow. In the same year *Bean-cake* was shipped, 4,553,367 piculs from Newchwang, 1,192,948 piculs from Chefoo, 583,095 piculs from Hankow, 423,447 piculs from Chinkiang, with total shipments of 7,030,325 piculs ; of this quantity 3,400,444 piculs went to Japan, and the balance, except 731,161 piculs for Amoy, went to Kwangtung.

Coal shipments in 1905 amounted to 193,759 tons from Tientsin and Chinwangtao, 16,887 tons from Kiaochow, 5,793 tons from Chungking, and 72,422 tons from Hankow, with a total of 290,477 tons. Of this 10,384 tons were shipped to Hongkong and Indo-China, 120,766 tons to Shanghai, and the balance to other Chinese ports, chiefly Chefoo, Wuhu, and Chinkiang. In 1909 the output of the Kaiping mines, for which the shipping port is Chinwangtao, was 1,226,000 tons.

Cotton hand-woven cloth was shipped by steamer in 1905 to the extent of 229,609 piculs, equivalent to about 100,000,000 square yards, of which 189,649 piculs originated in Shanghai. This went pretty much to every place where there are Chinese, the largest proportion to Manchuria, but 32,116 piculs to the Chinese colonies in foreign parts. In 1904 Newchwang imported in addition 82,667 piculs by junk.

Ground-nuts were shipped to the extent of 183,601 piculs from Tientsin, 109,042 piculs from Chefoo, 79,726 piculs from Hankow, and 489,353 piculs from Chinkiang, with total shipments of 978,519 piculs ; of this quantity 24,600 piculs went to foreign countries, and 912,555 piculs to Canton.

Hemp, Jute, and *Ramie* shipments amounted to 365,988 piculs, of which 153,005 piculs came from Hankow and

113,634 piculs from Kiukiang ; 134,002 piculs went to Japan and 128,441 piculs to other foreign countries, leaving 103,545 piculs for home consumption.

Medicines of the Chinese pharmacopœia were shipped to a value of Tls.1,082,247 from Chungking, Tls.1,050,853 from Hankow (much of it the product of Szechwan, coming by junk), with a total of Tls.4,854,835, which was distributed to every part of China, Tls.1,875,825 going to Hongkong for the Chinese there and in other parts of the outside world.

Musk comes chiefly from Tibet via Chungking, but 6,400 ounces reached its market in 1905 through Tientsin, in a total supply of 60,885 ounces. Of this, 29,717 ounces went to foreign countries, leaving an equal quantity for the delectation of Chinese nostrils.

Oil expressed from beans, ground-nuts, and the seeds of the *Camellia oleifera* and the *Aleurites cordata*, provides the Chinese housekeeper with fat for cooking and for illumination and oil for painting and for varnishing. Shipments in 1905 amounted to 1,030,701 piculs, of which 33,373 piculs (116,498 piculs in 1903) came from Newchwang, 168,333 piculs from Kiaochow, 419,444 piculs from Hankow, 171,310 piculs from Chinkiang, and 148,915 piculs from Shanghai. It was imported into every port where it is not produced.

Oil-seeds were shipped in 1905 to the extent of 1,581,514 piculs. Cotton-seed supplied 657,379 piculs, the entire amount going to Japan. Rape-seed shipments in 1902 were 223,149 piculs, but in 1905 only 28,919 piculs, the greater part going to Japan. Sesamum-seed was 895,216 piculs, of which 379,530 piculs went to Europe, chiefly to Germany, 39,911 piculs to Egypt, and 125,474 piculs to Japan ; the balance of shipments remaining for home consumption amounted to 320,000 piculs.

Silk in its raw state, when not exported to foreign countries, is generally woven in the producing district. Of silk piece goods the shipments in 1905 amounted to 26,926 piculs, valued at Tls.19,747,539. Of this 9,793 piculs went to Hongkong for further distribution, and 2,597 piculs to other foreign ports, leaving 14,536 piculs, valued at Tls.10,849,912, for home consumption in other than the original producing districts.

Sugar was shipped to the extent of 1,481,524 piculs, almost entirely from Kwangtung ports, and found its market in the Yangtze and northern ports. This was in addition to 4,156,663 piculs imported from abroad.

Vegetable tallow, expressed from the seeds of the *Stillingia sebifera*, was shipped, almost entirely from Hankow, to the extent of 167,160 piculs. Of this 67,277 piculs were shipped abroad, chiefly to Italy, leaving 100,000 piculs for home consumption.

Tobacco, leaf or prepared and cut, was shipped to the amount of 529,253 piculs, of which 216,704 piculs came from Hankow, 98,522 piculs from Kiukiang, and 182,346 piculs from Kwangtung ports, and it goes wherever there are Chinese. This was in addition to cigarettes, Chinese-made, valued at Tls.1,667,698, shipped coastwise, and cigarettes, valued at Tls.4,427,171, and cigars, worth Tls.381,466, imported from foreign countries.

CHAPTER XI

OPIUM

OPIUM presents a thorny subject to handle for any writer. If he is a partisan of the opium trade, his tendency is strong to leave the ground with which he may be familiar, that of commercial dealings and statistics, and to try to demonstrate the innocuousness of the drug as smoked by the Chinese—to compare it to the relatively harmless ante-prandial glass of sherry. If his mission is to denounce the opium traffic, he invariably seems impelled, by an irresistible inclination, to leave the high moral ground on which he is unassailable, and descend into the arena of facts and figures, with which he is not likely to be so familiar, and among which his predisposition will lead him to pass by or to misinterpret those which make against his case. The writer who tries to investigate the facts with no predisposition to either side, is likely to find himself branded as a trimmer by the one party and a Laodicean by the other, with no opportunity to defend himself. This chapter falls into the third category, and an attempt will be made to present the general facts of the history of opium in China, in such a way that either party, by judicious selection of passages, may find arguments with which to confute its opponents. There will be no attempt to elucidate the really vital point in the opium question, the moral aspect pure and simple.

THE POPPY *

Previous to the Tang dynasty (A.D. 618) the poppy was

* " The Poppy in China," by J. Edkins.

350

apparently unknown to the Chinese botanists and physicians. The first mention in literature is in the " Supplementary Herbalist " of Chen Tsang-chi, an author writing in the first half of the eighth century, who quotes from an earlier lost writer, Sung Yang-tze, a statement that " the poppy has four petals, white or red. . . . The seeds are in a bag (capsule described) . . . being like those of millet." At this time the Arabs had been trading with China for a full century. The second reference is in the " Book on the Culture of Trees " by Kwo To-to, a writer of the latter part of the eighth century living in the inland province of Shensi. The poet Yung Tao, a resident of Szechwan in the closing years of the Tang dynasty (ended 906), wrote a poem describing the poppy growing in the plains near his home.

MEDICINAL USE

In the " Herbalist's Treasury," composed by order of the Emperor by a commission of nine in 973, is a reference to the medicinal use of the poppy : " Its seeds have healing power. When men . . . they may be benefited by mixing these seeds with bamboo juice boiled into gruel, and taking the mixture." About the same period the poet Su Tung-po says in one of his poems, " the boy may prepare for you the broth of the poppy." His brother Su Che wrote " A Poem on the cultivation of the medicinal plant Poppy," in which he says : " I built a house on the west of the city. . . . The gardener came to me to say ' The poppy is a good plant to have.' . . . Its seeds are like autumn millet ; when ground they yield a sap like cow's milk ; when boiled they become a drink fit for Buddha. Old men whose powers have decayed . . . should take this drink. Use a willow mallet and a stone basin to bruise ; boil in water that has been sweetened with honey. (When depressed) then I have but to drink a cup of this poppy-seed decoction. I laugh and am happy. I have come to Yingchwan (his later home) and am wandering on the banks of its river. I seem to be climbing the slopes of Mount Lu (home of his boyhood) in the far west." In the Herbalist of Su Sung, prepared by order of the Emperor about the year 1057, it is stated that " the poppy is found everywhere. . . . There are two kinds, one with red flowers, one with white. . . . When the capsules have become dry and yellow, they may be plucked. . . . In cases of nausea it will be found serviceable to administer a decoction of poppy-seeds made in the following way. . ."

A medical writer, Lin Hung, probably of the twelfth century, makes the first reference to the use of the capsules, which contain the juice from which opium is prepared. He directs that the entire poppy head be taken, washed, and the juice pressed out and filtered, and then boiled and afterward steamed: the residue may then be taken out and "made up into cakes shaped like a fish." The result of this process is opium, mixed with the impurity of the vegetable substance of the capsule. Three other writers of the same period, Yang Shih-ying, Wang Chiu, and Wang Shih, refer explicitly to the merits of the poppy capsule in curing dysentery. Three writers on medical subjects of the thirteenth century, Liu Ho-kien, Li Kao, and Wei I-lin, and one of the fourteenth century, Chu Chen-heng, also describe the mode of preparing the "fish-cake" paste from the capsule and its use in the pharma-copœia. The last-named states " it is used also for diarrhœa and dysentery accompanied by local inflammation ; though its effects are quick, great care must be taken in using it, because it kills like a knife."

The first reference to scoring the fresh capsule *in situ* to obtain the inspissated juice, which by manipulation becomes opium, is in the writings of Wang Hi, who died in 1488 ; he says, " Opium is produced in Arabia from poppies with red flowers . . . after the flower has faded the capsule while still fresh is pricked for the juice." Wang Hi was Governor for twenty years of the province of Kansu, where he would come in contact with Mohammedans, from whom he could learn of Arab arts and industries. In the "Eastern Treasury of Medicine," a Korean work of the same period, is given an exact account of the method of scoring the capsule, gathering the exuded sap, and drying it in the sun, much as practised to-day ; and there can be little doubt that the preparation of opium was introduced into China through Arab channels by the end of the fifteenth century. The "Introduction to Medicine" of Li Ting, in the middle of the sixteenth century, gives an exact account of the method of preparing opium, under the name A-fu-yung. The Arabs, in taking the Greek name opium (ὄπιον), transformed it into *afyûn.* In China the provinces along the coast have transliterated the name opium into ya-pien, by which the drug is generally known ; but in the inland province of Yunnan, where the Mohammedan influence has always been strong, and the Mohammedan population predominated up to the Panthay rebellion (1867) and the resultant massacres, opium of indigenous production is to this day referred to in official documents, tax receipts, etc., as fu-yung, which, except as a truncated form of a-fu-yung, is unintelligible in Chinese.

OPIUM SMOKING

It may be said broadly that, while all other opium-using people take it by the mouth and stomach, the Chinese alone smoke it.

Opium smoking came in through tobacco smoking. As we have seen (Chapter IX.*) the Spanish occupied the Philippines from the west in 1543, and made their first attempt to trade with China in 1575 ; thereafter they left the development of the trade between China and Manila entirely to the Chinese. Through the Philippines the American narcotic, tobacco, was introduced at Amoy, and thence to Formosa, which was in process of colonisation from Amoy in that period. In the "Notes on the Conduct of Business " published about 1650, the year 1620 is given as the date of the introduction, about the time of the " Counterblaste to Tobacco " of King James the Sixth of Scotland and First of England. The Chinese Emperors were animated by the same feelings as King James, and the last of the Ming Emperors (1628–1644) prohibited tobacco smoking in his dominions. The first of the Manchu Emperors, before his occupation at Peking, while he was Emperor of the Manchus but not of the Chinese, issued in 1641 an edict on archery, in which he says : " To smoke tobacco is a fault, but not so great a fault as to neglect practice with the bow. As to the prohibition of tobacco smoking. it became impossible to maintain it because you princes and others smoked privately, though not publicly ; but as to the use of the bow, this must not be neglected." Other prohibitive edicts followed, but were quite as ineffective ; and to-day in China, with few exceptions, every man, woman, and weaned child is a smoker of tobacco : the " Society of Total Abstainers " (from wine, tobacco, and tea) is in times of trouble classed with the secret societies, for which extermination is the prescribed treatment.

Formosa is a land of jungle and malaria, and where malaria prevails opium is a natural resource, as exemplified by the opium pills of the Norfolk fen-men a short century ago. Of the tropical jungle we have a note of Jacobus Bontius, a Dutch physician of Java, dated Batavia, 1629, in which he says that " unless we had opium to use in these hot countries, in cases of dysentery, cholera, burning fever, and various bilious affections, we should practise medicine in vain." In Formosa malaria is deadly to this day, and the early colonists mixed with their tobacco various ingredients to neutralise the effects of the fever, among them opium and arsenic : the latter is still used by the Chinese in what is called " water tobacco," and is prescribed in cases of malaria by Western physicians when for any reason quinine is contra-indicated. Kaempfer visited Java in 1689, and in his account of Batavia is the first mention of an " opium-smoking divan," in which was smoked "opium diluted with water and mixed with tobacco"; and as the Dutch controlled the trade of Formosa from 1624 to 1662, it seems probable that the practice of smoking mixed tobacco and opium was introduced from Java. From Formosa the practice extended to the mainland through Amoy, the " metropolis " of the colonists. There is nothing to show when opium ceased to be mixed with tobacco for smoking. The only reference to the habit in Staunton's account of Lord Macartney's mission (1793) is that many of the higher Mandarins took opium, and that " they smoke tobacco mixed with other odorous substances, and sometimes a little opium."

The Emperor Kang-hi, in his course of settling the Empire, came to the conquest of Formosa in 1683, with his base at Amoy. Here the governing powers were first brought into actual contact with the evil ; but in an age when edicts were readily issued, no immediate steps were taken. The first prohibitory edict was issued by his successor Yung-cheng, in 1729, enacting severe penalties on the sale of opium and the opening of opium-smoking divans, and from this time dealing in opium became a crime.

Foreign Opium

At the time of this edict the importation of foreign opium amounted to 200 chests a year, introduced by the Portuguese trading from Goa, and by none others until 1773 ; English private merchants then engaged in the trade up to 1781, when the East India Company took it into its own hands. In the forty years up to 1767 the importation increased gradually from 200 chests to 1,000, a chest containing from 135 lbs. (free-trade opium, as from Malwa or Persia) to 160 lbs. (Bengal regie opium). The machinery of an Imperial edict cannot have been directed against so insignificant a quantity as 200 chests, the annual amount at the date of the edict ; and that it was not considered by the Canton authorities to be directed against the foreign importation, is shown by the gradual and unconcealed increase at the rate of 20 chests a year. A distinction was recognised and made between opium for medicinal use, and its sale for smoking ; and its introduction for the former purpose was permitted. In the " Hoppo Book " * of 1753, which is based on tariffs of 1687 and 1733, then still in force, opium is included as paying Tls.3 a picul, which is at the rate of 6 per cent. (the then official rate of levy) on a value of Tls.50 ; and in a valuation book of the same date (1755), the values of certain commodities are given, among them silk at Tls.100, tea at Tls.8, rhubarb Tls.1·50, musk Tls.150, and opium Tls.50. The inference is that the Canton officials were quite honest in holding that the prohibitory edict of 1729 did not apply to the importation of the foreign drug. The trade went on without restriction on the importation, and in 1773 the English merchants made their first imports from Calcutta, with the probable effect of increasing the amount introduced. In 1780 a new Viceroy was appointed to Canton, who had " the reputation of an upright, bold, and rigid minister," † and who determined to apply the Imperial restriction to the importation of the drug, as well as to its sale for smoking ; but the connection between this and the assumption of control of the opium traffic by the East India Company in the following year, is a matter of inference. The evils arising from the use of opium became more apparent from year to year, the import in 1790 having increased to 4,054 chests ; and in 1796, on the representation of the Viceroy, an Imperial edict was issued imposing heavier penalties on opium smoking. In 1800 an edict was issued prohibiting the importation of foreign opium and the cultivation of the poppy. From this date the traffic became contraband, and about the same time smuggling became organised by detailed arrangements

* " Journal China Branch of Royal Asiatic Society," 1882.
† " British Parliamentary Papers," 1783.

made between the importers and the officials at Canton
and elsewhere along the coast.

DRAIN OF SPECIE *

In addition to the high moral ground taken by the
Imperial Government in their desire to suppress the opium
traffic, they rest their case upon their statement of the
fact that the necessity of paying for the opium drained
the country of silver, giving as an instance the " average
annual export of Tls.10,000,000 in the ten years previous "
to 1839 ; and this instance, and the drain of silver deducible
from it, have been generally accepted in the histories.
This drain of silver is not proved by facts. The sum is
first to be discounted as being a fine-sounding round figure
useful to support a prohibitory edict ; and, being in a
Chinese official document, the statement must be interpreted strictly, and not taken to imply more than it says.
Assuming that in ten years shipments of treasure amounted
to upwards of Tls.10,000,000 annually, which was not the
fact, it does not follow that, on balancing exports against
imports, the net export was as much. Several foreign writers
of the time refer to the permits specially required for the
shipment of treasure, and there can be no doubt that any
reported export of treasure was derived from the records of
such permits without any offset or the introduction of alien
matters. It was before the day of banks ; and while it is
almost true that at that time each ship had to square with
hard cash its accounts for imports and exports, it is abso
lutely true of each merchant, whether in a season he had
one ship or several. India supplied the opium, but took
no tea and no considerable quantity of silk, and shipment
of treasure to India was inevitable. In the present day
that country sends to China commodities to the average
annual value of over Tls.80,000,000, and receives in return

* For a detailed consideration of this subject, see the author's
" International Relations of the Chinese Empire "—" The Period
of Conflict," chap. viii. § 35.

commodities not exceeding Tls.10,000,000 in value ; to-day the difference is adjusted by bank bills, but then the opium from India could not be paid for by tea shipped to England or America, but must be paid for in cash and the specie shipped, except in so far as it might be taken over by the East India Company against its bills on Calcutta, to provide funds with which to buy tea. Except for the opium of India and the spices of the Southern Isles, the rest of the world could provide little that China wanted. England could send a few pieces of camlet, probably not a hundredth of what was needed to buy a cargo of tea ; and from the English, American, Dutch, Portuguese, and other trade, poured in a stream of silver in the shape of Spanish dollars,* which to this day are current in Anhwei, and were current in Formosa up to 1895, in which year two and a quarter millions of them were introduced into the island for the tea season. The movement of silver was inward, not outward ; and the explanation of the fact that merchants of the highest repute brought themselves to engage in a trade which we have come to regard as disreputable, is to be found in the imperative commercial necessity of lessening the constant flow of silver from the depleted European market, and of substituting for it any commodity which the Chinese would consent to buy.

Opium Contraband

Opium was the one thing the Chinese would consent to buy, and buy it they did and continued to do, after the prohibitory edict of 1800, as they had before ; and arrangements were made with business-like method for circumventing the prohibition, allowing the buyers to get the drug they wanted, and securing what they considered their proper dues to the rulers of the land whose duty it was to see that the edicts were enforced. The edicts never were enforced ; for forty years there was no pretence at enforcing them in the spirit, and the restrictions of their

* See page 183.

letter had only the effect of covering the traffic with a veil of decency such that the importing merchants might engage in it, the officials might not have it thrust under their eyes, and the dealers might get their supplies with more trouble and at considerably more cost. The irregular dues levied over and above the official tariff were already heavy, but when it became necessary to pay for connivance in addition to the payments demanded for complaisance, they became heavier ; and they were distributed between the officials, Hoppo, Viceroy, Governor, Treasurer, and so on down the list, not as bribes in one payment to secure that eyes should be judiciously shut, but as dues levied on each chest divided in proper proportion to each official. As the trade was prohibited the dues received could not be included in the regular reports of revenue collected, and the regular New Year's gratifications sent in accordance with custom to the Ministers of State and the officials of the Court at Peking— heavier because of the greater amount of *lucrum* attaching to the provincial posts—had no peculiar odour attaching to them to betray their origin ; it was therefore to the interest of all officials concerned, below the Emperor and except an occasional honest statesman, that the prohibition should be enacted and that the traffic should go on. The Emperor might prohibit the trade, but the Emperor's representatives continued to sanction it.

On the issue of the prohibitory edicts it became impossible to continue the open storage of stocks in the factories at Canton, and the depots were established at Macao, which, it must be remembered, was under Chinese fiscal control until 1848 ; quantities were, however, still brought on in the importing ships and kept on board at the anchorage at Whampoa until they could be delivered to purchasers. This went on until 1820, when the order went out that no opium was to be stored in Macao or at Whampoa ; the importers then established store ships at Lintin Island, in the estuary of the Canton River. Up to this date the import had not in any year exceeded 5,000 chests.

When the edict of 1800 was issued, the East India Company ceased to carry opium on its own account. From that time it was officially responsible for the production of that portion of the drug which came from Bengal and for its sale in Calcutta, but had no direct concern with its transportation and sale in China, nor did it ever have any connection with opium from Malwa or from Persia.

During the Lintin period, opium (then regularly called " tea," and still ordinarily so termed at Canton) was sold by sample, and paid for invariably in hard cash against a delivery order. The importer had nothing else to do with sales for local delivery. The purchaser having arranged for the necessary protection from official interference, took his order to the receiving ship at Lintin, where he repacked into mat-bags, marked with his private chop, and took it away in fast boats with crews of sixty to seventy men. The trade would be temporarily interrupted on the arrival of each new official of high rank, until he had settled into his place ; and occasionally there would be a *brutum fulmen* of a proclamation ordering vessels " loitering at the outer anchorage " either to come into port or to sail away ; but never was Lintin mentioned by name, and never was a guard-boat so unmannerly as to poke its nose into the anchorage, though doubtless there were many watchful eyes round about.

Opium for the eastern part of Kwangtung was ordinarily sold at Canton, also always for cash, to be delivered by the seller ordinarily at Namoa, an island near Swatow, the station of the Commander-in-chief of the provincial coast forces. Hunter * describes a visit he made in 1837 in an American clipper schooner of 150 tons regularly despatched by his firm from Lintin to deliver their sales. On arrival at Namoa he found there two English brigs belonging to two English firms, engaged in the same traffic, and lying near them the " Admiral's flagship." The Admiral came on board, and all concerned went through some solemn

* " The Fankwae at Canton."

foolery, the object of which was to secure supplies for the schooner, on its way from Singapore to Canton, driven into Namoa in distress ; afterwards, at a more private interview opened by the direct question " How many chests have you ? " a bargain was struck, and non-interference provided for, on terms additional to those which were arranged by the purchasers at Canton. After this the opium, which had been packed in bags at Lintin, was delivered to junks flying a private signal, without further formality. The jurisdiction of the Canton Hoppo and Viceroy ended at Namoa, and farther up the coast the sweet simplicity of the Canton procedure could not be carried out in such perfect detail. The vessel in which Hunter returned came into Namoa from the north, and " her entire freight to Canton consisted of $430,000 in value of gold bars and sycee-silver."

This contraband traffic went on uninterruptedly until the end of 1838. In 1830 the annual import had increased to 16,877 chests, and in 1838 to 20,619 chests. The appointment of Lord Napier in 1834 as Ambassador of His Britannic Majesty, brought to the fore a different aspect of China's foreign relations, the right of foreign Envoys to treat directly with the representatives of the Empire, and, connected with it, the position of monopoly inherent in the Co-Hong, with which alone Envoy and merchant were to have any dealings ; but opium was no more in question from 1834 to 1838, during the time of Lord Napier and Captain Elliot, than it had been before. At Peking, however, there was renewed discussion of the evils arising from opium smoking, and of the still greater demoralisation from smuggling an article declared contraband by law ; and there was even serious consideration of a proposal to legalise the traffic in order to bring the evil under better control. The proposal was negatived, and the Emperor decided to enforce the edict issued by his father in 1800, and found a willing agent for the purpose in Lin Tse-sü. In this decision the Emperor may have been mistaken, he may have attempted to sweep back the tides of the ocean with a broom, but he was undoubtedly honest and intended that his will should be carried out. Lin was appointed Imperial Commissioner, and sent to Canton to carry out the will of his master, superseding *ad hoc* both Viceroy and Hoppo. Had it been only a question of opium, his mission was hopeless ; it was as if a Prohibition Government at Washington had sent Neal Dow to carry out a Maine Liquor Law in the state of Texas. But both he and his master had misjudged the situation ; when they said " opium," the English Envoy, backed by the English admiral, answered " equality," and equality it was, and not opium, which was settled by the treaty of Nanking. This treaty decided the equal status of officials of the two Powers, the abolition of the monopoly of the Co-Hong, and the adoption of uniform dues and duties ; but it left the Chinese government free to adopt its own measures for the regulation of the opium traffic. The English government did not undertake to perform preventive service for China, since others than English were already engaged in the trade, and others still could easily have taken it up ; but it forbade the establishment of an opium depot at the outset in Hongkong, and it afforded no naval protection to smugglers.

Commissioner Lin arrived in Canton on March 10th, 1839, and, after remaining inscrutable for some days, on the 18th issued a proclamation that the foreigners should deliver up all the opium in store and give a bond to import no more, on penalty of death. When they refused, the entire body of foreign residents, of all nationalities, were shut up in the factories, deprived of servants and of outside supplies of food and water, and informed that they were hostages for the due execution of the order. " Hostage " is an awkward word to use, and a still more awkward thing to be ; and in fear of death the merchants surrendered their opium, even bringing eight chests up from Macao. The total quantity surrendered was 20,291 chests, and the earnestness of conviction of the Emperor and his Commissioner is evidenced by the fact that this was effectually destroyed to the last ounce. Of the firms contributing the opium, the largest contributor was an English firm with 7,000 chests, then another English firm, then an American firm with 1,500 chests ; after them came English, Parsee, and other merchants, natives of India. Some fifty chests of Turkey opium in the possession of an American firm were not surrendered as not being from India. The only effect of the Imperial Commissioner's action, directed against the foreigner and not against his own countrymen, was to check the local trade for a time, but it did not do away with it : the demand remained, new supplies came forward, and the trade went on.

The loss of prestige by the Imperial Government not only inspired the smugglers with greater activity and less fear of the consequences, but caused the officials along the coast to throw off such modest feelings of restraint as they may have felt before. Then, in the decade 1850–1860, the spread of the Taiping rebellion over whole provinces, involving millions of people, caused vast misery, which drove many to the Chinese equivalent of " drink," filled the pockets of myriads with plunder to be spent in indulgence, and brought into the field on both sides armed forces whose chief occupation, then as in later times, was opium smoking. The result of this laxity and this increase in the demand was a perfect carnival of smuggling. Prior to Lin's mission the trade, though not legalised, was fully regulated, and it is a misuse of terms to apply the word "smuggling" to what went on then : the foreign merchant imported his opium without concealment, but, during the last twenty years of the period, instead of bringing it to his factory at Canton and storing it there or at Macao, he deposited it on store-ships at Lintin ; he sold it, generally speaking, and obtained payment at Canton, all subsequent proceedings being the concern of the purchasers, Chinese subjects ; and he delivered it on board his own ship, usually at Lintin, to a certain extent at definite points on the coast to the east and north, but always under official oversight. To a limited extent the sales were not effected at Canton, but at the points of delivery on the coast. After Lin's mission the trade was neither legalised nor regulated ; even such restraint as might come from publicity was absent, since at first the British authorities refused to permit the establishment of a depot in Hongkong. The result was to drive the importers into closer relations with the officials, who were in a position to impede the traffic at all places along the coast ; to what extent they, and to what extent the purchasers, made the actual arrangements, who was the active agent in perverting from their duty the only too willing representatives of the humiliated Emperor, is not known, because the whole traffic during this period is covered by a veil of secrecy and mystery. From this driving of the traffic away from the light of day, from the increased activity of the importers in supplying an increased demand, from the greater enterprise of the smugglers, whether they were foreign or Chinese, and from the greater laxity and depravity of the officials of China— from all these causes came two consequences : from the 20,619 chests of 1838 the import of opium increased to about 50,000 chests in 1850, and to 85,000 chests in 1860 ; and, as opium smoking had debauched the Chinese, the opium traffic debauched the foreign traders and dragged them down from their high estate.

It will be well to repeat, in a brief summary, the salient facts relating to opium. The poppy has been known in China for at least twelve centuries, its medicinal use for nine centuries, and that the medicinal properties lay in the capsule for six centuries. Opium has been made in China for four centuries. Tobacco smoking was introduced through the Spanish at the beginning of the seventeenth century, and the smoking of opium mixed with the tobacco through the Dutch in the middle of the seventeenth century ; there is no historical record to show when opium was first smoked by itself, but it appears to have nearly coincided with the prohibition of all opium importation in 1800. Foreign opium was first imported by the Portuguese at the beginning of the eighteenth century, and was first handled by the English in 1773 ; from 1781 to 1800 it was mainly in the hands of the East India Company. After that the principal importers were English, though there is nothing to show that traders of any nationality, who could lay hands on the drug, refused to deal in it ; it is on record that in 1839, on the occasion of the famous surrender, one-thirteenth of all the opium surrendered was given up by an American firm, and smaller quantities came from Parsees, who, though under British protection, would readily have transferred their protectorate to others, had there been sufficient motive. For the pandemonium of the period 1840 to 1860 the Chinese must be held primarily responsible ; the Emperor and his Commissioner Lin attempted the impossible in applying to foreign nations alone the restrictions which they could not enforce on their own subjects, so removing all regulation from a trade which they would not consent to legalise ; and his representatives, the whole length of the coast, acted in every respect, except as to turning their receipts into the treasury, as if the trade had been legalised. The disturbed state of the country from 1850 to 1860 weakened the authority of the government, and gave the officials an excuse and an opportunity for their laxity which they did not need, but it could not transfer the responsibility from the Imperial Government to the shoulders of foreign nations.

Opium Trade Legalised

The treaties made in 1858 as the result of the second war left the opium question still unsettled. The treaty of Nanking of 1842 was silent on the subject, leaving China to enact and enforce her own sumptuary and prohibitive laws, and to adopt her own preventive measures. The same silence was observed in the four treaties of Tientsin of 1858, in the British and French treaties imposed on China as the result of the war, and in the identical and simultaneous

American and Russian treaties which must be considered to be also the direct result of that war. But (to quote the premier treaty) Article XXVI. of the British treaty provided for the appointment of a Commission to revise the Customs tariff; and when, in November 1858, the Commission agreed on the tariff, opium was quietly inserted in it at a duty of Tls.30 per picul. Opium was included with the full consent of the Chinese negotiators; of this there is no doubt, for we have the testimony of Sir Thomas Wade and Mr. Laurence Oliphant, who were the representatives of the British Envoy on the Commission. That so burning a question as the opium trade should not be mentioned in those unofficial colloquies which accompany all negotiations was impossible; and that the wisdom of legalisation *cum* regulation was fully explained to the Chinese negotiators as a measure of political economy is made known to us by Oliphant. The first suggestion that the matter should be taken into consideration was made by the American Minister, Mr. William B. Reed, who came out to China with a strong bias against the opium trade, and with instructions from his government conceived in the same spirit, but who nevertheless became an advocate of the legalisation of the trade, from witnessing the abuses to which its contraband character gave rise.* With this changed view he wrote to Lord Elgin as follows:

> " I have more than once understood your Excellency to say that you had a strong, if not invincible, repugnance, involved as Great Britain already was in hostilities at Canton, and having been compelled in the north to resort to the influence of threatened coercion, to introduce the subject of opium to the consideration of the Chinese authorities. Yet I am confident, unless the initiative is taken by your Excellency, things must continue as they are, with all their shame ; and I appeal to your Excellency's high sense of duty,

* " Narrative of the Earl of Elgin's Mission to China and Japan," 1860, Vol. II., chap. xiii.

so often and so strongly expressed to this helpless though perverse people, whether we, the representatives of Western and Christian nations, ought to consider our work done without some attempt to induce or compel an adjustment of the pernicious difficulty. In such an attempt I shall cordially unite."

After alluding to the possibility of putting a stop to the growth of opium in India, Mr. Reed goes on to say :

" Of effective prohibition, and this mainly through the inveterate appetite of the Chinese, I am not sanguine ; and I therefore more confidently, though not more earnestly, call your Excellency's attention to the only other course open to us—attempt to persuade the Chinese to put such high duties on the drug as will restrain the supply, regulate the import, and yet not stimulate some other form of smuggling, with or without the connivance of the Chinese. The economical arguments in favour of this course are so fully stated in the accompanying paper that I need not allude to them further."

It was therefore decided that the matter should be brought to the notice of the Chinese Commissioners, who, however, required no long persuasion ; they were fully awake to the evils of what had become unrestricted trade in the drug, and their government needed the revenue which had for so long a time gone into the pockets of its servants. After approval by the French and American Envoys, the tariff was agreed to, including opium. At the same time it was recognised that opium was eminently an article of import which must be left to the unfettered discretion of the Chinese government to deal with ; and the fifth of the Rules of Trade appended to the tariff reads as follows :

" The restrictions affecting trade in Opium, Cash, Grain, Pulse, Sulphur, Brimstone, Saltpetre, and Spelter, are relaxed, under the following conditions :

" 1. Opium will henceforth pay thirty taels per

picul Import Duty.   The importer will sell it only at
the port.   It will be carried into the interior by Chinese
only, and only as Chinese property; the Foreign
trader will not be allowed to accompany it.   The
provisions of Article IX. of the Treaty of Tientsin, by
which British subjects are authorised to proceed into
the interior with Passports to trade, will not extend
to it, nor will those of Article XXVIII. of the same
Treaty, by which the Transit Dues are regulated.
The Transit Dues on it will be arranged as the Chinese
Government see fit ; nor in future revisions of the
Tariff is the same rule of revision to be applied to
Opium as to other goods."

The next step in the history of opium is found in the
Chefoo Agreement of 1876, by which the British government
accepted in principle a proposal that inland taxation (likin)
on the drug should be collected simultaneously with the
import duty, *i.e.* by the Imperial and not by the provincial
authorities. This was made effective by an Additional
Article signed on July 18, 1885, by which the amount of
likin was settled at Tls.80 per picul, making, with the
import duty, a total of Tls.110 per picul which the Chinese
government is entitled to collect ; and the establishment
in 1887 of the Kowloon and Lappa Customs, to control the
junk traffic with Hongkong and Macao, operated further
to the benefit of the Imperial exchequer by the restraint
thereby imposed on smuggling.

The only restriction imposed by China on the opium
trade and accepted by a foreign Power, other than the
inclusion of opium as " contraband " in the tariff annexed
to the American treaty of 1844, is contained in the Supplemental Treaty of 1880 between the United States and China,
of which Article II. is as follows :

" The Governments of China and of the United
States mutually agree and undertake that Chinese subjects shall not be permitted to import opium into any
of the ports of the United States ; and citizens of the

United States shall not be permitted to import opium into any of the open ports of China, to transport it from one open port to any other open port, or to buy and sell opium in any of the open ports of China. This absolute prohibition, which extends to vessels owned by the citizens or subjects of either Power, to foreign vessels employed by them, or to vessels owned by the citizens or subjects of either Power, and employed by other persons for the transportation of opium, shall be enforced by appropriate legislation on the part of China and the United States; and the benefits of the favoured nation clause in existing Treaties shall not be claimed by the citizens or subjects of either Power as against the provisions of this Article."

The only commentary on this agreement is found in the fact that when, in 1884–1885, temporarily and for reasons over which the American government had little or no control, the American flag reappeared on the coast and engaged in the carrying trade no attempt was made to enforce the restriction. A subsequent Act of Congress, approved February 23rd, 1887, supplied the legislation necessary to make the restriction effective.

The course of the trade in foreign opium since the legalisation is shown in the table on the next page. In 1863 Tientsin and Chefoo had been opened in the north, and Hankow, Kiukiang and Chinkiang on the Yangtze. In 1879 the recorded import, 82,927 piculs, reached its maximum. The opening of the Kowloon and Lappa Customs in 1887 may be assumed to have reduced smuggling in junk by between 10,000 and 15,000 piculs.

The second table shows the proportion of each kind of foreign opium imported during the past fifty years, viz. Bengal (Patna and Benares), the production of the Opium Régie of the government of India; Malwa, the free trade product of the states of Central India, feudatory to the British government but otherwise self-governing;

24

	1863.	1867.	1879.	1888.	1897.	1905.	1911.
	Piculs.	Piculs.	Piculs.	Piculs.	Piculs.	Piculs.	Piculs.
Manchuria ..	—	2,585	2,453	113	28	25	—
Chihli	3,708	7,898	5,181	1,555	918	225	—
Shantung ..	873	2,735	3,536	318	320	440	205
Hunan } ..	1,412	4,242	3,294	1,163	519	{ 240	99
Hupeh }						322	71
Kiangsi ..	1,993	2,202	2,153	3,077	2,483	1,715	1,491
Anhwei } ..	22,389	16,788	{ 3,141	3,400	1,557	1,626	1,228
Kiangsu }			{ 28,199	22,182	17,676	18,077	11,812
Chekiang ..	2,679	5,047	7,728	6,274	4,873	4,041	441
Fukien ..	9,821	9,238	8,903	13,039	7,877	6,600	4,280
Formosa ..	—	2,586	5,552	4,646	—	—	—
Kwangsi }						{ 22	94
Kwangtung } ..	7,212	7,627	12,787	26,845	13,058	{ 18,587	8,037
Other channels*	20,000	20,000	20,000	5,000	5,000	5,000	3,000
Total }	50,087	60,948	82,927	82,612	49,309	51,920	27,758
	70,087	80,948	102,927	87,612	54,309	56,920	30,758

* Other channels, *i.e.* by junk, either legitimately, but not reporting to the Imperial Maritime Customs, or smuggled. In 1905 a quantity unreported was introduced through Kwangchow-wan, estimated not to exceed 2,000 piculs. Of the official import into Kwangtung, the Canton delta ports in 1905 took 13,207 piculs, 8,150 piculs in 1897, and 17,776 piculs in 1888 ; before the opening of the Kowloon and Lappa Customs, in 1879 they took only 1,194 piculs, in 1867 only 2,111 piculs, and in 1863 only 3,469 piculs officially reported.

				BENGAL.	MALWA.	PERSIAN.	TOTAL.
				Piculs.	Piculs.	Piculs.	Piculs.
1863	..	..	..	15,120	34,967	—	50,087
1867	..	..	..	26,297	34,006	645	60,948
1873	..	..	..	24,300	40,910	587	65,797
1879	..	..	..	37,952	39,509	5,466	82,927
1883	..	..	..	27,504	34,632	6,032	68,168
1888	..	..	..	45,040	33,127	4,445	82,612
1893	..	..	..	32,416	28,694	6,998	68,108
1897	..	..	..	26,816	19,635	2,858†	49,309
1901	..	..	..	27,250	21,799	435	49,484
1905	..	..	..	34,195	16,034	1,691	51,920
1911	..	..	..	17,182	9,338	1,238	27,758
Average { Quantity	..			28,552	28,423	2,764	59,739
{ Per cent.	..			47·8	47·6	4·6	100·0

and Persian† (formerly also called Turkey), the product of
Persia. In comparing the figures it must, however, be
borne in mind that the province of Kwangtung ordinarily
prefers Bengal opium to the extent of fully three-fourths
of the foreign drug consumed, and that prior to 1887 much
of the supply for that province passed through channels
which did not lead to its inclusion in the figures given in
the table.

NATIVE OPIUM

Opium was produced in China before the vice of smoking
was introduced, and, in China as elsewhere, was valued for
its medicinal properties. There is no evidence to show
that, otherwise than medicinally, the Chinese ever took
opium in the shape of pills, as was for centuries the practice
in Central and Western Asia ; and the evidence is all against
the supposition that the Chinese smoked the drug because
they already produced it. Smoking came in independently,
and fed on foreign or native supplies indifferently, as evidenced by the fact that, at the date of the first Imperial
prohibition of the evil in 1729, the importation of foreign
opium was only 200 chests a year, and forty years later did
not exceed 1,000 chests. But, while it cannot be said that
an already existing production of native opium created the
evil of smoking, neither is it wholly true that the evil was
created by the introduction of foreign opium. The vice
came because opium existed in the world ; had there been
no native production, the foreign drug would have supplied
its food ; had there been no foreign importation, the native
supply would have sufficed, or would have become sufficient
for all requirements, even to satisfy the demands of a craving
which has extended to every corner and to all classes in
the Empire. It would therefore be a task leading to no
useful result, to search for statistics to determine if the

† Formosa, the chief consumer of Persian opium, passed under
the Japanese flag in 1895.

native production exceeded the foreign importation in 1729—we know it did ; or if it exceeded the foreign supply of 1800—it very probably, almost certainly did. Coming down to the nineteenth century, during its fourth decade, when the great question—to legalise the foreign trade or stamp it out—was under consideration, the native production was referred to in several memorials presented to the Throne. In 1830 it was stated that " the poppy is cultivated over one-half of Chekiang," a rhetorical exaggeration. In 1836 a memorial of Hu Nai-tsi proposed to legalise the traffic on various economic grounds, and, incidentally, because of the already great native production. This was opposed in a memorial of Chu Tsun, who was convinced of the evils of smoking, and based his objections largely on the amount of the home production, instancing that in his native province of Yunnan the annual production was many thousand piculs. The habit of smoking opium had been known in China for at least a century and a half, and it is probable that it had extended to the inland provinces ; while it is improbable that the 15,000 to 20,000 chests, which constituted the foreign supply, penetrated far from the coast, and it is not probable that they supplied much more than the provinces of Kwangtung, Fukien (including Formosa), and possibly Chekiang ; it seems probable that the foreign drug reached along the coast beyond the mouth of the Yangtze only after 1840. This is supposition, which is alien to the purpose of this chapter ; but it finds some support in the fact * that at Hankow, prior to the opening of the port in 1861, foreign opium was practically unknown, a few piculs only being introduced to satisfy Cantonese palates ; that prior to 1859 Hankow was supplied with opium from Shansi, but that these supplies were cut off by disturbances in that province, and in 1860 Hankow drew its supplies, to the extent of 2,000 piculs, from Szechwan and Hunan.

Statistics are unknown in China, the only statistics

* " Native Opium, 1863." Shanghai, 1864.

obtainable being those of the trade carried on under the cognisance of the Inspectorate General of Customs. Statistics relating to opium are especially unobtainable, since a commodity having so high a value in small bulk, and so heavily taxed, does not in general follow the ordinary trade routes, on which taxing stations are numerous, but is carried by armed bands over unfrequented mountain roads, on which the taxing stations are few and so poorly equipped as to yield readily to superior force, and accept a composition for taxes much lower than the official rate. All this leads to concealment on both sides, and, in estimating the present production of opium in China, inquirers have been driven to base their investigations on the observations of travellers and the opinions of people interested to discover the truth. The results of the investigations of many inquirers are given below for each province, divided into Coast Provinces, in which the original demand was chiefly met by supplies of foreign drug (the northern only since 1860); Yangtze Provinces, accessible to the foreign drug only since 1860; and Inland Provinces, which have never, to any known extent, been supplied with foreign opium. The figures and statements in the present tense are to be taken as referring to 1906.

COAST PROVINCES

Kwangtung produces little opium. At Canton in 1863 it was estimated that 1,500 piculs of native opium found a market, of which 800 came from Yunnan, 400 from Kweichow, 200 from Szechwan, and 100 were the product of Kwangtung, coming from the mountains of the northern part. There has been no great increase of poppy cultivation, and the production of opium in the province to-day probably does not exceed 500 piculs.

Fukien : opium is produced chiefly in the Tungan district, of which the output was estimated in 1863 at 500 piculs, and in 1879 at 1,000 piculs. The lowest estimate for the whole province to-day is 2,000 piculs.

Chekiang produces a considerable quantity, especially in the Wenchow and Chuchow prefectures, the production being estimated at 10,000 to 16,000 piculs in 1879, and at 4,500 piculs in 1887. It will be safe to put the output to-day at 5,000 piculs.

Kiangsu, in 1879, was estimated to produce 2,500 piculs of opium. There has recently been increased production in the Hsüchow prefecture in the north-western corner of the province, and the output of Kiangsu to-day cannot be less than 5,000 piculs.

Shantung imported 3,536 piculs of foreign opium in 1879; in 1888 this had fallen to 318 piculs, which is now the average amount. In 1887 it was estimated that the annual consumption of native opium was 8,000 piculs, mostly Shantung product. The production of the province to-day must be at least 10,000 piculs.

Chihli imported 7,898 piculs of foreign opium in 1867, and 5,181 piculs in 1879; in 1905 this fell to 225 piculs. Native opium was reported as coming from Shansi in 1863 in considerable quantities; in 1879 the production of Chihli was estimated at 3,000 piculs, and in 1887 it was reported to be "very large." Within forty years 7,500 piculs of foreign opium have been entirely displaced by native opium, and, allowing for increase in the population and extension of the habit, the consumption of the latter is now from 15,000 to 20,000 piculs. Some comes from Manchuria and some from Shansi, and the production of Chihli is probably 10,000 and certainly 5,000 piculs.

Manchuria has probably taken up the production of opium within fifty years past. Foreign opium was imported to the extent of 2,585 piculs in 1867, and 2,453 piculs in 1879; in 1888 the import was 113 piculs, and in 1905 was only 25 piculs. Native opium in 1863 came chiefly from Shansi, and it is on record that in that year 200 piculs were introduced into the city of Moukden. In 1879 the production of Manchuria was estimated at 3,000 piculs, and in 1887 at 8,000 piculs, and the quality was reported to be equal if not superior to that of foreign opium. The population has been greatly increased by immigration in the past thirty years, and, apart from the temporary effects of war, the output to-day may be estimated at 15,000 piculs.

For the Coast Provinces the annual production, estimated on a conservative basis, is 42,500 piculs.

YANGTZE PROVINCES

Hunan opium was known at Hankow in 1863 and before, and in 1879 the production was estimated at 1,000 piculs. Hunanese have filled the armies of China for fifty years, and returned soldiers have brought back the habit of heavy smoking. But little foreign opium is imported (240 piculs in 1905), and the production of opium in Hunan to-day is probably at least 3,000 piculs.

Hupeh consumed no foreign opium prior to 1861, and imported 4,242 piculs in 1867, and (including Hunan) 562 piculs in 1905. Native opium is, and has always been, introduced from other provinces, but there has also been a home production, estimated in 1879 at 2,000 to 3,000 piculs, and in 1887 at 3,000 : the output to-day is probably 4,000 piculs.

Kiangsi maintains its consumption of foreign opium of forty and thirty years ago. In 1863 the local production was estimated at 200 piculs ; there has been no great increase in poppy growing, and to-day the output probably does not exceed 500 piculs.

Anhwei imports to-day of foreign opium but half the import of 1879 and 1888. In 1887 the local production was estimated at 2,000 piculs, and to-day it is probably over 3,000 piculs.

For the Yangtze Provinces, accessible since 1861 by steamer, the annual production may be put at 10,500 piculs.

INLAND PROVINCES

Honan opium was known at Shanghai in 1863 ; in 1879 the production was estimated at 3,500 to 5,000 piculs, and in 1887 at 5,000 piculs : the output to-day is probably fully 5,000 piculs.

Shansi formerly supplied a large area with opium, from Hankow in the west and Shanghai in the east to Manchuria in the north. In 1879 the production was estimated at 4,000 piculs, and it will be safe to put it to-day at 5,000 piculs.

Shensi, as we know, cultivated the poppy in the eighth century ; and, as the practice of scoring the capsule to obtain opium was introduced through the adjoining province, Kansu, it may be assumed that Shensi was one of the first provinces to produce opium, and stood ready to supply the demand when it arose. In 1872 Baron von Richthofen records that " in some portions of the country it (the poppy) formed the most conspicuous winter crop." In 1879 it was estimated at Hankow, to which some part of the product was sent, that the annual output was 5,000 piculs ; and it would not be safe to put the output to-day at less than 10,000 piculs.

Kansu, according to Richthofen, " does not consume all the opium it produces, but exports considerable quantities both east and west, and imports none." With a population, largely Mohammedan, estimated at the lowest at 8,000,000, the production of opium must be over 5,000 piculs.

Szechwan must have early acquired the art of opium manufacture, bounded as it is to the north by Kansu and to the south by Yunnan, both centres of Mohammedan influence from early times to the present day ; and, when the practice of smoking the drug was introduced, it must have spread at once to the inhabitants of this mist-covered province, steamy in summer and chilly in winter. The universal testimony of travellers is that the people are, in general, heavy smokers, the consumption per capita being confidently stated to be three times that of the coast provinces. No foreign opium has ever been imported, and the poppy, cultivated certainly as early as the ninth century, is to-day grown everywhere; Mr. E. C. Baber (1878) says: "We were astounded at the extent of the poppy cultivation in Szechwan and Yunnan." Baron von Richthofen (1872) expresses the same astonishment, and estimates the production of opium at a minimum of 60,000 piculs and a probable output of 100,000 piculs. In 1904 the quantity passing by the river route to the east through Ichang was 36,856 piculs, and in 1905 it was 36,311 piculs. Of this quantity 11,011 piculs were imported and 11,025 piculs re-exported by steamer at Hankow in 1904, and 2,736 piculs imported and 2,492 piculs re-exported in 1905, the remainder of the Ichang transit going in the same way by junk; this furnishes an apt illustration of the well-known fact that opium in China comes into the light of day only when there is some obvious fiscal advantage to gain. In addition to the river route there are three main land routes, besides many unfrequented mountain roads, by which opium is carried to the east; and the total export from the province eastward must be well over 50,000 piculs, and is possibly upwards of 100,000 piculs. The recognised authority for Szechwan to-day is Sir Alexander Hosie. In his consular report for 1903 (presented to both Houses of Parliament, October 1904, Cd. 2247), he records the fact that " in the provincial capital, Chengtu, there is one opium-smoking saloon to every 67 of a population of 500,000 ; these saloons are open to men only, and women have to smoke in their own homes." As the result of a careful detailed calculation he states that the consumption of Szechwan-grown opium by the inhabitants of Szechwan is 182,500 piculs. If to this be added the probable export eastward from the province, we have a probable production of not less than 250,000 piculs.

Yunnan has long produced opium, the production in 1836 being stated to be " many thousand piculs." Baber (1878) says: "We were astounded at the extent of the poppy cultivation in Szechwan and Yunnan. . . . With a consciousness that I am underestimating, I estimate that the poppy fields constitute a third of the whole culti-vation of Yunnan." The province has to-day but two articles of importance with which to pay for extra-provincial products consumed—viz. opium and tin. The latter comes from one spot twenty miles from Mengtsz, and the value of the output in 1904 was Tls.3,200,000. Opium comes from all parts of the province and goes in all directions, that portion shipped for the use of the Opium Régie in Tonkin in 1904 amounting to 2,958 piculs, the quantity going by land into China being very much greater. Yunnan opium was known at Canton and at Chinkiang in 1863 ; in 1879 the production was variously estimated from 12,000 to 22,000 piculs ; in 1887 it was estimated at 27,000 piculs. A low estimate of the production to-day is 30,000 piculs.

Kweichow opium was known at Canton in 1863. In 1879 the estimates range from 10,000 to 15,500 piculs ; in 1887 one authority estimates it at 9,000 piculs, and another states "total production nearly as much as Yunnan." A safe estimate of the production to-day must be fully 15,000 piculs.

Kwangsi imports practically no foreign opium (22 piculs entered at Wuchow in 1905), and is a thoroughfare for Szechwan, Yunnan, and Kweichow opium for its own con-sumption, and in transit to Kwangtung. The poppy is also cultivated in the province, but to what extent is little known. The production of opium was estimated in 1879 at 3,000 piculs, and may be put at the same figure to-day.

For the Inland Provinces, not accessible at any time, except Honan, to the invasion of foreign opium, the annual production may be put at 323,000 piculs, making for the whole of China a total of 376,000 piculs.

It cannot be asserted that this figure is measurably exact ; but it may be safely asserted that the production of opium in China to-day * is, at the lowest, six-fold, and

* In 1906.

is more probably eight-fold, the quantity of the present import of foreign opium.

MORPHIA

For one vice, both for its introduction and its maintenance, foreigners must be held responsible. How or when the practice of injecting morphia was first introduced, except in hospitals, is not known ; it has been suggested that it arose from the well-meant administration of anti-opium pills containing the alkaloid, intended to satisfy the craving without the knowledge of the druggard that opium was administered in any form. However or whenever first started, hypodermic injections have taken hold, and the attention of the Chinese government has been drawn to the necessity of checking the evil. The first record of importation is in 1892 : since that date the quantities imported have been as follows :

	Ounces.			Ounces.
1892	15,761	1898	..	92,159
1893	27,993	1899	..	154,705
1894	43,414	1900	..	114,768
1895	64,043	1901	..	138,567
1896	67,320	1902	..	195,133
1897	81,716			

Up to April 1903 duty had been levied on import at the rate of 5 per cent. *ad valorem*, representing a tax of about Tl.0·08 per ounce ; then a prohibitory tax of Tls.3·00 per ounce, about 200 per cent. *ad valorem*, was imposed, and the imports declared to the Customs fell off as follows :

					Ounces.
1903	..	..	..	..	106,148
1904	..	..	..	..	128
1905	..	..	..	..	54
1911	..	..	..	..	501

An ounce of morphia will give from one to two thousand injections, according as they are for the requirements of druggards or the ordinary dose. The falling off in the later years given above is explained, not by a diminished demand, but by smuggling.

Opium Reform

During the past two centuries attempts have been made from time to time by the Chinese to check the evils resulting from the abuse of opium. In 1729 severe penalties were ordained against smoking opium or selling it by retail for that purpose. In 1796 this restriction was made more stringent and heavier penalties were imposed ; and in 1800 an edict was issued prohibiting absolutely the importation of foreign opium and the cultivation of the poppy in China. All these prohibitions were nugatory, owing to the direct connivance of the mandarins, who were interested in the revenue derived from a trade which had been declared to be illicit ; but in 1838 the Emperor, supported by a few high-minded officials, initiated an active crusade against the evil. This failed ; partly because the Emperor's agent, Lin Tse-sü, tried to ride rough-shod over all obstacles and came into collision with foreign interests having no connection with opium and held to be of greater importance than the upholding of China's sumptuary laws ; partly because its success was rendered impossible through the active connivance of every Chinese official who came into touch with the traffic. Other efforts, which did not get beyond the issuing of an edict, were made in 1851 and 1862 ; and in 1881 a tentative movement to that end was made by Li Hung-chang, who failed in showing that China would be able to check in any way the home production of the drug.

After 1900 public opinion in China was better informed. Education had impressed upon the minds of many Chinese a feeling that in matters in which China differed from the West she might be considered to occupy a position of inferiority, and this feeling made them sensitive to criticism or the suspicion of a sneering attitude. The government also reached a point on the path of reform so far advanced that it could again take up social reforms, and this time with a fair prospect of support from below, which had been denied to it on previous occasions. Foreign nations too had so far advanced in the development of public morality that it seemed probable that they were ready to abandon the *laissez-faire* policy of the nineteenth century—the attitude of " mind your business, and we'll mind ours." The impulse to reform was strong and the time propitious ; and on November 21st, 1906, an Imperial edict was issued, providing that within ten years all land then planted in poppy should by instalments be withdrawn from its cultivation ; that all smokers must take out a license, those under sixty years of age gradually reducing their consumption ; that restrictions should be placed on the sale of opium appliances and the extension of smoking divans ; that smoking be absolutely prohibited to all in the government service ; and that steps be taken for the gradual reduction of the import of foreign opium, and for its absolute cessation within ten years.

The countries chiefly concerned in the production were India and Persia. The latter has no treaty with China and is therefore not entitled to the privileges of extra-territoriality or to most-favoured-nation treatment ; and the British government promptly responded to the demand for support in this great moral movement, and, in December 1906, agreed to restrict the export from India by one-tenth in each year. The agreement was, however, to be in force only for three years, after which its continuance was to depend on the extent to which China had made effective her own reduction in the production of opium.

While the existing supply came mainly from India, or, in the case of Persian opium, through India, it was still open to other countries to produce and, under existing treaties, to their nationals to import the drug. Accordingly an international conference was held at Shanghai in February 1909, with the American Bishop Brent presiding, in order to arrive at a common agreement on the subject. The conference adopted resolutions recognising the " un- swerving sincerity of the government of China in their efforts to eradicate the production and consumption of opium throughout the Empire" ; and urging the various govern- ments represented at it to adopt regulations which would aid China in accomplishing her declared purpose.

The three years' probationary period having expired, the British government on May 8th, 1911, signed an agreement with China by which continued co-operation between the two was assured. On the one hand proof had been given that the cultivation of the poppy had been diminished in China even beyond the stipulated rate ; and, on the other, the import from India to China, which in 1907 had been taken as being 51,000 chests a year, had been reduced by law by an amount of 5,100 chests in each of the years 1908–09–10. Accordingly the new agreement provided for a continued reduction at this rate for the years from 1911 on to the end of 1917 ; and it was further agreed that Indian opium should not be conveyed into any province in which the production and import of native opium had been entirely suppressed, and that the tax on Indian opium should be increased from Tls.110 to Tls.350 per picul, " as soon as the Chinese government levy an equivalent excise tax on all native opium." Simultaneously the Chinese government im- posed a tax of Tls.230 a picul on native opium, this being taken as the equivalent tax, proportioned to the narcotic content.

A second international conference was held at The Hague in January, 1912, at which were represented Ger- many, America, China, France, Great Britain, Italy, Japan, The Netherlands, Persia, Portugal, Russia, and Siam. An international convention was agreed to and signed on January 23rd, by which it was provided :

That the Powers should enact effective laws or regulations for the control of the production and distribution of raw opium ;

That they should take measures for the gradual and effective suppression of the manufacture of, internal trade in, and use of prepared opium, and should prohibit its import and export ;

That they should pass laws to control the trade in and use of morphia, cocaine, and their respective salts ; and

That they should co-operate in preventing the smuggling of these drugs into and from China.

After the agreement of 1911 the reduction in the import of foreign opium was carried out. The quantity imported in each year, and the market quotations for Malwa opium in that year at Shanghai, were as follows :

	Import.	*Value per picul.*§	
1906 ..	54,225 piculs ..	Tls. 645	= £106
1912 ..	21,930 ,, ..	,, 2,000	= £300
1913 ..	18,138 ,, ..	,, 2,360	= £356
1914 ..	7,484 ,, ..	,, 6,000	= £820
1915 ..	4,447 ,, ..	,, 10,000	= £1,300
1916 ..	1,561 * ,, ..	,, 10,000–12,000	= £1,667–2,000
1917 ..	1,073 † ,, ..	,, 13,000–16,000	= £2,800–3,450
1918 ..	337 ‡ ,, ..	,, 20,000	= £5,280

At the end of 1918 there remained in bond at Shanghai a stock of 1,200 chests, which were bought by the Chinese government and publicly burned. From that date no further importation of foreign opium might be effected through legitimate channels.

The Empire had enforced the reduction in the cultivation of the opium poppy ; and, before the Revolution, it had been accepted as proved that the production and importation of native opium had entirely ceased in the whole of

* Including 416 piculs ⎫ imported from Japan into Dairen
†   ,,   225 ,, ⎬ and Kiaochow, both under Japanese
‡   ,,   333 ,, ⎭ control.
§ From " The China Year Book, 1919."

Manchuria and in the two provinces of Shansi and Szechwan ; and, from September 11th, 1911, the introduction of foreign opium into those areas was prohibited. It should be observed, however, that foreign opium had never entered into consumption in the two Chinese provinces ; and, if the enormous production of native opium in Szechwan had been entirely suppressed, the dislocation of trade occasioned thereby may serve to explain the rebellious state of that province just before and at the time of the Revolution. The clearing up of the provinces went on, however, and as each was declared to have been cleared, the importation into it of foreign opium was prohibited—in 1913 Chihli, Kwangsi, Hunan, Anhwei, and Shantung ; in 1914 Fukien, Hupeh, Chekiang, and Honan ; in 1915 far-distant Kansu and Sinkiang. This at the end of 1915 left only Kweichow, Yunnan, and Shensi, provinces which had never consumed foreign opium, and Kiangsi, Kiangsu, and Kwangtung, in which the foreign drug was legitimised until 1918.

Since 1906 the prohibition has been enforced. In some provinces this has been done against the dead-weight resistance of economic interest, in some the moral crusade has over-ridden all obstacles, in some the people have drifted and have yielded to an honest enforcement of the regulations. The moral crusade has behind it the full weight of the strong national feeling which created the Republic ; and, against many vested interests, against the innate apathy of the Chinese people, notwithstanding the poverty of the Treasury, that feeling has persisted in pushing the reform. The disturbed state of the country for several years has doubtless acted as a drag on progress ; but the young generation has grown up without having acquired the taste for the narcotic and with the feeling inculcated in them that the habit is a mark of a low civilisation ; many, very many, of the older generation have thrown off the habit and have recognised that in mind and in body they are better ; and the present situation is full of hope for the future, when peace and order are restored.

Shanghai Custom House, 1854-1893.

CHAPTER XII

THE INSPECTORATE OF CUSTOMS

THE foundations of the " Foreign " Customs were laid in the necessities of the Chinese government, and not in any demand by the foreign merchants that an improved revenue service should be provided for them. The forces of the Taiping rebellion, marching from Kwangsi in 1852, worked their way north through Hunan and thence down the valley of the Yangtze, destroying the fabric of Imperial government in all the provinces through which their devastating course was marked; twelve months later they entered Kiangsu from the west, and in September 1853 the Chinese city of Shanghai was captured by the Triad Society, a local body of rebels acting on the inspiration of the Taiping success. The limit of the occupation was the moat of the city, the foreign settlements, immediately adjoining, being defended by the foreign naval forces; and to this haven of refuge the Chinese officials all fled. The Custom House was thus closed by *force majeure*; and for a time there was no authority to collect the revenue from the important foreign trade of Shanghai. The merchants, then chiefly English and American, inherited the honourable traditions of the old factory days of Canton, and had in general no desire to evade the payment of their dues, which had been placed upon a just and moderate basis by the treaties of 1842 and later years; and the Consuls, newly armed with extraterritorial jurisdiction, conceived it to be as much their duty to control as to protect their nationals, control being rendered the more easy by the fact that but few Powers were involved. The first step taken to tide over the moratorium was an arrangement by which the foreign merchants declared to their Consuls the nature of the merchandise imported and exported, and deposited at the Consulates bonds for the duty leviable thereon, which, be it noted, was on a moderate 5 per cent. basis. This was found, for many reasons, to be irksome to the Consuls ; and, with the approval of the British, American, and French Ministers, then at Shanghai, an agreement was made on June 29th, 1854, between the Shanghai Taotai, Wu Kien-chang, who was a refugee in the English concession, and the three Consuls, the British, (Sir) Rutherford Alcock, the American, R. C. Murphy, and the French, B. Edan, the first article being :

> " RULE 1. The chief difficulty experienced by the superintendent of customs having consisted in the impossibility of obtaining custom-house officials with the necessary qualifications as to probity, vigilance, and knowledge of foreign languages, required for the enforcement of a close observance of treaty and custom-house regulations, the only adequate remedy appears to be in the introduction of a foreign element into the custom-house establishment, in the persons of foreigners carefully selected and appointed by the *tautai*, who shall supply the deficiency complained of, and give him efficient and trustworthy instruments wherewith to work."

Under this agreement a board of three Inspectors was nominated, British, Captain (Sir) Thomas F. Wade (afterwards British Minister to Peking), American, L. Carr, and French, Arthur Smith. Only one of the three, Captain Wade, had any knowledge of the Chinese language or any aptitude for the duties of his post, and on his shoulders fell the chief burden of organising the new office ; and, on his resignation a year later, his place was filled by Mr. Horatio Nelson Lay, who had an equal knowledge of Chinese and equally good powers of organisation. The board of three continued, but the actual control came into the hands of the working member of the board.

The attitude of the foreign merchants toward the new Inspectorate is shown by the representation addressed by the American merchants to their Minister, Mr. Peter Parker, upon his arrival in Shanghai :

" SHANGHAI, *August* 5, 1856.

" Sir,—We take advantage of your arrival at this Port to address you upon the subject of the continuation of the foreign inspectorship in the Chinese Custom-house here, in so far as it affects American trade.

" When established here in the fall of 1854, chiefly at the suggestion and by the efforts of the Honourable Mr. McLane, the affairs of the Custom-house were in much confusion in consequence of existing political troubles in this neighbourhood, and some remedy was ardently desired ; not only by those interested in securing to the Authorities their rightful dues, but by the great body of Merchants themselves, both English and American.

" The firms which we represent were unanimous in approving of an arrangement which promised to reform the abuses into which the Custom-house had fallen, and to put a stop to the irregularities prevailing.

" We understood, however, that the new institution was not intended to be permanent, unless continued political troubles and the concurrence of all the Powers interested induced the establishment of the same system at all the ports.

" The first and pressing cause for its establishment here has passed away, the authorities having fully reorganised their affairs and being able under their own system and superintendence to conduct those of the Custom-house with as much effect as elsewhere; and with this cessation of any necessity for its continuance, we cannot but perceive the great disadvantage in which we are placed by it in comparison with the other ports. Custom-house business in China under Chinese supervision is conducted with a facility which greatly aids in the despatch of business and the ready lading of ships when haste is of importance, while with the minute and in some respects vexatious regulations established by the inspectors, this advantage disappears, and this in itself is no small item in the account against us. Therefore, while expressing our desire in all cases and circumstances fully to meet our obligations under the Treaty, a desire we have proved to be sincere by our conduct on all former occasions, we feel ourselves called upon by the interests of the port and of those whom we represent, to press earnestly upon your attention the expediency and justice of abolishing the present system."

British opinion was divided, some of the merchants supporting the American representation, while others approved of the existing régime and pressed for its extension to all ports. The letter is noteworthy in three respects. It emphasises the unanimity with which the plan had been accepted, and it betrays a hankering for the flesh-pots of Egypt—for a return to the "facility" with which Custom-house business was conducted in China under Chinese supervision; it also marks the inherent weakness of the arrangement in the stricter control applied to one only of the ports open to foreign trade. The last consideration was held to be the most important when the Tariff Commission met and, in November 1858, agreed to Rules of Trade, of which the tenth (substituting French and American respectively for British) was, for all three, as follows:

" RULE 10. *Collection of Duties under one System at all Ports.* It being, by Treaty, at the option of the Chinese Government to adopt what means appear to it best suited to protect its Revenue, accruing on British trade, it is agreed that one uniform system shall be enforced at every port.

"The High Officer appointed by the Chinese Government to superintend Foreign trade will accordingly, from time to time, either himself visit, or will send a deputy to visit, the different ports. The said High Officer will be at liberty, of his own choice, and independently of the suggestion or nomination of any British authority, to select any British subject he may see fit to aid him in the administration of the Customs Revenue ; in the prevention of smuggling ; in the definition of port boundaries ; or in discharging the duties of harbour-master ; also in the distribution of Lights, Buoys, Beacons, and the like, the maintenance of which shall be provided for out of the Tonnage Dues."

This article foreshadowed the appointment of an Inspector General of Customs, and the obviously indicated person was Mr. Lay. Under his authority Custom Houses had been opened at seven ports when, in June 1861, he was granted leave of absence and returned to England. He resumed duty as Inspector General on May 9th, 1863, and was relieved from duty on November 30th of the same year. A man of marked ability, he conceived that he was destined to be the Clive and Dupleix, the Lally and Hastings, of a renovated China ; and when he failed to induce the Imperial Government to share this view, he fell. While in England he had been commissioned to procure a fleet of gunboats for the repression of rebellion and piracy ; and the demand of Mr. Lay and his commander, Captain Sherard Osborn, that this fleet should be directly and solely under their orders, was one that could not be acceded to. The fleet was accordingly paid off, the ships sold, and Mr. Lay " permitted to resign."

MR. ROBERT HART, " The I.G.," was appointed on June 30th, 1861, to exercise conjointly with Mr. G. H. Fitz-Roy the functions of Inspector General during Mr. Lay's absence from China. The appointment by the Prince Minister was communicated by a circular despatch signed by Mr. Hart and addressed to seven Commissioners of Customs, including Mr. Fitz-Roy, viz.:

At Tientsin, C. Kleczkowsky (French);
  ,, Chinkiang, J. K. Leonard (British);
  ,, Shanghai, G. H. Fitz-Roy (British);
  ,, Ningpo, Geo. Hughes (British);
  ,, Foochow, W. W. Ward (American);
  ,, Swatow, F. Wilzer (German);
  ,, Canton, Geo. B. Glover (American).

The appointment was in the following terms:

" The PRINCE OF KUNG,
      by Imperial appointment, Minister and Superintendent of Foreign Affairs,

issues the following Instructions:

" WHEREAS it is laid down in Article X. of the Supplementary Treaty and Tariff, that, in order to the protection of the Revenue, one system shall be adopted at every port, and that, if it seems good to the officer deputed to administer the Customs Revenue, he shall employ Foreigners to assist him, whom he shall procure without Foreign recommendation or intervention, &c.; and WHEREAS, the Inspector General LI-TAI-KWOH [Mr. LAY], now absent on sick leave, having introduced the Commissioners of Customs FEI-SZE-LAE [Mr. FITZ-ROY] and HEH-TEH [Mr. HART], under whose supervision Customs Revenue has been ably and satisfactorily administered at Shanghai and Canton, the said FEI-SZE-LAE and HEH-TEH were officially directed by the Imperial Commissioner,

HSIEH, to exercise conjointly a general surveillance over all things pertaining to the collection of Customs Revenue and Foreign Trade at the Treaty Ports : Now, therefore, the PRINCE instructs the said functionaries, FEI-SZE-LAE and HEH-TEH, that it will be their duty, officiating as Inspectors of affairs in accordance with the Treaties ; not allowing Foreigners to sell goods for Chinese, or the goods of Chinese to be clandestinely included in Foreign cargoes, with a view to the commission of frauds ; distinguishing carefully Imports from Exports, and Native from Foreign Produce, and preventing the one being confounded with the other.

" It will be their duty to report quarterly the amounts of Duties and Tonnage Dues collected, together with the expenses of collection ; their statements must be truthful, perspicuous, and accurate, and should be transmitted in duplicate, one copy being for the Board of Revenue, and the other for the Foreign Office.

" It will be their duty, inasmuch as it is impossible for the Chinese Government to form an estimate of the merits of the different Commissioners and other Foreigners employed in the public service, to take cognisance of the same, and make examination and inspection from time to time.

" As regards the salaries to be paid and the sums to be expended, the Chinese Superintendents of Customs and the Inspectors General will proceed conjointly to determine the same in accordance with the state of the Revenue at the ports, and with due attention to the prevention of waste and excess.

" For the transaction of all business connected with the various classes of Foreign merchant ships that arrive or depart, the Chinese Superintendents of Customs are commanded to consider it their duty to act in concert with the Inspectors General ; and the Inspectors General must make strict and faithful inquiry into all breaches of regulations committed by ships that presume to move about in contravention of law, and into all cases wherein smuggling is attempted or the revenue defrauded. Should any such irregularities and offences be allowed to occur, the Inspectors General will be held responsible for the same.

" The zealous and satisfactory manner in which business has hitherto been conducted, fully evinces that FEI-SZE-LAE and HEH-TEH are trustworthy and to be depended upon ; the PRINCE, therefore, hereby confers on them the requisite powers and authority, and commissions them to officiate as Inspectors General. The salaries they are paid by the Chinese Government are liberal, and the responsibilities of the office to which they are appointed are very serious ; it therefore behoves them to be just, energetic, and assiduous in the performance of their duties.

" The Foreigners employed in the Customs are not to engage in trade ; mismanagement or bad conduct must be followed by dismissal from the service.

" The Officiating Inspectors General must not disappoint the great confidence the PRINCE reposes in them, in appointing them to their present Office.

" Let this Instruction be carried strictly into execution !

" A Special Instruction addressed to the Officiating Inspectors General of Maritime Customs, FEI-SZE-LAE and HEH-TEH (Mr. FITZ-ROY and Mr. HART).

" HSIËN-FÊNG, 11th year, 5th month, 23rd day
" 30th June, 1861."

The office was in fact administered by Mr. Hart alone, with his headquarters, in 1861, June at Peking, July at Tientsin, September at Peking, November at Shanghai ; 1862, May at Canton, then back to Shanghai ; 1863, February at Canton, April back to Shanghai, where on May 9th he surrendered his office. Mr. Lay, resuming his office, established himself at Peking. Upon the substantive appointment of Mr. Hart, November 30th, 1863, he established his office at Shanghai, and in May 1864 transferred the Inspectorate General to Peking, where it has since remained. During his only two absences from China, in 1866 the office was administered by Mr. G. H. Fitz-Roy, and in 1878–1879 by Mr. (Sir) Robert E. Bredon conjointly, first with Mr. W. Cartwright, later with Mr. I. M. Daae.

Upon his appointment Mr. Hart found himself confronted by the difficulty that each Custom House had continued the decentralised system characteristic of Chinese administration, and that each Commissioner, acting conjointly with his Chinese colleague the Superintendent, looked to the provincial authorities and considered local needs, and was disinclined to conform without question to the leading given by the centralising office, the Inspectorate General. The ability and tact which he has shown so uniformly, and in so many instances since, were never more marked than in Mr. Hart's first decade of office, the Sixties, when he had to reconcile the Imperial Government to a form of administration which, though working in its interest, was distinctly alien ; to lead, with small powers of compulsion, subordinates of marked personality and of different nationalities to submit their judgment to his, and accept his instructions for their guidance ; and to introduce into Customs procedure the uniformity and system which are the necessary concomitants of effective administration. During that decade elementary questions were vital, and an unwise settlement could easily have undermined the foundations of the structure he was erecting. The Chinese Customs collect duty, not only on imports from foreign countries, but also on exports whether abroad or to another Chinese port, and on re-importation at a Chinese port collect an import duty ; they also collect tonnage dues on shipping, transit dues exempting from further taxation foreign imports conveyed inland and native produce from inland marts intended for export to foreign countries, and, since 1887, likin on foreign opium ; with all this complexity there had to be maintained simultaneously foreign and native control, foreign and native record, and foreign and native report. To introduce simplification into this complexity was the task of the first ten years, and among the questions to be decided were : the regulation of the coastwise traffic ; the provision that the original duty payment exempted imports from further tax, instead of the provincial system of refund and repayment on each reshipment ; the regulation of the inland transit trade ; the compilation and publication of statistics ; pilotage ; emigration ; the ton equivalents of various lasts and metric and other tons ; and, above all, the proper dovetailing of the foreign and Chinese sides of the administration ; and all these were settled on lines which have endured. Mention must not be omitted of the lieutenants who seconded the work of the Inspector General during this formative period. In addition to the seven mentioned before, who were Commissioners in charge of ports in 1861, it is right to record the work done in instituting this new experiment by, among others, E. C. Bowra, Chas. Hannen, Thos. Dick, A. Macpherson, and W. Cartwright, British ; E. C. Taintor, F. E. Woodruff, and E. B. Drew, American ; Baron de Méritens and A. Huber, French ; and F. Kleinwächter and G. Detring, German.

In all matters of procedure and regulation—in administration *ad rem*—the Inspector General has always referred to the Imperial Government, giving of course his views, and the instructions he has issued for the guidance of the Commissioners have always been based upon the instructions given to him by the government, sometimes, in important matters, after reference to and report by the High Commissioners of Trade, the Viceroys at Tientsin and Nanking acting *ex officio ad hoc* ; and the bilateral character of the Service is exemplified by the practice of issuing identical and simultaneous instructions through the Inspector General to the Commissioners and through the High Commissioners to the Superintendents. Originally the Inspector General's phraseology was " I have received the commands of H.I.H. Prince Kung to direct " ; it then became " I enclose for your information and guidance copy of a despatch from the Tsungli Yâmen directing," and this form (with the substitution from 1901 of the Wai-wu Pu, and from May 1906 of the Shui-wu Chu, for the Tsungli Yâmen) continued to be adopted for over forty years. Given an Inspector General loyal to the government he served, the most hostile scrutiny could detect no development of an alien *imperium in imperio*, and during a service of close on half a century not a breath of suspicion has even been thrown on the I.G.'s entire loyalty to those whose salt he ate.

In the administration *ad personam* the Imperial Government has never interfered. The aim in establishing the Inspectorate was, momentarily to secure from foreign traders a revenue which the disturbed state of the country might otherwise render precarious, and permanently to secure to the central government the advantages of Western system and organisation in one branch of its revenue ; and at the outset it was recognised that it was " impossible for the Chinese government to form an estimate of the merits of the different . . . foreigners employed in the public service." The Outer Barbarians could only be controlled by one of themselves, and the Chinese government having for that function found a man they could trust, trusted him. The appointment of a Commissioner in charge of a port, or his transfer to another post, has always been reported to the higher authorities ; but apart from this the Inspector General has been left to the exercise of his discretion in the appointment, promotion, and discharge of all placed under his orders, keeping in his own hands movements affecting foreigners, and leaving to the Commissioner at each port much of the control over the Chinese staff. During the period covered by the I.G.'s tenure of office there has been probably nowhere in the world any servant of the state so unfettered in the exercise of so large a patronage ; and the general testimony is that his rule has been a benevolent despotism tempered, at times, by Legation representations. His rule has in general been marked by great fairness: probably of no other man in the world, with so much personal power and such extended patronage at his disposal, can it be said, as it can of him, that his appointments of men connected with himself by ties of friendship or of relationship have been so few. In general, under the administration of Sir Robert Hart (he was knighted in 1882) there was developed a strong, loyal, honest, well-organised, and cosmopolitan service.

The Customs Service is now (1906) organised in four departments, the " Inspector General of Customs and Posts " being the directing head of all.

I. Revenue Department.
    1. Indoor Staff, the executive, controlling and clerical branch.
    2. Outdoor Staff, the inspecting and preventive branch.
    3. Coast Staff, the preventive cruiser branch.
II. Marine Department.
    1. Engineers' Staff, for construction of Lights, etc.
    2. Harbours Staff, for Coast work in general and Harbour work at Shanghai.
    3. Lights Staff, for operation of Lights.
III. Educational Department.
    1. Tung Wen Kwan at Peking, which after nearly forty years' good work was amalgamated with the Imperial University of 1902.
    2. Tung Wen Kwan at Canton.
IV. Postal Department (instituted in 1896 as a branch separate from the Revenue Department).

The growth of the Service and its cosmopolitan character may be gauged by the following comparative statements of the numbers in 1875 and in 1906 :

Staff.	1875.		1906.	
	Foreign.	Chinese.	Foreign.	Chinese.
I. Revenue Department :				
1. Foreign Indoor	126	—	343	—
2. ,, Outdoor	203	—	754	—
3. Coast Staff	19	145	54	672
4. Chinese Clerical	—	282	—	950
5. ,, Non-clerical	—	802	—	2,858
II. Marine Department :				
1. Engineers' Staff	9	—	7	} 310
2. Harbours Staff	14	—	32	
3. Lights Staff	43	—	59	267
4. Chinese employees	—	188	—	—
III. Educational Department :				
Staff	10	—	1	—
IV. Postal Department :				
Control and Clerical Staff	—	—	95	2,388
Non-clerical Staff	—	—	—	3,190
	424	1,417	1,345	10,635
Total	1,841		11,980	

Nationality.	1875.	1906.
American	46	88
Austrian	5	18
Belgian	4	10
British	265	738
Danish	9	42
Dutch	2	15
French	28	64
German	34	170
Greek	1	—
Hungarian	2	1
Italian	3	30
Japanese	—	21
Luxemburger	—	1
Norwegian	2	68
Portuguese	2	27
Russian	3	20
Siamese	—	3
Spanish	5	14
Swedish	12	49
Swiss	1	3

An attempt will now be made to give some idea of the nature of the work done by the Chinese Customs Service, differing, as it does, so much from the work done by corresponding organisations in other parts of the world.

On the entry of a ship, her papers are deposited with the Consul of her nationality, to be surrendered only upon issue of a provisional Customs clearance. The passing of the import cargo proceeds much as elsewhere, but note is to be taken of the fact that from point to point the foreign ship and the foreign merchant are covered by the privilege of extraterritoriality. Against an offending ship the Customs have only three remedies, all strictly limited by treaty. For clandestine trading she may be prohibited from further trading along the coast, a penalty which has never yet been enforced; and for having on board un-manifested goods—for a " false manifest "—she may be fined after joint investigation and decision by the Customs and the Consul concerned, the limit of fine being Tls.500. The third remedy is in the withdrawal of an extra-treaty concession made by the Customs; the treaties were made to fit the old sailing-ship conditions, and it is only in the modern steamer procedure that any means can be found for enforcing proper preventive measures, by the withdrawal of the privilege of clearing before the payment of all import duties on the ship's cargo, whereby the Customs are often forced to use a steam hammer to crack a nut. Against the merchant the Customs have even less power, and, in effect, any penalties for false declaration are enforced against the incriminated goods, and never against the offending merchant: to confiscate an importer's goods and to fine him in addition for a breach of Customs regulations is unheard of in China. This arises partly from the very considerable degree of protection accorded to foreign merchants by treaty, and partly from the fact that there is no competent tribunal before which a revenue case can be carried; the Chinese territorial courts are ruled out, the Consul is necessarily the advocate of his national, and the Commissioner of Customs is a party to the case.

Goods, having paid their import duty, are in most countries free to go anywhere ; in China movement is taxed at every point, and documentary protection must be accorded to imports at every point. This protection is given to foreign imports at any treaty port without further payment, provided that the original payment within three years past can be proved ; and so valuable is this protection that Chinese produce may be shipped to a foreign port, *e.g.* Hongkong and back to China, paying once duty on export and once duty on import, and a half duty on transport inland, and show a balance of profit over transport from the place of production direct to another place, perhaps only a couple of hundred miles away. At Shanghai the great volume of the re-export trade has caused the institution of a system of " Importers' Passes," by which the importer may convey his rights to a purchaser. When re-exported to another treaty port, either by the original importer or by the purchaser under a pass, the goods are covered by an " exemption certificate," without which they are liable to import duty at the second port ; and the exemption applies only to goods in their original packing. If again re-exported, goods are again covered by exemption certificate. If imports are intended for an " inland " place, *i.e.* any place not being a treaty port, the purchaser has the option of paying likin *en route*, or of paying half the import duty additional and obtaining a " transit pass inwards," and being then exempt from likin.

Chinese produce may be brought to a treaty port on payment of likin, or, if intended for shipment abroad, and only in that case, may be covered by a " transit pass outwards " on payment of a half duty. On shipment at any port export duty is paid, whether for a foreign or another Chinese port : in the latter case the goods are covered by a " duty proof." On arrival at a Chinese port a half duty is paid as " coast-trade duty." Upon re-export to any destination from this second port the coast-trade duty is refunded ; if re-exported to a third Chinese port, the goods are covered by a " duty-paid certificate," and on arrival the coast-trade duty is again paid. Going inland these goods have no transit pass privilege, and the greatest confusion results from the necessity of distinguishing between, *e.g.*, Swatow sugar shipped to Shanghai direct, thence re-exported to Hankow and thence going inland, and Swatow sugar going inland from Hankow after having reached there via Hongkong and Shanghai.

Upon payment of tonnage dues a "tonnage dues certificate " is issued to the ship, exempting from further payment for a period of four months, which is extended by the time spent in effecting repairs in a Chinese port.

Foreign opium, having paid duty and likin, is covered by labels affixed to each ball or small package, and exempted from all further payment so long as the labels are intact. Native opium is since 1906 treated in the same way whenever it comes under the cognisance of the Customs.

Since November 11th, 1901, the Native or Regular Customs have been under the supervision of the Commissioner of Maritime Customs at each port. To exercise this supervision over a Chinese office run by Chinese methods, operating on a purely Chinese trade, with the original Chinese staff, and with little or no aid from foreign agents, and without published regulations or a unified tariff, is to impose on the Commissioner a task of quite a different character from his ordinary work, varied and complicated though that be, and calls for the exercise of the diplomatic function as much as the executive. He must not rub too much the wrong way those who have previously exercised control ; he must not render too much discontented the staff whose irregular practices he is there to check : while facilitating work to the traders by the introduction of regularity, he will find that too much unaccustomed rigidity may lead to discontent and even to riot ; he must satisfy the representatives of the foreign

Shanghai Custom House, 1894.

Powers in whose interest, to secure funds for due payment of the indemnities, he is placed in control ; his measures must be such as not to alienate the Chinese government whose servant he is, while he is often called upon to enforce against them the provisions of their own treaties ; and all this he must do from a position which, in some respects, is rather advisory than executive.

In the control of the Foreign, as of the Native Customs, the Commissioner is freed from one responsibility, in that he does not handle the revenues. In a country in which the currency is a tangled mass of complexity, and banking is an exact science of great inexactitude, this would be an impossible function for the foreigner to assume ; and the Commissoner's function is only to obtain a receipt certifying to the payment to the properly constituted authority of the amounts due, and to report the revenue so collected. This authority is the Customs Bank, appointed by the Chinese government at each port, and revenues received by the bank pass directly under the control of the Chinese side of the Customs, the Superintendent and not the Commissioner. Malpractice by the bank might be made the subject of representation, but for effective action would be rather a diplomatic than an executive matter, the affair of the Consul concerned than of the Commissioner.

The Coast Service for preventive duty is composed of 6 revenue steamers, officered by a special Coast Staff, 4 revenue cruising launches, 21 revenue launches, and 9 sailing-craft, officered by men detached from the Revenue Staff. For movement from one district to another, and for general control, they are under the orders of the Inspector General ; for personnel and matériel they are under the Coast Inspector ; and for control, discipline, supplies, and work they are directly subject to the Commissioner in whose district they are. Besides their ordinary preventive duty, the revenue steamers are used in connection with new Lights work and for supplying Lights, and for coast work (surveying, etc.) as well.

26

The Marine Department is divided into the Engineers', Harbours, and Lights branches.

The Engineer-in-Chief is charged with the construction of new and maintenance of existing Lights, and the provision of illuminating and other special supplies. He reports direct to the Inspector General on new proposals and on Lights work affecting the whole coast, and through the Commissioner, who has joint authority, on work affecting only one district. Under the superintendence at first of Mr. David Marr Henderson and recently of Mr. J. Reginald Harding, there have been installed by this office and are now working 106 Lights (of which 14 are of the first order, and 39 are occulting, flashing, or revolving), 4 Light-vessels, and 22 Light-boats.

At the head of the Harbours Staff is the Coast Inspector, who supervises coast work, surveying, sea and river conservancy; selects the sites for new Lights; and is in technical control of all Harbours work and Pilotage for China generally. He reports direct to the Inspector General on matters affecting the whole coast, and through the Commissioner, who has joint authority, on work affecting one part or lying within one district. Subject to the direct control of the Commissioner, he has general control over the revenue steamers and their personnel. He is also charged with the general supervision—the direct control being with the Commissioner—over buoys (111 established) and beacons (105 established). Record must be made of the good work done by Captain A. M. Bisbee while he occupied this post. A Harbour Master, paid from Marine funds, exists only at Shanghai; elsewhere the duties of the post are performed by the Tide Surveyor, a Revenue officer who is, under the Commissioner, in direct control of the Outdoor Staff. The Harbour Master is the official charged with the supervision of pilotage, conservancy, movement of shipping in port, and similar matters; port regulations on these subjects are issued with the authority of his signature, but, as he is the subordinate of the Commissioner, while the hand is the hand of the Harbour Master the voice is the voice of the Commissioner. In all these matters the Commissioner is the buffer between many conflicting interests, over which he can often exercise only an influence and not an authority ; he may, for example, be appealed to for a decision on a foreshore case, where the Chinese territorial authorities and a Consul acting for his national may hold opposite and irreconcilable views, where the Harbour Master is in theory expected to apply the principles of Chinese law, but where neither he nor the Commissioner can enforce his authority on the rival parties. Such a case becomes then a question of diplomacy, bringing in the heavy artillery of Foreign Office, Legation, and Inspector General, unless the Commissioner can devise a *modus vivendi* acceptable to all concerned.

The Lights Staff consists of 58 foreign and 244 Chinese lightkeepers, the latter being subordinated at the larger Lights stations or in charge of the smaller stations. The maintenance of each light and the control of its staff are directly under the Commissioner of the district ; except that the Amoy Commissioner controls most of the lights in the adjoining districts—Foochow and Swatow, while the Shanghai lights and most of those in the Ningpo district are directly under the Coast Inspector.

The Educational Department (merged in the Peking University by Imperial Decree of January 11th, 1902) had only an indirect connection with the Customs. It was supplied with funds through the Customs, and the Inspector General nominated to vacant chairs in the Peking College, and frequently " lent " men from the Customs for temporary instructing duty ; but the College was built up and directed for many years by the venerable Dr. W. A. P. Martin, educator and sinologue. The College at Canton, which still survives, is smaller, and is under the direct control of the Commissioner, as *quasi* colleague of the Tartar General, appointments to its staff being made by the Inspector General.

The Postal Department will be more fully described in the chapter on the Post Office, and it will suffice here to show its connection with the Customs. In the early days foreign mails were sent along the coast by the primitive method of handing them to the steamer agents. The Customs organised a Postal Department for the transmission of its own mail matter, and in 1876 the postal facilities of the offices at Shanghai, Tientsin, and Peking, subsequently extended to Newchwang and Chefoo, were thrown open to the public, in order to provide uninterrupted communication with Peking and the north during the winter, when the northern ports were closed by ice. Communication was maintained by a trunk line of couriers from Chinkiang to Tientsin, a distance of 800 miles, and a postal service organised by Mr. G. Detring, Commissioner at Tientsin, was in full working order by 1878. This " Customs Post " was found to be a convenience to the public, and in 1882 the facilities were extended to all ports north of Fukien. In 1896 a decree was issued creating an Imperial Post, the organisation and management of which were entrusted to Sir Robert Hart. The new establishment was thus grafted on the Customs, which was called upon to provide men and funds for its development, and a new burden was laid on the shoulders of Inspector General and Commissioners. In the organisation of the Post, the Customs organisation was the foundation on which the structure was erected; the Customs district became the Postal district, the Commissioner of Customs became the District Postmaster, the Customs Accountant became the Postal District Accountant, and the net balance of Postal receipts and expenditure became a receipt or payment entry in the Customs " Unclassed " account—and invariably a payment entry. The life-blood of Customs energy was drained away, but without this aid a Chinese service could not have been instituted ; without it an exotic organisation would have been formed, having its roots in Western practice but not satisfying the needs of China, and with it has grown up a Service which has grafted Western methods on Chinese requirements. An enormous mass of organising work was thrown on the broad shoulders of the Inspector General of Customs and Posts, and on his lieutenant, the Postal Secretary ; and a no less enormous amount of organising on the Commissioners. It speaks volumes for the spirit which animates the Service that this unaccustomed work has been cheerfully undertaken and carried through. The Commissioner, as District Postmaster, is a Postmaster General for his district, which in most cases is of the size and with the population in many a European kingdom. He audits the accounts of each post office, and, with his accountant, prepares his district accounts ; he exercises a direct supervision over the working of the head office at his port, which serves as model for the other offices in his district, and is responsible that existing instructions and new procedure are properly understood and duly carried out ; he studies the needs of his district, and himself decides on opening new " agencies," corresponding to the fourth-class post offices of the United States and village grocery offices of England ; he refers to headquarters his proposals for opening " branch offices " or for raising the status of an agency ; and he is the medium of communication with the territorial officials and with foreign Post Offices established in his district. He is the responsible head of the district, and its working and personnel are subject to his authority. All this adds no small amount to the already extended work and responsibility of that Jack-of-all-trades, the Commissioner of Customs.

Nor is this all. The many departments of work which devolve on the Customs in China trench so often on matters outside even the extended sphere of the Customs Service, that it is naturally and inevitably brought into touch with questions even more remote ; where the foreign merchant has so privileged a position, and the relations between foreign and Chinese are so complicated and have so many ramifications, it would be difficult to define the exact limits of a Customs establishment working on and in a situation characterised by the principles of extraterritoriality. To exemplify this by action taken by the Inspector General would be to give a résumé of the foreign relations of China for forty years, and it will be enough to refer to matters, purely local, in which the Commissioner of a port may be called upon to intervene. The first recorded intervention was national rather than local, and constituted the several Commissioners the intermediaries for paying to the British and French governments the quarterly instalments of the indemnities due under the treaties of 1858 and 1860 ; the " 1st quarter " for this purpose began on October 1st, 1860, and the successive quarterly reports and returns to the Chinese government are still numbered from that date, the 184th quarter ending on September 30th, 1906. Following this precedent the Customs have often, both generally through the Inspector General and locally through the Commissioner, been made the financial and disbursing agent for the payment of indemnities or of principal and interest of loans. One such instance will suffice. In 1895 the Canton authorities issued an internal loan of Tls.5,000,000, the prospectus and bonds stipulating that the bonds, to bearer, should be countersigned by the Commissioner of Customs at Canton ; the proceeds of the loan be received by him ; the monthly instalments paid into banks to his order ; the coupons and drawn bonds paid by his cheque ; the register to be kept and bonds cancelled by him ; and in case of default the bonds should be received by him at face value in satisfaction of Customs duties. The Chinese government recognised that the Chinese public would not trust its agents of the official hierarchy, but would trust the Commissioner, and the loan was a success. In times of foreign complication the reading and experience of the Commissioner have been freely drawn upon to supplement the deficiencies of provincial officials, whose reading and experience offered them nothing to meet the exigencies of a novel situation ; and many a well-intended breach of international conventions has been averted, many an Asiatic incitement in dealing with a Western enemy has been withdrawn or modified, many a blunder based on Asiatic ignorance of modern conditions has been avoided, under representations made by the Commissioner and pressed upon the notice of the responsible officials. The application of the principle of extraterritoriality, too, brings within the purview of the Commissioner many cases which are not strictly Customs matters; and yet, apart from missionary cases, it may be said that there are few questions arising under this principle which do not touch in some way on commerce or revenue. In such cases it rarely happens that some one of the parties interested, the Chinese territorial authority, the Consul, or the foreign merchant, does not invoke the aid or the influence of the Commissioner, and it is one of his hardest tasks to limit the extent of his own interference. Even in cases where the apparent Customs connection is of the slightest, however, it has often been found of the greatest advantage to all concerned to have the representative of the foreign side of a Chinese administration available to act as intermediary; though a Chinese official, he is a foreigner, and though a foreigner, he is a part of the Chinese administration; he supplies to the Chinese that connection with foreign ways and principles in which they have in the past been lacking, and he supplies to the foreign Consul and merchant the intimate knowledge of Chinese legal and official machinery which they do not always possess; and, in the past at least, his position may be likened to that of the man in the middle of the see-saw, able to raise or to depress, as he may judge the right to lie on one side or the other. The general testimony is that this position of influence has not been used arbitrarily, either in favour of the Chinese government, whose servant he is, or in favour of the foreigners, to whom he is allied by birth and education.

In all these local matters the closest touch has always been maintained with the Inspector General. Commissioners have never failed to make the fullest reports to him, and from him have come the guidance and encouragement which have enabled them to grapple with questions beyond their ordinary capacity. He has seldom interfered unduly with " the man on the spot " ; but an illuminating sentence, coming from the experience acquired at the centre of affairs, has often supplied the missing thought unattainable by a more circumscribed knowledge.

As one of themselves, I say of my colleagues that among them are many of sturdy independence of thought ; that, one and all, they are animated in their conduct by the strictest rectitude ; and that, with all their independence and with their varying national characteristics, no one in all these years has ever impugned their entire loyalty to their chief and the government they serve, or the absolute impartiality of their administration.

The appointment of Robert Hart in 1861 as Officiating Inspector General was communicated to the Commissioners in charge of seven ports then open ; his substantive appointment in 1863 was communicated to thirteen ports ; and his last circular instructions were issued to Commissioners of Customs at more than forty ports, to six Likin Collectorates, and to four Postal Commissioners. The revenue collected for the Imperial Government by the Service organised by him increased from Tls.8,296,275 in 1865 to Tls.37,080,457 in 1906. The foreign trade under its cognisance increased from Tls.121,898,792 in 1865 to Tls.674,988,988 in 1905 ; to these figures must be added Tls.28,523,449 in 1865 and Tls.128,647,510 in 1905, as the value of the original exports of Chinese produce carried coastwise. This gives Tls.803,636,498 as the value of the trade handled by the Customs during 1905, but, with the necessity of continuing documentary protection at every stage, the work done by the Customs is by no means measured by this value. During 1905 permits and protecting documents on import, export, re-export, re-import or transit inland, were issued for goods valued at Tls.1,737,546,961.

Sir Robert Hart, the organiser of the Service which has done this work, was born on February 20, 1835. After graduating (A.B. and Senior Scholar) at Queen's University, Ireland, in 1853, he was appointed Supernumerary Interpreter to the British Superintendency of Trade at Hongkong in May 1854 ; and in May 1859 was granted special permission to resign in order to join the newly instituted Chinese Customs Service. He was appointed Officiating Inspector General in 1861 and Inspector General in 1863. In May 1885 he was appointed Her Britannic Majesty's Envoy Extraordinary and Minister Plenipotentiary to the Emperor of China and also to the King of Korea, but did not take up the appointment, and continued as Inspector General. His services to China and to the world have been recognised in a tangible way by the bestowal of many honours. From China he received in 1864 the brevet title of Provincial Judge, with civil rank of the third class ; in 1869 the brevet title of Provincial Treasurer, with civil rank of the second class ; in 1881 the red button of the first class ; in 1885 the order of the Double Dragon, second division, first class, and the distinction of the Peacock's Feather ; in 1889 Ancestral Rank of the first class of the first order, dated back for three generations, with Letters Patent ; in 1901 the brevet title of Junior Guardian of the Heir Apparent ; and in 1902 he was received in Audience by the Empress Dowager and Emperor. In 1908, on his departure on furlough, he was given the brevet rank of Shang-shu, President of a Board (*v.* p. 44). His native land has recognised the distinction he has conferred upon it by making him in 1879 a Companion of the Most Distinguished Order of St. Michael and St. George, in 1882 a Knight Commander, and in 1889 a Knight Grand Cross of the same order ; and in 1893 a Baronet of the United Kingdom. Other countries also have shown their appreciation of the value of his work, and he has received decorations, many of them Grand Croix or Grand Officier, from Belgium, Sweden, Austria, France, Italy, Portugal, Norway, Holland,

Prussia, and the Pope. From the United States has come the degree of LL.D., bestowed upon him by the University of Michigan. For native ability and power of organisation he may be compared, in one aspect or another, with John Lawrence and Alexander Hamilton. His monument is in the Service he created and his life-record is in the history of the foreign relations of China during a period of forty years of transition. Another sits in his chair,* another signs as Inspector General, but in the history of China there will be but one " I.G."

* Sir Robert Hart died on September 20th, 1911, and Sir Francis A. Aglen was appointed to succeed him as Inspector-General of Customs. Among the changes introduced by him, the most significant is the assumption of control over the actual collection of the revenue. This is now received by the Commissioners at the ports and held by them subject to the order of the Inspector-General.

CHAPTER XIII

THE POST OFFICE

An organised service for the conveyance of government despatches has existed in China for many centuries, the I-chan, or Government Service of Couriers, being mentioned in the records of the Chow dynasty, the beginnings of which date back 3,000 years. During the succeeding centuries the necessity was always felt of maintaining regular communication between the Emperor and his government at the capital, and his officials and garrisons in the provinces ; and what may be called postal communication was as fully organised in China as it was under Persian Kings or Roman Emperors. The I-chan is wholly maintained by the State through provincial contributions from ordinary local taxes; the cost being estimated in a joint memorial to the Throne in 1902 by the two Yangtze Viceroys, at some Tls.3,000,000 annually. The service is under the supervision of the Board of War at Peking. The direct control is exercised by the Cart and Chariot Department of the Board, and under it, the Horse Office controls the couriers and their horses, and the Despatch Office receives and forwards the official mails at the capital itself. At each provincial capital is a Director of Posts, a military officer appointed by the Board of War, and placed under the orders of the Provincial Judge, his duty being to see that despatches are transmitted without impediment. The actual forwarding is done by each District Magistrate from border to border of his district, and the cost is a charge on his budget. With the constitutional conservatism of Chinese officialdom in

411

matters of expenditure—in never letting go a good thing when they have it—the full machinery of the I-chan is still maintained, though, when available, steamers and railways are now utilised for the more rapid transmission of despatches.

The Wenpao Chü, or Document Office, is an offshoot of the I-chan, but quite independent of it. On the appointment of Ministers to foreign countries in 1875, it became necessary to arrange for the transmission of their despatches between Peking and Shanghai, where they could be deposited in and taken from the foreign Post Offices ; and offices were opened for this purpose at Tientsin and Shanghai. In subsequent years offices were opened at Yangtze ports from Hankow down, and at coast ports as far south as Canton ; and much of the work of the I-chan along the coast and on the Yangtze is done by these offices. Notwithstanding the development of the Imperial Post, the Wenpao Chü continues to function.

The only really Government Post open to the public, organised by Chinese officials, was established in Formosa. When, after the attack by the French naval forces in 1884–1885, the attention of the Imperial Government was drawn to the necessity of organising the island as a province, the Imperial High Commissioner and Governor, Liu Ming-chuan, introduced several startling innovations, among them a railway and a Post Office. For the latter it was at first proposed to adopt adhesive stamps and they were ordered from England in two denominations, red 3-cent for short distances, and green 5-cent for longer distances. The simplicity of an almost uniform tariff worked, as always in China, against its adoption ; and these stamps had a history unique in philately, being used for railway tickets. This Post Office was ultimately organised on the following lines :

1. Mails were carried by couriers on foot.
2. The postal routes were divided into stages, averaging a day's journey in length, or, say, 70 to 100 li.
3. Letters and packages were carried at the rate of 20 cash per tael per stage, with additional charges for delivery at places not on the main routes,

4. Postage stamps were of two kinds—official and ordinary. The former were supplied to public offices, free of charge, to be used on official mail matter ; and the latter were sold to the public. As regards stamps, the system was cumbrous. Stamps were not sold to the public indiscriminately. Any one who had a letter to forward, say from Tamsui to Tekcham, took it to the Tamsui district Post Office, where he prepaid 60 cash for the three stages, and got a receipt for his letter, the Post Office affixing the stamp. The letter was then sent on to Taipei, and thence to Tiongleck and Tekcham, receiving at each stage an additional stamp, probably as evidence of the responsibility of the affixing office.

This organisation fell on the cession of Formosa to Japan in 1895.

These are the postal organisations instituted by the government of China, and, except in Formosa, for the transmission of official despatches only. The people of China are essentially a literary and commercial people, and in both capacities are a letter-writing people ; and for centuries past they have attended to the transmission of their business and family correspondence with no more support or interference from the government than is given to any other commercial undertaking. This they did by "Letter Hongs," usually established by a remittance bank or a merchant's firm having its own business connections with certain other places, and having its own correspondence to forward, undertaking for a consideration to forward the letters of other people, and gradually extending their postal operations to other places in the same direction to which their ordinary business does not extend. Under this system very strong letter hongs have been developed, utilising every means of conveyance, and meeting in every way the wishes of the public ; maintaining fast special services where they are wanted, content with slow channels where economy is the first object, keeping open until after midnight when that hour is more suitable, and, most attractive in China, making the addressee pay a portion of the postage, usually half. The transmission of silver, bank drafts, and parcels is a most lucrative part of their business. They have a tariff, more or less fixed according to distance, ranging from 20 cash ($\frac{1}{2}d$.) to 200 cash ($5d$.) for each letter, but are not particular to an ounce or two in the weight ; and these rates may be reduced to an important customer or commuted for an annual subsidy, while smaller people will ordinarily pay more, and addressees are regularly mulcted in extra payments. On the whole the system has suited admirably the public which it serves, but has the fatal effect, from a national point of view, that it does not encourage postal development on lines not immediately profitable, the funds for this purpose, derived from the more profitable routes, being diverted to private pockets.

Any national and general postal organisation has thus two strong vested interests to encounter : the first, the official interest in the expenditure of Tls.3,000,000 annually in rendering a service which could be performed by other hands at less than half the cost ; the second, the commercial interest in a profitable business enterprise, under a government which never coerces the people but acts mainly by moral suasion and on the principle of "live and let live."

The Imperial Post was established by Imperial Decree on March 20th, 1896, as the result of a long experiment begun as far back as 1861 by the Inspector General of the Chinese Maritime Customs Service, Sir Robert Hart ; and Mr. T. Piry traces the development in his report on the Working of the Post Office for the year 1904 :

> " Early in the ' sixties,' during the first few winters after Foreign Representatives took up their residence at Peking, the Legation and Customs mails were exchanged between Shanghai and Peking, under the

auspices of the Tsung-li Yâmen, by means of the Government couriers employed for the transmission of official despatches. It was then found convenient to arrange that the Customs should undertake the responsibility of making up and distributing these mails, a practice which, for the overland service during the winter months, involved the creation of Postal Departments at the Inspectorate and in the Custom Houses at Shanghai and Chinkiang, and, similarly, for the transmission of mails by coast steamers during the open season, the opening of quasi-Postal Departments in the Tientsin and other coast port Custom Houses. At that early date it could be seen that out of this simple beginning might be elaborated a system answering other and larger requirements, on the principle of a National Post Office. This idea gradually shaped into form and had already so much ingratiated itself in the official mind that in 1876, when the Chefoo Convention was being negotiated, the Tsung-li Yâmen authorised the Inspector General to inform the British Minister, Sir Thomas Wade, that it was prepared to sanction the establishment of a National Postal System and willing to make it a Treaty stipulation that postal establishments should be opened at once. Unfortunately, through, so to speak, a conspiracy of silence, the insertion of the postal clause was omitted in the official text of the Treaty. and thus the project was postponed *sine die*. Meanwhile, however, the experiment was persevered with and warmly encouraged by the Imperial Commissioner Li Hung-chang, who promised to ' father ' it officially as soon as it proved a success. Hence the more formal opening of Postal Departments at various Custom Houses, the 1878 experiment of trying a Native Post Office alongside the Customs Post, and the establishment of Customs couriers from Taku to Tientsin, from Tientsin to Peking, and the Customs winter mail service overland from Tientsin to New-chwang, from Tientsin to Chefoo, and from Tientsin to Chinkiang, as also the introduction of Customs postage stamps in 1878.

" The growing importance of the Service thus quietly built up and its convenience for regular communications with Peking and between Treaty ports were not only appreciated by the foreign public, but were also recognised by the foreign Administrations having postal agencies in China. In 1878 China was formally invited to join the Postal Union. In the same year, while on a visit to Paris, the Inspector General was sounded by the French Minister for Foreign Affairs as to a possible way of withdrawing the French Post Office in Shanghai; and while, more than once, the British Postmaster General at Hongkong expressed his readiness to close the Hongkong Post Office agencies along the coast, arrangements were actually discussed for the absorption by the Customs Department of the Municipal Post Office at Shanghai. But no definite response to these overtures could be given, or final steps taken, before the Chinese Government had declared its intention to undertake national responsibilities; and the Customs Department continued to satisfy only certain wants and prepare the system for further development till, twenty years after the Chefoo Convention, the Decree of the 20th March, 1896, appeared. This Decree created an Imperial Post for all China, to be modelled on Western lines, the organisation and management of which were confided to Sir Robert Hart, who from that date has acted in the double capacity of Inspector General of Customs and Posts.

" This long hesitation on the part of the Chinese Government to formally recognise and foster an institution known to have worked with such profitable results in foreign countries, both from public and revenue standpoints, may be to some people a matter of surprise. But it must not be forgotten that from immemorial times the Chinese nation has possessed two postal institutions : one, the I-chan (or Imperial Government Courier Service), deeply rooted in official routine ; the other, the Native posting agencies, long used and respected by the people. Both give employment to legions of couriers, and are still necessary to the requirements of an immense nation ; they can neither be suppressed, transformed, nor replaced at a stroke. The Imperial decision therefore only gave final sanction to a new and vast undertaking, but abolished nothing ; it is through competition and long and persevering efforts that the two older systems must be gradually superseded and the implantation of the National Post Office patiently pursued."

The first notification of the extension to the public of the Customs postal facilities appeared in the Shanghai newspapers in the following terms :

CUSTOMS NOTIFICATION

WINTER SERVICE

Postage stamps and copies of Postal Tariff may be obtained on application at the Customs Postal Department.

(Signed) J. H. HART.

SHANGHAI, 16th December, 1878.

This winter service was organised by the Tientsin Customs Commissioner, Mr. G. Detring, in 1876, so as to maintain, with an overland courier service via Chinkiang, the postal communications with the outer world necessarily interrupted by the port of Tientsin being ice-blocked.

Mr. Detring sent to Shanghai one of his Writers, a Mr. Wu Kuan, who, under the control of the Shanghai

27

Commissioner, supervised the overland courier service to the north. This department, which was called the Shu Hsin Kuan, or Post Office, was opened on July 24th, 1878, and started with a staff of seventeen men

Under instructions issued in December 1882, the system was extended to all treaty ports north of Fukien, but still working on " Postal Department " principles, and this continued until the issue of the Imperial Decree in 1896. Up to this time Mr. Detring had, under the Inspector General, been mainly responsible for the organisation and development of postal work, under the designation of Postal Commissioner. In 1896 Mr. H. Kopsch was appointed the first Postal Secretary; he was succeeded in 1897 by Mr. J. A. van Aalst; and he in 1901 by Mr. T. Piry, to whom the present organisation of the Post Office is mainly due.

Under its present organisation the headquarters of the Imperial Post Office are at Peking, where all postal affairs are dealt with by the Postal Secretary under the Inspector General of Customs and Posts. There is also at Shanghai a Deputy Postal Secretary to attend to supplies. The Eighteen Provinces and Manchuria have been divided into postal districts, now fifty in number. Next to the headquarters staff come Postal Commissioners—now four, at Peking, Hankow, Shanghai, and Canton—exercising direct control over their own district and a supervising direction over neighbouring districts. The other treaty-port districts are under the Commissioner of Customs acting *ex officio* as District Postmaster; and the inland districts, six in number, are under District Inspectors stationed at the respective provincial capitals.

Each Head or Sub-Head Office has under it a certain number of subordinate offices; these are of three kinds :

Branch Offices, at which the Imperial Post Office maintains its own staff on its own premises ;

Inland Agencies, at which licensed Agents, who are usually substantial shopkeepers of the place and guaranteed, undertake all postal business, including the delivery of correspondence, in return for a fixed commission and certain other emoluments ; and

Box Offices—that is, small shops in which the Imperial Post Office places letter-boxes, cleared at certain times during the day, and where the owner, under license and guarantee, is allowed to sell stamps to the public in return for a small commission : ordinary postal business, including registration, can be effected at these shops, but the owners do not undertake delivery. Box Offices are placed in all large cities as adjuncts to the Head and Branch Offices situated there. In addition, in certain cities are to be found street pillar-boxes, which are cleared at regular intervals.

All Branch Offices established at important places undertake the transmission of small sums of money by means of a Money Order system, with a limit of $50 for places served by steam, and $10 for other places. The value of money orders issued in 1910 was $5,280,000.

The size of each postal district was originally determined by consideration of the distance, the density of population, and the means of communication available in the district ; but, the limits once defined, it has been left to Postmasters to extend to inland places within their districts on certain broad lines fixed by headquarters, and this extension, begun in 1901, is continued ; and it is intended to open and establish direct postal routes to as many as possible of the prefectural and district cities, and to bring every open place into postal communication, via the treaty ports or Peking, with the foreign mail termini at Shanghai, Tientsin, Canton, thence with Union countries and the outside world.

The result of this first period of extension has been that at this date the Imperial Post Office is to be found and all postal business can be transacted in every provincial capital of the Empire, in most prefectural and district cities, and in the more important smaller centres and towns throughout China. The total number of establishments on December 31st, 1906, was 2,096, and 5,357 at the end of 1910.

Communication between Imperial establishments is kept up by means of contract steamers (26,000 li) on the coast and large rivers ; by railways (15,000 li) where they exist ; by steam-launches, junks, or hong-boats (24,000 li) on the inland waterways ; and on the numerous overland routes, which now measure over 287,000 li (95,600 miles) in length, by mounted or foot couriers ; a total in 1910 of 352,000 li or about 117,000 miles.

The coast and river steamers and launches run on certain lines and between fixed points, and are availed of wherever possible. Railways are still in their infancy in China, but lines already open are used to their full extent. Hong-boats are chiefly used in the southern part of Kiangsu and northern Chekiang—a district with a large network of canals and small creeks, many of them unnavigable by launches. This part of China is also very densely populated, and although the Shanghai, Hangchow, and Ningpo districts are not extensive, they contain an unusually large number of post offices, a remark likewise applicable to the Canton delta districts.

Communication by couriers, of a kind to fulfil the requirements of a Postal Service built up on Western lines, has naturally been no easy matter in a vast country like China, presenting every variety of geographical features and where public roads are utterly neglected. Old-established trade routes are usually followed, even at the cost of extra distance, as offering greater safety for the couriers, and as capable of convenient subdivision into stages, from the number of towns and villages found on them. Stages are generally limited to 100 li (33 English miles), and the couriers run according to schedule on fixed days ; but on the main routes speed is accelerated as much as possible, daily despatch being ensured on them for light mails and an every-two-days or semi-weekly service for heavy mails.

For light mails night-and-day foot couriers are used in some parts and mounted couriers in others, raising the speed to 200 li (or 65 miles) per day. The couriers are the employees of the Imperial Post Office, and wear uniforms or badges.

As actually constituted, the staff of the Imperial Post Office included in 1906—

Foreign

Inspector General and Headquarters Staff	5	
Postmasters *ex officio*	33	
Postal Commissioners	4	
Postmasters, Deputy Postmasters, and Assistants	14	
District Inspectors	4	
Postal Officers	78	
Mail Escort Officers	6	
	—	144

Chinese

Inspecting Clerks	29	
Chinese Clerks—linguists	319	
,, non-linguists ..	674	
Postal Agents	1,361	
Writers	5	
Sorters, Letter-carriers and Couriers, and Miscellaneous	3,190	
	—	5,578
Total Foreign and Chinese ..		5,722

In 1910 the foreign staff numbered 120, and the Chinese staff over 14,000.

The functions of Postmasters are for the present fulfilled by the Commissioners of Customs authorised to act at the treaty ports as Postmasters *ex officio*, or, for a few ports, by separate appointees. Deputy Postmasters are additional at the largest ports. District Inspectors reside in the interior in charge of sub-districts or travel on tours of inspection of the inland establishments. Postal Officers supervise all Service details at Head Offices, and control from there all the routine work and active operations carried on by native hands throughout the districts. Chinese linguist clerks possess a practical knowledge of English, and do duty at Head Offices or act in charge of Branch Offices at places where foreign communities are found. Non-linguists are not required to know a foreign language, and work at Head Offices under the linguists, or in charge of various establishments inland. Grades and rates of pay are fixed, and all employees advance by promotion. Chinese clerks are all guaranteed, and the whole system, which, in the main, rests on their honesty and their efficiency, works satisfactorily, cases of loss, misbehaviour, or peculation being of extremely rare occurrence.

A uniform and elaborate system of accounts has been devised for recording all receipts and expenditure. Each Head Office, under foreign supervision, keeps the accounts of its district and renders them to Peking, where they are audited and passed to a General Account for the whole Service.

The organisation as above described, incomplete as it is yet, answers the most immediate requirements of postal work ; and the progress made these last few years—that is, since steady expansion began in 1901—vouches for the soundness of the system upon which it is established.

A few comparative figures will prove interesting.

	1901.	1903.	1906.	1910.
District Offices	30	34	38	49
Branch Offices	134	320	484	736
Agencies	12	609	1,574	4,572
Articles dealt with	10,500,000	42,500,000	113,000,000	355,000,000
Parcels : number	126,800	487,000	1,383,000	3,766,000
,, weight in lbs.	552,000	2,673,000	9,482,000	25,373,000
Letters in Native clubbed mails	7,300,000	7,267,500	7,892,000	7,409,000

Divided between the four large geographical divisions of China, the results for 1906 and 1910 can be summarised as follows:

	1906.			1910.		
	Estab-lish-ments.	Articles.	Parcels.	Estab-lish-ments.	Articles.	Parcels.
North China ..	696	37,000,000	397,000	2,174	151,000,000	1,837,000
Central China ..	415	17,500,000	248,000	1,002	53,000,000	571,000
Lower Yangtze ..	322	38,500,000	450,000	751	94,000,000	899,000
Southern China ..	663	20,000,000	288,000	1,430	57,000,000	459,000
Total ..	2,096	113,000,000	1,383,000	5,357	355,000,000	3,766,000

A few words must be said on the financial means of this large Service. It may not be generally known that, not only had the postal experiment started in 1861 to be carried on for over thirty years against numerous difficulties and without the avowed support of the government, but, even after its formal recognition in 1896, without any special pecuniary help from it. The Customs Service, under the leadership of Sir Robert Hart, had alone, from the beginning, to support this stupendous enterprise, lending to it the assistance of its staff and such resources as it could spare; the independent and quiet creation of an administration so new and so useful is the more wonderful in this immovable country, and it will not be the least of the services rendered by the Customs and its chief to China and her people. In the middle of 1904 the Chinese government, confident at last of the ultimate success of the National Post Office, granted the subsidies required to bring up this Service to a state of completeness. On June 12th, 1904, the Inspector General was notified by the Yamen that in future an annual grant of Hk. Tls.720,000 would be issued, payable in monthly instalments of Hk. Tls.10,000 at six of the treaty ports — Tientsin, Shanghai, Hankow, Foochow, Swatow, and Canton. This grant has not been received in full, not more than half being forthcoming, but it enables the Service to provide for its actual money deficiency. The Post Office is worked " on the cheap." Chinese cheap labour is utilised to the fullest extent compatible with paying a sufficient living wage to remove from the staff the necessity of supplementing it by peculation ; and in addition much is still provided from funds of the Revenue Department of the Customs. The salaries of the Inspector General, the Deputy Postal Secretary, the District Postmasters *ex officio*, the District Accountants, and many subordinate employees are not a charge on postal funds ; the mass of printed forms required, about thirty million in a year, are provided without special accounting ; office accommodation is provided on Customs premises at many of the smaller ports ; steamer mail subsidies are paid from Customs funds ; and it is probable that a complete severance of Customs and Postal expenditure would add to the latter some lakhs of taels a year.*

It must be acknowledged that the Postal undertaking has long passed the experimental stage. Large communities, foreign and Chinese, are now dependent on the Imperial Post Office for the transmission of their correspondence, and the public duties of the Service increase every day. New establishments are wanted in every direction, and at those now open the work is becoming heavier. The system hitherto followed, to stretch out lengthy lines of couriers so as to rapidly bring all large cities of the interior into communication with treaty ports, had to be carried on without special regard to the local exploitation of each great centre, and, as a consequence, many are still only provided with Agencies quite inadequate to their requirements. Every *fu* and *hsien* city † should now have its own and properly constituted Post Office, able, separately, to

* In 1911 the Post Office was severed from the Customs, and provided with its own budget.

† In 1910, in a total of 1,910 such cities, 1,680 were provided with Post Offices, leaving only 230 for the future.

undertake the establishment and control of agencies or box offices in all the localities in its neighbourhood. A larger staff and larger means are required for this, and it is obvious that until this is done much of the advantages and possibilities of the new system will be neglected. These considerations have been brought to the notice of the Chinese government, and effective official support in various directions is now assured. Doubts can no longer be entertained that the Postal programme is definitely accepted and welcomed in official circles, and we have seen in Shansi, Honan, Hupeh, and some other provinces the high provincial authorities issue, of their own accord, remarkable proclamations making known to the population the character and aims of the Imperial Post Office, and enjoining upon all to welcome and support it as the national institution. There is now no more trouble, on the opening of new establishments, to obtain local proclamations from the authorities of the place, and, in fact, Magistrates not unfrequently apply of themselves for the planting of establishments in their cities, and wherever protection is asked for offices or couriers it is readily granted. Indications are seen everywhere of the growth of the institution ; its low rates, quickness, and regularity draw the public more and more to its counters.

China has not yet formally entered the Universal Postal Union, but special Conventions entered into with Japan, France, Hongkong, and India place her, through the intermediary of the contracting Administrations, in exactly the same postal relations with all Union countries as if she had already joined it. Under these Conventions Chinese mail matter for abroad, franked in Chinese stamps, is handed over in open bags to the foreign Post Office at the foreign mail terminus port, and that Post Office, by date-stamping each cover, confers on it the right of admission into any Union country in the world ; on the other hand, the foreign Post Office hands over in a similar way its incoming correspondence for transmission through Chinese lines. There is thus between the Chinese and foreign Offices an exchange of services which are paid for, as is done by any two Union countries, on the basis of yearly statistics taken during the first twenty-eight days of May or November of alternate years, and which are settled at the established Union rates. For this exchange of services foreign governments have made ample provision. At Shanghai, where a reason for the presence of a few of them exists in the necessity of connecting with various national and subsidised lines of mail steamers, there are no less than six foreign Post Offices— British, French, German, American, Japanese, and Russian —and, to utilise fully the postal facilities of the port, the public may find it expedient to keep supplies of the postage stamps of seven nations. At other ports no such necessity now exists, but foreign Post Offices, from one to five (the American not participating), have been established at twenty-five ports, not including French Offices at Mengtsz and Chungking for an internal and purely Chinese postal traffic. Of these, the British offices were established many years ago to supply the need of merchants when no other postal facilities were offered to the public ; but, except at Shanghai, the others all date from the general scramble for political influence of the past two decades.

It should be remembered here that in dealing with international correspondence, China in every respect conforms to the rules of a Union country. In April 1896, shortly after the promulgation of the Imperial edict establishing the National Post, China addressed the Conseil Fédéral Suisse, notifying the creation of the Imperial Postal Service, and her formal intention to join the Union as soon as organisation permitted ; meanwhile her Post Offices, as they opened at the treaty and other ports, were to observe Union practice and rules. These declarations she confirmed again before the Universal Postal Congress of Washington in 1897, and ever since she has acknowledged, at these places, Universal Postal Union regulations and rates. Consequently, all international mail matter, to and from treaty ports and steam-served places, are passed free at Chinese Offices if fully prepaid at Union tariffs, and, when a tax is applied for insufficiency of postage, it is done in conformity with Union rules. To non-steam-served places, where communications have to be maintained by a costly service of land couriers, the rule remains the same for light articles—letters and postcards; but on printed matter and other heavy mail articles the Chinese Administration imposes a domestic charge, distinct from Union rates, to cover courier expenses. As regards more particularly mail matter arriving from British places at the penny postage rate or from the United States at American domestic rate, if received for distribution at Shanghai it is distributed free, but if received for further transmission through the Imperial Post Office system it is taxed in conformity with Union rules.

The native letter hongs present a far more difficult problem. Entrenched in monopoly and possessing a profitable vested interest in postal work, they obtain the backing which is always given in China to vested interests, and even the provision of cheaper postal facilities to the public does not prevail against their plea that " they are there, and wish to remain there." Compulsion and the monopoly of postal transmission to the Government Office are out of the question, and the Imperial Post has been driven to *invite* them to co-operate. Registration hurts no one, and they have been given practically free transport * for their closed mails—called " clubbed mails "—along the coast, and these mails they have consented to hand over for transmission. Unprofitable inland lines they have been willing to abandon, but for the profitable routes they fight tooth and nail. Between them and the National Post it is " a fair field and no favour," and the latter, with fixed rules and more or less fixed hours, is heavily handicapped against business agencies with flexible rules and no hours to speak of. The Chinese trader and official know no limi-

* A charge for transport was imposed from November 1906.

tation to their hours of business, and they patronise the agency which consults their convenience. The Post Office must close at some fixed hour, even if it is at 9 or 10 p.m. The business agency may remain open until 2 or 3 or 4 a.m. if thereby business is furthered, and makes a practice of collecting mail matter, even at those hours, from its clients' places of business. By these conditions the Post Office in China is driven to develop on lines of its own, without much regard to procedure elsewhere, and several innovations have been introduced experimentally. An "express delivery" system has been instituted at and between Peking, Tientsin, Shanghai, Hankow, Foochow, and Canton; house-to-house collection has been started in the business section of certain large cities; and, in general, every effort is made to increase postal facilities to meet the views of an exacting Chinese public.

POSTSCRIPT

What precedes has more particularly an historical value, showing the difficulties which had to be encountered in establishing a postal organisation in China, and the way in which they were met. The connection of the Post Office with the Customs was severed on May 28th, 1911, and it was placed under the Ministry of Posts and Communications (Yu-chuan Pu); after the establishment of the Republic it remained under the Ministry of Communications (Chiao-tung Pu), but with a separate organisation and a separate budget. At its head in 1911 was placed Li Ching-fang as Director-General, with Mr. Théophile Piry as Postmaster-General. In 1917, on the resignation of Mr. Piry, Yeh Kung-cho, Vice-Minister of Communications, was appointed Director-General of Posts, and Mr. H. Picard-Destelan Co-Director-General. Mr. Piry died in France in July 1918.

In 1918 the Chinese staff of the Post Office numbered 26,933, including 55 on the administrative staff, 3,698 literates, 1,623 sorters, 7,604 postal agents, and 13,953 postmen, couriers, office-boys, etc. To superintend this number there was a foreign staff consisting of 15 Commissioners, 18 Deputy Commissioners, 68 Assistants, and 6 Postal Officers, besides a few absent on leave or on war service.

In 1918 the number of official post offices was 1,763, and of agencies 7,604. Courier lines had increased to 449,000 li (150,000 miles), steamer and boat lines to 69,800 li (23,300 miles), and railway lines to 20,000 li (6,500 miles). Despite adverse conditions due to the civil war, the weight of mail matter carried by the post-boat fleet between Ichang and Chungking was 970,000 kilos.

The table on page 422, showing the rate of progress of the Post Office, is correct in that respect; but it is deceptive in showing the number of mail articles and parcels *dealt with*, each article being recorded on each occasion when it was posted, transmitted, or delivered by a post office. The more correct method is to record the number of articles posted, and on this basis the progress of the Post Office is shown by the following figures :

		1908.	1913.	1918.
Mail matter				
posted	No.	79,882,252	197,484,136	302,269,028
Parcels ⌠	No.	623,315	1,380,912	2,738,090
posted ⌊	Wt., kilos.	2,315,190	5,581,755	10,850,034

In 1918, of the total number of mail articles posted, no less than 25,131,528, or 8 per cent., were registered, express, or insured. Native clubbed mails, representing the effort of the mercantile postal agencies to maintain their business, fell in 1918 to less than half the 1910 figures.

Money orders were issued to the amount of $10,161,000 in 1913 and $35,335,800 in 1918. In the latter year orders of a value of nearly $3,500,000 were issued to the British Emigration Bureau at Weihaiwei alone, representing allotments payable in remote villages in Shantung and Chihli to the families of members of the Chinese Labour

Corps recruited for service in France; and $332,000 were issued to the French authorities.

The progress of the Post Office is shown most markedly in its finances. For the first fifteen years of its history, its maintenance was a burden on the energies and resources of the Customs; and for the first four years after its severance from the Customs its accounts showed an annual deficit, which had to be made good by the Treasury. Then came an annual surplus, though with no provision for capital expenditure for sites, buildings, vans, boats and property generally; and in 1918 the accounts gave the following results:

	Dollars.
Revenue	9,500,000
Working expenses	7,590,000
Surplus	1,910,000
Capital expenditure	813,000

Great credit is due to Director-General, Co-Director-General, and staff generally for such a result, after many years of deficits, and in a year in which postal work was impeded by civil war, by brigandage on an enormous scale, by the burning and pillaging of many post offices, by the murder of couriers, and by the misery and desolation brought to many millions of the people of China.*

* See page 74.

CHAPTER XIV

RAILWAYS *

FIFTY years ago China was the one great commercial country in the world which had no railways. Of the eighteen provinces of China proper, twelve were served, in all their populous parts, by waterways, providing safe and cheap transport for their commodities. The people at large asked nothing better ; the commercial classes had been satisfied with the junk, and were now quite content with the steamer ; and the officials dreaded the introduction of additional foreign innovations. In the summer of 1863, while Soochow was still held by the Taiping rebels, but with the armies under Li Hung-chang and Gordon in sight of its walls, a group of twenty-seven English and American merchants presented a petition to Li Hung-chang, as Governor of Kiangsu, asking a concession for a railway from Shanghai to Soochow. The Governor had come into close touch with foreigners and had realised their aggressiveness ; he had further realised the danger to the Chinese state from any extension of the privilege of extraterritoriality ; and he returned to the petitioners the answer that " railways would only be beneficial to China when undertaken by the Chinese themselves and conducted under their own management ; that serious objections existed to the employment of numerous foreigners in the interior ; and that the people would

* This chapter is an abbreviated reproduction of the chapter on Railways in " The International Relations of the Chinese Empire," vol. iii. It is given here since it is thought that this work may be read by many who will not see the history.

evince great opposition to being deprived of their land for that purpose." The petition was accordingly rejected.

In that same year an English engineer, Sir MacDonald Stephenson, paid a visit to China, and, from the incomplete information then available, without a personal inspection of the country, he laid down certain trunk lines. His lines, with the exception of that from Hankow westward through Szechwan and Yunnan to Burma, were those which have since been followed ; but it did not require a great engineer to make the proposals, and, such as they were, they were rejected. They served, however, as the text from which one friendly adviser after another exhorted the rulers of China to promote the welfare of their country by building railways. Mr. Burlingame in 1868 asserted that China was even then ready to engage western engineers to open mines and build railways ; but the attitude of the imperial advisers was expressed by the Grand Secretary Wensiang : " The only instruction we gave our envoy was to keep the West from forcing us to build railways and telegraphs, which we want only so far as they are due to our own initiative."

The Shanghai merchants were not dismayed by their first failure, and in 1865 they formed a syndicate to make a railway from Shanghai to Wusung, a length of ten miles. In 1863 this would have presented no difficulty, since the country to be traversed was then in the occupation of the English and French forces protecting Shanghai; but in 1865 the territory had reverted to the control of the Chinese civil officials, and only the warmest support from those authorities could have overcome the difficulties in the way of expropriating the land in a territory so covered with graves and cemeteries, objects of the highest reverence to all Chinese. The promoters then resorted to a subterfuge. They obtained permission to reconstruct the military carriage road from Shanghai to Wusung, and to acquire by private negotiation the land necessary to widen and straighten it. Their project was delayed by the financial situation in Shanghai consequent on the crises of 1866 ; but in 1874 the merchants, resorting to a subterfuge, announced their intention to lay rails for a tramway along their new " horse-road." The rails for the tramway arrived at Shanghai in December 1875, and work was at once begun on the permanent way of a line of 30-inches gauge ; but the Chinese soon learned that the tramway (horse-carriage iron-road) was in fact to be a railway (fire-carriage iron-road), with carriages drawn by a steam locomotive engine. The Chinese authorities protested on February 23rd, 1876 ; but the promoters persisted in their work, without the permit of the Chinese government, and without the approval of the Legation, which had approved a tramway but could not sanction a railway.

The line was completed from Shanghai to Kiangwan, five miles, and trains for passengers only were run from June 30th. The people flocked to the trains as to a circus, and the promoters congratulated themselves on the popularity of the new foreign raree-show, when, on August 3rd, a countryman walking on the line was killed under circumstances which suggested either extremely dense stupidity or a malicious intention to commit suicide, and thereby create a prejudice against railways. The people began to manifest great hostility ; and, in fear of an epidemic of similar accidents, the British authorities ordered that the running of trains should be suspended. On October 24th the Chinese authorities agreed to buy the undertaking for its actual cost, Tls.285,000. Traffic was then resumed by the promoters as security for their interest ; but, the purchase money having been paid on October 21st, 1877, the Chinese at once tore up the line and shipped off rails and rolling stock to Formosa. So ended in failure an attempt, based on subterfuge, to impose on China a railway which she did not yet want.

The next attempt was also based on subterfuge, but one carried through by Chinese for China, and avoiding the intrusion of a foreign interest which had been fatal to the previous ventures. Tong King-sing, the head of the

28

China Merchants' Steam Navigation Company, had in 1878 opened the Kaiping coal-mine to obtain a direct supply of coal for his steamers. The main shaft at Tongshan was twenty-nine miles from the nearest shipping port, Pehtang, and seven miles from Hsükochwang, the nearest point to which a canal could be made. The chief engineer, Mr. R. R. Burnett, proposed a railway from Tongshan to Pehtang; for this imperial sanction was obtained, and Mr. C. W. Kinder was placed in charge of the construction. The imperial assent was soon after withdrawn and the work stopped. Mr. Kinder then obtained permission to connect Tongshan with Hsükochwang by a tramway, the track to be of standard railway gauge, and the cars to be drawn by mules; and this line was begun in 1880 and completed in 1881. Meanwhile he had built a locomotive, of which the boiler had originally belonged to a portable winding engine, the wheels had been bought as scrap iron, and the frame was made of old channel iron; its total cost was $520 (£95). Orders came to stop its construction, but the Viceroy, Li Hung-chang, was interested and gave his approval; and on June 9th, 1881, the hundredth anniversary of George Stephenson's birth, it was christened the " Rocket of China." Its success was soon demonstrated, and in 1882 two locomotives were bought to work the seven-mile length of railway to the canal, which had meanwhile been dug to Lutai on the Pehtang River.

The next venture was made in Formosa. The war with France in 1884–1885 had shown the necessity of erecting the island into a province of the Empire; but it had also shown the importance of Kelung as a coaling port, and the vulnerability of that port to hostile attack from the sea. The first Governor, Liu Ming-chüan, an energetic army commander, realised the importance of protecting this port and the coal-mine near it, which had been opened in 1875; and he proposed to connect Kelung by a railway with Taipeh, the capital, a distance of twenty miles. Formosa was looked on as a detached province in which experiments might be tried, and the imperial assent, after some delay, was given at the end of 1886. In March 1887 the Governor in person, with the aid of the English engineer, and accompanied by his whole retinue, traced the line for the first four miles over the level plain. The line was to be built by Chinese for the Chinese, and there was no obstruction ; but the work was done by soldiers, and the labour conditions were so unsatisfactory that, in the first two years, five engineers-in-chief resigned in succession. The work was ultimately carried through under the supervision of Mr. Henry C. Matheson. The line to Kelung was completed in 1891, and that towards southern Formosa reached Teckcham (Sinchu), thirty miles from Taipeh, in 1893. The line was throughout the victim of Chinese official management ; it was starved in its construction, its equipment, and its working ; and the Japanese in 1895 took over little except fifty miles of badly laid track.

The Kaiping steam tramway was extended in 1886 to Lutai, a distance of twenty miles, at a cost of $135,000 (£25,000). This was done for the development of the coalmine, and the Viceroy Li Hung-chang's interest was excited ; but, though he saw clearly the commercial advantage, his interest was based on strategic grounds, and on those grounds he obtained the support of Ihwan, Prince Chun, father of the Emperor, and president of the newly established Admiralty. On March 15th, 1887, the prince memorialised the throne, urging that the railway be extended eastward to Shanhaikwan, and westward to Tientsin, and thence to Peking, " in order to facilitate the movement of troops and the transport of war material." An imperial rescript granted the memorialist's prayer, the work was taken in hand, and by April 1888 the line was completed to Tangku, and in August to Tientsin. The total cost of construction was about $19,000 (£3,000) a mile.

A third of the proposed line had now been built, eighty miles ; the western section, Tientsin to Peking, was also to be eighty miles ; and the eastern section, Tongshan to

Shanhaikwan, also eighty miles. It was now proposed to construct the western section before the eastern ; but the forces of reaction, and of opposition to Li Hung-chang and all his works, became active, and the Grand Council withheld its consent and called for the opinions of the viceroys and governors. Of the replies received, that from Liu Ming-chüan was most pronounced in support of the extension, its argument being based on strategic grounds. Chang Chih-tung, viceroy at Canton, opposed the extension, also basing his argument on strategic grounds ; and he advocated instead the construction of great trunk lines through the interior of the country, safely remote from attack by sea power, beginning with one from Peking to Hankow. This opinion prevailed, and Chang Chih-tung was transferred to Wuchang with orders to undertake his projected trunk line, building it of Chinese material and under Chinese direction, as he had proposed. He found himself unable to carry out his intentions, but, to provide for the future, he established the Hanyang steel works.

The extension to Peking was thus shelved ; and, because of the requirement to use only Chinese capital and Chinese material, the trunk lines were also shelved for an indefinite time. Li Hung-chang did not fear responsibility, and, on the authority of the original imperial sanction, he proceeded with the extension eastward to Shanhaikwan. The line to this point was completed in 1894 ; and, overriding an objection made by Russia to Mr. Kinder's surveying in Manchuria, Li Hung-chang pushed his line further eastward, reaching Chunghowso, forty miles from Shanhaikwan, on the outbreak of the war with Japan. The result of that war demonstrated the strategic value of railways, and the absurdity of building only those which were " safely remote from the sea " ; and the western extension was taken in hand. Peking was reached at the end of 1896. The management of this railway, purely Chinese except for the engineer staff, has been most competent. In 1906 the length of line operated, excluding sidings, was 588 miles, of which 141 miles had been paid for out of profits. In that year the total gross receipts were $12,191,189, the operating expenses $3,429,943, or 27 per cent., leaving a surplus of $8,761,246. The cost of construction and equipment was $47,970,000, or per mile of line $81,582 (£12,482 at exchange of 1898, £8,723 at exchange of 1906).

Russia, baulked of her aims in Korea, turned in 1895 to Manchuria as a sphere of influence, to be open to Russian exploitation, but to that of no other power. In that year it was tentatively agreed, and confirmed by a convention in September 1896, that Russia, providing the capital herself, might construct her Transiberian railway across Manchuria, on the line afterwards followed, and that China should have recourse only to Russian banks to finance her railways in Manchuria. By a later convention the railway already begun from Shanhaikwan to Moukden was kept free from Russian control; but other railways Outside the Portal were constructed by the Chinese Eastern Railway Company, a Russian corporation organised under Russian law. This corporation, partly from its own capital, but in much greater part from advances issued by the Russian Imperial Treasury, constructed two main lines—west to east, Manchuli-Harbin-Suifenho, 950 miles; north to south, Harbin-Talienwan (Dalny, Dairen), 646 miles; total 1,596 miles. By the agreement, China might redeem the lines in thirty-six years, and at the end of eighty years they were to revert to her without payment.

Russia's action in Manchuria initiated the era of international scrambling for railway concessions in China—the policy of " conquest by railways " as it was termed, which was afterwards, in 1909, merged in the policy termed " dollar diplomacy." The French had combined their industrial and financial interests into a " syndicate " in 1885, at the close of the Franco-Chinese war ; but now, in 1896, all the industrial nations entered the field with syndicates, which began to bid one against the other. There had already been some recognition of spheres of interest, and the competition for railway concessions led to a clearer definition of these spheres. In the end, during the year 1898, it was recognised that Russia had special and exclusive interests in Manchuria, and claimed them in North China ; but the latter claim was resisted. Germany claimed, and was accorded, an exclusive interest in Shantung ; the British government even voluntarily disclaimed any intention of penetrating that province through the portal of Weihaiwei. England claimed a special interest in the provinces bordering on the Yangtze ; but Germany refused to recognise any exclusive right, such as she arrogated to herself in Shantung, and other nations also claimed equal rights in the Yangtze basin. France claimed exclusive rights in the three provinces bordering on Tongking ; she also claimed rights in Szechwan, but they were not accorded to her. Japan claimed preferential rights in Fukien, the province fronting on Formosa. Finally, in 1899, Italy took steps which seemed to indicate an intention to claim rights over Chekiang ; but on this occasion the Chinese government stiffened its back, and offered a stout resistance to the Italian pretensions.

The Viceroy Chang Chih-tung found a difficulty in providing the funds for his Peking-Hankow railway, and, in October 1896, he received permission to obtain foreign capital. Negotiations were opened with the American-China Development Company, at the head of which was ex-Senator W. D. Washburn, and it undertook a rough survey of the route ; meantime a Belgian syndicate made counter offers which were more attractive, and the American syndicate, cold-shouldered by its own government, missed the prize which it counted its own. But the way of the Belgians was not smooth. Behind Belgium interested eyes, foreign and Chinese, discerned France and Russia ; other powers might or might not support the American pretensions, but they were all united in opposing the Belgian claims. The Belgian negotiations were then dropped, but they were renewed in July 1897 on the expressed condition that

" the money is all to come from Belgium, none from France or Russia will be accepted." In the face of much opposition these negotiations were again dropped.

In April 1898 the Peking government created a Bureau of Control for Railways and.Mines ; and at the same time the Belgian negotiations were resumed, resulting in the signature, on June 26th, of a contract for a loan and for working the line. The loan was for 112,500,000 francs at 5 per cent., issued at 90, and was to be paid off by twenty annual drawings beginning in 1909 ; the syndicate was further to operate the line for thirty years from 1898, receiving therefor 20 per cent. of the net profits, after deducting operating expenses and interest and amortisation of the loan. The line was completed in 1905, with a total length of 812 miles, including branch lines of 58 miles. The rails and iron fittings were bought from the Hanyang steel works. In October 1908 China exercised her right under the contract, and bought back the line by means of a thirty-year loan, issued through the Hongkong and Shanghai Bank and the Banque de l'Indo-Chine, for £5,000,000 at 5 per cent. for fifteen years and 4½ per cent. for the second fifteen years, issued at 94 ; and £450,000 at 7 per cent. and par repayable before 1920.

Shantung was claimed by Germany as her sphere of development. By a convention signed March 6th, 1898, the enclave of Kiaochow was ceded to Germany on lease, provisionally for ninety-nine years ; and in this China sanctioned the construction by Germany of two lines of railway in Shantung. An imperial German charter was granted in 1899 to the Schantung-Eisenbahn-Gesellschaft, with a capital of 54,000,000 marks, for a railway from Tsingtau to Tsinanfu : the shareholders were to be only German or Chinese ; the material used was to be German as far as possible ; and the German treasury of Kiaochow was to share in the profits after 5 per cent. had been paid to the shareholders. The company was also to have the right to build lines from Tsingtau to Ichowfu, and from Tsinanfu to

Ichowfu. The line from Tsingtau to Tsinanfu, 245 miles, with a branch of 36 miles to the Poshan coalfields, or 281 miles in all, was completed in 1904 at a cost of 52,900,000 marks of German capital. The success of the line is seen in the transfer of the trade of Shantung from Chefoo to Tsingtau, as shown by the following values of the total net import and export trade:

	1903. Tls.	1913. Tls.
Chefoo .	38,183,912 (72 per cent.)	31,641,224 (35 per cent.)
Tsingtau	14,598,411 (28 per cent.)	59,168,880 (65 per cent.)

In 1918 in war conditions, with Tsingtau under Japanese control, the figures were : Chefoo, Tls.30,835,885 (33 per cent.), Tsingtau, Tls.63,447,330 (67 per cent.). Whether the railway will ultimately be under German, Japanese, or Chinese control is, at this date of writing, not yet settled.

Yung Wing, a distinguished Cantonese, graduate of an American university, had in the years 1872-1881 been the Director of the mission which sent selected students to study at American universities ; and in 1897 he was authorised by imperial decree to undertake the construction, as a Chinese undertaking, of a railway Tientsin-Tsinanfu-Chin-kiang. This was at once opposed by the German envoy, who declared that Germany alone had the right to build railways in Shantung. Yung Wing, nevertheless, persisted, and in August 1898 contracted with an American syndicate for a loan of £5,500,000 ; this contract was not carried out, since Germany protested on the ground that her rights in Shantung blocked the way. A previous offer by a German syndicate had been rejected by China ; and the British syndicate, fearing political complications, was reluctant to undertake the line, although it led to the Yangtze basin. Finally, the British and German interests joined in a contract for the line, which was sanctioned by imperial decree in May 1899. Under this agreement the northern part, from Tientsin to the southern border of Shantung, was to be " constructed, equipped, and worked" by the Deutsch-Asiatische Bank, and the southern part by the British and Chinese Corporation, both as agents for the Chinese government.

This agreement was not carried out owing to the Boxer troubles of 1900 ; and, when negotiations were reopened in 1896, the Chinese government had adopted a new policy, and insisted on its right to construct and work all new lines through Chinese directors, while still inviting loans of foreign capital. A new contract was made in January 1908 with the Deutsch-Asiatische Bank, representing German interests, and the Chinese Central Railway Company, representing an alliance of British and French interests, for a loan of £5,000,000 at 5 per cent., issued at 93, followed in 1910 by another of £3,000,000 at 5 per cent., issued at 94·5 ; the southern terminus was changed to Pukow, on the north bank of the Yangtze, opposite to Nanking, to which the length of line is 674 miles. The loans were secured, not on the railway receipts, but on certain specified provincial revenues ; and it was provided that " the construction and control of the railway will be entirely vested in the Chinese government," . . . and " after completion of construction the Chinese government will administer both sections as one undivided government railway." The policy thus indicated, by which China asserted her right to control the expenditure of funds borrowed on her security, became known as " Pukow terms."

France claimed the three provinces bordering on Tongking as her sphere of development ; she also extended her claim to cover Szechwan, but this was not accepted by others. In 1895 France obtained the right to connect Langson with Lungchow, but this project was abandoned in 1900. In 1898 she obtained a concession for a railway from Pakhoi, and in 1899 for one from Kwangchowwan, both to the West River in Kwangsi ; neither of these was taken in hand. In 1897 an agreement sanctioned the construction by France of a line from the frontier to Yunnanfu, in continuation of a line to be constructed in Tongking from Hanoi up the Red River to Laokay. After many difficulties the line was completed in 1910, with a length of 289 miles and at a cost of 165,000,000 francs. Of this sum 76,000,000 francs were provided by a loan guaranteed by France, 63,580,000 francs by a subsidy from the government of Tongking, and 25,420,000 francs by the French company which undertook the construction and working. The effect on the trade of Mengtze is shown by the following figures :

	1910. Tls.	1913. Tls.	1918. Tls.
Imports ..	5,077,320	8,612,646	9,474,225
Exports ..	6,387,609	11,066,270	11,398,818

The American syndicate of Senator Washburn had failed to secure a concession ; but, in view of the territorial aspirations of at least four of the European powers which were manifested in the spring of 1898, the Chinese had strong reasons for seeking the support of capitalists in the United States, which had given no evidence of such aspirations. At the end of 1897 Sheng Hsüan-hwai memorialised the throne, asking sanction for a line from Hankow to Canton, and proposing that, as there were " serious objections to allowing England, France, or Germany to undertake the work," the contract should be placed in America ; and in April 1898 an agreement for the line was signed with the American China Development Company, at the head of which was Senator Calvin Brice. The loan was for £4,000,000 at 5 per cent., issued at 90 ; construction was to be done by the company for a commission of 5 per cent. on all outgoings except for land and earthwork ; and the line was to be worked by the company in consideration of receiving debentures equal to one-fifth of the cost, to secure the payment to it of 20 per cent. of the net profits. The survey, under the direction of Mr. William Barclay Parsons, gave a line 740 miles long, with branches of 100 miles, total

840 miles. The engineering difficulties were found to be so considerable that, in July 1900, a new agreement was made increasing the loan to 40,000,000 gold dollars, this agreement being declared to be a mortgage, with the railway as security. Subject to this mortgage, the line was to be Chinese property; and it was expressly stipulated that the Americans could not transfer their rights to other nations or the people of other nationality.

The Americans had now the contract for the southern half of the great medial line, Peking-Hankow-Canton; but, if the Chinese were desirous that the whole of that line should not come under Belgian control, the Belgians, with the other interests in the background, were no less desirous of obtaining that control. The Americans met many impediments. The American money market was upset by the Spanish war, the English by the South African War; China was thrown into confusion by the Boxer troubles and their consequences; and the death of Senator Brice knocked the bottom out of an undertaking which was now deprived of his support. This was the opportunity of the Belgians, and, through an American nominee, they acquired a controlling interest in the American company. China protested; the Belgians stood firm; but ultimately, chiefly in consequence of the Japanese victory over Russia, the principal supporter of the Belgian claims, the Belgians yielded and the control passed back into the hands of American interests. This did not settle matters, however, because of the hostility of the gentry and merchants of Kwangtung, Hunan, and Hupeh, based on a strong feeling of nationality; and the American company agreed in 1905 to sell the concession, and the work already done, back to the Chinese government for 6,750,000 gold dollars. To provide for this the Chinese borrowed from the Hongkong colonial government £1,100,000 at 4½ per cent. and par. The southern section, within the province of Kwangtung, has since then been " in course of construction " by the Chinese of Canton; the northern section was in 1911 entrusted to the Four-Power Group.

In 1898 England was led by one graceful concession after another to admit the utmost pretensions of other powers which asserted protectionist principles in their respective spheres of development, and was left with the privilege of competing, on an open-door basis, with all except Russia in railway development in the Yangtze basin. There, in May 1898, the British and Chinese Corporation obtained the contract for a railway, Shanghai-Soochow-Chinkiang-Nanking. Financing was delayed by the South African War, and then by the Boxer rising; but in 1903 an agreement was made for a fifty-year loan of £3,250,000 at 5 per cent. : the first issue was made at 90, the second at 95½. The line and its plant were to be the security; and the corporation was to pay Tls.1,000,000 (£125,000) for the Shanghai-Wusung railway, which had been built by the Chinese. The line, 210 miles in length, was completed in 1908. The contract provided that construction and operation should be under the control of a board of five commissioners, two Chinese, two English, and the (English) Engineer-in-Chief ; but, since the completion of the line, control of the operation has been vested in the Chinese president for the commission.

In August 1898, as compensation for what was regarded as the Chinese government's " breach of faith in the Peking-Hankow affair," the same corporation obtained concessions for a railway, Soochow-Hangchow-Ningpo, and for one Pukow-Sinyangchow (a point tapping the Peking-Hankow line). Owing to provincial opposition, the construction of these lines was not entrusted to the corporation, but in 1908 it undertook a loan of £1,500,000 at 5 per cent. for the former; the latter has been shelved.

The province of Shansi is one of the richest coal-fields in the world, and it has besides large deposits of iron-ore. In 1896 Commendatore Angelo Luzatti made a study of this field, and in 1897, to work it, he formed the Peking Syndicate—Anglo-Italian in its composition, but English in its capital. In May 1898 he obtained by imperial decree the sole right for sixty years to open and work coal and iron

mines and petroleum wells in certain districts of Shansi and
of Honan north of the Yellow River. The syndicate was
to pay a royalty of 5 per cent. of gross receipts, then 6 per
cent. was to be paid on capital, then 10 per cent. of net
profits to a sinking fund, and of the surplus 25 per cent. was
to be paid to the Chinese government and 75 per cent. to
the syndicate. The syndicate, using its own capital, might
" make roads, build bridges, open or deepen rivers or canals,
or construct branch railways to connect with main lines or
with water navigation," to carry its coal and iron. The
syndicate, with a subscribed capital of £1,520,000, proceeded
to develop mines and to construct to them a railway starting
from Taokow, at the head of barge navigation on the Wei
River. After being delayed by the Boxer rising, the railway
was completed in 1905 to (Pashan) Tsinghwa, a length of
90 miles. The Chinese then decided to buy out the rights of
the syndicate in the railway ; and, under two agreements of
July 3rd, 1905, the syndicate issued a thirty-year loan for
£700,000 at 5 per cent. and 90, and sold the railway for
£614,600 cash ; the line itself was the security, and it was
to be worked by the syndicate during the currency of the
loan.

Other lines were also taken in hand, each representing
some diplomatic pressure on the Chinese government.

(a) The Chengtingfu-Taiyuenfu Railway, connecting the
capital of Shansi with a station on the Peking-Hankow line.
For this an agreement was made with the Russo-Chinese
Bank in 1898, supplemented by a definite contract in 1902,
for a thirty-year loan of 40,000,000 francs at 5 per cent.,
issued at 90, guaranteed by the imperial government and
secured by the traffic receipts. The contract was later
transferred to a French syndicate. The line, of one-metre
gauge, is 151 miles long and was completed in 1907.

(b) The Kaifengfu-Honanfu-Sianfu Railway, parallel
to the Yellow River. In 1899 an agreement was signed with
a Franco-Belgian syndicate, La Compagnie Générale des
Chemins de Fer et Tramways en Chine, followed by a final

contract in 1903, for the section Kaifengfu-Honanfu, 115 miles. . The|contract of 1903 provided for a loan of 25,000,000 francs, to which a later contract of 1907 added 16,000,000 francs, at 5 per cent., issued at 90. This section was completed in 1909.

(c) Railway communication between Hongkong and Canton is solely a British interest, and that portion of the line, 28 miles, which is within the limits of the colonial territory is, for financing and construction, a British affair. The line from the frontier to Canton, 85 miles, was taken in hand by the Chinese of Canton. In 1907 a contract was made with the British and Chinese Corporation for a thirty-year loan of £1,500,000 at 5 per cent., issued at 94, secured on the railway and guaranteed by the Chinese government.

Other smaller lines have been taken in hand by the Chinese themselves, and in general without foreign financial aid or government guarantee; but their length is not considerable.

The Russo-Japanese war of 1904-1905 resulted in the transfer to Japan of much of the Russian interest in Man-churian railways. Russia retained the whole of the Tran-siberian line, west to east from Manchuli to Suifenho, 950 miles; of the north and south line she kept the northern section to Kwanchengtze, 132 miles, but the lines south of that point, 514 miles, went to Japan. In addition, it was agreed with China in 1905 that Japan, providing the funds herself, might build a line from Mukden to Antung on the Korean frontier, a length of 189 miles. Two other lines were to be built by Japanese for China, half the cost being provided by China, the remaining half being lent by Japan at 5 per cent., viz.: Sinminfu-Mukden, 48 miles (loan £33,300); Kwanchengtze-Kirin, 75 miles (loan £225,000). For her lines in Manchuria Japan in 1906 organised the South Manchuria Railway Company, with a capital of 200,000,000 yen (£20,000,000), of which half was provided by the Japanese government, and £4,000,000 by a 5 per cent. thirty-five-year lôan issued in London in 1906.

Szechwan was a subject of rivalry between England and France : the latter hoped to tap its trade from Tongking, the former from Burma, by railways through Yunnan ; and England would benefit the more by a continuance of traffic along the course of the Yangtze. In 1905 an Anglo-French syndicate, the Chinese Central Railways Company, was formed to undertake railways in the Yangtze basin ; the American financial interests were invited to co-operate, but were not then inclined to accede. In 1909 the German syndicate was admitted to form a tripartite group, and in the same year the Americans demanded that they should be admitted to share. In May 1910 an agreement was made in conference at Paris for dividing the Hukwang railways, including the Hankow-Szechwan line and the northern portion of the Hankow-Canton line, equally between the members of the " Four-Power Group," viz. :

For England, the Hongkong and Shanghai Bank.

For Germany, the Deutsch-Asiatische Bank.

For France, the Bank de l'Indo-Chine.

For the United States, the American Group (composed of Messrs. J. P. Morgan & Co., Messrs. Kuhn, Loeb & Co., the First National Bank, and the National City Bank, all of New York).

It may here be said that the Four-Power Group, in the interest of China, asserted its sole right to provide all loans for the purposes of the Chinese government, and to exercise a supervision over the expenditure of their proceeds ; that, for this function, it became the Six-Power Group by the adhesion, on their demand, of Russia and Japan ; and that, in March 1913, on the inauguration of President Wilson, it became the Five-Power Group by the withdrawal of official support from the " dollar diplomacy " of the American group.

In May 1911 the Four-Power Group obtained the contract for the Hukwang railways. The contract provided for a present loan of £6,000,000, and a later loan of £4,000,000, at 5 per cent., guaranteed by the Chinese government, and secured on the traffic receipts and on certain salt and likin taxes of the Hukwang provinces, Hupeh and Hunan. The four banking interests were to take the loan in equal shares and without responsibility for each other. The construction and control of the lines were to be entirely and exclusively vested in the Chinese government; in the construction Chinese material was to be used as far as possible; and for it the Chinese were to appoint engineers:

> English for the section Hankow-Ichanghien (on the southern border of Hunan);
> German for the section Kwangshui-Ichang;
> American for the section Ichang-Kweichowfu.

Extension into Szechwan beyond Kweichowfu was left to be the subject of future agreement. An additional railway, Hankow-Kingmenchow, did not come under this contract, but was entrusted to a Chinese company employing Chinese capital.

A table of the railways on Chinese territory is given in Appendix G.

APPENDIX A

FOREIGN DEBT OF CHINA OUTSTANDING DECEMBER 31ST, 1911.

(Exchange at 3s. per tael.)

Title.	Issued.	Principal Amount.	Rate of Int.	Charge 1911.	Principal paid off to Dec. 1911.	Principal outstanding Dec. 1911.
National Loans :		£		£	£	£
1. Loan E, Tls.767,200 ..	1886	115,080	7	8,400	87,780	27,300
2. Hongkong and Shanghai Bank, Tls.10,900,000	1894	1,635,000	7	197,835	1,308,000	327,000
3. Arnhold, Karberg & Co. (Nanking Loan) ..	1895	1,000,000	6	84,600	733,300	266,700
4. Cassel Loan	1895	1,000,000	6	84,600	733,300	266,700
5. Hongkong and Shanghai Bank	1895	3,000,000	6	248,000	2,400,000	600,000
6. Franco-Russian Loan (Fr.400,000,000) ..	1895	15,820,000	4	836,669	4,452,527	11,367,473
7. Anglo-German Loan ..	1896	16,000,000	5	960,479	3,602,575	12,397,425
8. Ditto	1898	16,000,000	4½	831,688	1,977,375	14,022,625
9. Hongkong and Shanghai Bank	1905	1,000,000	5	61,250	800,000	200,000
10. Japanese Loan ..	1911	1,000,000	5	50,000	—	1,000,000
11. Telegraphs Loan ..	1911	500,000	5	25,000	—	500,000
Indemnities (1901) :						
12. Series A.		11,250,000	4	574,425	1,493,862	9,756,138
13. Series B.		9,000,000	4	520,470	—*	9,000,000
14. Series C.		22,500,000	4	900,000	(1915)†	22,500,000
15. Series D.		7,500,000	4	300,000	(1916)†	7,500,000
16. Series E.		17,250,000	4	690,000	(1932)†	17,250,000
		124,570,080		6,373,416	17,588,719	106,981,361
Railways						
17. Imperial Chinese Rly.	1899	2,300,000	5	169,626	402,500	1,897,500
18. Shansi Rly.	1902	1,600,000	5	80,000	(1931)†	1,600,000
19. Kaifeng-Honanfu Rly.	1903–7	1,640,000	5	82,000	(1915)†	1,640,000
20. Shanghai-Nanking Rly.	1904–7	2,900,000	5	145,000	—	2,900,000
21. Taokow-Tsinghwa Rly.	1905	700,000	5	35,000	(1935)†	700,000
22. Canton-Hankow Rly.	1905	1,100,000	4½	49,500	(1915)†	1,100,000
23. Canton-Kowloon Rly.	1907	1,500,000	5	75,000	(1920)†	1,500,000
24. Shanghai-Ningpo Rly.	1908	1,500,000	5	75,000	(1919)†	1,500,000
25. Tientsin-Pukow Rly.	1908–10	8,000,000	5	400,000	(1919)†	8,000,000
26. Peking-Hankow Rly.	1908	5,000,000	5	250,000	—	5,000,000
27. Ditto.	1910	450,000	7	31,500	(1916)†	450,000
28. Manchurian Rys. (Japanese)	1909	258,300	5	12,915	—	258,300
29. Hukwang Rys. ..	1911	6,000,000	5	300,000	—	6,000,000
		32,948,300		1,705,541	402,500	32,545,800
Total Liabilities ..		157,518,380		8,078,957	17,991,219	139,527,161

* Redemption to begin 1911, but delayed by Revolution.   † Redemption to begin.

APPENDIX B

A FEW typical instances are given below, showing the nature of the cases which come before the foreign Courts in China, and the way they are dealt with.

BRITISH SUPREME COURT

SHANGHAI, *May 21st*, 1906.

Before SIR HAVILLAND DE SAUSMAREZ, *Judge*

A. PAVLOW v. BARON WARD

This was an adjourned rehearing with regard to the defendant's set-off of Tls.40,000.

Mr. L. E. P. Jones appeared for the plaintiff, and Mr. A. S. P. White-Cooper for the defendant.

Mr. Jones said that at the last hearing the Court had asked him for an assurance that there was another Court in Shanghai which was competent to deal with Baron Ward's claim against Mr. Pavlow in the event of this Court dismissing it ; and on the strength of the correspondence which he had filed counsel was now able to give the assurance that the Russian Consular Court had the necessary jurisdiction in the case.

Mr. White-Cooper said he had not yet any evidence available, and asked for the hearing to be adjourned till June 15th. The Tls.40,000 had been retained by Mr. Kristensen ; it had never been in the hands of Baron Ward.

His Lordship said the state of the case was that there would have to be some issue determining the amount to be set off. It had been held that the plaintiff was entitled to set off something, but the amount had not been ascertained. A new trial was to be had as to the propriety of the sum of Tls.40,000. At the trial before the full Court the Assistant Judge said : " I therefore agree there ought to be a new trial as to this issue, which I would frame somewhat as follows : ' What is the proper sum to be set off in respect of the Edendale transaction ? ' " Then, his Lordship supposed, the order was drawn up.

Mr. Jones said that the defendant had had ample opportunity afforded him of coming to the Court and proving his claim. He had failed to do that, and counsel applied that that claim be dismissed, that the order be amended accordingly, and Baron Ward be now left to take such steps as he thought fit against Mr. Pavlow in the Russian Court.

His Lordship said he had considered the matter very carefully, and what he would do would be this : grant an adjournment until June 15th and fix that date peremptorily so that, in the event of the defendant not appearing to substantiate his defence, he would immediately fail, and the judgment, as modified by the order of November 16th, 1905, and the order of the Full Court would stand. As regarded this particular claim something had been said by Mr. Jones as to its nature. His Lordship had looked very carefully through the record of the case and also the report, and had been unable to find that it had been seriously argued at any time that this was a counter-claim and not a set-off. At the same time, looking at the Order in Council, Article 151(3), " Cross-action.—A counterclaim shall not be brought in the Court against a plaintiff being a foreigner," his Lordship felt clearly, from what had occurred, that the plaintiff in this case did not consent to a counter-claim being brought against him in that Court ; and it was perfectly evident to his Lordship's mind, on the terms of the Order, that if he did adjudicate on a counter-claim which was not properly before the Court the Court would be exercising jurisdiction which it did not possess, and therefore any judgment which might be passed in the matter would be necessarily void, or could be attacked and easily upset. He thought therefore that if it was made to appear to him, either at once or on June 15th, that this was a counter-claim and not a set-off, then he ought not to exercise jurisdiction. If, however, it should prove to be a set-off on argument, then it seemed to him that would substantiate the defence, and the Order in Council did not modify the right in any way to raise such a defence as a set-off. In this particular case, the proceedings had gone on so long and had so nearly reached an end, and the findings of the jury were very explicit now that they had been dealt with in the judgment of the Full Court, that he thought clearly he ought to entertain this set-off if it proved to be a set-off and not a counter-claim. Therefore he would grant an adjournment until June 15th, and the case would be set down peremptorily for that date ; but in the meantime, or at the trial, if plaintiff's counsel chose to move that this Court did not entertain this claim on the ground that it had no jurisdiction to do so, he would entertain the motion. He had felt it necessary to say this about the counter-claim and the set-off because he did not want it to be thought that he was assuming jurisdiction which ought properly to be exercised by the Russian Consular Court, but he felt that he was bound by the statute ; if he was wrong, of course there was occasion for an appeal, and if the Russian authorities were not satisfied with the judgment, of course, after it had been reviewed by the Privy Council, they could move for a new Order in Council.

The Court then rose.

SHANGHAI, *May 3rd*, 19c6.

Before SIR HAVILLAND DE SAUSMAREZ, *Judge*

JOSEPH JOHN GILMORE *v.* HENRY BENNERTZ

The hearing of this case was concluded. Mr. W. N. Symonds appeared for the plaintiff and Mr. Loftus E. P. Jones for the defendant.

Mr. Jones said the only other evidence which he would like to put before the Court was a copy of the judgment which was given in the case against Mr. Bennertz in which Tsau was plaintiff. The case was heard before the Consular Court at Changsha. Counsel also had a copy of the claim made by Mr. Bennertz upon which this Tls.5,200 was paid ; also a letter from Mr. Fraser, British Consul-General at Hankow, with regard to that claim.

Defendant was recalled. Witness put in a claim for an indemnity, and the document produced was a despatch he received from Mr. Fraser in relation to the matter. (Counsel read the despatch to show that there were no profits contemplated in this indemnity ; it was solely made up of Tls.400 a month compensation.) Witness said at the time Mr. Gilmore left Changsha for Hankow the liabilities of the business exceeded Tls.5,200 ; and at the time the indemnity was received the liabilities exceeded Tls.5,200.

Mr. Symonds put in a letter written by Mr. Woo to Mr. Gilmore dated April 20th, 1906, in which he said the matter was -setted between Bennertz and Gilmore before the latter left for Hankow. Woo proceeded to relate the understanding which he said was come to.

Witness, in reply to Mr. Symonds, said he was not satisfied with an indemnity of Tls.5,200. The Tls.25,000 was not the rest of the indemnity.

Mr. Symonds produced a statement in Mr. Giles's hand-writing of the payments witness had made out of the Tls.25,000 up to February 15th, 1906. Counsel pointed out that according to this statement there was a balance of nearly Ts.1,700. What had witness done with that ?

Defendant said the Tls.1,700 had been spent in meeting expenses of liquidation of Chinese debts in Changsha. There was still a small balance which he had been using to pay his expenses in Shanghai since March.

Mr. Jones and Mr. Symonds then briefly addressed his Lordship on the case.

JUDGMENT

His Lordship proceeded to deliver judgment as follows :

The dispute in this case has arisen out of an enterprise undertaken by the parties on the opening of the port—I call it a port so as not to use a compromising word with regard to the city, or fu, or whatever it might have been—of Changsha, for foreign trade. Up to this time, or immediately preceding this time, the parties were carrying on business at Hankow. The plaintiff thought there might be an opening and he went up to Changsha to look about him, and in consequence of his negotiations there he thought an opportunity occurred of starting a business, and he in consequence communicated with the firm of Bennertz & Esternau, with whom he appears to have been in communication, in Hankow. The details of what happened do not seem to me to very much affect the matter, but the result of it all was that the plaintiff remained in Changsha and the defendant came up, and they did in fact start business. But previous to that certain negotiations were entered into and a company was sketched. I think that is about all that happened as regards that company. It was sketched out, and certain steps no doubt were taken to fill in the details of the sketch, but I do not think they ever amounted to enough to give that company any real consistency. The consequence is that where I find a reference to the action of the company in Changsha I look upon it as simply indicating the business to be carried on by these people in the company, and who were realities, and who continued to be connected with the trade name. There were certain Chinese, but they one after another fell out, and in the end the two parties to this action were the only two people who can be described as people having anything to do with this company, and they do appear to have carried on business under the name of Bennertz & Co. and the Chinese hong name of Yu Hung-tih. That is the name which continued throughout, and it appears to exist still. Difficulties arose, and I do not see that it makes any difference to the present action as to whether these difficulties arose through the nature of things or from personal objection to the defendant on the part of the Chinese, as suggested by the plaintiff. From whatever source they did arise, the business did not flourish, and after about a year things were so bad that the plaintiff left Changsha because he thought it was useless to go on, and he returned to Hankow. A claim was later made for the intervention of the British authorities in Peking, and they did intervene, with the result that payment of Tls.5,200 was made. I think it is quite clear from Mr. Fraser's letter, which was put in, how that sum was arrived at and the purpose for which it was paid. It was to be, shortly, for compensation for disturbance ; and the person who had approached the British authorities was the defendant in this action, and, therefore, naturally it was to him that the communications of the British Consul-General at Hankow were addressed. The terms of the communications between the British Consul and Mr. Bennertz would, of course, in no way affect any liability which Mr. Bennertz was under to third parties —that is to say, parties other than himself and the British government—in the distribution of this sum. That appears to be the way the Tls.5,200 was paid. As regards the various sums which were from time to time expended in this business, I am unable to find that there was any capital found by either of the parties ; I think they each managed to scrape along as best they could in Changsha, paying their own expenses and hoping things would improve. Unfortunately they did not. Then comes the 29th of June, when there was an interview ; when the plaintiff decided that, as he had something definite to go to at Hankow and nothing definite to remain for at Changsha, he had better go to Hankow. On the evidence before me I have come to the conclusion that these two parties did do business in partnership from the date of this contract, namely July 4th, 1904, down to June 29th, 1905, and that on that date the partnership was dissolved by mutual consent. I will finish the story first, before I come to the terms of that partnership. I think that after that the business was carried on by Mr. Bennertz alone. He came down to Shanghai to see what he could do ; the whole of the responsibility was upon him ; he was the only person looked to by the Chinese authorities in Changsha ; and the plaintiff does not appear to have taken any steps with respect to the business, and except with regard to a loan on one occasion—which amounted to very little—he does not appear to have done anything with reference to this partnership or the affairs of the defendant. Unfortunately things did not improve. Mr. Bennertz did not seem to get on any better with the Chinese than before, and Changsha seems to have opened its doors to foreign trade in an extremely reluctant manner. The end of it was that Mr. Bennertz appeared at Changsha with a considerable amount of goods which he had been able to secure in Shanghai and things had to be finally settled up. The result was that an agreement came to be made between Mr. Bennertz and the Chinese in which the sum of Tls.25,000 was paid for the stock-in-trade which he had there, and various other things which are enumerated in this agreement, and he was to clear out—all connection between him and Changsha was to cease. I consider this agreement was made personally between the Chinese and Mr. Bennertz—not Bennertz & Co., but Mr. Bennertz himself and the parties in Changsha who paid him the Tls.25,000. I need not go into the different terms of this agreement, but I think what I have already stated, and the document itself will enable any one who comes to take the accounts to see how the money should be applied. I think there is only one other thing. I think that the Tls.25,000 was intended to cover not only the debts which Mr. Bennertz himself had contracted in Changsha, both before and after the time that this partnership was dissolved, but I think it also was intended to clear up any debts which had been contracted, and which might still be outstanding to the partnership while it existed. Therefore, assuming for the moment that the Tls.25,000 was more than enough to cover all claims, then I think the Tls.25,000 should be applied in wiping them all out, and any balance of the Tls.25,000 would have to be considered as belonging to Mr. Bennertz, subject to any contracts which he might have with other parties. The Tls.5,200 stand in a different position. Assuming, as I say, that the Tls.25,000 was sufficient, that Tls.5,200 definite compensation would remain to be divided between the two parties.

Now as to the terms of the contract. They appear to me to be embodied in this agreement of July 4th, 1904, in so far as they were at that time put into force. Mr. Gilmore was so far as was possible made a partner in the firm of Bennertz & Co. As a matter of fact, that firm never having come seriously into existence, the fact that he was made a partner in it did not give him any claim, because Bennertz & Co. having no property, there was nothing for him to have a claim to. But the partners —the plaintiff and the defendant—did carry on business under the form of Bennertz & Co., and, from all the documents before

me, there is no doubt they were carrying on business in partnership. There is or there might be, in consequence of this sum
for disturbance, something to be divided, and it will be divided
on the terms on which the partners agreed to trade. We have
the definite statement here that of whatever profit Henry
Bennertz touched, he should pay 25 per cent. to the plaintiff.
There is the suggestion that an agreement was come to on
June 29th that the sum of one-third instead of one-quarter should
be paid to Mr. Gilmore out of this sum paid as indemnity, but
there appeared to be the stipulation that Tls.3,500 should first
be paid to the Chinese. There are various other matters which
certainly are somewhat complicated, and which I should expect
to find reduced to writing. We have the version of it given by
the plaintiff, which no doubt represents his own view, and there
is on the other hand a denial of it by the defendant, and I cannot
come, on the evidence before me, to the conclusion that the
original agreement of one-quarter of the profits was varied by
anything that took place on that occasion. It will have to be
ascertained what accounts come under this exhibit " Q "—the
deed of January 30th, this year, by which the Tls.25,000 was paid.
I think this includes all debts due by the partnership, as well as
by the defendant, to the people who are enumerated in this
deed. There are, for instance, the Chinese in Changsha, and the
firms in Shanghai, and there are certain others. I will take
for instance the sum of Tls.64, which is a small sum due to
Messrs. Hall & Holtz in Hankow, and this probably would not
come under that. I give that as an example, but I do not
decide that. This is a point which I shall have to take in
Chambers, or must be considered by whoever takes the account.
I mention that as it is a small sum and it does not matter much
whichever way it goes. If the Tls.25,000 is not sufficient, then
it will have to be divided, the various sums will have to be
paid, so far as I can see, pro rata, and if after that there are
partnership debts—debts between July 4th, 1904, and June 29th,
1905—then, of course, these will have to be liquidated out of
the Tls.5,200. I think if there is any balance on the Tls.25,000
—I do not think there is the least likelihood that there will
be—then the matter will have to be referred to me again as to
its division. It is not quite clear now, and I should like to hear
counsel more fully as to what ought to happen to any balance
of the Tls.25,000. I think, as it was to cover everything, the
plaintiff is entitled to a certain amount. I do not think he is
entitled to a quarter, but I think he is entitled to any amount
which might be assessed as sufficient and proper. I think that

direction is sufficient. The accounts may be so reduced that they might come before me in Chambers, and I might be able to come to a decision at less expense to the parties and in a very short time, because I know about it ; and if it is referred to anybody else there will be some question of nicety as to some of these sums, and they would probably have to be sent back to me for direction. I would like to hear counsel further especially in the case of Tsau's debt. I shall want to know a little more about that, but so far as I can see this money which has been expended by Mr. Bennertz in purchasing goods for the trading of his company will have to be paid out of this Tls.25,000. If it is proved that this amount for provisions is a purely personal debt in no way connected with the company, it ought not to be set off against the Tls.25,000 ; but at the same time from what I can see, and in looking at the contents of the agreement and the way in which the business was carried on, the Tls.25,000 was meant to cover Tsau's debt. Still, at the same time, I do not think I have anything before me which would make me say definitely whether it ought to be paid. I have given my direction, and I think that the outstanding points may be so reduced that I can come to a conclusion very shortly.

Mr. Symonds, on behalf of his client, said he would be pleased to refer the matters of account to his Lordship.

His Lordship—You will have to get the accounts in order first. In my judgment, I really say what is wanted is that Mr. Bennertz should show how the Tls.25,000 has been spent, and if he has gone beyond that to pay the debts of the firm, he will have to show that the Tls.5,200 has been expended on the remaining debts of the partnership.

Mr. Jones asked his Lordship if he would deal with the question of costs at this time.

His Lordship—I will deal with that when I deal with the accounts. If I find the money substantially misapplied by Mr. Bennertz, he will have to pay costs ; but on the other hand, if the inquiry was uselessly raised, it will be the other way.

His Lordship then rose.

SHANGHAI, *December 3rd*, 1906

Before MR. F. S. A. BOURNE, *Assistant Judge*

DIEDERICHSEN JEBSEN & CO. *v.* THE CHINESE ENGINEERING AND MINING CO., LTD.

Mr. J. H. Teesdale appeared for the plaintiffs and Mr. A. S. P. White-Cooper for the defendants, Mr. Loftus E. Jones watched the case on behalf of the Holland China Trading Co., interested parties.

Mr. Teesdale said that his Lordship was not sitting when counsel made his application, last Saturday week, for an injunction restraining the defendant company from parting with the possession of certain cargo stored at their wharf and of the shipping documents relating to it. The injunction was granted, and counsel now merely made application for pleadings. The case would probably be rather complicated, and several legal points were likely to be involved. It was possible that evidence would have to be given on questions of law—not necessarily British law—which would have to be gone into thoroughly, so that he applied that pleadings should be delivered in the usual way, and that his Lordship should fix a date on which he had to deliver his statement of claim.

Mr. White-Cooper, in reply to his Lordship, said he had nothing to say. The defendants simply held the goods as warehousemen, and if the plaintiffs set up a better title to them than the Holland China Trading Co., they would deliver to them. At present the defendants had no interest in the subject-matter of the goods except as warehousemen.

His Lordship—And you, Mr. White-Cooper, have an undertaking that any costs you may be put to will be paid by the plaintiffs ?

Mr. White-Cooper—Yes.

His Lordship—Won't this case have to be fought out in another Court ?

Mr. White-Cooper—As far as one can see, the contract would appear to be governed by Dutch Law.

His Lordship granted the application for pleadings, the statement of claim to be filed within fifteen days.

The Court then rose.

SHANGHAI, *September* 20th, 1906

Before SIR HAVILLAND DE SAUSMAREZ, *Judge*, AND MESSRS. T. GRAYSON (*foreman*), F. W. RAWSTHORNE, W. E. BLADES, T. H. W. CHARNLEY, G. W. NOEL, D. C. KERR, G. C. DEW V. H. LANNING, G. H. RENDALL, W. FLEMING INGLIS, JAMES JONES, AND G. R. BARRY (*Jurors*)

REX *v.* PETER SYDNEY HYNDMAN

Peter Sydney Hyndman, bookkeeper, was charged that on September 1st feloniously, wilfully, and of malice aforethought, he did kill and murder Harry Smith.

When formally charged, prisoner, in a low voice, pleaded
" not guilty."

*   *   *   *   *

Addressing the prisoner his Lordship said : Peter Sydney
Hyndman, you have been convicted of the crime of manslaughter.
The jury have taken, I am glad to say, a lenient view of your
conduct on this occasion. They thought that the provocation to
which you were subjected so wrought on your emotions and your
feelings that for the moment your will was suspended, and that
the intent which would be presumed from your acts did not exist.
At the same time I cannot help feeling that you were more
rash in this matter than you were justified in being. The case
of a husband who finds his wife whom he believes to be faithful
to him in a position of that kind is one which might excuse him
almost from receiving any punishment at all for taking such
sudden and violent vengeance on the man. I cannot feel that
you are in that position, and, though I do not consider your
crime one of great enormity, I must pass upon you a sentence
which will let the community know that the foolish and reckless
carrying of firearms is not to be encouraged, and that when a man
does put himself in the position in which you put yourself, he
must take the consequences of his own acts. I sentence you to be
kept in prison for eighteen calendar months with hard labour.

BRITISH POLICE COURT

SHANGHAI, *December 4th*, 1906

Before MR. G. W. KING, *Police Magistrate*

ASSAULT BY A SIKH CONSTABLE

HOW TO EVADE AN AGREEMENT

Dungah Singh, Indian P.C. 199, was charged with assaulting
and beating one Chang Ah-cum at No. 216, Fearon Road, at 5.15
p.m. on December 2nd.

Inspector Bourke prosecuted, and intimated to the Court
that the accused was on duty at the time the assault took place.

*   *   *   *   *

His Worship (addressing accused) said : I consider the
evidence given by the prosecution to be true ; that you did do
what you are said to have done. In an ordinary case, perhaps,
it would be meet to give you a fine only, because the assault is not
a grave one. I cannot overlook the fact that at the time you
were on duty, and from the fact that you were on duty and that
you did what you are accused of having done, I believe you

had ulterior motives ; that your desire was to get out of the Police Force. The evidence of the Jemadar seems to point to that too, and you yourself have made no effort to contradict his evidence. I have taken into consideration your past record, both as you claim to have been in the Cavalry and also in the Police, more especially in the Police. There has been no previous conviction against you, but in spite of that I must send you to prison. You were a policeman on duty in uniform, and you have disgraced your uniform ; you are put there to keep order, and you go and make disorder. You might attain your object of getting out of the Police—of course that does not lie with me—but you will first have to go to prison for one month with hard labour.

IN THE AMERICAN CONSULAR COURT FOR THE DISTRICT OF HANGCHOW

HANGCHOW, *March 15th*, 1906

Before FREDERICK D. CLOUD, ESQ., *American Vice-Consul-in-charge, Acting Judicially*, AND J. H. JUDSON, ESQ., AND J. STEINACHER, ESQ., *Associates*.

In the matter of SUN ZAI-LING, YEE TSUNG-LIEN, SUN YU-LING, *and* CHOW DING-HO, *Plaintiffs, v.* THE SOUTHERN METHO-DIST MISSION, AND THOMAS A. HEARN, AND EDWARD PILLEY, *Defendants.*

In this action A. S. P. White-Cooper, Esq., appeared for the plaintiffs, and F. M. Brooks, Esq., of the law firm of Andrews & Brooks, represented the defendants.

JUDGMENT

This is an action brought by certain Chinese citizens against the Southern Methodist Mission, an American institution, repre-sented by Thomas A. Hearn and Edward Pilley, of Huchow, to recover certain alleged temple lands which have been purchased by, and are now in the possession of, the Southern Methodist Mis-sion, in which the plaintiffs allege that the said mission is in wrongful possession of the said temple lands ; that as a result of repeated protests against such possession by the plaintiffs, the de-fendant mission, or certain representatives of the defendant mis-sion, entered into an agreement of compromise with the plaintiffs whereby, and according to the terms of which, certain lands were to be restored to plaintiffs on condition of, and in con-sideration of the said plaintiffs paying to the defendants the sum of Tls.2,000 ; that the plaintiffs have duly paid to the defendants the said consideration of Tls.2,000, which sum of money is still in the possession of, or under the control of the defendants, but that the said defendants have illegally, wrongfully, and in breach of the terms of the agreement, refused to abide by and carry out its terms and surrender the land agreed therein to be surrendered to the plaintiffs ; that by reason of the defendants' wrongful breach of this agreement, and by reason of the defendants' wrongful trespass on the said land, the plaintiffs have suffered damages through (1) the defendants' wrongful actions above mentioned ; (2) the deprivation of the said temple lands and trespass thereon ; (3) and the loss of Tls.2,000 ; and that the defendants had notice and well knew that the land in question belonged to the temple and could not lawfully be purchased by defendants.

Wherefore, it was the plaintiffs' prayer that the defendants be required to carry out the terms of the said compromise agreement, or that the defendants be ordered to forthwith vacate and give immediate possession of the land wrongfully inclosed ; that the defendants be ordered to pull down, forthwith, any buildings erected on the said land and to restore the land to its condition prior to such wrongful trespass ; that the defendants be ordered to pay the sum of Tls.1,000 as damage for such trespass, and in addition to return the sum of Tls.2,000 paid the defendants by the plaintiffs, and that defendants be ordered to pay the costs of this action.

In answer the defendants have admitted that the plaintiffs are Chinese subjects, but have specifically denied each and every other allegation of the plaintiffs. And answering further, the defendants allege that all of the land possessed and inclosed by the Southern Methodist Mission at Huchow was procured legally, and according to treaty rights between America and China ; that the plaintiffs well knew, while the defendants were acquiring the said land, of the facts, and purposes for which it was sought ; that the plaintiffs well knew of the purchase of said land, and of the improvements in progress on the same from time to time, but that the plaintiffs did not make any protest against such improvements while they were in progress ; that the alleged agreement referred to by the plaintiffs was never signed by the defendants but by parties who never had the right, nor the authority, directly or indirectly, either in fact or in law, to bind the defendants, and that when said agreement was presented to the defendants herein for their signatures, said defendants immediately repudiated the same and refused to sign it ; that the sum of Tls.1,000 or Tls.2,000 or any other sum of money had never been paid to them by the plaintiffs, or by any one else, but that certain Chinese officials had paid into the American Consulate certain moneys which were still subject to the order of the said officials ; and further, that the plaintiffs in this action well knew that defendants had legally acquired this land, and stood by, well knowing that defendants were improving the said land, and having made no protest during that time, were now bringing this action for the purpose of harassing and interfering with the work carried on by defendants to their damage in the sum of Tls.5,000.

Wherefore, it was the defendants' prayer that this action be dismissed with costs, and that defendants may recover damages against the plaintiffs in the sum of Tls.5,000.

The facts in this case, as established in Court, are quite clear. In the spring of 1902 the Southern Methodist Mission, through its representatives, the defendants in this action, made known to the proper local officials of Huchow their desire to purchase land within the city of Huchow for mission purposes. These representatives desired to purchase land in a certain portion of the city and made their desire known to the aforesaid officials. These officials, the Prefect and Magistrate, expressed the wish that the defendants select another tract of land, stating that the tract they had chosen was wanted by the officials and gentry of Huchow on which to build native schools. The said officials then pointed out a section of the city known as Hai Tao, as being largely unoccupied land, where the defendants were at liberty to acquire as much land as might be needed for the mission. The Prefect went so far as to delegate certain gentry to assist the mission in obtaining the land from the several owners, and in perfecting the titles thereto. Proclamations were issued by the Magistrate having jurisdiction over the land, announcing the fact that the mission wanted to purchase the land, and calling upon the owners thereof to come forward and negotiate with the defendants for the sale of their various tracts. Eventually a considerable tract of " waste land " was found which had no owners. The Magistrate was informed of the fact, who issued a proclamation stating that the mission desired to acquire this " waste land," and if there were any owners thereof they should come forward. And although these proclamations were posted for a period of two months, yet no one came forward as owners of the land, nor could any such owners be found. Thereupon the defendants purchased the land from the Magistrate himself. There was perfect satisfaction on all sides relative to this transaction, nor have the plaintiffs attempted to show that the Magistrate exceeded his authority in thus disposing of " waste lands," or that any one objected to his doing so. The Magistrate gave defendants a proper receipt for the consideration of the transaction, and published the facts relating to the sale to the people of Huchow by means of a special proclamation.

The defendants having obtained all the land desired for mission purposes, sent their title-deeds to the yâmen to be registered and stamped. The deeds remained in the yâmen, some five months, when they were returned to the defendants, having been properly registered and stamped. These various transactions also received the written approval of the various authorities concerned, including the Provincial Governor.

The acquisition of all this land by the defendants was not accomplished without long delays—something over a year's time being required for its completion. The negotiations were carried on openly, and the people of Huchow were made acquainted with the fact that the defendants were buying the land, through the medium of the Magistrate's proclamation ; this, the plaintiffs have not disputed. Nor does the evidence show that the people, or the gentry of Huchow, made or offered any protest against the acquisition of this land by the mission until after all the negotiations had been completed and the land so purchased had been inclosed by the defendants within a wall. Nor is there any evidence to show that in the acquisition of this land the defendants deviated, in the least, either from the letter or the spirit of the provisions of the treaty between the United States of America and China governing such matters.

As to the allegation of the plaintiffs that a portion or portions of the aforesaid land is Confucian temple land, the Court must hold that it is incumbent upon the said plaintiffs to show; by a preponderance of evidence, that such is the case ; but this the plaintiffs have failed to do.

The fact that the ruins of what the plaintiffs allege to be those of an ancient Confucian Library are characterised by numerous carvings of the Lotus flower, which is a characteristic emblem of Buddhism and of Buddhistic ornamentation ; that the said ruins, or foundation stones, are situated a considerable distance away, and in another ward, or division of the city, from the group of buildings recognised, and confirmed by the officially written topographies of Huchow, as constituting the Confucian temple property ; that the defendants have produced documentary and other evidence showing that the real site of the ancient Confucian Library (the Tsen Ching-ko) is not situated on any land now enclosed by, or in possession of the mission, but is entirely outside of, and is a considerable distance away from the property of the said mission, is sufficient evidence to convince the Court that the said Confucian Library site (Tsen Ching-ko) is not situated on the defendants' premises, and that none of the land now held by the defendants is Confucian temple land.

The plaintiffs have endeavoured to force upon the defendants the terms of an agreement of compromise, which agreement had been signed by certain representatives of the Southern Methodist Mission, whereby a portion of the mission's land was to be turned out of the defendants' enclosure. The facts are that one member of a committee of three members, appointed by the mission to deal with this matter, two of whom are the defendants in this action, signed this said agreement as indicating to the other two members his opinion of the case, and not in any manner as trying to bind the other two members to the agreement. However, when this agreement was presented to the defendants who were named therein as parties to the agreement, they refused to sign it, or to carry out its terms; and it has been shown by evidence that to do so would be grievously injurious to the plans and future work of the mission. And since the provincial officials have offered, upon their own motion, written testimony to the fact that the Tls.1,000 named as the consideration of this agreement, and that the Tls.1,000 presented to the mission for charitable purposes had been provided for by themselves, and does not, nor ever did in any manner belong to the plaintiffs, and the further fact that the defendants have never accepted or been in possession of this money, it is evident that plaintiffs are not entitled to bring action against the defendants for its recovery.

According to solemn compacts between China and the United States of America, the Southern Methodist Mission, as well as all other American missionary societies, have the right to purchase, or lease land in perpetuity, at Huchow, as well as at all other places within the Chinese Empire. And when they have obtained their land, and secured properly executed title-deeds, they are entitled to enjoy full and complete possession of all such land without annoyance or molestation of any nature.

The petition of the plaintiffs is hereby dismissed at plaintiffs' costs.

The defendants' prayer for damages is disallowed, as this Court has no jurisdiction to award damages against Chinese subjects, and leaves defendants to follow plaintiffs into a regularly constituted Chinese tribunal.

(Signed) FREDERICK D. CLOUD,
American Vice-Consul-in-Charge,
Acting Judicially.

J. STEINACHER, }
J. H. JUDSON, } Associates.

INQUEST

SHANGHAI, *December 7th, 1906*

Before MR. W. P. BOYD, *American Vice-Consul-General-in-Charge, Acting as Cuban Coroner*

A SAD ENDING

An inquest was opened at 2.30 p.m. yesterday at No. 2, North Honan Road, to inquire into the circumstances attending the death of Miss Loura Leslig, *alias* Cossette Denvers, a Cuban subject, aged thirty-two years, who died in bed at her residence, between the hours of 10.30 and 11.30 p.m., the 5th inst., from laudanum poisoning.

* * * * *

The Coroner brought in a verdict that deceased came to her death on December 5th, 1906, between the hours of 10.30 and 11.30 p.m., by taking an overdose of laudanum, self-administered, with suicidal intent.

GERMAN CONSULAR COURT

SHANGHAI, *December 7th, 1906*

Before MR. L. HEINTZE, *Vice-Consul*

THE MUZZLING ORDER

V. Blinkman, No. 72, Range Road, was charged with allowing his dog to be at large unmuzzled on the Range Road on the 30th ultimo, contrary to Municipal Regulations.

Inspector Bourke stated the nature of the charge.

Defendant was fined $3 or in default one day's detention.

JAPANESE CONSULAR COURT

SHANGHAI, *December 7th, 1906*

Before MR. D. YAMAMOTO, *Police Magistrate*

BREAKING THE RULES

One Nejita was charged with keeping a house of entertainment, to wit, a shooting gallery, at No. 513, Miller Road, without a license and contrary to Municipal Regulations.

30

Inspector Bourke stated the nature of the offence.
Accused was severely cautioned and ordered to close the place at once.

SHANGHAI, *December 4th*, 1906
Before MR. D. YAMAMOTO, *Police Magistrate*

JACK ASHORE

A festive sailor from the N.Y.K. steamer *Chiyoda Maru*, named M. Yasuda, was charged with having been drunk and disorderly on the Broadway, and damaging property to the extent of 50 cents, about 10 p.m., the 3rd inst.

Inspector Bourke related the nature of the charge.

Tsang Zen-fah, the complainant, gave evidence of the accused having been drunk and doing damage to witness's goods.

Accused was fined $3 and ordered to pay the amount of damage done.

RUSSIAN CONSULAR COURT

SHANGHAI, *December 3rd*, 1906
Before MR. C. KLEIMENOW, *Consul-General*

ALLEGED ARSON

A. M. Silkiss was charged on a Russian Consular warrant with having feloniously and wilfully set fire to his premises and dwelling-house known as the Tivoli Hotel at Nos. 9 & 10, Boone Road, about 11.30 p.m., December 1st, 1906, with intent to secure insurance money thereon, and thereby endangering life and property.

Inspector Bourke appeared to prosecute.

Extensive evidence was taken, but, the press not being admitted, we are not able to give a report of the proceedings.

SHANGHAI, *December 7th*, 1906
Before MR. C. KLEIMENOW, *Consul-General*

ALLEGED ARSON

A. M. Silkiss was brought up on remand charged on a Russian Consular warrant with having feloniously and wilfully set fire to his premises and dwelling-house known as the Tivoli Hotel, at Nos. 9 & 10, Boone Road, about 11.30 p.m., December 1st, 1906, with intent to secure insurance money thereon, and thereby endangering life and property.

Det. Insp. McDowell prosecuted on behalf of the police.

On the Court resuming this morning, the evidence was concluded, and his Honour disposed of the case as follows : This Court having no power to deal with a case of this nature, the Court has decided to submit the whole of the evidence, together with the plans of the premises in question, to the Supreme Court at Vladivostock. In the meantime the prisoner would be released on depositing the sum of Tls.8,000, including diamonds, jewellery, etc., as well as being bound over in the sum of $4,000 in two sureties of $2,000 each.

SHANGHAI, *December 12th,* 1906

Before MR. L. BRODIANSKY, *Vice-Consul*

WHO'S WHO ?

Alec Alexander, No. 56, Broadway, arrested on a Russian Consular warrant, was charged with being a pimp, and living and trafficking on the proceeds of prostitution.

Inspector McDowell appeared to prosecute on behalf of the police.

Accused was examined at some length, and not being able to produce any papers or satisfactory evidence that he was a Russian subject, the Court refused to recognise him or assume any responsibility over him.

The accused was next taken to H.B.M.'s Police Court, where he was also refused recognition.

Accused was therefore taken back to the Station, where he was locked up, pending a decision as to what should be done with him. Later in the day accused was taken to the Mixed Court, where he was remanded till Friday, the 14th inst.

Alec Alexander, No. 56, Broadway, who was arrested on a Russian Consular warrant a few days ago, was charged at the Mixed Court to-day, the court room being cleared and the case tried in camera, with being a pimp and living and trafficking on the proceeds of prostitution. Inspector McDowell appeared to prosecute on behalf of the police. The Inspector made a statement as to how the case was first brought to his notice. An Englishwoman, who had been decoyed out to the Far East by the accused by false promises, gave evidence as to how she came out and became an inmate of a house of ill fame. Accused was eventually sentenced to fourteen days' imprisonment and to be afterwards deported from Shanghai.

APPENDIX C

THE following letter gives the attitude of the British government in respect to intervention by missionaries in the interior on behalf of their Chinese converts.

MISSIONARIES AND CHINESE OFFICIALS

To the Editor of the " North China Daily News "

SIR,—Under instructions from H.M. Minister at Peking I beg to hand you herewith for publication copy of a circular dated August 31st, 1903, addressed by Sir E. Satow to H.M. Consular Officers in China.

I am, etc.,
PELHAM WARREN,
Consul-General.

October 31*st*, 1906.

CIRCULAR

H.B.M. LEGATION,
PEKING, *August* 31*st*, 1903.

SIR,—Cases have come to my notice in which missionaries have addressed themselves directly to Chinese officials, either verbally or in writing, on behalf of their Chinese converts, instead of acting through the proper channel, which is one of H.M. Consuls or the head of H.M. Legation.

Such intervention I presume would be defended on the ground that some action has been taken in regard to the convert which is in violation of Article VIII. of the Treaty of Tientsin.

It is necessary, however, to point out that missionaries are not accredited agents of the British government for the enforcement of the Treaty, and Article VIII. was not intended to confer upon missionaries any right of intervention on behalf of native Christians.

I do not see any objection to a missionary addressing the local Chinese authorities directly on any matter affecting himself

468

personally, such as for instance a robbery that has been committed at his house, or any similar private affair.

If, however, a missionary has to complain on behalf of himself that his teaching is interfered with, or that a Chinese preacher or convert has been interfered with or persecuted, his proper course is to lay the facts before the Consul of the district in which he resides, who after due examination will make such representations to the Chinese authorities as the case may require.

His Majesty's Consuls are not authorised to delegate their duties in this respect to missionaries.

I have reason to know that this view is shared by the managing bodies of British Protestant Missionary Societies who carry on Mission work in China, and I understand that it is accepted and acted on by most of the missionary bodies in China.

The fact that a missionary or the convert on whose behalf a complaint is made resides at a distance from one of H.M. Consuls is not sufficient reason for the missionary taking upon himself the duty of the Consul, and his intervention could only be justified when there was imminent danger of an extreme character threatening the safety of converts.

I have accordingly to request you to act upon what is laid down in this Circular, and to acquaint missionaries with its contents whenever it seems likely to be departed from.

I am persuaded that if missionaries uniformly refrain from direct intervention on behalf of native Christians, and confine their action to representing to H.M. Consuls cases of actual persecution, such a course will redound to the preservation of peace between converts and non-converts, and to the spread of a genuine Christianity among the people of China.

I am, etc.,

(Signed) ERNEST SATOW.

APPENDIX D

CLAN fights between Catholic and Protestant converts are common in Chekiang, not uncommon in Kwangtung, and not unknown in other provinces. One such fight broke out in November 1906 at Haimen, in Chekiang, regarding which an unbiassed Chinese informed me that the people of Haimen are notorious for piracy and turbulence, that generally in these disputes both Protestants and Catholics are equally to blame. and that on this occasion the Catholics were the aggressors. The two partisan versions of the occurrence are given below.

THE PROTESTANT VERSION

RESCUE OF PROTESTANTS

TAI-CHOW FU, CHEH, *November 13th*, 1906.

For the past few days we have been living in great suspense. The little Protestant community at Haimen, surrounded by hundreds of Roman Catholic robbers who were under the command of the native priest Nyun, was in imminent danger of being massacred. The foreign priests resident at Haimen seemed to be in entire sympathy with the native priest, and the Mandarins felt themselves unable to protect the Protestants. At the beginning of the attack on Friday the Protestant preacher applied to the Military Mandarin for an escort to take the Protestants to Tai-chow Fu, but the Chen-tai replied that it was not necessary for them to go, as he was quite able to protect them there. The request was then made for a few soldiers to come inside the Protestant compound, but this also was refused.

Soon the town was at the mercy of the Roman Catholic army, variously estimated at 800 to 2,000 strong, and the Mandarins became powerless to deal with them. The Tong-ling was unhorsed, made a prisoner, and kept in the Roman Catholic compound. Another military officer was beaten by one of the priests, and the Major-General had to go in person to obtain their liberation. He did this by promising to behead one of the military officers who had been active against the robbers, and to pay $3,000 to the Roman Catholics for rifles taken from the robbers by order of the Tong-ling. Houses and shops belonging to Protestants were pillaged, and passengers to and from the boats were robbed. A Protestant inquirer was caught and held for ransom. He was told that if he did not furnish 100 jars of Chinese wine he would be killed. He gave them 90 jars and was allowed to escape. Some of the members and inquirers had narrow escapes from being shot. The son of an inquirer was shot through the thigh, and one of the robbers was accidentally shot dead by another Roman Catholic.

On Saturday evening the Mandarins sent word to the Protestants that they could not protect them, but would send an armed escort to take them to Tai-chow city. A fleet of five gunboats sailed with them from Haimen. At a point, 40 li from Haimen, two of the gunboats returned, leaving three boats to carry the refugees the remaining 80 li to Tai-chow city.

In company with two foreign missionaries and the Mandarin under whose escort they had travelled, they went to visit the Prefect, who said that the Protestants had shown themselves superior to the Roman Catholics, and had acted splendidly in the great trouble caused by the Roman Catholics. He also said they must not return to Haimen until the trouble was over.

Testimony of the Protestant member whose shop was pillaged by an armed Roman Catholic band :

" I was upstairs above the shop when the armed band entered my shop. My assistant told them I was upstairs. They called me, and I asked who they were. They said, ' Come down and see.' I looked out and saw the men armed with long pistols and big knives, and became alarmed. I shouted, ' I will come down at once,' and then ran out at the back door and hid in a neighbour's house. Here I remained for an hour or so, until after they had pillaged my shop ; then the Chen-tai passed, and I went out and asked him for protection. He sent seven or eight soldiers to escort me to the Protestant compound. Here I remained from Friday till Sunday morning. The Protestant compound was surrounded by a band led by Li Ti-song. This man struck the Tong-ling when he rode up to disperse the mob, upon which the Tong-ling proceeded to the R.C. compound, where he was detained to make him promise $3,000 to pay for rifles which had been taken from some of the Roman Catholic robbers by his order. The Roman Catholics also demanded execution of an officer who had acted under the Tong-ling's orders. The Tong-ling was eventually rescued by the Chen-tai.

" On Saturday, at 5 p.m., the Chen-tai said we must leave Haimen, as he could not protect us here, and he would provide an escort to take us to Tai-chow city. About an hour later we all were escorted to gunboats, but the head-wind was so strong that the boats could not start, and most of us returned to the Protestant compound. My wife and little children went to hide in a neighbour's house.

" On Sunday morning, at 10 o'clock, those of us in the Protestant compound were again escorted by the Chen-tai and his soldiers to three gunboats. We then sailed for the city, and were escorted by two other gunboats for 40 li, as it was feared that the Roman Catholics might follow and attack us. We all arrived safely at Tai-chow city on the following day—Monday."

Testimony of a Mandarin who escorted a party of the refugee Protestants from Haimen to this city :

In reply to my questions he said he lives in Haimen. He estimates the number of the attacking party of Roman Catholics at about 1,000, but says it is very difficult to form an exact estimate. They came in squads, and mostly belong to the south of Haimen. Each squad is under a leader. The larger half of them have not rifles but carry clubs. The others have breech- and muzzle-loading rifles and pistols and swords. They were called up by the R.C. priest Nyun. Each squad has its own commissariat.

" The first I heard of them was on Friday morning, November 9th, when they commenced looting Protestant houses and shops. The town of Haimen was soon in terror and all the shops were closed. The following morning the Protestant church premises were surrounded by the Roman Catholics. The Tong-ling came along on horseback, and one of the Romanists pointed his rifle at him. This enraged the Tong-ling, who ordered his men to seize the rifles. Twenty or thirty rifles were seized and two Romanists were taken prisoners. The Tong-ling then rode towards the west gate, and in passing the premises of the R.C. church he was stopped and invited to enter. He did so, and the gates were at once shut and he was made a prisoner. Two of his men were also made prisoners. Word was at once carried to the Chen-tai, who came and had him liberated. The Roman Catholics demanded the liberation of their two men who were apprehended, and they were set free. The government troops stationed at Haimen number 120 regulars under the Chen-tai, and about three hundred Militia under the Tong-ling, but these Mandarins are afraid to harm the Roman Catholics because the R.C. bishop would accuse them to the Provincial Governor (Fu-tai) and they would lose their rank, ' kong-ming.' "

The Provincial Governor (Fu-tai) having wired to settle the combatants without violence, the military stored their rifles and went about unarmed. All the shooting was done by Romanists, who accidentally shot one of their own men. Many of the Roman Catholics assembled under arms are well-known robbers.

The following is a diary showing the principal events that occurred in connection with the Roman Catholic attack at Haimen.

Friday, November 9th

Hundreds of armed men, under the command of the native Roman Catholic priest Nyun, suddenly appeared in the streets of Haimen. They looted the houses and shops of Protestants. The owners fled to the Protestant compound. The Protestants asked for an escort to Tai-chow city, but the Military Mandarin said they would protect them in Haimen. The son of a Protestant inquirer was shot through the thigh. The Protestant preacher sent an open note by a messenger to the foreign missionaries here. It is as follows : " Eight hundred Roman Catholic soldiers armed with rifles and swords have just pillaged the houses and shops of Christians (names given) and are building the wall. The Military Mandarin is powerless to restrain them. I do not know about killed and wounded. We hope you will rescue us quickly. "

Upon the arrival of this messenger, at 5 p.m. on Friday, a telegram was sent to C.I.M., Shanghai, and to British Consul, Ningpo, as follows : " Hundreds armed Romanists attacked Haimen Protestants. Killed, wounded, unknown. Houses pillaged. Tidal wall occupied." Foreign missionaries visited Prefect, and found that he already knew the situation, and that the District Magistrate and two Deputies from the Prefect were preparing to start for Haimen. It was learned that the Major-General (Chen-tai) at Haimen had previously warned the city Magistrate of a Roman Catholic plot to attack the Protestants on the following day—Saturday. Evidently, therefore, the attack began a day sooner than the Major-General expected. The Protestant city pastor left for Haimen in company with the returning messenger.

Saturday, 10th

The Protestant pastor arrived at Ko-ts, three miles from Haimen, and was furnished with an escort of eight soldiers to guard him to Haimen. The escort deserted him before he reached Haimen, but the chair-bearers carried him safely into the Protestant compound.

He learned that the Governor (Fu-tai) had ordered the military to disperse the Romanists without violence. The soldiers were therefore without arms. At 4.15 in the afternoon he succeeded with considerable risk in sending off a telegram, which we received in this city about 5 o'clock. It is as follows : " This morning the robbers surrounded the Protestant compound twice. Chen-tai is unable to restrain them." At 5.30 a telegram was sent to the British Consul, Ningpo, as follows :—" Haimen telegram says premises still surrounded. Mandarins powerless." At 8 p.m. received a telegram from British Consul, Ningpo —" You are on no account to take part in lawless violence. Do your best to restrain your converts. Similar message is being sent to priest by bishop." Meantime events were thickening at Haimen.

Immediately after the telegram was dispatched at 4.15 the Romanists started a desultory fire, and the General commanding the Militia (Tong-ling) rode along to stop them. A robber pointed his rifle at the Tong-ling, who with his men were unarmed. The Tong-ling ordered one of his officers to seize the rifles and swords of this squad. Twenty-seven rifles and swords were seized. The robber chief, Li Ti-song, retaliated by bringing up more men and seizing five of the Tong-ling's men. The Tong-ling rode off in the direction of the Roman Catholic compound to complain to Priest Nyun, the Commander-in-Chief of the Roman Catholic forces. Nyun got him inside the Roman Catholic premises, made him prisoner, demanded $3,000 for the rifles and swords his men had captured, and the execution of the military officer who had captured them. The Romanists accidentally shot one of their own men dead.

About 5 p.m. the Chen-tai went to the Protestant compound and said he could not guarantee protection any longer, but would furnish an escort to take all the Protestants to Tai-chow city. He then went to the R.C. compound and secured the liberation of the Tong-ling.

About 6.30 p.m., under a military escort, the Protestants were taken to gunboats, but a tempest was blowing and the boats could not start. Some of the refugees remained on the boats, women and little children hid in neighbours' houses, and most of the men returned to the Protestant compound for the night.

Sunday, 11th

At 10 a.m. the Protestant refugees were escorted by the Chen-tai and soldiers to the three gunboats, which sailed for Tai-chow city, 40 miles distant. Other two gunboats were sent as an additional escort for 10 miles, as it was feared that the robbers might follow in boats. When half-way to Tai-chow city, a party of Roman Catholics were sighted, but no attack was made.

5 p.m. People arriving at the city by steam launch from Haimen reported passing Protestant refugees in three gunboats about fifteen miles below the city.

Monday, 12th

9 a.m. First party of refugees arrived safely. Praise God. They report that others are on the way and that the Protestant community of Haimen will probably all be here about noon to-day, as they all sailed together on Sunday morning from Haimen.

Telegram from British Consul, dated Ningpo, Monday, 10 a.m.: " Catholics state that they have dispersed out Protestants still assembled together with aggressive intentions. Is this true ? " A reply was sent to the British Consul from Tai-chow Fu at 11 o'clock as follows : " Protestant community officially sent here under escort. Left Haimen Sunday morning. Unable to protect there. Premises in charge of Chen-tai."

Last of the three gunboat parties arrived about noon. We are informed that a body of Romanists left this city in answer to a telgram from Haimen on Saturday night to attack refugees *en route*. They had lacked courage at sight of the gunboats. The Romanists say they must have the life of the Protestant preacher.

2 p.m. All the refugees except the women and children visited the Prefect, who said they had shown themselves superior to the Roman Catholics, and that they must stay here till he saw it safe for them to return to their homes.

8 p.m. An inquirer arrived from Haimen said the R.C.'s had caught him, and demanded 100 jars of wine as ransom for his life. He managed to get 90 jars of wine for them, and they allowed him to escape. He says a large force of armed men from the north bank of the river was crossing to join the Roman Catholic army to-day.

Thursday, 13th

8.30 a.m. A Thanksgiving Service to God for the escape of the refugees was held in the China Inland Mission Chapel. Psalms 37 and 124 were read, and prayer was offered for the persecuting Roman Catholics.

At Haimen the Roman Catholics are searching for those who have shown sympathy with the Protestants. Many have fled from the town, others are in hiding, and business is paralysed. One man was caught and taken to the R.C. premises to be tortured. The Mandarin succeeded in getting him liberated. Attempts were then made to catch his son, who escaped, and fled to this city, arriving here by steam launch with District Magistrate and Tong-ling at six o'clock. He says some of the armed bands have dispersed, others have come, and they reside principally in the R.C. compound.

The Roman Catholic army is composed of bands of men, each under a leader, and each band has a distinctive badge, The Commander-in-Chief is the native Roman Catholic priest, Nyun, and the principal leaders are : (Eleven names given).

Several of these are well-known robber chiefs ; at least two of them are only recently liberated from prison.

THE CATHOLIC VERSION

After the disturbance over the chestnuts, in which the Protestants summoned the brigands in order to pillage a Catholic's house and deliver from jail by force of arms a criminal arrested by the Magistrate, the parties interested were extremely excited. It had only need of another incident to cause an explosion, and the Protestants were soon to furnish it.

At Haimen the Catholic Mission owns a piece of land on the river front which surrounds the Protestant church. Houses are being built there for the support of our charitable institutes. One of these houses being built behind the Protestant church, it was now necessary to build a wall around it as it was to serve as a warehouse. In order to avoid all occasion of fresh discord the wall was to be built four feet from the church, but when the masons came to commence the work they were stopped by the Protestant church master, Ko Siao-tsen, and his band, who, ready to fight, claimed the property as theirs.

Instead of resisting violence by violence we preferred to bring the case before the local authorities. Civil and Military Mandarins were immediately appointed by the Prefect of Tai-tcheou-fou,

Mr. Tchang, to examine the case. Their first act was to demand the titles of ownership from the Protestants. Now, the latter have none to give, no, not even for their church, which stands on a site formerly used as a place of capital punishment, and was partly occupied by them, partly given to them by a famous brigand named Tchang. They answered, however, first saying that the deeds were at Ningpo ; the second time they said they were at Shanghai ; and the third time they showed a false paper which they had manufactured after taking the measurement of their church's land.

The Mandarins afterwards examined the titles of ownership in the possession of the Catholic Mission, which are incontestable, and all were unanimous in acknowledging our rights, adding that we could build the wall. This decision being given, the workmen returned on November 9th to continue work on the wall ; but Ko Siao-tsen, the Protestant master, the evening before, had already assembled eighty armed men in the church for the purpose of opposing the work. They rushed at the workmen and threatened to shoot them if they would not quit. The workmen retired.

It was market day ; the news soon spread to the outskirts of Haimen, and a great number of Catholics assembled, being exasperated by the incessant provocations of Protestants and by former insult and injustice.

The next day, Saturday, November 10th, the workmen returned to their labour with a guard of Christians to defend them. Two hours after the Mandarins asked that the work be stopped, promising to settle the question immediately. About four o'clock that evening a delegate paid our missionaries a visit and offered the following conditions of peace :

1. That the Protestant master Ko would be sent away from Haimen and forbidden to return.

2. The wall would be built the next day and the lines drawn without any change.

3. If Protestants thereafter wished to take revenge, the delegate and Colonel Tsao would take upon themselves the responsibility and would answer for all.

The missionaries accepted these conditions and immediately ordered the Christians to disperse. The latter were still in the port in the act of eating when they perceived two vessels coming towards them from the other side of the river. They were full of pirates and armed Protestants, who as soon as they landed opened fire on the Christians. The latter were obliged to defend themselves, and put to flight their assailants. Then there took place a deplorable encounter between the Christians and Colonel Tsao's soldiers, caused by the bad-will of an under-leader commonly called Siao Lao-yi. He was formerly a pirate, who, having made his submission, is now in command of some soldiers who themselves are more or less second-hand pirates. He had been sent to the port with fifty soldiers to separate the combatants. When he saw his former companions of brigandage fleeing, he ordered his men to charge the Christians and disarm them, and he himself fired. Ten were wounded, of whom one died.

Shortly after this bloody fight Colonel Tsao paid the missionaries a visit, saying that if any had been killed, the guilty parties would be executed ; if depredation had taken place, the damages would be compensated. General Ou was present and put the blame on the soldiers. Sub-prefect Siao did so likewise, as also all the witnesses of this bloody brutality committed against men who were justly defending their lives and who, faithful to instructions given them, offered no resistance to the soldiers. Siao Lao-yi is greatly to blame, and merits punishment.

As for reproaching the Christians with having firearms, that is ridiculous in a country in which, to the knowledge and before the very eyes of the Mandarins, all the inhabitants carry arms to defend themselves against the pirates, who, thanks to the inactivity of those in power, abound there—brigandage and assassination are continual.

Peace reigns there now, since the Mandarins expelled the pirates of Peyen and sent away under good escort the Protestant master Ko Siao-tsen. But I received a telegram this morning, November 16th, stating that he returns this very day at the head of a large number of robbers. What will happen, and what can we do ?

The other side of the relations between Roman Catholic and Protestant missionaries is seen in the following communication sent to the *Shanghai Mercury* by a Protestant missionary in Szechwan.

SUI-FU, VIA CHUNGKING, SZECHWAN

(*From our Correspondent*)

November 28th, 1906.

DEATH

It is with sorrow that I have to record the passing away of one of the Roman Catholic Fathers who has laboured in this land for over thirty years, twenty of which he has spent in this city.

Père Beraud has had a very busy time of it here, for besides looking after the members' spiritual welfare, he has built two large churches, one within and one without the city, both of which will remain as his monument for years to come. He passed away on November 11th, from an apoplectic stroke, and was buried in the Priests' Cemetery at Ho-ti-k'eo, some twenty miles from here. Père Beraud is especially remembered for his great kindness to your correspondent during the terrible time of the 1895 riots, when night after night he crept round about midnight to see how we were faring, and to sympathise with us in the difficulties of our situation. Such acts speak louder than words, and can never be forgotten.

APPENDIX E

On December 11th, 1905, a serious organised riot occurred at Shanghai, the provoking cause of which is described in the following narrative.

THE OUTBREAK AT THE MIXED COURT

FIGHT BETWEEN POLICE AND RUNNERS

EXTRAORDINARY INCIDENTS

The tension between the Municipal authorities and those of the Mixed Court reached a climax on Friday morning, when an attempt to carry out contradictory orders from the Bench led unfortunately to an exchange of blows between the municipal police and the native runners.

There was a preliminary to Friday's occurrence on the preceding day, when the Magistrate (Mr. Kuan), after making another futile protest against the presence of the police cadet in Court, and his supervision of the proper execution of the sentences of the Court, retaliated by sending a runner to the Central Police Station to see that they did their duty there properly. The selected runner spent a long and presumably rather tedious day in the courtyard of the Central Police Station. where he was allowed to remain unmolested. We understand, indeed, that a letter was sent from the Council to Mr. Kuan congratulating him on the interest he had suddenly taken in police administration, and offering his representative every facility for gaining useful information.

Circumvented in this attempt in his policy of annoyance, a policy which Mr. Kuan has himself declared he has orders from the Taotai to pursue, it would seem that only the opportunity was wanted to force matters to a more serious issue. There are indications, in fact, that Friday's disorder was premeditated. Early in the session the Magistrate had a difference with the British Assessor (Mr. Twyman) over a case which had, he said,

480

been ordered for hearing on another date, and which he now refused to hear. The real trouble came, however, when two women and three men were put before the Court on charges of kidnapping girls from their homes in Szechwan. Fifteen young girls, who were to be the witnesses in the case, had been cared for by the municipal police, and were brought to the court in their charge. When the case came to be remanded, the Assessor marked the charge sheet " Children to go to the Door of Hope pro tem." and instructed the police to take them there. Mr. Kuan, however, wished to keep the children in the Mixed Court cells, and gave his orders to the runners to take them away. The runners went to remove the children, but the police, under instructions from their cadet officer, Mr. Fenton, refused to give them up. There was some hustling, and one of the runners struck Inspector Gibson in the eye. This started a general fight, in which the police were victorious and carried off the children and prisoners to their vans in the yard.

During the fight Mr. Ching, the Assistant Magistrate, was heard shouting from the Bench to the native municipal constables and detectives, in Chinese, that they were Chinese subjects, and if they resisted the Magistrate's orders they would be severely punished. The native constables, however, appear to have considered their first duty lay to their employers.

The riot was sufficiently serious to induce Mr. Fenton to go to the telephone to send a message for reinforcements. He had used the instrument an hour before, and it was then all right, but now the mouthpiece was nowhere to be found. This may have been a coincidence merely. At all events it did not render the telephone unusable. The gates of the compound leading into the road were, however, shut and locked. The Magistrate, Assistant Magistrate, and Assessor were then standing in the middle of the court. Mr. Fenton went to ask that the gates be opened to allow the vans to go out, whereupon the Magistrate turned on him in a perfect fury, and told him that he might break the gates open, and destroy the court itself. " You may trample on my body," he added, and then strode away. The gates were subsequently opened, and the children removed. The sitting of the Court had, of course, been abruptly suspended.

So far as is known the only casualties in the fight were sustained by Inspector Gibson and a runner, both of whom were slightly damaged.

A wild statement is being industriously circulated that Mr. Ching was hit over the head by one of the police.

31

THE CHINESE VERSION

The Chinese view of the disturbance on Friday in the Mixed Court is represented in the following letter from " One who was present." The original letter is in Chinese.

" It has always been a part of the Regulation of the International Mixed Court for female criminals to be confined in the Mixed Court prison. Mr. Twyman, the British Vice-Consul, has, however, repeatedly wanted to send these females to the foreign gaol, and on this account it has been a subject of repeated opposition on the part of Mr. Kuan, the Magistrate of the Mixed Court. The latter has also petitioned the Shanghai Taotai to back up this opposition. This is on record.

" On the morning of the 8th instant, Mr. Kuan, Magistrate, Mr. Ching, Assistant Magistrate, and Mr. Twyman, the British Assessor, were trying cases brought by the police, among which was one in which a certain Mrs. Li Wang-shih was charged with kidnapping children. According to the evidence, this woman claimed to be the wife of an official, and that she, accompanied by four others, had arrived in Shanghai from Szechwan ; that she had with her five little girls which she had purchased in Szechwan as personal attendants, but which the police had wrongly charged her with having kidnapped. In view of the wrongful accusation Mrs. Li Wang-shih asked that her accusers be punished. It was found, in the course of the trial, that the defendant had arrived in Shanghai in the steamer *Poyang, en route* to her home in Kwantung, and that the luggage brought by her amounted to over one hundred pieces. As for the children, the defendant declared that she had documents proving *bona fide* sales to her of them, etc. As this evidence appeared to refute the charge of the children having been kidnapped, the Magistrate consulted with the Assessor as to the advisability of remanding the case, sending the children to the ' Door of Hope,' and keeping the defendants under the custody of the Mixed Court *ad interim*. The British Assessor, however, determined to have the defendants confined under remand in the foreign (municipal) gaol. The Magistrate replied that as he had not received any instructions from the Taotai to change the regulations, he could not consent to this. An argument ensued, and, neither side being willing to give way, the Magistrate accordingly ordered his runners to follow the regulations and hand the female defendants to the charge of the Court female gaoler. Upon this the Vice-Consul ordered the police inspectors and all the constables present to use force in getting away the defendants. In the *mêlée* that ensued two runners of the Court, Chang Ta'i and Chou Yu-ch'ing, and several onlookers were hurt, and when the Magistrate called out to the police to stop striking, one of the inspectors went so far as even to threaten him with a club.

" About this time there was a large crowd of people outside the gates, who, hearing of the disturbance, tried to rush in. Fearing a riot against the police on the part of the mob, the Magistrate ordered the gates to be temporarily closed in order to prevent outsiders from coming in. Following on this the police forcibly took away the defendants, male and female. Nothing can render a worse insult to the dignity of an independent country than such treatment of its officials.

" Finally the two runners who were hurt by the police have been examined by a special officer sent by the Shanghai Taotai and also by Dr. Ransom, the latter granting a certificate as to the condition and nature of injuries received by the runners in question."

The London *Times* of November 1st, 1906, contains a letter on this subject from the Rev. W. Arthur Cornaby, Corresponding Secretary of the Christian Literature Society for China, who has peculiar opportunities for knowing what the Chinese think on public questions.

CHINESE GIRL SLAVERY AND THE SHANGHAI MUNICIPALITY

To the Editor of " The Times "

SIR,—I have been asked to send you some particulars, hitherto unpublished in England, concerning the Shanghai riot of last December and its sequel. I am in touch with Chinese public opinion from long residence, and latterly the editorship of a weekly newspaper in Chinese.

Until toward the end of last year all the Chinese complaints which reached me were concerning the Chinese side of the Mixed Court, and especially the notorious " runners " of that Court. The Chinese of Shanghai felt they were not sufficiently protected by the fact of a Western assessor sitting to watch the cases. They deemed the French settlement system to suit them better, where the Western was the judge and the Chinese Mandarin the assessor. And not until the case of a woman from Szechwan, with eighteen young girls, being arrested by the Western police on suspicion of kidnapping, did the native papers and talkers and merchant guilds take sides (before the case had been tried) with the Chinese Mandarin against the police and municipal council. This is to be explained by the following facts.

A riot in Shanghai was threatened as early as July 9th last year (1905) in a Chinese document, handed to certain members of the Municipal Council and others, by a league of Chinese owners of certain unmentionable property, who appended their names, fourteen in all, to that document. They deprecated anything being done to check their trade, or even to regulate it, as their Chinese patrons " would express their feelings in such an uncontrolled fashion as to cause great inconvenience to the foreign residents of the settlement " if any measures were attempted.

The number of inmates of the houses referred to, as estimated by the property-owners themselves, is " not less than four or five thousand." And as many of these girls break down in health, the numbers are recruited by the agency of kidnappers and slave-dealers in many centres, notably along the Yangtze, from Hankow westward. Daughters of prominent native Christians have been among those kidnapped for this trade, and the Chinese have repeatedly affirmed that hardly one foreign steamer leaves Hankow for Shanghai without some " slaves " from Szechwan. The women who escort them pose as " ladies with personal slaves," and are protected by the league of Shanghai property-owners, backed by the merchant guilds (which latter were so much in evidence before last December riot)—so the Chinese of Central China have affirmed for over a decade now.

Then, as there has been no tracing the missing daughters after they have been transferred from native boats to the foreign steamers, rumours have been dangerously current in past years that foreigners are connected with the trade, and paid to protect the " ladies " from Mixed Court investigations. Indeed, seven years ago I was myself mobbed, at a spot one hundred miles up the Han river, as being a " foreign kidnapper," which made it all the more interesting to be among those mobbed in Shanghai last December in the anti-rescue riot. Only the local Chinese feeling seems to have been reported in England, but so many Chinese families along the Yangtze Valley have lost their brightest girls that very much of the respectable public opinion out of Shanghai has been with the municipal police rather than on the side of " the patriots of Shanghai." And, happily, his Excellency, Chow Fu, Viceroy of these Liang Kiang provinces, saw the true national bearings of the case at the time, as opposed to local vested interests. He was forced to " save the Chinese face " by taking the " patriotic " side, but proceeded to draw up a memorial to the Throne for the total abolition of girl-slavery throughout China. This was twice reported to have been approved, but as no Imperial edict has been forthcoming, he has now (September 24th) memorialised the Throne once again with intent to get the measure put through. This will affect millions of young girls physically and tens of thousands morally. And when his memorial becomes definite law, we may even see the local property-owners appealing to the Municipal Council to protect them from the local Chinese authorities, which will be a new departure in the tangled history of the Mixed Court of Shanghai.

I am, Sir, your obedient servant,

W. Arthur Cornaby.

Christian Literature Society for China, Shanghai,
September 29th.

APPENDIX F

REGULATIONS PROHIBITING OPIUM SMOKING

(Issued November 21st, 1906)

Article I. To limit the cultivation of the poppy is the way to eradicate the evil. The poppy obstructs agriculture, and its effect is very bad. In China, in the provinces of Szechwan, Shensi, Kansu, Yunnan, Kweichow, Shansi, and Kianghuai, the poppy is widely cultivated, and even in other provinces there are places where poppy cultivation is largely pursued. Now it is decided to prohibit and root out the habit of smoking opium within ten years. It is therefore necessary to limit the cultivation of the poppy so as to effect the prohibition. Viceroys and Governors of provinces have to instruct the Magistrates of departments and districts to report upon, after registering, the actual area of land used for cultivation of poppy. Unless land has been hitherto used in the cultivation of the poppy it is not to be used for that purpose in future. For the land already being cultivated with the poppy special title-deeds must be obtained. Of the land at present in use for the cultivation of the poppy one-ninth must be annually withdrawn from cultivation, and if such land is suitable, other crops are to be cultivated thereon. Magistrates of departments and districts are to pay surprise visits in order to ascertain whether there is any violation of this regulation.

By this means the cultivation of the poppy will be exterminated in nine years.

Any person violating the rule will forfeit his land, and any person ceasing to grow the poppy and adopting some other crop before the time required in the decree shall be considered as meriting special reward.

Article II. The issuing of certificates will prevent the possibility of new smokers. The bad habit of opium smoking has now been indulged in for such a long time. About three or four tenths of the natives smoke opium. Therefore we must

486

be lenient to those who have already acquired the habit, but must be strict for the future. First of all, all the officials and gentry and licentiates shall be prohibited to smoke opium, so as to show examples to the common people. Those who smoke opium, without distinction, whether he be an official, one of the gentry, or a servant, shall report the fact at the local yâmen. If the place of their living is remote from the local yâmen, they may report themselves to the police bureau or to the gentry of that place, who will collect such applications and send the same to the local yâmen. The local officials then will issue a proclamation ordering them to fill up a form with their names, age, residence, profession, and the amount of opium each smokes per day ; such forms will be ordered to be sent in at a fixed date according to the distance of the residence from the yâmen. After the forms have been collected at the yâmen a list will be compiled, and one copy of the same will be handed over to the higher yâmen, and certificates will be issued under the official seal. Such certificates will be of two kinds : one for those who are over sixty years of age and another for those who are under sixty years of age. Those who receive the second kind of certificate are not allowed to receive the certificate of the first kind when they reach sixty. In the certificate the name, age, native address, amount of daily consumption of opium, as well as the date of the issue of the certificate, are mentioned to certify that they are allowed to buy opium. If there are any who, having no certificate, buy opium secretly, such persons will be duly punished. Once a registration has been made and certificate been issued no future application will be allowed.

Article III. By ordering gradual reduction of the amount of smoking opium, a cure of such habit may be effected. Those who are over sixty years old are treated leniently because of their age, but those who are below sixty and have received a certificate of second kind are ordered to reduce the amount of smoking annually either by two-tenths or three-tenths, and to determine the date of ceasing to smoke opium. Those who cease to smoke and obtain the guarantee of their neighbours will be presented to the local officials, who will also inquire into the case, and then the name will be erased from the book of registration and the certificate will be returned to the officials. A list of such withdrawals will be sent to the higher yâmen for record. The date of prohibition of opium is quite lenient, and therefore if there is any one who does not give up the practice within term, such person shall be severely punished. If there is any one who has a certificate of the second class and does not stop smoking, if he be an official, he will be cashiered; if he be a licentiate, his title will be taken away; and if he be an unofficial person, his name will be registered. These names will be sent up to the higher yâmen to be placed on record, their names and age will be put up in the street, and their residence will be made public, and no honorary positions will be given to them. They are not allowed to be reckoned as equals of the general public.

Article IV. By closing the opium shops the source of the evil can be cleared away. Until the terms for the date of prohibition come it is impossible to close the shops where opium is sold. However, there are opium shops where are many lamps for smoking opium, and many youngsters are induced to come there and gather together with many bad characters. Therefore such shops shall be closed by local authorities within six months, and the owners shall be ordered to change their occupations. If they do not close their shops in time, these shops shall be officially closed by sealing the door. The restaurants and bars shall not keep opium for the use of their customers, and the guests shall not be allowed to bring in any opium pipe in order to smoke opium in these places. If there are any who violate the rule, they shall be severely punished. Those who sell opium pipes, opium lamps, or other utensils for opium smokers, shall be prohibited from selling these goods after six months, or they shall be severely punished. The taxes on opium lamps shall not be collected three months after date.

Article V. By registering each shop where opium is sold, the exact number of them can be known. Though the shops where opium is sold cannot be closed at once, yet they can be gradually closed and no new shops be allowed to be opened henceforth. In every city, town, or village, the shops where opium or opium dross is sold are to be investigated by the local officials, and their numbers shall be duly registered and kept on record. Certificates shall be issued, which certificates will be reckoned as permits to follow that business, and no more new shops shall be allowed to be opened. These shops shall show the certificates whenever they buy their merchandise, or they are not allowed to sell the same. These shops shall report upon the quantity of opium and opium dross they sell at the end of each year, and report the same to the local officials, who will keep the same on record. After calculating the total amount of opium and opium dross consumed in a district, annually, the proportion of annual reduction necessary for the abolition of opium smoking in ten years shall be calculated. Any surplus at the end of that time shall be destroyed, and double its value forfeited as a fine.

Article VI. The government shall manufacture medicine to cure the bad habit. There are many prescriptions for curing the habit of smoking opium, and each province shall select the best medical students to undertake research for the best cure suited to the circumstances of each province. Such cures shall be made in pills, and shall in no case contain opium or morphia. After being manufactured such pills will be distributed to each prefecture, sub-prefecture, department, and district, at reasonable prices, and then these will be handed over to the charitable societies or medicine shops, where the cure will be sold at cost price. Whenever there are any poor people who cannot afford to buy the medicine, the cure may be given to them gratis. It is also granted to local gentry to manufacture the cure in accordance with the official prescription, so as to have the cure distributed as widely as possible. If there is any one who will distribute the cure for charity's sake, and if such cure has the proper effect, the local officials shall give them reward.

Article VII. The establishment of anti-opium societies is a worthy proceeding. Lately, many persons cured have voluntarily organised an anti-opium society, and have endeavoured to eradicate bad habits. This is really praiseworthy. Therefore the Viceroys and the Governors of provinces shall instruct the local officials, with the local gentry, to organise anti-opium societies, and to endeavour to stop the opium-smoking habit in the locality. Then prohibitions will surely have better effect. Such society shall be purely for the anti-opium smoking, and the society shall not discuss any other matters, such as political questions bearing on topical affairs or local administration, or any similar matter.

Article VIII. The local officials are relied upon to use their utmost endeavour to carry into effect these regulations, and with the effective support of the local gentry there should be no difficulty in carrying out the prohibition. The Tartar Generals, the Viceroys, and the Governors of provinces shall make up a list of people who smoke opium, and those who cease to smoke annually, and the number of pills which are used as cure, together with the number of anti-opium societies. These lists, when compared, will easily give the comparative results of each province, by which the responsible officials will be either rewarded or reproved accordingly. The annual statistics shall be sent to the Government Council, where their merits will be duly dealt with. In the city of Peking the police authorities, officers of gendarmerie, and the officials of the city are held responsible. If in any district opium smoking is stamped out before the expiry of the ten years' limit, the officials of that district should be duly rewarded. The petty officials are to be warned to have no irregularities in reducing the area in which the poppy is cultivated, in issuing certificates for opium shops and shops where opium and opium dross are sold, or in dealing with those who smoke opium. Any such irregularity will be followed by severe punishment, and any who receive bribes will be punished on a charge of the crime of fraud.

Article IX. The officials are strictly prohibited from smoking opium so as to set examples to others. The prohibition within ten years is for the general public. The officials shall be examples to common people, and therefore they shall stop such bad habits before the general public, and such prohibitions shall be strictly enforced upon the officials and the punishments upon them shall be more severe. From now all the officials without distinction of rank, metropolitan or provincial, military or civil, who are over sixty and suffering from opium-smoking habits, are exempted from the prohibition just as are the common people, for they are too far gone for cure. However, those who have not reached sixty years of age, princes, dukes, men of title, high Metropolitan officials, Tartar Generals, Viceroys, Governors, Deputy Lieutenant Military Governors, the Provincial Commanders-in-Chief, as well as Brigadier Generals, being all officials who are well treated by the Throne and high in rank and position, are not allowed to conceal their affairs, and if they smoke opium, they shall report themselves and the dates when they should stop the same. During the cure of the habit these officials shall not retire from their official duties, but shall appoint acting officials ; and when they have proved themselves cured of opium smoking, they may return to official duties. Moreover, they shall not be allowed to take opium under the pretence of illness longer than the terms promised. The rest of the officials in metropolitan or provincial service, either military or civil, substantive or expectant, shall report themselves to their principal officials in regard to these matters, and they shall cease to smoke within six months, at the end of which time they will be examined. If there are any who cannot be cured in time, they shall give reasons, and if they are hereditary, they shall retire and, if they be ordinary officials, they will retire with original titles retained. If any conceal their actual conditions, such officials shall be impeached and be summarily cashiered as a warning to others. If there are any who are misreported by higher officials, they may memorialise and the case will be tried accordingly. Those who are the professors and students of ordinary schools and colleges or of military or naval schools and colleges are also hereby ordered to cease smoking within six months from date.

Article X. The prohibition of the import of foreign opium is one of the ways to root out the source of opium smoking. The prohibition of cultivation of the poppy and of the opium-smoking habits are within the jurisdiction of the internal administrations. Foreign opium, however, concerns foreign Powers. The Waiwupu is hereby instructed to negotiate with the British Minister to Peking to enter into a convention to prohibit the importation of opium gradually within a certain term of years, so as to stop such importations before the term for the prohibition of opium smoking. Opium is imported from Persia, Annam, Dutch colonies, and other places besides India, and the Waiwupu shall also open negotiation with the Ministers of these treaty Powers. In case of a Power where there is no treaty China can prohibit the importation by her own laws. The Tartar Generals, Lieutenant Generals, Viceroys, and Governors shall order the Commissioners of Customs to find a way to stop such importation from the frontiers either by water or by land. It is also known that morphia is injected, and the habit is worse than opium smoking. It is mentioned in Article 11 in the Anglo-Chinese Commercial Treaty, and in Article 16 of the American-Chinese Commercial Treaty, that except for medical purposes no morphia shall be imported to China, and it is also strictly prohibited to sell or manufacture morphia or syringes for injecting the same by Chinese or foreign shops, so as to stop the bad habit.

These regulations shall be promulgated by the local civil and military officials in cities, towns, and villages, for the informations of the general public.

LIST OF THE RAILWAYS ON CHINESE TERRITORY IN 1915, COMPLETED, UNDER CONSTRUCTION, OR ACTUALLY CONTRACTED FOR

Compiled mainly from information supplied by the Ministry of Communications, Peking

Railway.	Length completed.				Under Construction.	Capital Cost.	Bonded debt incurred.	
	Main line.	Branch lines.	Sidings, etc.	Total.			Amount.	From what source.
	Kilom.	Kilom.	Kilom.	Kilom.	Kilom.		£	
FOREIGN RAILWAYS								
Transiberian (Manchurian Section)	1,529	—	—	1,529	—		—	Built by Russian capital
North Manchurian (Harbin-Kwanchengtze)	212	—	—	212	—	12,225,000	—	Do.
South Manchurian (Kwanchengtze-Dairen)	705	122	?	827	—	1,300,000	—	Do. (transferred to Japan)
South Manchurian (Mukden-Antung)	304	—	?	304	—	20,000,000	—	Built by Japanese capital
Shantung Railway	394	59	?	453	—	2,645,520	—	Built by German capital
Yunnan Railway (1 metre gauge)	465	—	—	465	—	6,600,000	—	Built by French capital
	3,609	181	—	3,790	—	42,770,520	—	
CHINESE GOVERNMENT RAILWAYS								
Changchun-Kirin	128	—	23	151	—	619,359	225,000	Japanese
Peking-Mukden	845	114	264	1,223	—	5,821,752	{ 33,300 / 2,300,000	Japanese / British
Peking-Kalgan (Changkiakow)	211	27	84	322	—	1,294,031	—	
Kalgan-Suiyuan	191	—	36	227	—	955,326	—	
Peking-Hankow	1,214	94	272	1,580	—	10,257,980	5,000,000	Anglo-French

492

Railway						Capital cost	Gold / bonded	Nationality
Shansi Railway (1 metre gauge)	243	—	81	324	—	2,309,215	1,600,000	Franco-Russian
Taokow-Tsinghwa	150	2	32	184	—	728,114	700,000	British
Kaifengfu-Honanfu	185	—	18	203	?	1,335,578	1,000,000	Franco-Belgian
Tientsin-Pukow	1,013	98	205	1,316	—	9,423,728	9,800,000 }	German / Anglo-French
Hukwang Railways	—	—	—	—	abt.1,000	—	} 6,000,000	British / German
Hankow-Canton	—	—	—	—	abt.1,000	—		French / American
Hankow-Canton (in Kwangtung)	—	—	—	—	abt. 235	—	—	
Pingsiang-Chuchow	97	—	10	107	—	474,304	1,100,000	British
Shanghai-Nanking	311	16	70	397	—	3,043,615	—	British
Shanghai-Hangchow-Ningpo	258	6	55	319	125	1,562,025	3,050,000	British
Canton-Kowloon	143	—	20	163	—	1,670,841	1,500,000	British
Canton-Samshui	49	—	22	71	—	326,249	1,500,000	British
	5,038	357	1,192	6,587	2,360	39,822,117	33,808,300	
CHINESE COMPANIES								
Amoy-Changchowfu	28	—	—	28	22	216,000	—	
Swatow-Chaochowfu	40	—	—	40	—	337,460	—	
Sunning-Kongmoon	60	—	—	60	—	259,137	—	
	128	—	—	128	22	812,597	—	
TOTAL	8,775	538	?	10,505	2,382	40,634,714	33,808,300	

Notes :—Gold commitments converted at exchange : 25 francs = 20 marks = 10 yen = £1 sterling.

The capital cost of the Chinese Government Railways was stated in silver dollars and has been converted at nominal exchange 10 dollars = £1 sterling.

Bonded debt is the original amount without deduction for amortisation.

The bottom line gives the length of all railways, but the capital cost is that of Chinese lines only.

INDEX

32